ANTI-JUDAISM IN THE NEW TESTAMENT

To Lenny
With best wishes
May we see the redemption of all Israel
Gerry Sigal

ANTI-JUDAISM IN THE NEW TESTAMENT

Gerald Sigal

Copyright © 2004 by Gerald Sigal.

Library of Congress Number: 2003097474
ISBN :   Hardcover   1-4134-3307-3
           Softcover   1-4134-3306-5

All rights reserved. No part of this book may be reproduced or transmitted in any form or by any means, electronic or mechanical, including photocopying, recording, or by any information storage and retrieval system, without permission in writing from the copyright owner.

This book was printed in the United States of America.

To order additional copies of this book, contact:
Xlibris Corporation
1-888-795-4274
www.Xlibris.com
Orders@Xlibris.com
21848

CONTENTS

INTRODUCTION 7
1. THE FORMATION OF NEW TESTAMENT
   RELIGIO-POLITICAL THEOLOGY 18
2. SELLING "THE CHRIST" 49
3. "TRUE JEWS" AND "CHRIST-KILLER JEWS" 56
4. THE LETTER TO THE HEBREWS 72
5. THE GOSPEL OF MARK 76
6. THE GOSPEL OF MATTHEW 115
7. THE GOSPEL OF LUKE AND THE BOOK OF ACTS 149
8. THE GOSPEL OF JOHN 173
9. THE BOOK OF REVELATION 213
10. WHAT HAPPENED TO THE DISCIPLES
    FOLLOWING THE DEATH OF JESUS? 215
11. THE CRUCIFIXION OF THE JEWS 268
BIBLIOGRAPHY 311
SCRIPTURAL INDEX 319
SUBJECT INDEX 337

INTRODUCTION

Critiquing New Testament anti-Judaism

This volume is a systematic critique of the anti-Jewishness of the New Testament. Its primary purpose is to delineate what the New Testament authors intended to convey to their respective audiences concerning the Jewish people. That is, this volume is concerned with the initial meaning intended by the New Testament authors and how this intended meaning directly and with forethought contributed to Christian anti-Judaic[1] thought and action. We will investigate how and why the New Testament authors created this anti-Judaic climate.

Analysis of the Gospel stories demonstrates that anti-Judaism is woven into the fabric of a significant part of the New Testament narrative. This narrative has provoked bitter condemnation and persecution of Jews. The Jewish people were cast in the role of a dark satanic force as a systematic denigration and demonization of the Jews took place. It is to its harsh and bitter polemic against the entire Jewish people that one must ascribe the accusations of the Jews being Christ-killers and children of Satan and the later embellishments of Jews as host desecrators, ritual murders, and well-poisoners.

Post-New Testament developments of Christian anti-Judaism are not central to this study. In pursuing our investigation we will make a distinction between what was originally intended by the New Testament authors and the usage made of their works to meet the anti-Judaic needs of the subsequent church. Conclusions reached by later interpreters that have often been attributed to the authors of the Gospels are not our primary concern. It is not a question of how, or to what extent, the New Testament passages concerning Jews and Judaism were misused or misread in later centuries, but of what they were meant to mean in the first place. Thus, our focus will be on what the authors meant to convey to their respective contemporary audiences about the Jews.[2]

What would the New Testament's audience have understood from the information its various authors provided? What meaning would a reader derive from a particular text? Is the New Testament anti-Jewish or is it merely an accurate report of events as they took place? Answers can only come through an examination of the relevant passages in their specific literary contexts, as well as in the context of the struggles, aspirations, and theologies of the early church. Special attention must be paid to the relationship between the church and the Roman authorities, on the one hand, and the synagogue, on the other hand, at the time the various books of the New Testament were written and to polemics within the early church community.

The New Testament was not written solely to condemn the Jews. But, in the process of developing the several story lines that evolved into the four respective canonical Gospels, the early church adopted a decidedly anti-Judaic stance. Consequently, in its final form, instances of anti-Judaic sentiment are found in much of the New Testament, the Gospels in particular. This animosity has to do as much with politics as with theological doctrine, relations with the Roman imperial authorities as with displacing Jews and Judaism.

If pre-Gospel traditions already included anti-Judaic elements, they were now systematically exploited. There was a growing need to explain why Israel, God's chosen people, had rejected Jesus and the message of his disciples. How could this be reconciled with God's will? In presenting Jesus as the Messiah and Christianity as superseding Judaism, Paul and the authors of the Gospels and Acts, in particular, indict the Jewish people for the death of Jesus and spread antipathy of Jews and Judaism as part of a program to achieve Christian ascendancy. The historicized core myths that provide the basis for the New Testament missionary program were shaped and reshaped to show that the church possessed full authenticity and validity contra Jews and Judaism.

The New Testament authors strive to obscure the dividing line between fact and fiction. Nevertheless, it is clearly a work broadly touched by the craft of fiction. Besides fabrication *ex nihilo*, the editorial process of creating the Gospels and other books of the New Testament resulted in modification or transformation of the very meaning of the pre-Gospel materials. Whether or not the New Testament represents the view of Jesus' earliest followers, or even those of Jesus himself, is not our primary concern. What is important is that whatever the origin of the material comprising its contents this is what was incorporated into the text and this is the literary material with which we must work.

The Gospels encourage their readers to develop a negative view of the Jews. This is accomplished through specific statements made throughout their respective narratives. Examples are found in the description of the alleged plot to kill Jesus (Mark 11:18, Matthew 26:3-4, Luke 20:20, John 11:48-53), the emphasis on the supposed "wicked" nature of the Jews themselves (Matthew 23, John 8), and on the moral responsibility of the Jews for the death of Jesus (Matthew 27:25). Thus, the Jews are identified as being evil, guilty of murder, and unrepentant. In contrast, Jesus is identified as the "Christ" and the "Son of God." He is depicted as good-hearted, interested only in the welfare of others, and innocent of any wrongdoing.

If we let the New Testament speak for itself, we find two themes dominate the New Testament's concept of the Jews. The first of these concerns a claim to a common biblical heritage for Jews and for the followers of Jesus. Acknowledging the distinctive status of ancient Israel, the New Testament authors claim continuity for Christianity with that biblical faith of Israel. From this perspective, they postulate that prior to the coming of Jesus, Jews had an exclusive claim to spiritual legitimacy—that in a sense, Christianity and Judaism were one. The second theme declares the Jewish fall from grace and the resulting Christian spiritual monopoly. It is alleged that Christianity has become the legitimate inheritor of the true faith and of God's promises to Israel. Essential to this theme is an enumeration of those acts and events through which Jews are shown to have lost their spiritual prerogative. This second perspective disposes of the unique position of the Jews in God's providence. It provides an image of Jews as renegades from the true faith, cruel persecutors of the faithful, and the very crucifiers of Jesus, God's anointed son; it leaves Christianity as the only surviving heir to spiritual legitimacy.

The earliest written Christian polemic against the Jews is found in 1 Thessalonians 2:14-15. There, Paul declares that "the Jews, who killed both the Lord Jesus and the prophets, and drove us out; they are not pleasing to God, but hostile to all men." It is the Jews, as a nation, that Paul condemns as murderers of both Jesus and the prophets, and as his persecutors. Consequently, God rejects them. The underlying bitterness Paul shows toward the Jews in this passage is unparalleled even in Paul's other writings. It is also the sole reference in Paul's letters to the allegation that the Jews were guilty of killing Jesus.[3] Paul provides the basis for the recurrent New Testament theme that the Jews, as a nation, are alone responsible for the execution of Jesus. In this earliest known "Christ-killer" polemic to be found in Christian literature, Paul identifies the Jewish national rejection and slaying of Jesus as an endemic trait that had earlier precedent in their killing of the prophets. The Jewish people as a nation is characterized as the archetypal persecutor of God's messengers be they Jesus, the prophets, or the Christian preachers. This was followed in time by the Gospel of Mark, which introduced the anti-Jewish theme that was later adopted by the Gospels of Matthew and Luke. To these was added the Gospel of John, with its intense anti-Jewish viciousness.[4]

Some readers may feel that this work is overly critical of the New Testament and its authors. Nevertheless, biblical and non-biblical documentation and even the New Testament attest to these facts. One need only investigate the post-New Testament presentation of certain themes—such as the central role of the Jews in the trial of Jesus (Matthew 27:25), the portrayal of the Jews as the devil's children (John 8:44), the popular meaning attached to the word "Pharisee,"[5] and the labeling of Judaism as legalism[6]—for proof that the New Testament authors achieved their anti-Jewish objectives.

There are some Christians who without examining the question of whether the New Testament itself contains anti-Judaic passages see the anti-Judaic roots of Christianity as stemming, not from that document, but from Christianity's teachings of its own traditions.[7] There are other Christians who, although they know better, would rather keep silent concerning the New Testament's role in creating the hostile climate in which persecution and degradation of the Jews are perfectly acceptable. They devise stratagems to avoid acknowledging exactly what it is that they know. That is why it is all the more commendable that there are some Christians who admit to the injustice done the Jewish people by the New Testament.[8] Nevertheless, there is still great resistance by the majority of Christian theologians, clergymen, and laymen to acknowledging the presence of anti-Jewish passages in the New Testament and the repudiation of those verses.[9] It is hoped that with time, honesty will prevail.[10]

A ray of hope

It should be noted, however, that although the New Testament prepared the way for centuries of persecution of those Jews who did not accept Jesus and church leaders of all denominations of Christendom consistently reiterated its anti-Jewish themes one cannot infer that all Christians hate or persecute Jews. Many are truly embarrassed by the vicious anti-Jewish contents of the New Testament and its results. Many have risked their lives and many have even died protesting against anti-Jewish persecution. It is to their everlasting credit that they were able to resist adherence to the anti-Jewish aspects of the New Testament.

Notes

[1] *Judaic* refers to everything having to do with Jews and Judaism.

2. Some of the new translations of the New Testament have the effect (whether intentional or not) of intensifying anti-Jewish prejudices. For example, the King James Version of Titus 1:10 reads as follows:

> For there are many unruly and vain talkers and deceivers, specially they of the circumcision.

The *New English Bible Version* (Oxford University Press and Cambridge University Press, 1970), a translation authorized by all the major Protestant Christian denominations of Great Britain (including among others the Church of England, the Baptists, the Presbyterians, and the Methodists) and the Catholic Church, renders this passage as:

> There are too many, especially among Jewish converts, who are out of control, they talk wildly and lead men's minds astray.

Why did the translators use the word "Jewish" in a context where the word is not found in the Greek text and where therefore its use creates an unnecessary negative connotation? Furthermore, does the original passage specifically refer to Jewish converts as opposed to Gentile Christians who practiced circumcision, or perhaps to Samaritan converts?

> In a further illustration, the King James Version renders John 11:19 as:

> ... many of the Jews came to Martha and Mary to comfort them.

This is one of the few passages in the Fourth Gospel where "the Jews" do not appear in a negative sense. *The New English Bible* renders this passage as:

> ... many of the people had come from the city to Martha and Mary to console with them.

Why did the translators remove the term "the Jews" from this context and replace it with the term "the people"? The Greek New Testament does not warrant such a reading. What do these changes mean? These changes in the text serve no purpose other than to increase the anti-Jewish teachings of the New Testament and perpetuate further anti-Jewish propaganda even beyond that already found in the *textus receptus*.

3   Mainly because the specific accusation that the Jews killed Jesus does not appear elsewhere in the Pauline letters, there is speculation among modern New Testament scholars that 1 Thessalonians 2:14-16 is a later interpolation.

4   The Gospels of Matthew, Mark, and Luke (but not John) are often referred to as the Synoptic Gospels because of similarities in their presentation of the life and teachings of Jesus. There is some identical and a great deal of similar material contained in the first three Gospels, as well as materials peculiar to each. The Fourth Gospel is not included because it differs markedly in content, style, and thought from the other three. Almost the whole of Mark is contained respectively in Matthew and Luke, and it appears that the authors of the latter two used Mark in writing their own works. Matthew and Luke, it is believed, used Mark; then each combined the sayings of Jesus according to his own understanding with other pre-Gospel traditions and added his own innovations. Consequently, there are striking agreements as well as wide differences among the respective narratives produced by these authors.

5   "Pharisee" is defined as: "a formal, sanctimonious, hypocritical person," a definition obviously dependant on Matthew 23. (*Funk and Wagnalls Standard College Dictionary*, New York: Funk and Wagnalls, 1973, p. 1011)

6   The persistence of this understanding of Judaism among New Testament scholars is documented in E.P. Sanders, *Paul and Palestinian Judaism*, Philadelphia: Fortress Press, 1977, pp. 33-75.

7   Thus, in the mid-1960's Gregory Baum, a Catholic priest (and the son of Jewish parents) maintained that the New Testament texts are not themselves tainted by anti-Judaism but that the later interpretations of the church gave them this coloring. He wrote: "It is *unthinkable* for anyone who accepts the gospel as the ultimate revelation of divine love that part of the New Testament was designed to encourage contempt of any people and contribute ... to the growth of misunderstanding and hatred in the world." (Gregory Baum, *Is the New Testament Anti-Semitic?* New York: Paulist Press, 1965, p. 6.) It should be noted that he later reversed his opinion.

8   For example, Gregory Baum, who earlier had stated emphatically that there were no anti-Jewish trends within the New Testament, has since become convinced of the anti-Judaic polemics of the Gospels, especially the Gospel of John. For his change of position, see his *Religion and Alienation: A Theological Reading of Sociology*, New York: Paulist Press, 1975, pp. 78ff. also see his "Introduction" to Rosemary Reuther, *Faith and Fratricide*, pp. 2-3.

Baum writes that Reuther changed his mind by demonstrating that the canonical texts themselves are already colored by an antagonism toward the religion of Israel. Baum writes: "I was ... convinced that the anti-Jewish trends in Christianity were peripheral and accidental, not grounded in the New Testament itself but due to later developments, and that it would consequently be fairly easy to purify the preaching of the Church from anti-Jewish bias. Since then, especially under the influence of Rosemary Reuther's writings, I have had to change my mind" (p. 3). John M. Oesterreicher, a Catholic priest (and the son of Jewish parents), in his *Anatomy of Contempt* (South Orange, N.J.: Seton Hall University, n.d.), strongly reproved Reuther for her "lopsided exegesis" and endeavored systematically to sustain Baum's earlier position. Concerning Reuther, see Alan Davies, Ed., *Anti-Semitism and the Foundations of Christianity* (New York: Paulist Press, 1979), which is a collection of essays reflecting on the issues raised by her work.

9   An example of this resistance is found in the Second Vatican Council document, *Declaration on the Relationship of the Church to Non-Christian Religions* (*Nostra aetate* ["In Our Times"], final version approved October, 1965, p. 4).

> Even though the Jewish authorities and those who followed their lead pressed for the death of Christ (cf. John. 19:6), neither all Jews indiscriminately at that time, nor Jews today, can be charged with the crimes committed during his passion. It is true that the Church is the new people of God, yet the Jews should not be spoken of as rejected or accursed by God as if this followed from holy Scripture. Consequently, all must take care, lest in catechizing or in

> preaching the Word of God, they teach anything which is not in accord with the truth of the Gospel message or the spirit of Christ.
>
> Indeed, the Church, reproves every form of persecution against whomever it may be directed. Remembering, then, her common heritage with the Jews and moved not by any political considerations, but solely by the religious motivation of Christian charity, she deplores all hatreds, persecutions, displays of antisemitism, leveled at any time or from any source against the Jews. (Austin Flannery, Gen. Ed., *Vatican Council II: The Conciliar and Post Conciliar Documents*, Northport, NY: Costello Publishing Co., Rev. Ed. 1992, p. 741.)

In reading this document, one is compelled to notice the *great omission*. In listing the very conditions this council deplores the document makes no admission of the part played by the New Testament in creating "hatreds, persecutions, [and] displays of antisemitism." Instead, it denies that very fact. Thus, this declaration misses the point. The point is not whether one believes today that all Jews, past, present, and future were mysteriously present, demanding that Jesus be crucified, but that this is the message the evangelists intended to convey. And, as we see from history, they did it very effectively.

A further example comes from a three-day symposium on the origin of anti-Semitism held at the Vatican in October 1997. Its purpose was to examine Christian thought for prejudice against Judaism, as well as against Jews. In the text of the Pope's comments, released by the Vatican, Pope John Paul II condemned anti-Semitism as "totally unjustifiable and absolutely condemnable" and called it a pagan refutation of the essence of the Christian doctrine. But, he makes no apology for Vatican silence during the Holocaust and for its centuries-old tolerance of anti-Semitism among its clergy and, until the late 1960's, in its liturgy.

The Pope acknowledges that certain Christian teachings helped fuel anti-Semitism but stops short of admitting direct New Testament or church culpability in creating anti-Jewish prejudice. Instead, he maintains that certain Christian teachings, based on "wrong and unjust" interpretations of the New Testament, had helped contribute to the Holocaust and the persecution of Jews in Europe over the centuries. Indulging in culpability shifting the Pope states, "In the Christian world—I do not say on the part of the church as such—the wrong and unjust interpretations of the New Testament relating to the Jewish people and their presumed guilt circulated for too long, contributing to feelings of hostility toward these people." He then explains that "These contributed to soothing consciences to the point that when a wave of persecution swept Europe fueled by pagan anti-Semitism—which in its essence was equal to anti-Christianism—next to those Christians who did everything to save the persecuted at the risk of their own lives, the spiritual resistance of many was not that which humanity expected from the disciples of Christ." (*The New York Times*, "Pope Ties 'Unjust' Teachings to Anti-Semitism," November 1, 1997, p. A6.)

The direct role of the New Testament and the church in the spread of anti-Jewish feeling among Christians is sidestepped. Pope John Paul II refers directly to those who risked their lives to save the persecuted but makes a judicious statement that "the spiritual resistance of many was not that which humanity expected from the disciples of Christ." This is a rather innocuous way of describing those that with brutal forethought aided and abetted murder.

In a special Mass at the Vatican (March 12, 2000), Pope John Paul II apologized for historical transgressions committed by Roman Catholics in the name of the church. This apology has significant limits. It is offered on behalf of the "children of the church," but not the church itself. This apology is accompanied by a thirty-one page document which "explains that the church is holy, but is stained by the sins of its children, and requires 'constant purification.' It implies but does not directly address the delicate issue of whether past church leaders also erred . . . The document also cautions against judging past generations by today's moral or religious standards . . ." (Alexandra Stanley, "Pope Asks Forgiveness for Errors of the Church Over 2000 Years," *The New York Times*, March 13, 2000, p. A10).

Both the Pope and the document failed to refer to the transgressions of the church itself or to past popes, cardinals, and clergy and the part they played in periods distinguished by forced conversions, the Crusades, and the Inquisition. The apology was confined to the sins committed by the ill-defined "children of the church," but not the church itself. It remains "holy" and above the misdeeds of its adherents—clergy and laymen alike—done in its name. This self-serving "cleansing" also does not address the role of the New Testament in the formulating of church policies toward Jews and Judaism.

[10] To this end, Jesuit scholar Raymond Brown wrote in his study of Johannine Christianity: "It would be incredible for a twentieth-century Christian to share or to justify the Johannine contention that 'the Jews' are the children of the devil, an affirmation which is placed on the lips of Jesus (8:44); but I cannot see how it helps contemporary Jewish-Christian relationships to disguise the fact that such an attitude once existed" (Raymond Brown, *The Community of the Beloved Disciple*, New York: Paulist Press, 1979, pp. 41-42).

1.
THE FORMATION OF NEW TESTAMENT RELIGIO-POLITICAL THEOLOGY

Gospel authorship

Composed forty to seventy years after the crucifixion, the Gospels[1] are theological-political works that assume the form of historical biography, but they are not history. They are representatives of a literary development which based itself on pre-Gospel traditions (both oral and written) that were available to the rapidly developing, church.[2] In composing the four canonical Gospels the older layers of pre-Gospel tradition were modified by theological needs and by the evangelists' imaginations. An historical Jesus was not the source of much of what was attributed to the Christological Jesus. The notion of Jesus was a peg on which those who became his followers hung theological beliefs held initially independent of him or developed after his death. Following his death, the historical Jesus was the victim of those who tailored what he had said and did during his lifetime to fit their own political and theological needs and when that was not sufficient they fabricated totally new material. The Gospel of Mark is often assumed to be the most historically reliable Gospel because of its less complex style and its being written closer to the time of Jesus than the others (c. 70 C.E.). It also served as the model for the respective Gospels of Matthew and Luke, each of which contains additional material. The Gospel of John represents a different pre-Gospel tradition and exhibits significant Samaritan influence (as do parts of Luke-Acts).[3] In no case can the historical accuracy of any Gospel be taken for granted.

Some Christian commentators have stated that the Gospel writers could not be anti-Jewish because they themselves were Jews. The question of New Testament authorship is problematical. It is not known who were the original authors of the respective Gospels. Authorship claims are based on second century conjectures and are not necessarily historically accurate.[4] As such, it is a matter of speculation to identify the authors of the respective Gospels, or, for that matter, to pinpoint the locations where these men called by Christian tradition Matthew, Mark, Luke, and John wrote the original manuscripts. It follows that there is disagreement concerning the ethnic origins of the Gospel writers. Whether the author of the Gospel of Mark was a Christian of Jewish or Gentile origin is a subject of controversy. In any case, he wrote for and favored the Gentiles while disparaging the Jews. The author of the Gospel of Matthew is said to have been a Jewish-born Christian. He, too, was decidedly anti-Jewish in his narration. The author of the Gospel of Luke and the Book of Acts was most likely a Greek Gentile and he displayed an anti-Jewish bias as well. There are indications that he used some Samaritan Christian sources in both his Gospel and Acts. The Gospel of John is for the most part the outcome of the work of Gentile Christians[5] who used material obtained from Christians of both Samaritan and Jewish origins. In its original composition it was most likely a Samaritan oriented Gospel. The Gospel of John is generally known as the most notoriously anti-Judaic of the Gospels. Even if these writers were Jewish by birth, it does not follow that they did not harbor ill feelings against the Jewish people. Moreover, the various documents constituting the New Testament were edited at a time when the church consisted largely of Gentiles and was engaged in a polemical battle with Judaism.

The authors of the Gospels were not interested in writing a

mere historical account of the life of Jesus. The evangelists were primarily interested in promoting belief in Jesus. They wished to persuade their respective audiences that Jesus was the only means by which one could achieve salvation from sin. The evangelists' goal was to convince their audience, readers and listeners alike, of the truth of their message. Pre-Gospel traditions attributed to Jesus' actual life were of interest to the Gospel authors only in so far as they could be utilized to further this goal.

The Gospels' authors exercised strong creative control over the pre-Gospel documents and traditions they utilized. By interweaving these pre-Gospel traditions with their own theological needs and imagination, the evangelists developed works of historical/theological fiction. They ordered and edited their respective narratives significantly to meet the needs of the communities for whom they wrote. As such, the Gospels reflect not only the traditions of the early church but also the reaction of the Gospel authors' respective communities to contemporary difficulties, especially with Jewish and Roman authorities. Thus, in composing their respective works, the evangelists were not simply recording historical fact nor were they strictly creative novelists. They were, in effect, imaginative writers of theological fiction set within an historical framework, practitioners of fictionally enhanced non-fiction.[6] In their respective literary compositions, the authors of the New Testament wanted to show that Jesus had distanced himself from both the Jewish people and Jewish law and that the church now took their place. The New Testament attack is twofold; it is directed against both the Jewish belief system and those Jews who remain loyal to that belief system.

Supersession

The New Testament authors introduced a doctrine of supersession in delineating Christianity's relationship to Jews and Judaism.[7] They claimed that Christianity was the legitimate heir of the original covenant and that the Christian church had displaced Judaism to become the true "sons of Abraham" (Galatians 3:7) and "the Israel of God" (Galatians 6:16). "For they are not all Israel," Paul declares, "who are [descended] from Israel; neither are they all children because they are Abraham's descendants" (Romans 9:6-7). The goal of these verses is to show that God has created a new Israel, the church, to inherit the promises made to the old Israel, which has failed to keep its covenant with God. Judaism's mission and message have become obsolete; those who believe in Jesus now exclusively hold its former divinely favored status.

Essential to enabling Christianity to claim exclusivity in God's sight was the fabrication of an anti-Judaic myth. By using anti-Jewish motifs, the New Testament authors replaced Israel by the church. To do this, it was necessary to make God and Jesus anti-Jewish as well. Thus, was created the New Testament's anti-Judaic myth of an Israel scorned by God (e.g., Matthew 21:43) and reviled by Jesus (e.g., John 8:44).

Disassociation after 70 C.E.

In the aftermath of the bitter Roman-Jewish War, Christians intensified their efforts to disassociate themselves from the rebellious Jewish people in the eyes of the Roman authorities. Christians were in an awkward position. They were, after all, a group who worshiped a Jew who had been executed by crucifixion, the Roman punishment for sedition. To be associated, in such a way, with rebels, added to the pagan animosity and the suspicion felt toward Christians. Consequently, it frustrated missionary endeavors among the Empire's inhabitants. Concerned with getting acceptance of the Christian message in the Roman Empire the Gospels' authors wanted to show the Roman authorities that Christians were not Jews. The war had destroyed the influence of the Jerusalem church. This left Paul's non-Jewish followers in clear command of the church. The main body of the church was no longer Jewish and, except for its historical background, had no need to keep any ties with Judaism and the Jewish people. Christianity had been and remained a messianic movement, but they now developed a different, "non-political" type of messianism to evade the threat of

Roman accusations that they are a seditious movement. However, this did not prevent sporadic Roman persecution of Christians.

Foremost, the developing church needed to show it was the new "spiritual Israel." However, it also needed to sift out of the pre-Gospel oral tradition any incidents that showed Jesus to be an active rebel against Roman governance. The canonical Gospels conceal his anti-Roman agitation by reinventing Jesus' activities. They turn the conflict between Jesus and Rome into a struggle solely between Jesus and the Jews.

Most Jews rejected Christian claims and adhered to the Pharisaic/rabbinical continuity of ancient Judaism. Christian failure to attract most Jews exacerbated their bitterness and increased their invectives against those they blamed for the death of Jesus, first the Jewish authorities and then with increased ferocity, the Jewish people as a whole. Christians could not understand why the Jews had not joined the Jesus movement in greater number. They had been expected to do so more than any other group. On the part of Christians, therefore, the so-called "nonbelieving" Jews' rejection of the messianic faith was seen as a provocation and a challenge to Christian conviction. With the Jewish defeat in the war against Rome, Christian religious animosity turned into political expediency. In the post-war period Christians also did not want to be thought of as Jews because of the *fiscus Iudaicus*, the tax placed on the Jews as punishment for the revolt. This tax was a financial burden on those who had to pay it.

Beginning with the first Jewish revolt against Rome (66 C.E.) and extending into the postwar period a new urgency was added to the Christian desire to be recognized as a separate entity from Judaism. They sought to avoid repressive measures and negative feelings directed at the Jewish people because of the war. One such measure was the *fiscus Iudaicus*. Following the destruction of the Temple in Jerusalem the annual tax that Jews paid to the Temple treasury was transformed into a poll tax called the *fiscus Iudaicus*. It became a tax placed on the Jews as punishment for the revolt. The Jews of the Roman Empire now had to pay this tax to the Temple of Jupiter Capitolinus. Josephus writes, "On all Jews, wheresoever resident, he [Vespasian] imposed a poll-tax of two drachmas, to be paid annually into the Capitol as formerly contributed by them to the temple at Jerusalem."[8] Thus, a sacred duty was turned into an onerous symbol of subjugation. The tax, equal to two drachmas (or denarii) a person per year, was required of all those who practiced Judaism including full proselytes. Introduced by Vespasian, in 71 C.E., it was increased first by Domitian (81-96 C.E.) and later by Hadrian (117-138 C.E.). Domitian, harsher in his treatment of the Jews than his father, Vespasian, or his brother Titus, rigorously enforced the collection of the *fiscus Iudaicus*.[9] Domitian also encouraged informers to expose proselytes to Judaism, and sentenced the latter to death for atheism (that is, for denying the imperial cult) if they persisted in practicing Judaism. Suetonius comments that during Domitian's reign:

> Besides other taxes, that on the Jews [a tax of two drachmas a head] was levied with the utmost rigor, and those were prosecuted who without publicly acknowledging that faith yet lived as Jews, as well as those who concealed their origin and did not pay the tribute levied upon their people. I recall being present in my youth when the person of a man ninety years old was examined before the procurator and a very crowded court; to see whether he was circumcised.[10]

To avoid inclusion among those required to pay the poll tax born-Jewish Christians and Gentiles who adhered to Gentile forms of Christianity stepped up attempts to emphasize to the Roman authorities the Christian distinctiveness from Judaism.

Jews in the Hellenistic world

From the time of Alexander the Great, Jews began to settle in the cities of Asia Minor. By the first century of the Common Era, Jews achieved a unique position in relation to their Roman overlords. Jewish communities were given the right to live under Jewish law and to be exempted from offending imperial laws. Thus, the Romans continued the religious toleration enjoyed by the Jewish population of the Hellenistic kingdoms, at the time they were incorporated into the Empire.[11] Roman tolerance of Judaism was advisable considering the large proportion of Jews among the population of the eastern regions of the Empire.[12] As a rule, Jews were nonconforming and non-compromising in religious matters, refusing to adhere to governmental demands which conflicted with their sacred traditions.[13] This resistance to change was balanced by adaptability to new conditions and absorption of ideas and influences from outside. Jews did not deny or evade the rightful claims of secular government. Support for the law of the land was a sacred duty (Jeremiah 29:7), at the same time they countenanced no tampering with any of Judaism's other sacred duties.[14]

Jewish loyal nonconformity was officially recognized. Jews were excused from offices and practices that involved idolatry. These special privileges angered some pagans. Consequently, classic exponents of anti-Judaism, as exemplified by those pagan authors of antiquity who attacked the Jewish people and Judaism in their literary works, mainly criticize Jewish "exclusivism." Nevertheless, anti-Jewish enmity among intellectuals was not necessarily the norm. However, among the masses there was widespread anti-Jewish sentiment.[15] Essentially, hostility stemmed from pagan resentment of Jewish separatism and privilege resulting from their religious beliefs and the attraction Judaism had for many non-Jews. Dietary laws, circumcision, the Sabbath, prohibition of intermarriage, and not worshiping idols, or the emperor were among the complaints. The large number of non-Jews who, attracted to Judaism, abandoned their former practices in favor of Jewish observance angered many pagans. Thus, Jewish resistance to the Hellenization of Judaism and the success of Jewish proselytism were at the core of pagan anti-Jewish sentiments.[16]

There was an overall governmental tolerance of the Jews in the pre-Christian Greco-Roman world. Incidents of pagan anti-Judaism were random and generally spontaneous. Although there was hostility to the Jews and violent outbreaks did occur, they were seldom centrally directed and organized. There were some notable exceptions, as in the concerted bloody attack on the Jews of Alexandria in 38 C.E.[17] This violent incident was endorsed and assisted by the Roman governor Flaccus,[18] "who, if he wished," Philo writes, "could have by himself suppressed in a single hour the tyranny of the mob."[19] Generally, the Roman government's policy toward the Jews was not greatly influenced by the anti-Jewish authors or masses. However, the outbreak of the Roman-Jewish War exacerbated relations between Jews and the Roman authorities in some parts of the Empire. Once the pagan masses saw the apparent weakening of government support for Jewish privileges, massacres by anti-Jewish mobs took place, notably in Alexandria, Caesarea, and cities in the province of Syria.[20] Yet, such outbreaks did not spread throughout the Empire. Following the war, the Roman administration once more restrained the mobs and a restoration of Jewish rights took place.[21]

Despite pagan anti-Judaic literary expressions, there was no singular ideological theory to consolidate hatred. That distinction was left to the anti-Jewish ideology developed by the New Testament. Considering the Jews as a devilish people, it accused them, as a whole, of killing Jesus and held them collectively responsible for his death. The need to discredit and condemn the Jewish people, Judaism, and the Jewish religious authorities did not end with the New Testament. Later, this ideology of hate was sharpened by some of the church fathers and given official governmental approval when Christianity became the state religion of the Roman Empire. Patristic anti-Jewish vilifications were written with little interest in real Jews or Judaism, rather they were fabricated from the polemics of the New Testament.[22]

Pagan and Christian anti-Judaism: the differences

Some Christian scholars maintain that anti-Judaism is essentially pagan and that it predates the Christian era by centuries. Hatred of the Jews, it is said, is a pagan legacy that entered Christianity as greater numbers of Gentiles adopted the Christian faith. Yet, Christian anti-Judaism cannot be explained based on pagan animosity to Jews. There is no ideological continuum between pagan anti-Jewish sentiments of the pre-Christian Greco-Roman world and similar feelings among Christians. No legacy of anti-Jewish doctrine was bequeathed to Christendom from the pagan world. Expressions of Christian anti-Jewish sentiment were not dependent on or necessarily a result of pagan anti-Jewish sentiment. Christian anti-Judaism did not arise from earlier and deeper origins—it was not so much dependent on pagan attitudes as it was on the beliefs and policies that shaped and directed the nascent church. There were certainly areas of large-scale anti-Judaism among the Empire's pagan inhabitants, and this attitude was carried over when these pagans became Christians. However, Christian anti-Judaic sentiments were not a simple continuation of pagan hostility toward Jews. Christianity nurtured and reshaped pagan (and Samaritan) enmity against Jews and Judaism. The church incorporated certain contemptuous accusations of pagan anti-Judaism into its own attacks, but its anti-Jewish approach was unique. Pre-Christian anti-Jewish pagans may have provided a receptive audience for Christian polemics against the Jews. However, it was the New Testament centered religious hostility of Christianity that demonized the Jews. The anti-Jewish thrust of the Gospel of John, in particular, exemplifies this demonization. The Johannine narrative provides a rationale and theological base for future racial antipathy toward the Jewish people.[23]

Christianity saw itself as standing in a different relationship to Jewish heritage than did paganism. Pagans who were enemies of the Jews and Judaism were contemptuous of Jewish heritage and, as such, made no claim to it.[24] They cared not at all for Jewish Scriptures or their contents, Christians did. Because of the distinctive claims of Christianity, it challenged Judaism as no paganism could ever hope to do. The conflict between the two faiths was due in part to the use of the same source of revelation to uphold their respective claims. As the church developed its theology, it simultaneously developed its anti-Judaic outlook rooted in the New Testament. The continued existence of Judaism and of a competing biblical interpretation challenged the foundations of

Christian faith. Church leaders and church civil rulers also saw active Jewish proselytizing as a threat to Christianity. The church and the rabbis both claimed to have the true understanding of the biblical text: Only one could be right.

Blaming the Jews/exonerating Pilate

As Christianity spread in the Roman Empire, it was faced with the problem that the Romans had killed Jesus. The church could not deny that the Romans were his executioners. It dealt with this problem by transferring the responsibility to the Jews. Pilate, the imperial representative, had arrested, tried, sentenced, and executed him. But, Jesus was not a threat to the Empire. Nor, indeed, were the Romans responsible for his death. The New Testament authors did not deny that the Romans actually killed Jesus, but they accused the Jews of being ultimately responsible for what the Romans had done by Pilate and his soldiers. The Jews, not the Romans, were presented as the actual enemies of Jesus. A fictionalized account of a trial was devised whereby the Roman governor of Jerusalem had judged Jesus' claims as harmless and desired to set him free. He decreed the death sentence only after the failure of serious attempts, on his part, to free Jesus. In the end, Pilate succumbed under pressure from the Jews.

According to the authors of the Gospels, the circumstances leading to Jesus' execution revolved around religious disputes between him and the Jewish religious authorities of his day. There is no record of any conflict between him and the Roman authorities. In fact, reference to the Romans in the Gospels is minimal. All criticism of the Romans is suppressed; they are scarcely mentioned. The Jesus of the Gospels is remarkably silent on the issue of their presence in Judea and Galilee and there is no mention of Roman oppression. In fact, in all of the four Gospels the word "Roman" occurs only once (John 11:48). The role of the Romans in Jesus' arrest, trial, and execution is minimized. Nowhere are they condemned for the crucifixion. Instead, the evangelists portray the rapacious, brutal Romans as naive background figures manipulated and misled by the Jews into executing Jesus. In creating a political theology, the New Testament singles out the Jews, and the Jews alone, as the national entity ultimately responsible for the death of Jesus.

The Roman governor, Pontius Pilate, who condemned Jesus and the Roman soldiers mentioned in the Gospel narrative as carrying out that sentence are exonerated. The Romans are depicted as unwilling participants in Jesus' execution. It is said that although the Romans carried out the execution, the Jews manipulated them into doing it. The role of the Romans in the death of Jesus is minimized and they are exonerated. Jewish leaders are assigned responsibility in bringing about Jesus' execution. But, implication of Jewish leaders is not enough. By the introduction of fictitious events and historic inaccuracies, the instigators, those responsible for Jesus' execution, are said to be the Jewish people as a whole. It does not matter that the great majority of contemporary Jews, whether in the Land of Israel or in the Diaspora, had never heard of Jesus. They and their progeny are said to be forever responsible for Jesus' death.

The Gospels show a determination to gloss over Roman culpability for the execution of Jesus. Instead, the Jews are portrayed as the prime movers from beginning to end in bringing about Jesus' crucifixion. According to Luke 23:13,18, the "chief priests and the rulers and the people" united in demanding Jesus' execution. In particular, the alleged conspiracy of Jewish priests, scribes, elders, rulers, Pharisees, crowds, people, and nation to kill Jesus are traced in the Gospels and Acts in great detail. They are accused of bringing false charges against the innocent Jesus (Mark 14:56) and maneuvering the Romans into executing him (John 19:12). The Gospels allot a minimal role to Pilate and the Roman soldiers in the death of Jesus. In Mark 11:18 it is the chief priests and scribes who are said to fear Jesus after he attacks the Temple. They sought to destroy him (Mark 3:6, 14:1). In Matthew 21:14-15 the same groups are indignant over Jesus' welcome in the Temple by those shouting, "Hosanna to the son of David." Luke 19:39 and John 12:19 say his growing following among the people disturbs the Pharisees. Luke 20:19 identifies the "they" who try to arrest Jesus after the parable about the vineyard in Mark 12:12 as the scribes and chief priests, while Matthew 21:45 says it was the chief priests and the Pharisees. In John 18:3, the soldiers who arrest Jesus in the garden are said to come from the chief priests and the Pharisees. John 11:47-53 portrays the Pharisees as gathered in the Sanhedrin to plot Jesus' death in collusion with Caiaphas, the High Priest. Discussions concerning the level of involvement by Jewish religious authorities in events culminating in Jesus' execution become almost irrelevant under the shadow of the New Testament's total unmitigated inclusion of all Jews as being responsible for the death of Jesus.

Roman concerns and involvement are not addressed honestly. This is especially evident from the tendentious rewriting of the events surrounding the crucifixion. Matthew's unique exoneration of Pontius Pilate, the Roman prefect (or procurator[25]), provides an opportunity to see the Matthean flare for fantasy at work. According to the author of Matthew, "Pilate said to them [the Jews], 'What then shall I do with Jesus who is called Christ?' They all said, 'Let him be crucified!' And he said, 'Why, what evil has he done?' But they kept shouting all the more, saying, 'Let him be crucified!' And when Pilate saw that he was accomplishing nothing, but rather that a riot was starting, he took water and washed his hands in front of the crowd, saying, 'I am innocent of this man's blood; see to that yourselves'" (Matthew 27:22-24). This passage represents a significant instance of political engineering of the alleged events known as the passion[26] narrative. It carried with it serious repercussions for the Jewish people of later centuries. This version of the story is not found in the older form of the Roman trial episode encountered in the Gospel of Mark or, for that matter, in any other Gospel.

It is possible that some Jewish priestly authorities provided assistance to the Romans in arresting Jesus. It is even possible that they willingly sought his death. After all, his attack on the Temple most certainly did not endear him to the Temple hierarchy. There also exists the possibility that if they did assist in the apprehension of Jesus it was because Pilate coerced them. In its effort to explain away the execution of Jesus for anti-Roman sedition, the early church invented or exaggerated the story of the Jewish authorities' involvement and/or responsibility in Jesus' death. In the Gospels' final redaction, responsibility for Jesus' death was made to lay not just with a minority of Jewish individuals, whether priests, scribes, or Pharisees, but with the entire Jewish people.

The process of transferring guilt from the Romans to the Jews did not suddenly happen after 70 C.E., when the Gospels were first compiled, but much earlier. The Gospels' general antagonism was an accentuation of hostilities toward non-Christian Jews already visible in Paul's letters and presumably percolating in other Christian circles as well. The Christian tradition recorded in the Gospel narratives concerning the role of the priestly authorities in the execution of Jesus had developed prior to the Temple's destruction and the loss of priestly authority. But, when the Gospels were written, authority for transmitting Jewish tradition lay with the Pharisees and they became subject to special attack within the Gospel narratives. The Pharisees provided religious resistance to Christian missionary activity following in the wake of the catastrophe of 70 C.E. They were depicted anachronistically by the Gospel authors as the leading protagonists in opposition to Jesus. The negative portrayal of the Pharisees was, in actuality, a criticism of Judaism itself for they were its primary spokesmen. As the Jewish leadership contemporaneous with the Gospels' redaction, the Pharisees bore the brunt of the Gospels' attack on Jewish authority, just as in much of the pre-Gospel tradition the attack centered on the priestly authorities.

The New Testament sources, in one way or another, portray every faction of the Jewish populace as entering a conspiracy to bring about the arrest, conviction, and crucifixion of Jesus. Pilate, described in the historical sources as especially cruel, is presented as a mild mannered judge who made a futile attempt to free Jesus. Thus, the Romans are absolved, their hands literally washed clean of any guilt (Matthew 27:24) and the Jews freely take responsibility upon themselves (Matthew 27:25). Years earlier, Paul had already made the accusation implicitly all-inclusive: all Jews, all places, for all time are at fault (1 Thessalonians 2:14-16).

Some Christian commentators make a distinction between the seething discontent under the Roman prefecture in the years preceding the Roman-Jewish War and the prefecture of the earlier period in which Jesus lived. This lack of distinction between the two periods, these commentators say, has led to the mistaken conclusion that Jesus was a political revolutionary. What is more, they contend that in the first half of the first century Roman rule was considered a welcome respite from the vicious religious and political struggles and misrule of the pre-Roman period. This description is extended to assume that the prefecture of Pontius Pilate was not all that unbearable and that the excesses described by Philo, Josephus, and Tacitus are prejudicial, exaggerated if not totally unfounded. As it relates to Judea, Tacitus (c. 100 C.E.), despite his aversion to Pilate, describes the reign of Emperor Tiberius (14-37 C.E.) from a Roman perspective as a peaceful period. He writes, "During the reign of Tiberius things [in Judea] remained in a state of tranquility."[27]

Apparently, Judea and Galilee were not on the verge of revolt while Pilate was governor (26-36 C.E.). There were no major anti-Roman uprisings recorded at this time, but a number of incidents of Roman provocation and bloodshed did occur. Roman rule was by no means welcome or accepted by the majority of the Jewish population in Judea and Galilee during this period. In fact, the populace detested Roman rule. Pilate, in particular, does not receive a positive rating in first century non-Christian sources and can only be vindicated when scholars ignore the overwhelming evidence against him. Pilate exacerbated Roman-Jewish relations by his callousness and ruthless brutality. The incident concerning the Roman standards[28] and the episode of the aqueduct[29] were but two instances exemplifying his viciousness and insensitivity.

In the Barabbas episode, the Gospels' anti-Jewish theme is vividly portrayed. The harmless Jesus stands meekly before the screaming Jewish mob, in which all the divisions of the Jewish people are represented, all united in the demand, "Crucify him!"

Pilate, a weak but kindly man, full of compassion, stands by helplessly. The Romans are not to blame for the execution, it is not the governor, or the imperial power he represents, that is responsible, but the Jewish mob and their leaders. The Gospel narratives relate that Pilate found Jesus not guilty and wanted to release him. It is said that Pilate was opposed to Jesus' condemnation but was coerced by Jewish pressure to agree to it. His plans to free Jesus, the Gospels maintain, were foiled by the Jewish crowd's (alternately, "people," "nation") demand that Barabbas (literally, "Son of the Father"), a convicted insurrectionist and murderer, be freed instead.[30] This was supposedly in accordance with a custom (recorded nowhere else) by which a prisoner chosen by the people was released "at the feast" (Mark 15:6-15, Matthew 27:15-26, Luke 23:16-25, John 18:39-40).

The Gospels' description of Pilate's actions is fantasy. Pilate would never succumb to a threat that if he released Jesus he was "no friend of Caesar" (John 19:12). He could easily explain to the emperor the execution of a known rebel, Barabbas, and the release of a harmless religious preacher, Jesus. If he allowed the Jewish leaders their way, as found in the Gospel narrative, it would make him vulnerable and fearful and render his rule ineffective. That the Roman prefect of a rebellion-prone province would submit to the demands of a local crowd and release what the New Testament describes as a known insurrectionist and murderer while executing a harmless prisoner he wished to free is incredible. What would the emperor's reaction be to such a stupidity? Surely, Pilate knew that he would suffer the consequences for such a breach of duty.[31]

How does the Barabbas tale serve the religio-political purposes of the early church? The aim of this deceptive story is to absolve the Romans, through their chief representative, while indicting the entire Jewish people for murder through both their priesthood and their own words. If, as the Gospel accounts of the trial maintain, Pilate believed Jesus to be innocent, he was completely free to exercise his power to acquit him. Instead, he condemned him. Why? It was not because he was coerced, helplessly in the clutches of the Jewish leaders. The historical evidence indicates that Pilate was a brutal individual who would not hesitate to order the crucifixion of anyone who claimed to be a messiah, that is, the king of the Jews. The Gospels' portrayal of Pilate as easily intimidated by the Jews should be tempered by Philo's description of Pilate as "naturally inflexible, a blend of self-will and relentlessness."[32] This was in addition to "his vindictiveness and furious temper."[33] His prefecture was infamous for "the briberies, the insults, the robberies, the outrages and wanton injuries, the executions without trial constantly repeated, the ceaseless and supremely grievous cruelty."[34] This is a man who would not fear being accused before Caesar of ordering the execution of a would-be king. What he would fear is the accusation that he permitted a known insurrectionist and murderer to go free. Therefore, he would never release a known rebel such as Barabbas. Surely, there were other prisoners from which to choose one to be released. There was nothing to prevent Pilate from freeing another prisoner, or any number of prisoners, instead of the particular prisoner chosen by the Jews, if that is what he wanted to do. But, the church needed to suppress the truth. The freeing of Barabbas story, as developed in the pre-Gospel tradition, explains why Pilate, despite his judicial power to do otherwise, did not free Jesus. At the same time, this episode, whatever its origins, plays a pivotal role in placing the blame for Jesus' death on the Jews.

Pilate's cruel behavior was consistent throughout his prefecture and well attested to in contemporary literary sources. Nevertheless, in the Gospels, the Jewish people are blamed for Jesus' execution while Pilate is portrayed as attempting to prevent an injustice. The Gospel authors would have us believe that Pilate suddenly changes his usually vicious character, and out of kindness or a sense of justice, wants to save Jesus who claims to be the king of the Jews. These authors avoid mentioning that the Romans considered Jesus dangerous. And so, Matthew has Pilate become "innocent of this man's blood" through a symbolic washing of hands (Matthew 27:24), Mark has him question "what evil has he done?" (Mark 15:14), Luke has him reluctantly turn "Jesus over to their will" (Luke 23:25), and John has him say, "I find no guilt in him" (John

18:38). When one discounts the Gospels' self-serving accusations against the Jews and the absurdity that Pilate was merely the victimized agent of a Jewish plot, one realizes that the Romans had the greatest interest in suppressing an individual who thought himself to be a king and opposed their governing the land. Moreover, Mark's Pilate shows awareness that the crowd demanding the release of Barabbas also considers Jesus to be its king. Addressing the crowd, Pilate says concerning Jesus, "Do you want me to release for you the King of the Jews?" (Mark 15:9). This is not a mere sarcastic remark for Pilate then asks concerning Jesus, "Then what shall I do to him *whom you call King of the Jews?*" (Mark 15:12). Yet, the authors of the Gospels would have us believe that Pilate contemplated releasing Jesus, who the crowd considered a king!

First century Christians, as reflected in the Gospels, found it expedient to maintain that the Jews demanded Jesus' death despite Pilate's wishes to free him. It is difficult to imagine a greater discrepancy as that between the ruthless Pilate described in the writings of Philo and the weak-willed, vacillating figure depicted in Mark 15:1-15—the basic passage which set the model for subsequent Christian portrayals. The Gospels' Pilate frets, his wife advises him not to harm this man, he confers with the crowd of Jews, and he appeals on Jesus' behalf. Finally, unable to withstand the demands of the crowd, he has Jesus executed. According to the Gospels, Pilate believed that Jesus was innocent (see Mark 15:14, Matthew 27:23, Luke 23:13-16, John 19:12-16). Thus, the evangelists claim it is only because of the relentless demands of the Jewish people and their leaders that he reluctantly orders the execution. These components of the story of Jesus' last hours result from a Christian desire to smooth relations with Rome and to portray Jews as their actual adversaries. What is more probable is that Pilate had determined that Jesus' actions were threatening law and order. Therefore, he demanded Caiaphas' cooperation in apprehending Jesus, had Jesus scourged and interrogated, and, then, condemned him to death with not a second thought.

A story was concocted which portrays Pilate as wanting to free Jesus because he was "aware that the chief priests had delivered him up because of envy" (Mark 15:10). But, Pilate was not interested in the religious disputes of the Jews. He was not at all concerned about those who kept the Jewish ritual or ignored it. He was not interested in the religious arguments of the Pharisees or Sadducees or in any dispute they might have with this Jesus. But, he was very interested and very much concerned about any hint of a political revolt against Roman governance. It makes no sense to maintain that Pilate interfered in a purely religious dispute between Jesus and the Jewish religious authorities. Therefore, the Jews are made to bring false charges against Jesus and to force the hapless Pilate into going along with their plan or suffer their vindictiveness as well. The fact is that there was no trumped-up charge of sedition presented by the Jewish leaders. Pilate already considered Jesus guilty because of his own words and actions. He regarded Jesus, who considered himself as king of the Jews, a political threat and, therefore, dangerous to the stability of Roman rule. His concern about Jesus was not religious, but political. Jesus denounced paying taxes to Rome (Mark 12:17, Matthew 22:21, Luke 20:25), rode into Jerusalem as a messianic king (Mark 11:7-10, Matthew 21:4-11, Luke 19:35-39, John 12:12-15), seized the Temple courtyard (Mark 11:15-16, Matthew 21:12, Luke 19:45, John 2:14-16), and claimed to be king of the Jews in Pilate's presence (Mark 15:2, Matthew 27:11, Luke 23:3, John 18:37). These were the deeds of a political insurrectionist, not a benign religious preacher. Yet, by their very nature, they most certainly had religious repercussions as well. In response to Jesus' words and actions, the Roman governor, Pilate, who at least in regard to Jewish rebels was definitely "a friend of Caesar," knew exactly what had to be done to preserve Roman sovereignty. Political rebellion was to be immediately crushed. To this end, Pilate placed himself in complete control of the situation. Thus, the Romans put Jesus to death, not because of his overall teachings, but because of specific politically inflammatory statements and acts which attracted crowds and crowds were unpredictably dangerous. For their part, the Jewish authorities might have feared that his actions would precipitate an insurrection that would lead to devastating consequences for the entire people. The Jewish authorities were well aware of Roman brutality. Most would have been old enough to witness events after the Roman suppression of the relatively minor rebellion in Judea following the death of King Herod (4 B.C.E.). At that time, Quintilius Varus, the Roman Legate of Syria, crucified 2,000 Jews.[35] Indeed, fears concerning massive retaliation were realized during Titus' siege of Jerusalem in 70 C.E. when, according to Josephus, the Roman army crucified as many as 500 Jews a day for several months.[36]

In contrast to the historical Pilate, the New Testament portrait of Pilate that emerges is one of an individual sympathetic to a victim of an internal Jewish religious dispute who he realizes is falsely accused of being a political foe of the Empire. Pilate, pressured by the Jewish mob and Jewish leaders reluctantly agrees to their demands. Disregarded by the Gospels' Pilate is what should have been his major concerns: Jesus' call to his audience not to pay taxes to Caesar, his staging of a royal entrance into Jerusalem, and his pre-planned riotous attack on the Temple just before the Passover festival. Yet, to believe the evangelists, these are of no concern to Pilate even when Jesus answers positively to his query: "Are you the king of the Jews?" (Luke 23:3). All Pilate can say is, "I find no guilt in this man" (Luke 23:4). He is not even concerned that Jesus' physical actions were along the same lines as the contents of his preaching: "He stirs up the people, teaching all over Judea, starting from Galilee, even as far as this place" (Luke 23:5). Either Pilate had no concern for the Roman Empire's security and his own well being or the Gospels hide the truth.

The early church downplayed that after a speedy interrogation with no witnesses and with no real trial procedure Pilate had Jesus quickly executed. Stories of Pilate's reluctance to execute Jesus and his weakness of character are creations of New Testament apologetics. Their purpose is to reduce the conflict between the nascent church and the Roman authorities.[37] But, in truth, it was because of a claim to the kingship of Israel that the Romans crucified Jesus as a political criminal. The Roman governor knew quite well why he condemned him. This much is evident from an analysis of the Gospel narrative. The actual extent to which the Jewish authorities of Jerusalem willingly cooperated with the Romans or agreed with the condemnation is another matter. But, it has become so obscured by New Testament polemics that it can never be known with any certainty.

Theological engineering of the New Testament text

There are those who would deny that the New Testament laid the foundation for Christian hatred and persecution of the Jewish people. They argue that anti-Judaism can be traced to the New Testament only tendentiously or if that work is incorrectly interpreted. However, to deny that there is anti-Jewish sentiment expressed in the New Testament is to disregard all literary, theological, and historical data to the contrary. In fact, one does not have to leave it to personal, theological, or emotional considerations to decide if the New Testament teaches hatred of the Jewish people. The decision as to whether or not the New Testament contains anti-Jewish teachings can be based solely on the information provided by the New Testament itself.

Some authors attempt to dilute the anti-Jewish accusations explicitly expressed in the New Testament by saying that all men and women, past, present, and future contribute to the death of Jesus. Therefore, they argue that neither the Jews alone or in conjunction with the Romans are responsible for the crucifixion of Jesus. These commentators maintain that all mankind was, and is, responsible for this deed. The Jews of that generation merely acted as representatives of mankind, Jew and Gentile alike, in every generation. They contend that people are responsible for the crucifixion each time they reject God or knowingly reject what, as defined and taught by Christianity, God wants. Accordingly, it is said to be wrong to fix blame solely on one group of people.

Statements that generalize guilt for Jesus' death into a worldwide phenomenon, are not supported by relevant New Testament texts. The New Testament accusations speak for themselves. The New Testament assigns a marginal guilt solely to those Romans actually present and immediately has the dying Jesus forgive them for their deed. At the same time, New Testament texts hold all Jews, of every generation, responsible for Jesus' death. In the New Testament, all the Jews contemporary with Jesus and all subsequent generations are ultimately made to carry the entire burden of guilt. Consequently, it is the Jews, and they alone, of all the peoples of the world, who have been called "Christ killers"; they alone have been persecuted for the death of Jesus. These basic facts make the accusation of mankind's collective guilt meaningless.[38]

Such theological engineering might sound appealing but it does not conform to the New Testament text. Moreover, it cannot excuse away the fact that only one group of people, the Jewish people, have actually been persecuted and held accountable for Jesus' execution. Jews, who blame the New Testament's authors for anti-Jewish persecution, need not apologize. History supports the accusation.

Spreading the Gospel: "To the Jew first"

The New Testament, with its passages of wrath directed against Jews and Judaism, prompted centuries of anti-Judaic hostility. These passages were the inspiration for centuries of the most unspeakable inhumanity and barbarism. Jews lived in social and economic conditions that were humiliating and crushing and were the victims of forced conversions, medieval disputations, expulsions, and death at the hands of those Christians who sought to "bring the Jews to Christ." The New Testament furnished a theological basis for an attitude of hostility toward Jews that erupted repeatedly in insidious programs of conversion combined with physical acts of oppression. In explanation of Jewish suffering, the Christian answer was that it was due to divine displeasure for having rejected Jesus. Consequently, the Jews were to be wanderers, relentlessly pursued. But the solution to their problems, the oppressor's circular reasoning maintained, was the Gospel. To find peace and acceptance they needed only to accept Jesus as their Messiah.

For centuries, zealous Christians have tried to convert Jews.

Their profession of love for the Jewish people led more often than not to Jews being racked, hacked, beaten, and burned. In their zeal to qualify Jews for entrance into heaven, they have put them through hell on earth. Despite all the attempts to have Jews "saved" through the redemption supposedly found in Jesus' "covering blood," the only blood that ever covered most Jews was their own. The centuries of anti-Judaic extremism sprouting from the New Testament seedbed are without parallel in their violence and consequences. Yet, despite all efforts to the contrary, the Jewish people have survived.

Notes

[1] *Gospel.* One of the first four books of the New Testament, describing (often in variant accounts) what is supposed to be the life, death, and resurrection of Jesus. *Gospel* may also refer to the teachings of Jesus and the apostles.

[2] The Jesus movement or church was never a unified body. Certainly, by the late first century, what we call "the church" was factionalized into numerous and theologically diverse groups.

[3] As will be shown in subsequent chapters, there is evidence of Samaritan anti-Jewish sentiment having influenced several New Testament authors. The author of John, in particular, relied on Samaritan folk-hatred of the Jews in developing his own anti-Judaic attack. But, the result was only remotely related to the Samaritans or their counter-charges against Jews and Judaism. What the author developed was a distinctly Christian product with claims on Israel's heritage equally alien to Samaritans as to Jews.

[4] In this work, a Gospel volume sometimes will be referred to solely by the name of its traditionally assigned author. This does not imply acceptance of the position that the Gospel was written by that individual. It is merely a stylistic convenience.

[5] Hereafter the respective authors of the Gospel of John will, generally, be referred to in the singular.

[6] The canonical Gospels were not the only Gospels written. Other examples are the Gospel of Thomas, the Gospel of Peter, the Gospel of Philip, the Secret Gospel of Mark, the Gospel of Mary Magdalene, the Gospel According

to the Hebrews, and the Gospel According to the Ebionites. Gospel genre represents diverse theological and philosophical beliefs concerning the person, mission, and death of Jesus. The church fathers have handed down fragmented details from the Gospels used by the Ebionites and Nazarenes. These sects may have been closer in belief to Jesus and the Apostles than were Stephen and Paul and their followers. The Ebionites and Nazarenes and their literary works were declared heretical by the Gentile dominated church and destroyed.

[7] Rosemary R. Reuther (*Faith and Fratricide*, New York: Seabury Press, 1974) expresses the view that Christian anti-Judaism had been fundamental to the early Christian movement's understanding of itself as "true Israel" and of Jesus as the Jewish Messiah.

In discussing supersessionism, a study document (not an official position paper) approved by the General Assembly of the Presbyterian Church (U.S.A.) acknowledges that "The long and dolorous history of Christian imperialism, in which the church often justified anti-Jewish acts and attitudes in the name of Jesus, finds its theological base in this teaching."

(*A Theological Understanding of the Relationship between Christians and Jews: A Paper Commended to the Church for Study and Reflection*, New York: Office of the General Assembly of the Presbyterian Church [U.S.A.], 1987, p. 3)

[8] Josephus, *Jewish War* VII. 6. 6 [218].

[9] The *fiscus Iudaicus* continued to be imposed upon the Jews for nearly three centuries under both pagan and Christian emperors until it was abolished in 361 C.E. by the Emperor Julian, who had the tax lists burned so that the tax might not be reimposed.

[10] Seutonius, *The Lives of the Caesars: Domitian* 12. 2.

[11] Jewish sovereignty in the Land of Israel ended with the Roman conquest of Jerusalem in 63 B.C.E.

[12] Some scholars estimate that the Jews of the Roman Empire numbered between four to seven million people.

[13] Josephus writes, "Religion governs all our actions and occupations and speech: none of these things did our lawgiver leave unexamined or indeterminate" (*Against Apion* II. 16. [171]).

14 The eventual introduction of the imperial cult into the eastern Mediterranean region intensified the division between Jews and pagans. With the waning of belief in the ancient pagan gods, it became increasingly commonplace for rulers to be worshiped as gods. This was especially true of the spread of the Roman imperial cult. As far as most Jews were concerned, any compromise between Judaism and the pagan imperial cult was inconceivable. This deification of rulers sharpened the contrast between Jews and pagans.

15 See, Louis H. Feldman, *Jew and Gentile in the Ancient World: Attitudes and Interactions from Alexander to Justinian*, Princeton, NJ: Princeton University Press, 1993. Feldman explores the relationship between Jews and Gentiles from the fourth century B.C.E. through the sixth century C.E.

16 Roman authors who mention Jews, even incidentally, frequently refer to their proselytizing activity (see Molly Whittaker, *Jews and Christians: Graeco-Roman Views*, Cambridge: Cambridge University Press, 1984, pp. 85-91).

In one of his satires, Juvenal (60?-140? C.E.), scoffs at the Roman father who turns from paganism to Judaism. The father eats no pork, observes the Sabbath, and worships only a God in heaven and his son undergoes circumcision, is contemptuous of Roman laws, and studies Jewish law:

> Some, sons of a father who observes the day of the Sabbath, worship nothing but clouds and a spirit in heaven, and differentiate not between human flesh and that of the swine from which their father abstained. Soon they shorten their foreskin. Trained to hold Roman law in contempt, they study with care Jewish law to obey and to revere it, and all that Moses transmitted in a secret book. It forbids them to show the right way to any but those who accept the same rites, and permits them to guide to the well (of their wisdom) the circumcised only and none of the others. At fault is the father, however, who every seventh day turned lazy, taking no part in the tasks and duties of life (*Satire* 14. 96-106).

The law-ordered life of an observant Jew with its ethical teachings and conduct was often very appealing to his Gentile neighbors. Josephus writes, concerning the Greeks: " . . . many of them have agreed to adopt our laws; of whom some have remained faithful, while others, lacking the necessary endurance, have again seceded" (*Against Apion*, II. 10 [123]). Attraction to Judaism was to be found in every strata of non-Jewish society. Josephus describes Poppea, Nero's wife, as "a worshiper of God . . . who pleaded on behalf of the Jews" (*Jewish Antiquities* XX. 8. 11 [195]). He also mentions that most of the women in Damascus were converts to Judaism (*Jewish War* II. 20. 2 [560]).

17 Philo describes this anti-Jewish outbreak as resulting from a long-standing Egyptian hostility toward the Jews. " . . . [J]ealousy is part of the Egyptian nature, and the citizens were bursting with envy and considered that any good luck to others was misfortune to themselves, and in their ancient, and we might say innate hostility to the Jews, they resented a Jew [Herod Agrippa] having been made a king just as much as if each of them had thereby been deprived of an ancestral throne" (Philo, *Flaccus* V. 29).

18 Flaccus was appointed prefect of Alexandria and Egypt *circa* 32 C.E.

19 Philo, *On the Embassy to Gaius* XX. 132. Because of his actions, Flaccus was recalled to Rome in disgrace, banished, and eventually executed (*Flaccus* XII. 103-XXI. 191).

20 For example, Josephus reports that following the outbreak of the Roman-Jewish War " . . . the people of Damascus, learning of the disaster which had befallen the Romans, were fired with a determination to kill the Jews who resided among them. As they had for a long time past kept them shut up in the gymnasium—a precaution prompted by suspicion—they considered that the execution of their plan would present no difficulty whatsoever; their only fear was of their own wives who, with few exceptions, had all become converts to the Jewish religion and so their efforts were mainly directed to keeping the secret from them. In the end, they fell upon the Jews, cooped up as they were and unarmed, and within one hour slaughtered them all with impunity, to the number of ten thousand five hundred." (*Jewish War* II. 20. 2 [560-561]).

21 The shifts in Roman policy are illustrated by Josephus. He describes conditions in Antioch after the war began. Antiochus, an apostate Jew, stirred up the masses to massacre the Jews of the city and to force the survivors to violate the Sabbath. To enforce Sabbath-breaking he enlisted the aid of the local Roman general who provided troops for this purpose (*Jewish War* VII. 3. 3 [46-53]). Antiochus incited another attack after the revolt was over.

This time there was a different Roman reaction. The Roman deputy-governor restrained, "with great difficulty," the rioters' fury (VII. 3. 4 [54-59]). When Titus passed through Antioch he was requested by its pagan residents to expel the Jews. He refused this request as well as their further petition to revoke "the privileges of the Jews." Thus, Josephus writes, "But this, too, Titus refused . . . leaving the status of the Jews of Antioch exactly as it was before . . ." (VII. 5. 2 [100-111]).

[22] Thus, charges that the Jews posses a devilish nature and the accusation of deicide form the core of most anti-Jewish diatribes by the church fathers.

[23] Hyam Maccoby credits the pagan world with a greater role in shaping Christian anti-Judaic sentiment. Maccoby identifies three sources of Christian anti-Semitism: (1) pre-Christian Gnosticism and its anti-Semitic mythology, (2) the ancient mystery-cult myth of a god murdered by an evil force or rival god, and (3) a supersessionist theology in which the church replaces Israel as the vehicle of God's promises. In Maccoby's view, what is most significant is not that Christian anti-Semitism has roots in mystery religions and Gnosticism but that Christianity has been the chief conduit through which these pagan ideas have passed into Western consciousness. (Hyman Maccoby, *The Sacred Executioner: Human Sacrifice and the Legacy of Guilt*, London: Thames and Hudson, 1982. Maccoby writes that anti-Semitism is embedded in Christianity at the deepest level: " . . . Christian anti-Semitism derives not from some accidental and inessential layer of Christianity but from its central doctrine and myth, the crucifixion itself." (Hyman Maccoby, "Theologian of the Holocaust," *Commentary* 74 [December, 1982], p. 36)

Anti-Semitism, according to the *Encyclopedia Judaica*, means "all forms of hostility manifested toward the Jews throughout history" (Binyamin Eliav, "Anti-Semitism," *Encyclopedia Judaica*, Jerusalem: Keter Publishing House, vol. 3, 1971, col. 87). The *Encyclopedia Americana* defines anti-Semitism as, "prejudice and discrimination against, or persecution of the Jewish people." It adds, "Although most Arabs and Ethiopians are classified as Semites, 'anti-Semitism' only applies to Jews" (Raphael Patai, *The Encyclopedia Americana*, "Anti-Semitism," Danbury, Conn.: Grolier, vol. 2, 1992, p. 74). Therefore, the blunt term "Jew-hatred" is, in some contexts, preferable to the genteel euphemism "anti-Semitism." After all, it is not Semites that most anti-Semites despise!

The neologism, anti-Semitism, is derived linguistically and was coined in 1879 by Wilhelm Marr, a German anti-Jewish agitator. The term is supposed to lend "scientific" responsibility to hatred of the Jews as a race, a prejudice allegedly uncontaminated by "pre-enlightenment" religious bigotry. It was a sign of bigotry, anti-Semites argued, to be biased against Jews because of religion. But they maintained the Jews were of an inferior race, and that to recognize that alleged fact was not bigotry but scientific.

To describe the anti-Judaism of antiquity by use of the term "anti-Semitism" is anachronistic and misleading. Mostly, the division between Jews and other people in the Greek and Roman world was based on religio-cultural differences not race. The term "anti-Semitism" should not be used for the first century situation when there was nothing resembling the modern-day phenomena. However, the Gospels of Matthew (Matthew 27:25) and John (John 8:44) do lay a theological groundwork for an anti-Jewish racial theory.

In the post-Holocaust era, it was politically incorrect for those who hate Jews to admit to anti-Semitic feelings in the public form. Therefore, the term "anti-Zionist" has often supplanted "anti-Semite" as the self-appellation of choice of the more sophisticated Jew-hater. Such individuals often deny that they are, in actuality, anti-Jewish. After all, they maintain, it is not their fault that most Zionists are, as it happens, Jews. As to the Holocaust that made it unfashionable to call oneself an anti-Semite, that, they claim, is part of the Zionist plot—a fiction to gain sympathy for the state of Israel.

The terms, "anti-Judaism" and "anti-Semitism" have been used to describe anti-Jewish attitudes in the New Testament. Compare, for example, Samuel Sandmel, *Anti-Semitism in the New Testament?* (Philadelphia: Fortress Press, 1978); and Peter Richardson, Ed., *Anti-Judaism in Early Christianity*, vols. 1 and 2 (Waterloo: Wilfred Laurier Press, 1986, 1987).

Some Christians make a distinction between "anti-Judaism" and "anti-Semitism." For example, Edward Flannery defines "anti-Judaism" as a "purely theological reality . . . which rejects Judaism as a way of Salvation but not Jews as a people." It is "intellectual in nature . . . bereft of hatred or stereotyping of Jews"; it is a "theological offensive" against Judaism, which constitutes "fair and irenic polemics." "Anti-Semitism," on the other hand, always "include[s] a note of hatred or contempt of the *Jewish people as such*" (Edward Flannery, "Anti-Judaism and Anti-Semitism: A Necessary Distinction," *Journal of Ecumenical Studies* 10 [Summer, 1973], pp. 582-583). Although many Christians have acknowledged "anti-Judaic" sentiments in the Gospel of John, very few are willing to label those sentiments "anti-Semitic." Flannery's definition of "anti-Judaism" does not come close to describing "the Jews" as portrayed in the Fourth Gospel. The Gospel of John is neither "bereft of hatred or stereotyping of Jews" nor are its polemics "fair and irenic." More realistic is the observation of Eldon Jay Epp. He writes that while the "denigration of the Torah" by Paul and the "maligning of the Pharisees" in the Synoptic Gospels have led to "pernicious consequences," the "vilification of the Jews" as a whole by the Gospel of John "must be accounted more heavily responsible for those consequences." His conclusion is that "[It] is difficult to apply to the Fourth Gospel's anti-Jewish attitudes and to their distinct impact upon the reader any other term than 'anti-Semitic'" (Eldon Jay Epp, "Anti-Semitism and the Popularity of the Fourth Gospel in Christianity," *Central Conference of American Rabbis Journal* 22 [Fall, 1975], p. 49). The Johannine anti-Judaic demonization of "the Jews" is essentially religious in nature, but contains racial overtones expressing the contemptuous attitude usually associated with anti-Semitism.

A. Roy Eckardt comments: "If it is unfair and inaccurate to lump the New Testament indiscriminately under anti-Semitic literature, nevertheless some of the seeds of anti-Semitism are contained therein.... I believe that James Parkes puts the matter fairly: Although anti-Semitism today contains aspects which have nothing to do with Christianity, we who are Christians cannot deny our responsibility 'for the creation of the instrument' which anti-Semites 'now use without us.'" (A. Roy Eckardt, "Theological Approaches to Anti-Semitism," *Jewish Social Sciences*, 32 [October 1971], p. 282; James Parkes' remark is from an address to the London Society of Jews and Christians entitled, "The History of Jewish-Christian Relations," March 1961 [unpublished].

An important study reviewing the work of those scholars who, on the one hand, dismiss the importance of Christian belief, attitude, and behavior "as a source of anti-Semitic feeling in the modern world" and, on the other, those scholars who find a close relationship between "Christian faith and anti-Jewish sentiment" is that of Stephen R. Haynes ("Changing Paradigms: Reformist, Radical, and Rejectionist Approaches to the Relationship Between Christianity and Antisemitism," *Journal of Ecumenical Studies*, 32 [Winter, 1995], pp. 63-88).

[24] See Josephus' *Against Apion* and Philo's *On the Embassy to Gaius*.

[25] Pilate's formal title was *Praefectus* (Greek, *eparchos*) *Iudaeae*, "Prefect of Judea" rather than "procurator" (Greek, *epitropos*—see *Jewish War* II. 8. 1 [117]). A partial Latin inscription found in archeological excavations at Caesarea, Israel, in 1961, reads in part:

[PON]TIUS PILATUS
[PRAEF]ECTUS IUDA[EA]E

The unbracketed words, or parts of words, represent the intact Latin inscription, but everything else was not represented on the stone inscription when found. The Gospels describe Pilate as *hegemon*, "governor," of Judea (Matthew 27:2, Luke 20:20). Perhaps the titles were somewhat interchangeable.

[26] *Passion* refers to the respective Gospel narratives describing the suffering of Jesus in the period following the Last Supper and including the crucifixion.

[27] Tacitus, *Histories* 5. 9.

[28] *Jewish War* II. 9. 2 [169-174].

[29] *Jewish War* II. 9. 2 [175-177].

[30] Barabbas is called a *lestes* (John 18:40). Although *lestes* can mean robber, in this case, it most likely refers to an insurrectionist (Josephus constantly uses it to describe the Zealots.). The two men who were crucified with Jesus are described as *lestai* (Matthew 27:38). Their being sentenced to be crucified shows that they were not mere robbers, but seditionists and that *lestai* is better rendered as "rebels," "guerrillas," or "insurrectionists."

[31] According to Harold W. Hoehner (who calculates that Jesus was executed in 33 C.E.), "Pilate was an inflexible and ruthless character as long as his mentor Sejanus was in power" (Harold W. Hoehner, *Chronological Aspects of the Life of Christ*, Grand Rapids: Zondervan Publishing House, 1977, p. 11). Before

his downfall, Sejanus was virtually in control of the Roman government. In Hoehner's opinion, once Sejanus, a vicious Jew hater, was executed (d. 18 October 31 C.E.) Pilate had everything to fear (see Hoehner, pp. 105-114). As Hoehner reconstructs events, Pilate appears to have a weak character in the Gospel narratives because he has just been severely rebuked by Tiberius Caesar, in the votive shields incident. He fears, Hoehner contends, that the Jewish leaders' threat (John 19:12) could lead to another rebuke and his dismissal from office. This explanation of Pilate's behavior, as depicted in the New Testament, is simply speculation on Hoehner's part. Even if initially shaken by Sejanus' fall from power, Pilate would soon have to regain his confidence if he expected to continue to rule Judea effectively. In fact, when Pilate was dismissed in 36 C.E. it was precisely because of ruthless actions he had ordered.

32 Philo, *On the Embassy to Gaius* XXXVIII. 301. Philo was Pilate's contemporary.
33 Philo, XXXVIII. 303.
34 Philo, XXXVIII. 302.
35 *Jewish Antiquities* XVII. 9. 10 [295].
36 *Jewish War* V. 9. 1 [449-450].
37 There were other attempts to show that the followers of Jesus were at peace with Roman governance. Paul is said to have advised, "Let every person be in subjection to the governing authorities. For there is no authority except from God, and those that exist are established by God. Therefore, he who resists authority has opposed the ordinances of God; and they who have opposed will receive condemnation upon themselves" (Romans 13:1-2). The author of 1 Peter counseled, "Submit yourselves for the Lord's sake to every human institution: whether to a king as the one in authority; or to governors as sent by him for the punishment of evildoers and the praise of those who do right" (1 Peter 2:13-14). These authors wished to show that the followers of Jesus were good and loyal citizens; the Roman Empire had nothing to fear from them.
38 Gerald O'Collins reminded his readers that we all share in the guilt of those who condemned Jesus, because of the "primal lust for evil which lays its hand on everyone" (Gerald O'Collins, *Interpreting Jesus, Introducing Catholic Theology 2*, London: Geoffrey Chapman; Ramsey, N.Y.: Paulist Press, 1983, p. 79). He contends that we must recognize in ourselves those "degrading flaws that—given the required circumstances—could even make me join

forces with those who directly killed Jesus" (*Ibid.* p. 78). Such words ring hollow. It is not the world, or specifically the Romans who are held accountable for Jesus' death. It is the Jews who are said to have "directly killed Jesus"; it is they alone who have been accused and persecuted for that death. More to the point is the observations expressed by Rosemary Reuther. Noting that most Christian discussions on anti-Semitism have been limited to an acknowledgment of its presence as an "element which is accidental to Christianity," she questions whether this attitude is not something which is deeply rooted in the "theological structures of the New Testament itself." Reuther recognizes the general reluctance of ecclesial authorities to face the issue. Therefore, she writes: "This careful hedging on New Testament territory was particularly apparent in the Vatican Council II decree on the Jews. In theological terms, it was willing to go only so far as to repudiate the idea of a special guilt vis-à-vis the death of Jesus resting on the Jewish people for all time. Since Christianity takes the death of Jesus as a sacrifice for sin on behalf of all mankind, it was easy enough to shift the discussion onto this framework, to assert that the Jewish guilt in this regard was only an instance of the general guilt of all mankind, not one pertaining to Jews alone. But this statement was framed in such a way as to prevent the raising of any questions about anti-Semitic attitudes within the New Testament itself. Whatever attitudes toward the Jews might be found in the New Testament were unimpeachable, both theologically and historically. This was territory which could not be challenged!" (Rosemary Reuther, "Theological Anti-Semitism in the New Testament," *The Christian Century*, vol. 85, no.7, February 1968, p. 191).

2.
SELLING "THE CHRIST"

To understand the New Testament attack on Jews and Judaism one must first have an understanding of Paul's belief that the end justifies the means. Paul presents his missionary program in word and deed in his letters and actions. In one of his letters he writes:

> Some, to be sure, are preaching Christ even from envy and strife, but some also from good will; the latter do it out of love, knowing that I am appointed for the defense of the gospel; the former proclaim Christ out of selfish ambition, rather than from pure motives, thinking to cause me distress in my imprisonment. What then? Only that in every way, whether in pretense or in truth, Christ is proclaimed; and in this I rejoice, yes; and I will rejoice. (Philippians 1:15-18)

In Philippians 1:17, Paul admonishes those who disagree with him and who preach Christianity for what he claims is their own personal ends. However, he does find reason to praise them in that these Christian adversaries of his are, when all is said and done, proclaiming "Christ." In Philippians 1:18, Paul praises the proclamation of Jesus to the world and it does not matter to him if this proclaiming is done "in pretense or in truth" so long as it is done. Paul maintains that in his preaching he is telling the truth: "I am telling the truth in Christ, I am not lying, my conscience bearing me witness in the Holy Spirit" (Romans 9:1), "Now in what I am writing to you; I assure you before God that I am not lying" (Galatians 1:20). Yet, Paul admits in Philippians 1:18 that he believes lying is a legitimate means for achieving his purpose.

In order to understand that there could be no other valid interpretation of verse 18 one must first study Paul's word usage in the preceding verses. In verse 17, Paul declares that some of his contemporaries were preaching Jesus "out of selfish ambition."[1] The Greek word is *eritheias* (genitive case).[2] The King James Version's rendering, "of contention,"[3] is based on the older theory that *eritheia* comes from *eris*, which is correctly translated "strife" in verse 15. Today, however, most scholars of Greek reject this view agreeing that the true meaning of *eritheias* is "selfishness," "self ambition," "self-seeking." A proper translation then would be, "out of selfish ambition."

With an understanding of the meaning of the word, *eritheias*, we can now understand what Paul is saying in Philippians 1:18. The Greek word *prophasis*, "pretense" (verse 18), comes from *prophemi* "speak forth," that is, in a manner that gives the outward appearance of being true, but is often untrue. Examining the context in which verse 18 appears, it is obvious that Paul is decrying that his opponents have chosen to preach Jesus "out of selfish ambition" (verse 17) with mixed and impure motives to enhance their own ends. He, however, envisions his own ministry to have been undertaken in a selfless manner. Nevertheless, although he upbraids them for their impure motives he still rejoices in that they were preaching Jesus, no matter what their motives (selfish-ambition) or methods (lying). So compelling was Paul's missionary zeal that in the end he does not mind if the ostensible presentation was often untrue. Thus, he says: "Whether in pretense or in truth Christ is proclaimed, and in this I rejoice, yes, and I will rejoice." This is a corollary to Paul's advice to born-Jewish Christian missionaries on how to infiltrate and seduce the Jewish community. Proclaim your Jewishness when it suits your purpose of getting the Jews to listen to your message without hostility. Thus, Paul said:

> For though I am free from all, I have made myself a slave to all, that I might win the more. And to the Jews I became as a Jew, that I might win Jews; to those who are under the Law, as under the Law, though not being myself under the Law, that I might win those who are under the Law; to those who are without law, as without law, though not being without the law of God but under the law of Christ, that I might win those who are without law. To the weak I became as weak, that I might win the weak; I have become all things to all men, that I may by all means save some. And I do all things for the sake of the gospel, that I may become a fellow-partaker of it. (1 Corinthians 9:19-23)

In the course of Paul's missionary effort, if it served his purpose, he spoke to a Jew as if he himself was *just* another Jew. Paul became *as* a Jew, "that . . . . [he] might win Jews." He gave the appearance of believing and worshiping in accordance with the Jewish way (Acts 13:15, 21:26, 28:17) when in fact it was mere pretense. He defended himself by asserting that he strictly observed the customs of his people (Acts 25:8, 26:5, 28:17).[4] He gave the appearance of being Jewish, but his beliefs were not Jewish. Paul no longer felt himself to be Jewish; he acted Jewish to gain access to the Jewish community "as a Jew." In essence, however, he negated his Jewishness and became an enemy of all things Jewish. He looked at his Jewish heritage as being nothing but "excrement" (Philippians 3:4-8; cf. *Jewish Wars* V. 13. 7. [571], *Sirach* 27:4). Yet, the nature of his missionary approach dictated that he should *not* always make his true feelings apparent. Paul would not be forthright if it would inhibit his main goal of converting the Jew or Gentile. Paul's literary legacy reveals that he despises those Jews who did not accept his teachings about Jesus.

Paul's letters and the information provided by the Book of Acts leave no doubt about clashes between Paul on the one hand and Jews in both the Land of Israel and the Diaspora on the other. He was accused by them of "teaching all people everywhere [things that are] opposite to the [Jewish] people, the Law, and this holy place [the Temple]" (Acts 21:28). In addition, many members of the church, described as "zealous for the Law" (Acts 21:20), disapproved of the way Paul's missionary program dealt with the Law of Israel. It was not only that he did not require that his Gentile converts adhere to the Law and the customs but it appears from his personal actions that he encouraged Jewish Christians in the Diaspora to discontinue them as well.

When Paul visits Jerusalem, James and the elders tell him that the Jewish followers of Jesus have heard "that you teach all the Jews which are among the Gentiles to forsake Moses, saying that they ought not to circumcise their children, neither to walk after the customs" (Acts 21:21). Therefore, they urge him to join four men who were going to the Temple to complete their Nazarite vows. Paul is to purify himself along with them so all will know "that you yourself are in obedience to the law" (Acts 21:24). It is assumed that if he publicly observes the Torah it would effectively reassure those who doubted Paul's fidelity to the Law and the ancestral customs. Paul follows their advice (Acts 21:23-24). Paul's apparent conformity to the Law does not fool those Diaspora Jews who recognize him in the Temple. They know him better, having heard his words and witnessed his actions in other settings. A riot ensued as they sought to remove him from the Temple and kill him (Acts 21:27-28).

Paul conformed to the Law or discarded it according to the company, Jewish or Gentile, in which he found himself. Among Jews, he might observe the Jewish dietary laws or holy days although he, himself, considered all days alike (Romans 14:5-6). When visiting Jerusalem, he probably practiced Judaism in conformity with his prescribed course of action to "Give no offense either to Jews or to Greeks or to the church of God; just as I also please all men in all things, not seeking my own profit, but that of the many, that they may be saved" (1 Corinthians 10:32-33). Whatever James and the elders may have thought of Paul's seeming conformity the Law, for his part, he had his own agenda when it came to observing the Law. In any instance where he observed the Law, Paul never compromised his own principle of expediency. He always acted in accordance with his own stated policy: "... to those who are under the Law, as under the Law, though not being myself under the Law, that I might win those who are under the Law" (1 Corinthians 9:20).

Paul's advocating that Gentile converts to Christianity were not governed by the Law was correct. The Torah was given only to the people of Israel, not to the other nations of the world. Therefore, non-Jews had no obligation to observe that Law. However, his teachings went further. Paul operated from and wrote his letters to communities of mainly non-Jewish Christians. Nevertheless, there is evidence that he advocated Jewish non-observance of the Torah's commandments and especially attempted to dissuade Jewish-born Christians from observance of the Law. As we have seen, the Jerusalem church confronted Paul with this accusation (Acts 21:21). It is difficult to imagine that his antinomian statements (Romans 14:14-15; Colossians 2:16, 2:20-22) were not meant to apply to Jews as well. This is especially true in light of his complaint against Cephas (Peter): "But when Cephas came to Antioch, I opposed him to his face, because he stood condemned. For prior to the coming of certain men from James, he used to eat with the Gentiles; but when they came, he began to withdraw and hold himself aloof, fearing the party of the circumcision" (Galatians 2:11-12). Certainly, he did not criticize other Jewish-born Christians who observed Jewish law and custom provided they agreed with him that these practices were no longer divine requirements but were voluntary actions that might be obeyed or ignored as expediency directed. For Paul, observance of Jewish ritual was only for outward appearances in order to accomplish the goal of spreading the gospel. As such, observance of the Law by Jewish-born Christians was appropriate if it was done as an expedient. This was his reasoning in the case of his circumcising of Timothy ("the son of a Jewish woman who was a believer, but his father was a Greek"—Acts 16:1); being circumcised made him of greater usefulness in Paul's ministry. "Paul wanted this man [Timothy] to go with him; and he took him and circumcised him because of the Jews who were in those parts, for they all knew that his father was Greek" (Acts 16:3). Circumcision is merely to be performed for the practical purpose of reaching the Jews with the gospel message, but not as a religious rite. Paul's readiness to be conciliatory toward Jewish sensibilities is in accordance with the *expediency principle* (1 Corinthians 9:20, 10:32-33). Thus, Paul was consistent within the parameters of his deviousness.

Paul considers circumcision useless; nevertheless, he did not advocate reversing the signs of circumcision (*epispasm*). But, he did not advocate its continued practice. "Is any man called being circumcised? Let him not become uncircumcised. Is any called in uncircumcision? Let him not be circumcised. Circumcision is nothing, and uncircumcision is nothing; but the keeping of the commandments of God" (1 Corinthians 7:18-19). He apparently criticized the use of circumcision only when it was undertaken as a religious obligation for he warned that circumcision carried with it the obligation to keep the whole Jewish law (Galatians 5:3). He maintains, "You have been severed from Christ, you who are seeking to be justified by the law; you have fallen from grace" (Galatians 5:4).

By the very nature of his example, we see Paul had no use for the Law other than its utility in spreading belief in Jesus. The Law was to be observed by Jewish-born Christians only to the extent that it could bring other Jews to belief in Jesus. The declaration, "Whether in pretense or in truth, Christ is proclaimed, and in this I rejoice" served as Paul's guideline throughout his apostolic career. Paul's statement in Philippians 1:18 as well as that in 1 Corinthians 9:20-23 validates any means used to obtain the conversion of the unbeliever. The only parameters governing what is proper at any given time are determined by what is most suitable under the circumstances.

Notes

[1] Some later manuscripts reverse the order of verses 16 and 17.
[2] The term is derived from a verb meaning, "to work for hire." H.A.A. Kennedy writes: "Originally, the character of a worker for pay. Now that which degraded

the hired worker, in the estimation of antiquity, was his labouring wholly for his own interests, while it was a sign of the noble to devote himself to the common weal" (H.A.A. Kennedy, "The Epistle to the Philippians," *Expositor's Greek Testament*, Ed., W. Robertson Nicoll, New York: George H. Doran Co., vol. 3, n.d., p.425). Arndt and Gingrich state that before New Testament times the word is found in Aristotle, "where it denotes a self-seeking pursuit of political office by unfair means" (W.F. Arndt and F.W. Gingrich, *A Greek-English Lexicon of the New Testament and Other Early Christian Literature*, Chicago: University of Chicago Press, 1957, p. 309).

3   The King James Version reverses the order of verses 16 and 17.

4   During the Second Commonwealth era, affiliation with a religion and its adherents was often expressed through the use of the words "custom" and "law" (2 Maccabees 4:11, 6:1; *Jewish Antiquities* XVI. 7. 6 [225]; B.T. *Sukkah* 56b; B.T. *Pesaḥim* 96a.

3.
"TRUE JEWS" AND "CHRIST-KILLER JEWS"

Following the death of Jesus the first communities of his adherents consisted of Jews who saw in Jesus the hoped-for Messiah. However, the Christianity of the New Testament is in essence based on the teachings of Paul and his predominantly Gentile followers. Paul was not actually one of Jesus' followers. He used the earthly Jesus as a peg upon which to hang his otherworldly "Christ." Moreover, his theological creation belongs to the world of the Greco-Roman mystery religions, not Judaism. Indeed, within a short time, the resultant form of Christianity he created had little in common with the religion of Jesus himself. The Pauline churches represented a variant blend of Judaism and Hellenistic religion. The first Gentile adherents to the Jesus movement were most likely among the Godfearers. These were Gentiles who accepted Judaism's teachings, ethics, Scriptures, and main practices such as the Sabbath, but were not circumcised and did not follow all the ceremonial laws of Judaism. In turn, they undoubtedly bore Christianity to pagan relatives and friends. What made Paul's teachings popular was the claim that by accepting Jesus as their savior from sin, the Gentiles could partake of all the blessings of the Law without having to actually be obedient to its requirements.

But, Paul did more than claim that Gentiles who believed in Jesus could be "grafted" into the people of Israel (Romans 11:17). He maintained that they along with like-minded Jews, "the remnant" (Romans 11:5), constituted the "true Israel" (Romans 9:6-8). This was the foundation of what became Paul's anti-Judaic stance. Thus, he taught that Jews are no longer the people of God because they had repudiated God's Messiah. He claimed that Jesus brought complete freedom from Jewish law to all those who believe in him as their personal savior from sin.

Paul boasted that he "was circumcised the eight day, of the nation of Israel, of the tribe of Benjamin, a Hebrew of the Hebrews; as to the Law a Pharisee" (Philippians 3:5). But, he taught that with the death of Jesus, circumcision was no longer spiritually meaningful; it was now a "mutilation" (*katatome*) of the flesh (Philippians 3:2). He declared that there was no longer any need for Jewish national existence: "For they are not all Israel who are descended from Israel; neither are they all children because they are Abraham's descendants, but: 'through Isaac your descendants will be named.' That is, it is not the children of the flesh who are children of God, but the children of the promise are regarded as descendants" (Romans 9:6-8). These postcrucifixion "children of the promise," Paul says, are "called, not from among Jews only, but also from among Gentiles" (Romans 9:24). In addition, Paul maintains that with the death of Jesus there is no longer a need for the Torah: "The Law has become our tutor to lead us to Christ, that we may be justified by faith. But now that faith has come, we are no longer under a tutor. For you are all sons of God through faith in Christ Jesus" (Galatians 3:24-26). Most telling is Paul's comment that he considered everything that mattered most in his previous life within Judaism to be nothing but "dung" (*skybala*) compared to his possessing "Christ" (Philippians 3:8).

According to the Book of Acts, Paul identified himself to a Jewish crowd in Jerusalem as "a Jew, born in Tarsus of Cilicia, but brought up in this city, educated under Gamaliel, strictly according to the law of our fathers, being zealous for God, just as you all are today" (Acts 22:3). Paul referred to his Pharisaic background when it seemed useful to him. Thus, for example, when he was brought before the Sanhedrin to answer charges of improper conduct, he declared, "Brethren, I am a Pharisee, a son of Pharisees" (Acts 23:6).

In this particular instance, his strategy was to create dissension between the Pharisees and Sadducees comprising the Council (Acts 23:7). But, if he ever was one, Paul was no longer a Pharisee. Paul may have had a Pharisaic education, but he abandoned his vital Jewish roots on joining the church. His Hellenistic outlook and disparaging remarks about Jews and Judaism, exemplified by the doctrines he taught placed him in opposition to the Pharisees and the fundamental precepts of Judaism as upheld by all Jews guided by the Torah. Paul's characterization of Jews as murderers and haters of humanity (1 Thessalonians 2:15) fostered a climate of hostility toward Jews. Almost all members of the church congregations Paul wrote to were of Gentile origin.

The way in which Paul interpreted the Hebrew Scriptures brought him into conflict with the biblical exegesis and the oral tradition of the scribes and Pharisees as well as with the Sadducees. What he claimed the Scriptures say, and the liberties he took in his association with Gentiles, were anything but in agreement with any Jewish interpretation and application of God's Law. In order to show that the Scriptures foretold Jesus as the Messiah Paul threw out the special election of Israel, embodied in the Torah, and the literal observance of the commandments of God. Even when he employed traditional methods of interpreting Scripture the results achieved were not in harmony with the Torah.

Paul's judgment upon the Jews and Judaism is an integral part of his christocentric eschatology. He is profoundly anti-Judaic. His theology establishes the Christian claim of supersession over Judaism. The concept that Christians have replaced Jews in the latter's relationship to God is a major theme in his preaching. Paul developed the notion that the church, Jews and Gentiles believing in Jesus, replaced "unbelieving" Jews in the covenant. He contrasts the "new covenant," a thing of the spirit, with the "old covenant," which is restricted to a written form. "The letter kills," Paul exclaims, "but the spirit gives life" (2 Corinthians 3:4-6). To Paul, obedience to the Torah is equivalent to being under a curse; he contrasts it with faith, through which the baptized Gentile lays valid claim to inclusion in Abraham's lineage (Galatians 3:5-14). To this end, he defines a Jew as someone who is one inwardly, not outwardly through circumcision of the flesh. The true Jew is not by descent or by observance of God's commandments, but by the heart, by the spirit (Romans 2:25-29). Accordingly, Israel "according to the flesh," biological Jews and Jews by choice are not the "true Jews." The "true Jews" are the Christians, both Jews and Gentiles. The true people of God, the "called," the "co-heirs with Christ," the "children of the promise" (Romans 1:7, 8:17, 9:8), the "believers," whether Jews or Gentiles, are the ones who have accepted Jesus as the Messiah. The term "Israel of God" (Galatians 6:16) appears as the designation for the new Christian community, in contrast to "Israel according to the flesh" (1 Corinthians 10:18). Thus, it implies that the Christian community is the true spiritual Israel, an eschatological Israel made up of those who believe in Jesus.

Before the advent of Christianity the Jews had been first in God's favor, that is, they were God's chosen people. Now the priority of being first in God's favor has passed from the Jews to the Christians. Paul cites Isaiah 10:22, with certain modifications, "Though the number of the sons of Israel be as the sand of the sea, it is the remnant that will be saved" (Romans 9:27). Paul believes that Israel's unbelief in Jesus cut them off from participation in the covenant. The remnant that believes in Jesus will be saved; the descendants of Abraham are not all Jews per se, only the remnant who believe in Jesus. Since the coming of Jesus, Paul contends, the Jews have been in a state of blindness and disobedience to God. However, he states, it is their offense that makes possible the inclusion of Gentiles in the new Israel. It is into this Gentile new Israel that the remnant of Jews will be eschatologically absorbed (Romans 11:11-32). According to Paul, the Christian church was the successor to Israel and the inheritor of the Abrahamic promises. Christians are "spiritual" Jews (Romans 2:29), Abraham's offspring (Romans 4:16), the "Israel of God" (Galatians 6:16), the true circumcision (Philippians 3:3). In the theological controversies in which he was a participant, Paul maintained that Gentile believers were equal to Jews who also believed in Jesus. The titles and attributes of the people of God applied fully to the Gentile Christians as well.[1]

Paul's doctrine of justification by faith apart from the law (especially Romans 9-11) where he discusses Israel's rejection of the Gospel established, in part, the church's justification for its despising of Jews and Judaism. Paul explains that "God has not rejected His people" (Romans 11:1). Is not Paul, himself, an Israelite of the tribe of Benjamin (Romans 11:1)? But, what does Paul mean when he uses the phrase "His people"? He explains that there is now "a remnant according to God's gracious choice" (Romans 11:5). God does not reject the Jewish people per se. What He has rejected, Paul says, are those who reject Jesus. According to Paul, God accepts only the remnant of Israel that believes in Jesus. Thus, Paul concludes, "What then? That which Israel is seeking for he has not obtained, but those who were chosen [the church] obtained it, and the rest were hardened" (Romans 11:7). Paul reserves his respect and love only for those Jews who follow Jesus.

As we have seen above, Paul did not believe that physical descent from Abraham guaranteed Jews a place in the Abrahamic covenant. This is nothing new. He simply employed the biblical idea of the remnant, the faithful few who believe and survive while the others perish (Romans 11:4-5, 7, 10; cf. 1 Kings 19:18). The concept that simple heredity did not ensure an individual's standing within the covenant is found in Judaism. By disobedience to God's commandments, one may place oneself on the outside of the community of Israel. The prophet Hosea declares, "When Ephraim spoke with trembling, he became exalted in Israel; but when he became guilty through Baal, he died" (Hosea 13:1). Ephraim died a spiritual death long before it suffered national destruction. God's graciousness comes to all individual Israelites who are faithful. What was radically different in Paul's belief was that Gentiles who believed in Jesus were now engrafted into a spiritual Israel made up of a mixed group of Jewish and Gentile followers of Jesus. Physical descent from Abraham lost all importance.

Paul expects that in time "all Israel will be saved" (Romans 11:26). In what sense does he use the phrase "all Israel"? It could refer to either Paul's notion of the "true spiritual Israel," that is, believers in Jesus, or it could refer to the Jewish people taken as a national unit, or to every single Jewish person. The phrase, "all Israel," is used in contemporary rabbinic literature to mean the totality of Israel without necessarily implying every single individual in the national unit. That is, it means "all"—except for those not included. This is, most likely, the sense in which Paul used it. The "all" in Romans 11:26 does not refer to all Israel in its entirety, but, rather, as in Romans 11:7, to a "remnant" of Israel that in becoming Christian remains in divine favor when the majority of Israel was rejected. Thus, he is once more speaking of a born-Jewish Christian "remnant" not "all Israel" as inclusive of every single individual Jew. This so-called "remnant" is Paul's "true" Israel. All other Jews he rejects as not being part of the so-called "true" Israel. Thus, for Paul those Jews who do not believe in Jesus have become a non-people with no reason for existence. The community of Israel will be dissolved. In its place, Paul speaks of the mystery (Romans 11:25) of God's election that includes both Jews and Gentiles in "the Israel of God" (Galatians 6:16). It is this "Israel of God" that Paul declares "will be saved" not the "Israel of the flesh."

What did Paul teach concerning the relationship of Gentile Christians to Jews who believe in God and seek to obey His will but do not believe in Jesus? Two passages (Romans 11:16-25 and Galatians 4:21-31) illustrate Paul's belief concerning the relationship of fleshly Israel to the new cosmic order. In the simile of the olive tree and its branches, Paul illustrates the relationship between the Gentile church and Israel (Romans 11:16-25). There is the holy root of the olive tree—Israel (Jewish Christians). There are also branches that were broken off from the original root of Israel (Jews who do not accept Jesus) and wild branches that were grafted in their place (Gentile Christians). Paul is simply saying one thing: Israel as a people has forfeited its privilege and is no longer the people of God; the Gentiles were graciously elected and are now along with the holy root of Israel (Jewish Christians) the people of God. Paul reminds the Gentiles of their insertion into the holy root, Israel. He makes them aware of their new position within the sacred root. He tells them that God is able and willing to re-engraft the original branches into the original olive tree (that is, those

Jews who will accept Jesus in the future). However, Gentile Christians and Jewish Christians are now God's chosen people. Accordingly, that into which the Gentiles have been engrafted is not the Jewish people per se, but those Jews who believe in Jesus. For some strange reason, Jews had to first reject Jesus before God could bring the Gentiles into belief. Following that period of unbelief, Paul says, the Jews would come to belief in Jesus: "a partial hardening has happened to Israel until the fullness of the Gentiles has come in; and thus all Israel will be saved" (Romans 11:25-26). Paul does not suppose that so-called "unbelieving" Jews are on an equal footing with Christian "believers." To a limited extent he regards the Jews as the olive tree onto which Gentiles are grafted (Romans 11:17 ff.) and he cannot contemplate the end of salvation history without the salvation of the Jews as a nation (Romans 11:25-32). Nevertheless, the "unbelieving" Jews are for him now in a state of disobedience and "unbelieving" Israel's election is presently, what one commentator calls, a "non-functioning election."[2]

Paul sees the Jews in a paradoxical situation. They are the elect, yet they are the disobedient elect with respect to faith in Jesus. Thus he writes: "From the standpoint of the gospel they [the Jews] are enemies for your sake, but from the standpoint of God's choice they are beloved for the sake of the fathers; for the gifts and the calling of God are irrevocable" (Romans 11:28-29). Paul's answer to the imaginary problem he has devised is self-serving and not always consistent. He expects the ultimate "salvation" of the Jews, but the anticipated inclusion of the Jews among "God's faithful people" will for him be connected to the acknowledgement of Jesus as the Messiah by a surviving remnant. In the meantime, Paul says that in a certain sense the Jews are still chosen. However, his negative stand on the continued validity of the Law (Galatians 3:11, 6:15; Romans 3:20) and his condemnation of those Jews that do not follow Jesus (Galatians 3:10, 2 Corinthians 3:14-15, Romans 9:31-32) illustrates most profoundly his basic feelings toward the Jewish people as a whole: The chosen "remnant," Paul anticipates, will accept Jesus, and become part of the church. The rest will be, like the broken branches of an olive tree, discarded.

Yes, Paul is saying, "the gifts and the calling of God are irrevocable" but they are now given to the spiritual children of the "fathers" the new Israel.

In Galatians 4:21-31, Paul alludes to the biblical story of the bondwoman Hagar and her son Ishmael (Genesis 21:9-21). His intention is to deny that the Jewish people and the Torah have any further importance to God. In their place stands the church as the people of God. As Paul describes events, the Jews are "cast off" as Hagar and Ishmael had been, with no part in Abraham's inheritance. In this allegorical interpretation Abraham's two wives, Hagar ("the bondwoman") and Sarah ("the free woman") represent the major protagonists—the Jews and the church respectively. Hagar represents the covenant of Sinai "bearing children who are to be slaves" (Galatians 4:24) and "correspond to the present Jerusalem, for she is in slavery with her children" (Galatians 4:25). This is the Jewish people and the Law who are "cast out" without inheritance. In contrast, Christians are the children of "the free woman" Sarah; they like "the Jerusalem above is free; she is our mother" (Galatians 4:26). They "like Isaac, are children of promise" (Galatians 4:28). Thus, Isaac is treated as a typological forerunner of Christians and their freedom from the Law. Hagar and Ishmael are typological forerunners of the Jews and their bondage to the Law. Those who believe in Jesus are "children of the promise" (Galatians 4:28); those who are physically descended from Abraham but who do not believe are not the inheritors of the promise but the children of slavery (Galatians 4:30). Paul's point is clear. In "Jesus Christ" Christians *are* Israel, while those who claim descent from Israel but do not have the faith of the new Israel are not. The Jews who do not believe in Jesus as the Messiah are thrown out from God's presence. To serve his purposes, Paul neglects to mention that in the Genesis story (Genesis 16 and 21) God also protected and multiplied Ishmael.

Paul's negative feelings toward Jews who do not accept Jesus as Messiah are expressed throughout the letters to the Romans and Galatians (especially Romans 9 and Galatians 3-4). He has nothing but disdain for non-Christian Jews and the Torah; peace and mercy are for the "Israel of God," that is, Christians. Paul distinguished between those who are Abraham's physical offspring and those who are his spiritual heirs. According to Paul, Jewish people who do not accept Jesus are stripped of their identity, inheritance, and, as such, their right to an independent future. "For they are not all Israel who are descended from Israel" (Romans 9:6); "Surely you know that it is those who are of faith that are sons of Abraham" (Galatians 3:7); "And if you belong to Christ, then you are Abraham's seed, heirs according to promise" (Galatians 3:29); "For we are the true circumcision, who worship in the spirit of God and glory in Christ Jesus and put no confidence in the flesh" (Philippians 3:3). The use of the first person plural, "we," shows that his identification is not with biological Jews but, rather, with those Jews and Gentiles who accept Jesus and whom he calls "the true circumcision."

Paul also establishes the fundamentals for rejection of the argument that the Romans are responsible for the execution of Jesus. The Gospels, written a generation after Paul, simply improved upon his work. In their narratives, the theme that the Jews are solely responsible for the death of Jesus becomes a recurring motif. 1 Thessalonians 2:14-16, authored by Paul (c. 51 C.E.), is the earliest written accusation that the Jews killed Jesus. It may be assumed that Paul held to the notion that the Jews killed Jesus long before he wrote this letter. In this passage, we are mainly concerned with verses 14-16 which read, "For you, brethren, became imitators of the churches of God in Jesus Christ that are in Judea, for you also endured the same sufferings at the hands of your countrymen, even as they did from the Jews, who also killed the Lord Jesus and the prophets, and drove us out; they are not pleasing to God, but hostile to all men, hindering us from speaking to the Gentiles that they might be saved; with the result that they always fill up the measure of their sins. But wrath has come upon them forever." This passage has had deep and long lasting consequences. Paul's accusation that the Jews killed Jesus and the prophets is chronologically the opening salvo of the anti-Jewish theme that runs through the New Testament. His words are in themselves both passionate and hateful. In effect, by the way in which he uses the term, "the Jews," Paul essentially divorces himself from the Jewish people in a manner characteristic of the Gospels, especially that of John. Paul imputes responsibility to the Jews for the death of Jesus by speaking of their "killing" Jesus, not of their crucifying him. His emphasis is intended to draw attention away from those that physically crucified Jesus and advance the Christian canard that "the Jews," as a people, are the ones directly responsible for the execution of Jesus. To this end, he also accuses them of being killers of the prophets. Paul's indictment, as later reiterated in the Gospels, is that it was the Jews who actively and insistently pressured the Romans to execute Jesus. As such, the Jews bear the responsibility for Jesus' execution.

Some New Testament commentators have suggested that this passage is an interpolation. These critical scholars have regarded 1 Thessalonians 2:14-15 as an interpolation because nowhere else in the extant letters of Paul does he give any clear indication that he holds the Jews responsible for Jesus' death. However, the Book of Acts relates that in his sermon at Antioch he stated: "For those who live in Jerusalem, and their rulers, recognizing neither him nor the utterances of the prophets which are read every Sabbath, fulfilled these by condemning him. And though they found no ground for putting him to death, they asked Pilate that he be executed" (Acts 13:27-28).

It has also been contended that 1 Thessalonians 2:14-16 is an intrusion into the text that interrupts the overall message. It is thought that verse 17 must have originally followed directly upon verse 13. But, what may seem incongruous to some modern critical scholars need not have been a problem for Paul when he authored this passage.[3]

In disagreeing with the interpolation theory, there are those who maintain that the comma that separates "the Jews" from "who also killed the Lord Jesus" (verses 14-15) and thereby makes the clause nonrestrictive is unnecessary in the original Greek. With the comma removed, they render the text as, "the Jews who killed the Lord Jesus." This adjustment restricts Paul's invective to a limited number of Jews. Perhaps only to those who, according to the trial narratives, accused Jesus before Pilate. However, the removal of the comma after "the Jews" in 1 Thessalonians 2:14-15 does not rescue Paul from the charge of accusing all non-Christian Jews of complicity in the murder of Jesus.

In disagreement with the interpolation and unnecessary comma theories is the fact that Paul does not restrict his attack to only the limited number of Jews said to have been directly involved in Jesus' trial before Pilate. According to the author of Acts, Paul blames not just the Jewish rulers but every Jew living in Jerusalem. "For those who live in Jerusalem, and their rulers, recognizing neither him nor the utterances of the prophets which are read every Sabbath, fulfilled these by condemning him. And though they found no ground for putting him to death, they asked Pilate that he be executed" (Acts 13:27-28). Concerning 1 Thessalonians 2:14, it has been observed that "One could translate *Ioudaioi* here as 'Judeans,' since it was Jews of Judea who persecuted the Judean churches, and not 'the Jews' in a more general sense—although it is 'the Jews' in a more general sense who form the antecedent to the relative (participial) clauses of vv 15, 16."[4] This is instructive, for showing that Paul's remarks are not confined solely to condemning the Judean Jews contemporary with Jesus and himself. In verses 15-16, Paul explicitly says that these same Jews who killed Jesus also killed "the prophets." That is, "the Jews" who killed Jesus are held responsible for the death of the prophets who were killed in prior centuries. Therefore, Paul maintains that Jewish guilt for these alleged offenses is a genetic inheritance for each generation to bear responsibility. In addition, "the Jews" have hindered Paul and others from preaching to the Gentiles. But, this activity took place in Asia Minor, not Judea. Therefore, this accusation includes the Jews of a wider geographic area than merely Judea. Paul's indictment is not only of Judeans, or all Jews, contemporary with Jesus or himself, but also of all Jews for all time and all places who do not accept Jesus. Paul considers contemporary non-Christian Jews responsible for Jesus' death as well as the death of the prophets of past generations. But, did he consider future generations of Jews to be guilty of the death of the so-called "Christ" who it is claimed was more than just a prophet? Timeless Jewish culpability is expressed in the statement that "wrath has come upon them forever" (1 Thessalonians 2:16). The indefinite period expressed by "forever" gives no indication of ever being lifted from those Jews who do not accept Jesus.

In the period just prior to the first exile "the chiefs of the priests, and the people" are said to have "mocked the messengers of God, and despised His words, and scoffed at His prophets, until the wrath of the Lord arose against His people, until there was no remedy" (2 Chronicles 36:14-16). But, there is no accusation in this passage that this behavior usually included the killing of prophets. In fact, the killing of prophets was an infrequent occurrence in the history of Israel. Only two recorded incidents of prophets being killed are found in the Hebrew Scriptures, Zechariah, the son of Jehoiada, stoned by order of King Joash (2 Chronicles 24:20-22) and Uriah, the son of Shemaiah, slain with a sword by king Jehoiakim (Jeremiah 26:20-23). Elijah's numerically ambiguous statement that "they have killed your prophets" (1 Kings 19:10) refers to an action performed by idolatrous Israelites from the northern kingdom of Israel. But, the people living in the southern kingdom of Judah were not held accountable or punished for the sins of those people living in the northern kingdom of Israel. Jesus' accusation of "prophet killers" is directed at Jews descended from those who, at the time of Elijah, were living in the kingdom of Judah and were therefore not included in Elijah's statement. The accusation of "prophet killers" is a deceptive New Testament diatribe unjustly directed at the Jewish people. It is part of a series of malicious statements designed to make pariahs of those Jews who do not believe in Jesus. Thus, these children of the devil (John 8:44) are to be punished for the death of all righteous people killed from the beginning of humankind (Matthew 23:35, Luke 11:50). This parody on the biblical principle of collective responsibility has its climax in the statement attributed to "all the people" that "his blood be on us and on our children" (Matthew 27:25). In contrast to the New

Testament canard that the Jews are "prophet killers," it has been observed that "practically all the kings of Israel and Judah had a deep reverence for the men of God, even when they bore ill tidings for the country or for the royal house. Such was the force of public opinion (since neither the kings nor any single class had concentrated power) that attempts to punish prophets, however subversive their preaching, were rare. Jezebel's threats against Elijah, the expulsion of Amos from the kingdom of Israel, Jehoiakim's execution of Uriah, the sufferings of Jeremiah, and the enforced silence of Judean prophecy during the reign of Manasseh (the unnatural death of Isaiah is mentioned only in a late Talmudic source) are merely exceptions."[5] Rabbinic literature mentions that Manasseh killed Isaiah[6] and a group of Jews killed Jeremiah in Egypt.[7] The Talmud records that "Our Rabbis taught: 'Forty-eight prophets[8] and seven prophetesses[9] prophesied to Israel . . . .' Were there no more prophets than these? . . . There were actually very many, as it has been taught, 'Many prophets arose for Israel, double the number of [the Israelites] who came out of Egypt,' only the prophecy which contained a lesson for future generations was written down, and that which did not contain such a lesson was not written."[10] Whether or not the biblical citations of two respective killings of prophets are counted in conjunction with the two recorded in rabbinic writings, the number of prophets killed out of the total number of known prophets who prophesied hardly warrants the accusation of "prophet killers."

Paul's phrase, "and drove us out" (1 Thessalonians 2:15), makes culpability contemporaneous with him and thus an on-going trait of the Jews. This trait explains why, "wrath has come upon them forever." In time, the Jesus of the Gospels reiterates Paul's charges, in verses 14-16, that "prophet killer" is a descriptive national characteristic of the Jewish people. The Jews have reproduced the pattern of killing the prophets in the killing of Jesus and in persecuting those who proclaim his message.

Paul continues with the phrase "they are not pleasing to God, but hostile to all men" (1 Thessalonians 2:15). Not only do their past acts displease God, but that displeasure continues into the present. Paul then announces that the Jews are "hostile to all men." He borrowed this anti-Judaic polemic from the pagan world. The pagan misunderstanding of Jewish exclusiveness was expressed in similar phraseology. The Roman historian, Tacitus (55?-118? C.E.), for example, says of the Jews, "toward all others [that is, not of their own people] they cherish hatred of a kind normally reserved for enemies.[11] The Egyptian, Apion, a contemporary of Paul, spread the calumny that Jews swear by the Creator to show no good will to any alien, least of all to Greeks."[12] The Jewish persistence in maintaining the traditional way of life was misunderstood and ridiculed and increased pagan suspicion that Jews were hostile toward Gentiles. Thus, the accusation, *odium generis humani*, "enemies of mankind." Paul uses similar phraseology in a context that makes it refer to the Jews who remain faithful to the Torah and do not follow Jesus. In Paul's attack, "hostile to all men" is descriptive of Jewish opponents of the gospel message which is being sent to save Gentiles (1 Thessalonians 2:16). He claims the Jews have filled their cup of sin to the brim and now God's "wrath has come upon them forever [*eis telos*, "to the uttermost," "to the very end"]" (verse 16). Punishment was now final. According to Paul, Israel, after the killing of their God given Messiah and after refusing to believe the message of his resurrection, is no longer the people of God. God's election has now been taken away from Israel and given to those Gentiles that embrace Jesus. Henceforth, the Jews are to bear the consequences of their sin of rejecting Jesus. It follows that the Christians should consider all the historical catastrophes that befall the Jews as a punishment of God. The "Old Covenant" is at an end and its blessings are transferred to the church (Luke 20:16; cf. Acts 13:46).

In sum, Paul proclaims that the "true" Israel is the spiritual Israel composed of the Jews and Gentiles who follow Jesus. He says Jews may become part of spiritual Israel (the church) through faith in Jesus, the same as everyone else. "If you are Christ's, then you are Abraham's seed, heirs according to promise" (Galatians 3:29). The church, Paul declares, is the Israel of the promise, not the Israel of the Sinai covenant. Only those individuals who believe in "Christ Jesus" are the real children of Abraham and heirs to God's promise to him. The people of Israel who do not accept Jesus as their Messiah and Savior are condemned to eternal suffering through the wrath of God for rejecting and murdering Jesus. Only those who "do not continue in their unbelief" (Romans 11:23) and accept faith in "Christ" are saved. It is only to this limited extent that Paul says God has not rejected His people, that is, Israel of the flesh.

Paul's supersessionist doctrines became the backdrop for the repressive and often violent climate to which Jews have been subjected at the hands of Christians and Christian acculturated pagans. The accusation of "Christ killer" (and "prophet killer") first encountered in 1 Thessalonians 2:14-15 is not an anomaly. It is a polemic found in other New Testament contexts as well. Paul's writings, along with the Gospels and Acts, became the New Testament literary blueprint for indicting the Jews and they alone eternally for the death of Jesus. Is it any wonder that the Jews of every generation not only have been blamed for the death of Jesus and declared guilty of murder, but have been hounded and persecuted by those Christians and Christian acculturated pagans who believed that in this way they were doing God's work?

Notes

[1] E.P. Sanders has maintained that Paul's disagreement with Judaism is because "*real* righteousness is being saved by Christ, and it comes only through faith." Paul "*explicitly denies that the Jewish covenant can be effective for salvation* . . . . In short, this is what Paul finds wrong in Judaism: it is not Christianity." (E.P. Sanders, *Paul and Palestinian Judaism*, Philadelphia: Fortress Press, 1977, pp. 551-552 [italics in original])

[2] A. Roy Eckardt, *Elder and Younger Brothers*, New York: Scribner's, 1967, p. 58.

[3] New Testament scholars are divided on the issue of how many of Paul's letters ought to be considered authentic. They also cannot agree on the identification of interpolations incorporated into those letters that are thought to be the work of Paul.

4   F.F. Bruce, *Word Biblical Commentary: 1 and 2 Thessalonians*, Waco, Texas: Word Books, 1982, p. 46.
5   Salo Wittmayer Baron, *A Social and Religious History of the Jews*, New York: Columbia University Press, vol. 1, 1952, pp. 78-79.
6   According to Talmudic sources, "Manasseh slew Isaiah" (B.T. *Yevamot* 49b, B.T. *Sanhedrin* 103b, J.T. *Sanhedrin* 10:2 [Zhitomer edition 37b]).
7   A Midrash quoted in *Midrash Aggada* on Numbers 30:15, reads as follows: "The Jews in Egypt stoned Jeremiah . . ." (Louis Ginzberg, *The Legends of the Jews*, Philadelphia: The Jewish Publication Society of America, vol. 6, 1968, p. 399).
8   Rashi's commentary to B.T. *Megillah* 14a lists forty-eight prophets.
9   The seven prophetesses listed are Sarah, Miriam, Deborah, Hannah, Abigail, Hulda, and Esther.
10 B.T. *Megillah* 14a.
11 Tacitus, *Histories* 5. 5. 2.
12 Josephus, *Against Apion* 2. 121.

4.

THE LETTER TO THE HEBREWS

The author of the Letter to the Hebrews[1] wishes to demonstrate the absolute superiority of Christianity over Judaism. It is not clear whether his main purpose is to attack Judaism itself, convince Jewish converts to Christianity not to return to Judaism, or to discourage Judaizing by Gentile converts. Some scholars suggest that the letter was originally written to Samaritan Christians.[2] In any case, in order to accomplish his goal the author concentrates his attack on the intrinsic institutions of Judaism. He maintains that the so-called old covenant was imperfect: "For the Law, since it has a shadow of the good things to come and not the very form of things, can never by the same sacrifice year by year, which they offer continually, make perfect those who draw near" (Hebrews 10:1). This Law has been rendered obsolete: "When He said, 'A new covenant,' He has made the first obsolete. But whatever is becoming obsolete and growing old is ready to disappear" (Hebrews 8:13). As such, the "old covenant" has now been superseded by a new and better covenant: "For if that first covenant had been faultless, there would have been no occasion sought for a second" (Hebrews 8:7). This new covenant is centered on Jesus as its perfect high priest (Hebrews 6:20): "Who has become such not on the basis of physical requirement, but according to the power of an indestructible life" (Hebrews 7:16).

At first glance, the Letter to the Hebrews appears as a sustained and systematic attack against Judaism itself rather than the Jews as a people.[3] The author, himself, was most probably a Jewish convert to Christianity deeply influenced by Samaritanism.[4] He may have been a missionary to the Samaritans, but, nevertheless, uses the Prophets and the Writings (which the Samaritans rejected) as well as the Torah, in presenting his arguments. Judaism was his religio-cultural background, but, at the time of his writing this polemic, his Jewishness no longer existed. For him, Judaism was obsolete and over, ready to disappear wherever its "shadowy" form still existed. On careful examination of the author's attack, it becomes apparent that it had wider implications. It is true that there is no direct attack on the Jews as a people, but the further implications of the attack on the institutions of Judaism are clear. If Judaism is obsolete, what need is there for a Jewish people? As far as the author of Hebrews is concerned, Jews, defined by their beliefs as a separate people, were obsolete and ready to disappear into the amalgam of Christianity.

Notes

[1] Although the Samaritans called themselves "Hebrews" the title of this letter has not been directly connected to them.

[2] John Macdonald has observed that "The affinities of the Epistle to the Hebrews with the Samaritan teachings are in some respects so close that it is not an irresponsible act to suggest that the Epistle was written to Samaritan Christians." (John Macdonald, *Theology of the Samaritans*, Philadelphia: The Westminster Press, 1964, p. 421).

Charles H.H. Scobie notes that:

> The writer [of Hebrews] . . . expound[s] his own highly original christology. Like Stephen and John he rejects a Davidic christology; though well aware of the tradition of Jesus' descent from Judah (vii.14), having mentioned the fact he proceeds to ignore it completely. Once again it can be

argued that he presents a christology which could be accepted by Samaritan Christians for whom Davidic messianic conceptions were anathema. The writer's own christology is centered in the idea of priesthood, a subject of special interest to Samaritans, whose high priest was a more important figure in the total life of the community than was the case in Judaism . . . .

The theory that the recipients were Samaritan Christians would explain the curious fact that in all the discussions of priesthood, sanctuary and sacrifice the author shows no interest in contemporary Judaism nor in the Temple which stood up to A.D. 70. His arguments are based on the Pentateuch and on the Tabernacle, a fact which has so impressed a host of modern interpreters that they have convinced themselves that the letter was written to Gentile Christians! The Samaritans rejected the Jerusalem Temple but connected their sanctuary on Gerizim with the Tabernacle. Confirmation of this may perhaps be found in . . . [the following] observation . . . . The author of Hebrews describes in ix. 3, 4 how, in the Tabernacle, the golden altar of incense stood within the Holy of Holies; this, however, is not the case, according to the description given in Exodus. In the SP [Samaritan Pentateuch], however, Exod. xxx. 1-10 (the description of the altar of incense) comes between Exod. xxvi. 35 and Exod. xxvi. 36, so that it follows immediately upon the description of the veil which separates off the Holy of Holies. The misunderstanding evidenced in Heb. ix. 3, 4 can thus be understood if the writer based his knowledge of the Tabernacle on the SP. (Charles H.H. Scobie, "The Origins and Development of Samaritan Christianity," *New Testament Studies*, 19 (1972-73), pp. 411, 412-413)

[3] Scobie writes "the theology of Hebrews has remarkable connections with the theology of Stephen's speech though it represents a different line of development than the Fourth Gospel . . . . Hebrews represents in a highly developed form the theology of one branch of the Stephen-Philip movement."

(Scobie, pp. 412-413) This theology displays an intensely anti-Judaic bias while exhibiting many beliefs that are in agreement with Samaritanism.

4   Scobie comments that "It is much more difficult to regard the writer as a Samaritan Christian. His dependence on Philo, or at least on the type of Hellenistic Judaism represented by Philo, is difficult to deny. Unlike Stephen, he uses the non-Pentateuchal books extensively, and his view of the reunion of God's people reflects the idea of the eschatological ingathering of the tribes to Mt Zion, even if this is reinterpreted in terms of the 'heavenly Jerusalem' (Heb. xii. 22)." On the other hand, it may be that Hebrews was originally a Samaritan Christian document which underwent a certain amount of Judaizing before entering the Christian canon.

5.
THE GOSPEL OF MARK

Most New Testament scholars believe that the Gospel of Mark was the first of the canonical Gospels to be written (c. 70 C.E.). The author combined earlier pre-Gospel material with his own fertile imagination. His attack on the Jews and Judaism is not as fully developed as that found in the later Gospels. He wants to show his readers that Jesus, though born a Jew, has no essential connection with the Jewish people and their religion. His intent is both politically and theologically motivated. Consequently, he seeks to distance Jesus from Jewish messianic concepts while advancing the notion of Jesus as the divine Savior of Mankind.

There was no way of denying that Jesus was condemned and executed by the Roman authorities, charged with the crime of claiming to be king of the Jews. The author of Mark sought to create a narrative that could plausibly explain this away. He sets himself to the task of explaining the reason for the crucifixion of Jesus so as to make it appear that Jesus was not guilty of sedition although this was the charge on which he was convicted (Mark 15:26).

To explain away the real cause of Jesus' execution the evangelist's writing takes a sinister direction. Writing (most likely) in the city of Rome, in the aftermath of the Roman-Jewish War, he sought to depoliticize Jesus, to hide the political element of Jesus' career, and make the Christian community acceptable to the Roman authorities. In order to do this, the author of Mark accuses the Jewish authorities of bringing a false indictment against Jesus before the Romans. He writes that at Jesus' interrogation before Pilate, "the chief priests began to accuse him [Jesus] harshly" (Mark 15:3). However, the author informs his readers that Pilate "was aware that the chief priests had delivered him up because of envy" (Mark 15:10). It is here, in his assignment of responsibility for the execution of Jesus that the evangelist's anti-Jewish strategy becomes most pronounced. Jesus' trial before Pilate is explained as a Jewish plot. As the trial narrative progresses blame is removed from Pilate and placed directly on the crowd of Jews present (Mark 15:1-14).

Throughout his narrative, the author of Mark seeks to weaken the connection between Jesus and the Jewish people. He cannot fully disassociate Jesus from the Jewish people but he can differentiate between those who believe in Jesus and those who do not. The Jewish people reject Jesus, generally, and, in particular, his own family rejects him. He comes home and his family thinks that he is insane: "And he came home . . . . And when his own people heard of this, they went out to take custody of him; for they were saying, 'He has lost his senses'" (Mark 3:20-21). When his family attempts to contact him, he repudiates them.

> And his mother and his brothers arrived, and standing outside they sent word to him, and called him. And a multitude was sitting around him, and they said to him, "Behold, your mother and your brothers are outside looking for you." And answering them, he said, "Who are my mother and my brothers?" And looking about on those who were sitting around him, he said, "Behold, my mother and my brothers! For whoever does the will of God, he is my brother and sister and mother." (Mark 3:31-35)

That Mark's Jesus cuts himself off from his own family, not only from his people, has political significance. Jesus' denial of the importance of his familial relationship is a severance of any connection with Davidic messiahship and its contemporary anti-Roman implications. Jesus underscores his reaction to the reception his message received in his hometown and among his family when he later declares that "A prophet is not without honor except in his home town and in his own household" (Mark 6:4).

In order to show that Jesus had no objection to Roman governance the author of Mark makes it appear that Jesus favored paying taxes to Rome: "And they sent some of the Pharisees and Herodians to him, in order to trap him in a statement. And they came and said to him, 'Teacher, we know that you are truthful, and defer to no one; for you are not partial to any, but teach the way of God in truth. Is it lawful to pay a tax to Caesar, or not? Shall we pay, or shall we not pay?' But he, knowing their hypocrisy, said to them, 'Why are you testing me? Bring me a denarius to look at.' And they brought one. And he said to them, 'Whose likeness and inscription is this?' And they said to him, 'Caesar's.' And Jesus said to them, 'Render to Caesar the things that are Caesar's and to God the things that are God's.' And they were amazed at him" (Mark 12:13-17; see also Matthew 22:15-22, Luke 20:20-26). In first century Judea burdened with oppressive taxation that statement could mean nothing less than that everything belongs to God and nothing belongs to Caesar. Therefore, pay no taxes to an unlawful ruler who violates and degrades God's holy land economically, politically, and religiously (Haggai 2:7-8; Exodus 19:5, "for all the earth is mine"). Seen in this light, Jesus' statement expresses the vision of political and religious power distribution to be established with the arrival of the kingdom of God. The extent of the historicity of this encounter between Jesus and the Pharisees and Herodians is not known. In any case, however, the author of Mark set the incident in a context in which Jesus endorses paying taxes to Rome.[1] In doing so, the author claims the question was asked of Jesus by the Pharisees and the Herodians in order to entrap him politically. Thus, he shows Jesus favorable to Rome while the Pharisees and Herodians are hostile to Jesus.

Whether Jesus was for or against paying taxes to Caesar, the very choice of the question that is asked of Jesus in this episode indicates that Roman taxation was a controversial issue.[2] The complaint that Jesus ate with tax collectors (Mark 2:16, Matthew

9:11, Luke 5:30) further illustrates the mood of the time regarding Roman taxation.[3] Surely, some of the religio-political revolutionary movements that gain prominence in the years of the later prefecture (44-66 C.E.) already have their rudimentary origins in the anti-Roman controversies that arose during the years of the early prefecture over Judea (6-41 C.E.). (The two periods are separated by the four-year reign of the Jewish king Herod Agrippa I.[4]) Burdensome taxation was a long-standing issue[5] but only one of the major points of contention. Roman governance had embittered many people religiously and politically toward that rule and those who supported it.[6] The absence of revolution during the years of 6 C.E. to 41 C.E. speaks more of Roman efficiency in the suppression of dissent than an absence of discontentment. The lack of historical records should also not be discounted. The author of Mark mentions an anti-Roman uprising taking place shortly before Jesus' crucifixion, but gives no details as to its cause: "And the man named Barabbas had been imprisoned with the insurrectionists who had committed murder in the insurrection" (Mark 15:7). This need not have been a widespread revolt. In Luke 13:1, mention is made of "the Galileans whose blood Pilate had mingled with their sacrifices," but no details as to the extent or cause of the trouble is given.

The Marcan account is foremost a theological document and is far from being simply historical. In itself, writing a formal gospel document for publication was a theological admission that Jesus was not coming back as soon as the church had originally expected. The author set himself to the task of explaining Jesus' teachings to his Gentile audience. The timing of the appearance of this compilation brought with it the necessity of answering some difficult and embarrassing political and religious questions. Inherent in the tale that he wove was the church's answers to some of these burdensome questions. The answers were restructured to reflect a pro-Roman Jesus under siege politically and religiously by the Jews. How is it that a loyal subject of the Empire should find himself condemned for sedition? All the rebel groups in the Land of Israel opposed Roman taxation. Yet, how is it that one who put himself at risk by defending the right of Caesar to collect taxes in the province should fall victim to a method of execution reserved by the Empire for the most despicable criminals and political rebels? The power invested in the chief Roman administrator of the province should have prevented an injustice. What prevented the Roman prefect from exercising his power to free an innocent man? To answer these questions the myth of a Jesus unopposed to Roman rule, who is hounded by a Jewish religious opposition, was created. The Jesus story had to be cleansed of any positive association with rebellious Jewish factions that had opposed Roman rule. As a result, any Christian tradition that was to appear in the document that eventually came to be called the Gospel of Mark had to be presented so as to minimize or delete altogether any compromising association between Jesus and anti-Roman forces.

The author of Mark was writing in the early seventies of the first century of the Common Era, immediately following the Roman-Jewish War. The Zealots were a political party that played a prominent role in that war. Since the party's founding, in the early years of the century, it advocated violent uprising against Roman rule and self-government for the Jews.[7] There is at least one Zealot (or former Zealot) among Jesus' disciples. The author seeks to hide the fact that among Jesus' most intimate group of disciples was one who was identified by the sobriquet "the Zealot." Some scholars maintain that the Zealot party did not yet exist. Nevertheless, there were already some individuals and groups prepared to revolt against Rome, who were known as zealots. This presented a problem since, at the time the Gospel of Mark was written, Christians were attempting to explain that although Jesus was executed for sedition he was not a rebel against Roman rule. Admitting the truth would have been politically embarrassing and a danger to the Christian community. As a result, the author of the Gospel of Mark lists a Simon the Cananaean [Greek, *ton Kananaion*] as one of Jesus' disciples without explaining the meaning of the title "the *kananaios*" (Mark 3:18; see also Matthew 10:4). In the Greek transliteration, appearing respectively in Mark and Matthew, there is a phonetic similarity with the Hebrew word for

"Zealot," *kanna*, but no translation of the term is given. This is strange because the author of Mark customarily explains the meaning of transliterated Hebrew or Aramaic words, for example, *Boanerges*, "Sons of Thunder" (Mark 3:17) and *qorban*, "offering [to God]" (Mark 7:11). By not rendering *ton kananaion* he did away with having to explain why someone identified as a Zealot was to be found in the inner circle of a Jesus unopposed to Roman rule. (It has been suggested that this term refers to a native of Cana, but then it ought to be written *Kanaios*.) The Hebrew, *kanna*, is correctly rendered in Luke 6:15 and Acts 1:13 as *ho Zelotes*, "the Zealot," that is, a member of the Zealot party. However, there is no mention of the Zealot party, as such, in the New Testament.

It is possible that others among the twelve disciples had previously been, or still were, members of the Zealots or similar groups. Some Old Latin versions of Matthew 10:3 list one Judas Zelotes in place of the name Thaddaios as a disciple of Jesus.[8] In addressing Peter, Jesus calls him Simon Baryona (Matthew 16:17). Understanding *bar* as being derived from the Aramaic *bar*, "son of," *Baryona* is commonly rendered as "son of Yonah." This is highly unusual since the word is not written in Matthew as two words, but as one. Other New Testament names in which *bar* is the first syllable (for example, Barabbas, Barjesus, Barnabas) are first names, not patronymics. In addition, there is no reason to assume that "Baryona" refers to a second given name, that is, that Peter's original given name was Simon Baryona bar . . . . If *Baryona* means "son of Yonah," it is strange that *bar* was left in the Aramaic. Elsewhere, the author of Matthew indicates "son of" by using the genitive case (Matthew 10:2, 3). In the Fourth Gospel, Jesus refers to "Peter as Simon the son of John" (John 1:42; 21:15, 16, 17). Perhaps, this is the result of a misreading of "son of Yonah" (the Hebrew for "John" is Yochanan). Some manuscripts have *Baryonah* in John 21:15, 16, 17 (chapter 21 is a later addition to the Gospel).

The name "Simon the son of John," in John 1:42, may indicate Peter's father's actual name or may be an attempt to conceal Simon Peter's rebel affiliation. Simon may originally have been referred to as Simon Biryona, "Simon the Outlaw." In Aramaic the definite article, *alef*, is affixed at the end of nouns. Thus, *biryon*, "outlaw," when written with the definite article becomes *biryona* ("the terrorist"). The *Biryonim* were a Jewish group that engaged in extremist actions against the Romans and their Jewish collaborators during the Roman occupation. It is also possible that Judas[9] Iscariot was a member of the Sicarii ("Assassins," from the Latin *sica*, "a curved dagger") and that the name *Iscariot* derives from the word *sica*, that is, *ho Iskariotes* is a corruption of *ho sikarios*[10] The Sicarii were an anti-Roman group affiliated with the Zealots. They carried out political assassinations of their opponents with daggers carried beneath their clothes. Some dismiss the suggestion that Judas was a member of the Sicarii because Josephus gives the date of their origins to be during the prefecture of Felix (52-60 C.E.).[11] But, this does not rule out that similar groups may have existed at an earlier period or that the mention of *Iscariot* is due to anachronistic Gospel usage.

It has been argued that "Zealot" is used in the Gospel of Luke and in the Book of Acts in a religious sense, with the meaning "one zealous for the Law"[12] However, this is not accurate. When the term Zealot is used alone, without an additional phrase, such as, "of the Law," it always has a political meaning. The definite article shows that *Kananaios* was a title. If *ho kananaios* were meant to describe Simon's nature, Mark would have given an example of how this disciple was zealous. Instead, contrary to his usual practice, he does not explain this Aramaic term. He wished to avoid mentioning that its Greek equivalent was *ho Zelotes*, since his readers would then understand it to mean a member of the Zealot party.

As we see, the author of Mark is careful to avoid depicting Jesus or his followers as being anti-Roman. He also wants to show that the Romans, unlike the Jews, showed no interest in arresting Jesus. Writing in Rome shortly after 70 C.E., the author had good reason for not wishing to draw attention to the fact that Jesus had been arrested by Roman soldiers for sedition and subsequently executed on that charge. Therefore, in describing the arrest of Jesus, he describes the composition of the arresting party as coming from "the chief priests and the scribes and the elders." In addition, he substitutes "a crowd with swords" (Mark 14:43) for a more definite expression analogous to the *speira* ("cohort") of John 18:3 which would identify the arresting party as Roman led and to a large degree Roman in content.

According to the Marcan account of the so-called Jewish "trial" of Jesus, "the chief priests and the whole Council," that is, the high priest, all the chief priests, the elders, and the scribes (Mark 14:53) tried to obtain testimony against Jesus in order to put him to death but they could find none (Mark 14:55). The trial links the decision to kill Jesus with some saying or activity regarding the Temple (Mark 14:58, Matthew 26:61). Some witnesses did come forward to say he threatened the Temple, but their testimony was not consistent (Mark 14:59). The author of Mark has already indicated that Jesus has caused some disruption in the Temple. Did he threaten the Temple as some testified (the Marcan author labels this testimony as false)? The charge appears again as Jesus hangs on the cross (Mark 15:29, Matthew 27:40). The author of Luke-Acts has Stephen accused (also by "false witnesses" [Acts 6:13]) of saying, "this Nazarene, Jesus, will destroy this place [the Temple]" (Acts 6:14). The Gospel of John, however, does have Jesus make a remark to "the Jews" concerning destruction of the Temple, "Destroy this Temple, and in three days I will raise it up" (John 2:19). The author of John interprets the statement as, "he was speaking of the Temple of his body" (John 2:21), that is, a reference to Jesus' supposed resurrection after three days. This shows that there were pre-Gospel traditions, rightly or wrongly, attributed to Jesus, concerning violent action he promised to take against the Temple. Mark, followed by Matthew, denies Jesus made such remarks. The author of Luke-Acts also treats this threat of Temple destruction by Jesus as a false accusation. Only the author of John admits Jesus said something concerning destroying the Temple. Whether he quotes Jesus verbatim is another question. The Johannine version reinterprets the remark that is found in the so-called false accusations so that Jesus does not say he will do the destroying. It is "the Jews" that do the destroying. The author of John then explains that Jesus was not referring to the Jerusalem Temple but, rather, to his own body ("destroyed" by "the Jews"). Thus, in the Gospel of John, there is no threat by Jesus against the Temple, only one by "the Jews" against the "temple of his body." Apparently, a saying about the destruction of the Temple was current in pre-Gospel tradition and perhaps was an embarrassment to the church. Its prevalence in the tradition is seen in the several ways in which it has been preserved (Mark 14:58; Matthew 26:61; John 2:19; and the Apocryphal Gospel of Thomas, logion 71: "I shall tear down this house and none shall be able to build it up again.").

In Mark's story, the witnesses failed to agree about Jesus' threat to the Temple. Consequently, the Jewish authorities, under the leadership of the high priest, could not establish a case against Jesus. Undaunted, the high priest remains committed to seeking Jesus' death (Mark 14:55). Failing to prove the original charge that Jesus threatened the Temple the high priest undertook a new line of questioning. He adopts the tactic of seeking to convict Jesus of claiming certain titles and being, because of his self-assertions, guilty of blasphemy. The high priest questions Jesus as to whether he was "the Christ" and "the Son of the Blessed One" in phraseology actually taken from later Christology. Jesus is convicted of blasphemy for claiming for himself the titles "the Christ" and "the Son of the Blessed One" (Mark 14:61). The Matthean account substitutes "the Son of God" (Matthew 26:63) for "the Son of the Blessed One." The Marcan high priest's question, "Are you the Christ, the Son of the Blessed One?" assumes that these two appellations go together and explain one another. Jesus' affirmative answer brings a cry of "blasphemy," from the high priest, as he rends his clothes. The rest of Mark's Council, equally anxious for a death penalty, vote in agreement.

According to the Gospel of Mark, the high priest asks Jesus, "Are you the Christ, the Son of the Blessed One?" Jesus accepts the two titles, "Christ" ("Messiah") and "Son of the Blessed One" as applying to himself (Mark 14:61), and the high priest then charges him with blasphemy (Mark 14:64). But, did the high priest ask this question? The conjunction of "Christ" ("Messiah"), "Son of the Blessed One," and "blasphemy" in the same context could not go back to a question made by the high priest. A careful examination of this episode reveals the titles to be anachronisms. The titles charge is a development of mythmaking that took place in the decades following Jesus' execution. It is during this period that Christianity gave Jesus both designations and construed them in a manner that Jews considered irreverent. "Son of the Blessed One," in particular, would come to mean to Christians that Jesus was not a mere mortal but rather an angelic being.

The words attributed to the high priest are a Christology that is a product of later Christian creativity. The Marcan high priest's phraseology attaches to "Christ" and "Son of the Blessed One" a combined significance that they did not have prior to the development of the church's Christology. The Marcan record of the verbal exchange between the high priest and Jesus could not be part of an actual trial proceeding. The question attributed to the high priest, "Are you the Christ, the Son of the Blessed One?" would not have had the same irreverent connotation in the third decade of the first century that it had with the development of the church's Christology. Joining them as they appear in the respective Gospels of Mark and Matthew is a later Christology that would have been unknown to the high priest. The entire episode has nothing to do with an actual confrontation between the high priest and Jesus just prior to Roman condemnation. Its sole purpose is to show that the Jews are responsible for the death of Jesus.

Besides the anachronistic nature of the Marcan high priest's question, there are other questionable elements in this episode. Unable to convict Jesus on a charge of threatening the Temple, the Marcan high priest asked the loaded question, "Are you the Christ, the Son of the Blessed One?" In the Marcan trial scene, the titles become an expedient for getting a conviction. Yet, claiming to be the Messiah and/or the Son of the Blessed One [God] did not, in and of themselves, constitute blasphemy. Was this the best they could do in charging him? Surprisingly, there is no mention of his Temple attack, his earlier royal entry into Jerusalem, or his teachings about the coming kingdom and his place in it. Since they were of particular interest to security minded imperial Rome, these episodes and teachings involve a political aspect of Jesus' activities that the Marcan author wished to squelch. But, they would be the crucial issues in a Roman decision to apprehend Jesus. Skepticism of Marcan veracity cannot end here. The Marcan high priest tears his clothing: "And tearing his clothes, the high priest said, 'What further need do we have of witnesses?'" (Mark 14:63). Tearing one's clothing is a biblical sign of mourning. Showing the signs of mourning in the context of the Marcan story has a dramatic affect. However, a biblical injunction specifically forbids the high priest from tearing his clothes (Leviticus 21:10). Did the high priest transgress the law by tearing his clothes, did he charge "blasphemy" when no such charge was biblically warranted (cf. Leviticus 24:15-16)? Or, was this emotional expression one more part of the Marcan cover-up of Jesus' violent actions and of the Roman reaction to Jesus' self-assertions? By accusing the Jewish authorities of making false charges and causing Jesus' condemnation the author of Mark sought to deflect any criticism of Jesus or the Roman authorities. All indications are that this author, or his sources, used a great deal of imagination in creating this "trial" episode. What the high priest actually thought and did is not known with certainty. What is found in the Gospels is distorted by the anti-Judaic polemic directed, in particular, against the priestly authorities. The direction of this attack centers on the Jewish leadership of the antebellum period. As the pre-war leadership, the priesthood came under special condemnation by the church. When the author of Mark wrote, it was still not clear that the leadership position had now passed to the Pharisees/Rabbis. He, therefore, continues to direct the major attack against the priesthood, although he or a later redactor did give the Pharisees a negative role as well. Subsequent Gospel authors revised the material more extensively to give the new leadership a wider role in the opposition to Jesus.

Evidently, Jesus' arrest must have had something to do with his premeditated attack (Mark 11:11) on the Temple (Mark 11:15-16, 18). Yet, not a single allusion to this event is made in the trial accounts. The author of Mark makes it clear that the Temple attack led to some reaction from the Jewish authorities. He writes, "And the chief priests and the scribes heard this, and began seeking how to destroy him; for they were afraid of him, for all the multitude was astonished at his teaching" (Mark 11:18). It is strange that such a serious offence does not deserve mention at a trial where the judges call for witnesses to come forward with any knowledge they may have of infractions of the law by the accused (the request made in the middle of the night). Apparently, the author of Mark thought it wise not to dwell on the incident. One might inquire further as to the extent of Roman interest in the fracas.

As part of the evangelical cover-up of the seriousness of Jesus' Temple attack there is no mention of intervention by the Jewish Temple guard (cf. Acts 4:1-3). The Roman soldiers who could observe the Temple enclosure from their vantagepoint in the Antonia fortress would most likely not readily enter the Temple enclosure as it could in itself precipitate a riot. When they did enter, it was only into the outer court, known as the Court of the Gentiles. This is where the moneychangers were located. We can see from Acts 21:31-39 how swiftly the Romans could descend on the pilgrims standing in the Temple courtyard. However, there is no mention of any Roman attempt to intervene in Jesus' Temple attack. Pilate would never tolerate such an incident to go unpunished. Some Christian commentators have remarked that there would have been no reason for either the Jewish Temple guard or the pagan Roman soldiers to interfere with a symbolic prophetic gesture. But, how would the Temple guard or Roman soldiers tell the difference between a disruptive prophetic gesture and a riotous revolutionary act?

Because of the editorial cover-up by the respective Gospel authors, it must remain in the realm of speculation that Jesus was anticipating a Roman intervention in the Temple attack. However, all the evidence points in that direction. He evidently expected that this confrontation was to mark the onset of a series of clashes that would inaugurate his seizure of power and the establishment of the kingdom of God. Apparently, Jesus did not meet with the success he envisioned in his Temple attack, and in the confusion was forced to escape. At this point, Pilate demanded that the Jewish authorities immediately apprehend Jesus and turn him over. As such, what John describes, following Jesus' capture, is not a Jewish trial preceding the Roman trial but an interrogation carried out before Jesus was handed over to the Romans. The evangelists cannot admit to this series of events; it would destroy the image of Jesus they are projecting. These events bring into question the respective roles played by Jews and Romans in the circumstances surrounding the crucifixion of Jesus as narrated in the Gospels. Early Christianity passed on a modified version of Jesus' Temple attack precisely because of its consequences; namely, it led not only to a direct conflict with the Temple authorities, but also with the Romans as well. Christian tradition left out Roman concerns. They sidestepped the fact that the rebellion-conscious Roman authorities were antagonistic toward anyone who disrupted the public order.

The high priest, as depicted in the New Testament, is politically in an unenviable position. He is the main spokesman representing his nation before the imperial authorities. Then along comes someone who attempts to stir up the masses by mixing a seditious brew of religion and politics. Jesus thought of himself as a king (Mark 15:2). This self-claim is announced in his manner of entry into Jerusalem and especially when it is combined with his teachings on the "kingdom" and the significant role he expected to play in it. Jesus was dangerous, not for theological reasons, but for attempting to cause a civic unrest, which Roman troops would quell with great loss of life. What was the high priest to do to safeguard the people? The author of John attributed to the high priest an appropriate, if not actually historical, statement, "it is expedient for you that one man should die for the people, and that the whole nation should not perish" (John 11:50).

What role did the Roman governor, Pilate, or Roman soldiers play in the death of Jesus? The author of Mark admits that it was Pilate, who really condemned Jesus and Roman soldiers who actually carried out the execution, but are they ultimately responsible? Pilate is portrayed as a weak crowd pleaser reluctantly succumbing to

Jewish demands and the indifferent soldiers as merely obeying orders (Mark 15:14-16, 20, 24). But, although the Romans had executed Jesus, they are not held culpable. It was the Jews, as a whole, who were truly responsible. Manipulated by the chief priests, the Jewish crowd is portrayed as enthusiastically calling for Jesus' execution. In the end, it is this Jewish crowd who Pilate wishes to satisfy and the soldiers are simply carrying out its demand.

Some Christians maintain that the Gospel of Mark distinguishes between the leaders of the Jews (Pharisees, scribes, elders, priests) and the Jewish people as a whole. They explain that in specific instances, the author of Mark accuses one faction of Jewish leadership or another of plotting Jesus' death, but not Jews in general. According to this view, the author of Mark finds fault with the Jewish leaders, not with the Jewish people. However, such distinction, if it exists, is not maintained consistently throughout that Gospel. First, the author establishes that certain leadership groups conspired to eliminate Jesus: "And the Pharisees went out and immediately began taking counsel with the Herodians[13] against him, as to how they might destroy him" (Mark 3:6). He proceeds to widen his attack to include the ordinary townspeople of Jesus' hometown (Mark 6:2-6). By the time of Jesus' trial before Pilate, the author of Mark not only accuses the "chief priests," who are said to have instigated the "crowd," but the "crowd" as well, for responsibility in the condemnation of Jesus. Thus, at the behest of the "chief priests" it is said the "crowd asks Pilate to release Barabbas" (Mark 15:11),[14] and it is the crowd who it is claimed shouted, "Crucify him" (Mark 15:13). Therefore, "Wishing to satisfy the *crowd*, Pilate released Barabbas for them, and after having Jesus scourged, he delivered Him over to be crucified" (Mark 15:15). This verse is of great significance. It is not the Jewish leaders alone who are condemned but all Jews who do not accept Jesus. They constitute the main target of Mark's anti-Jewish attack. As Mark's Gospel describes the situation, it was at the insistence of a Jewish "crowd," a representative cross section from all strata of Jewish society, that forced Pilate to execute Jesus. Mark does not go as far as Matthew's spurious self-indictment by the "people" outside Pilate's residence (Matthew 27:25), but he too makes it clear that he considers all Jews who do not follow Jesus as responsible for the latter's execution.

Even prior to the passion narrative, the author of Mark prepares his audience for the accusation that the Jews are solely responsible for the death of Jesus. This is illustrated in the parable of *The Wicked Tenant Farmers* (Mark 12:1-12; see also Matthew 21:33-45, Luke 20:9-16). The owner of a vineyard rented it out to tenant farmers and left the country. When it was time to collect his part of the harvest from the tenant farmers, he sent a servant. The tenant farmers beat that servant and then another servant whom the owner sent. A third servant the tenant farmers murdered, and did the same with subsequent servants sent by the owner. The owner then sent his beloved son, thinking that the tenant farmers would hold him in esteem, but they murdered him.[15] Therefore, the owner of the vineyard was going to come and destroy the tenant farmers and give the vineyard to others. In this parable, the "owner" is God, the "tenant farmers" are the Jews, the "servants" are the prophets, the "son" is Jesus, the "vineyard" is God's favor, and the "others" is the church. The intent of the parable is the denigration of the Jews and the announcement of their displacement in God's favor by the church. At no point in the parable, with its motif of unappreciative and unrelentlessly wicked murderers of God's messengers, is there the slightest hint of condemnation of the role played by the Romans in the death of Jesus. All criticism of the Romans is suppressed.

The author of Mark is ambivalent concerning who "knew he had spoken the parable against them" (Mark 12:12). Conflating the three Synoptic versions of the story, it is obvious that the chief priests, scribes, and Pharisees on hearing the parable from Jesus, will understand that it referred to them (cf. Matthew 21:45, Mark 12:12, Luke 20:19). However, that did not mean that the condemnation was reserved solely for Jewish leaders and not for the entire people. The leadership was said to have heard and understood what Jesus preached. At the enunciation of the parable, the leaders feared the reaction of the people if they seized Jesus.

This seems to speak well for the people, but only for a moment. The parable speaks of an event yet to come, the death of the "son." The "tenant farmers" murder the owner's son. As the passion narrative unfolds it parallels the parable. In the Marcan trial narrative before Pilate, the crowd of people joins with the leadership to demand the execution of the "son." It is the crowd's wish for Jesus' death that Pilate intends to satisfy (Mark 15:15). The Marcan message is clear. The Jewish people as a national unit are responsible for the death of Jesus. They are synonymous with the murderers described as the "tenant farmers"; they are to receive the punishment depicted at the end of the parable.

Matthew's Jesus, in relating this parable, further clarifies the subject of the denunciation. The "tenant farmers" symbolize the nation's unfaithfulness. The whole nation of Israel has lost God's favor and not simply some factions of Jews. "The kingdom of God," Matthew's Jesus declares, "will be taken from you and given to a nation [*ethnei*] producing the fruit of it" (Matthew 21:43). The thought expressed is that the kingdom of God will be taken from the Jewish people, not just their leaders, and given to the church, the "new Israel," that will entirely supplant the Jewish people. Everything that biblically distinguishes the Jews as God's people is now claimed for those who comprise the church. Thus, it is said of the church: "But you are a chosen race, a royal priesthood, a holy nation, a people for God's own possession, that you may proclaim the excellencies of Him who has called you out of darkness into His marvelous light; for you once were not a people, but now you are the people of God; you had not received mercy, but now you have received mercy" (1 Peter 2:9-10). For those who accept Jesus the New Testament authors promise God's mercy, but to the Jews who remain loyal to the God of Israel no mercy is to be forthcoming, neither from God nor from those generations nurtured on the anti-Jewish verses of the New Testament. The Jews and Judaism are delegitimitized with no independent usefulness in God's purposes. The Jews are set up for the kill; all that is needed is for the church to become powerful enough to carry out the dictates of the New Testament.

The tenant farmers' parable sums up Mark's political and theological agenda. Blame for the execution of Jesus is placed solely on the Jews; the Gentile church has superseded the Jews and Judaism, and the Jewish people, the national entity, having rejected Jesus, is condemned as a unit.

The Gospel of Mark was as much a political apologia as a religious one. Writing in the aftermath of the Roman-Jewish War, the author of Mark found it undesirable to portray Jesus as a Davidic descendant. The Romans were very much aware that for decades the focus of Jewish aspirations centered on the establishment of a religio-political kingdom of God governed by the messianic descendant of David. Therefore, when the author of Mark wrote this Gospel, he felt that claiming Jesus was a descendant of David was not in the best political interests of the Christian community. The Marcan Jesus says:

> How is it that the scribes say that the Christ is the son of David? David himself said by the Holy Spirit; "The Lord [*kyrios*] said to my Lord [*kyrio mou*], 'Sit at My right hand, until I put your enemies beneath your feet.' David himself calls him 'Lord,' how is he then his son? (Mark 12:35-37).

Attributing the questions of Mark 12:35 and 12:37 to Jesus, the author of Mark derides the scribes and their teachings concerning the Davidic descent of the Messiah, "the Christ." As such, the Marcan Jesus not only distances himself from Jewish beliefs, but also assures the Romans that he does not have a physical connection with the rebel-supported House of David.[16]

The author of the Gospel of Mark still has to explain why there are those who refer to Jesus as being of Davidic lineage. He writes that Bartimaeus, a blind beggar, calls out, "Jesus, son of David, have mercy on me" (Mark 10:47). The Marcan narrative is not providing support for a Davidic descent for Jesus. On the contrary, it maintains that those who had no direct Davidic lineage could speak of "our father David," with the implication that they were the "spiritual" sons of David (Mark 11:10, cf. Acts 4:25).

Therefore, the title, "son of David," the Marcan author would have his audience understand, is nothing more than a respectful form of address, irrespective of one's ancestry.

The great majority of controversies involving the Pharisees and Jesus that appear in the Synoptic Gospels focus on the question of the viability of the Law. The Gospels were all written after the death of Paul, and many of the pre-Gospel traditions were influenced by a negative Pauline understanding of the Law. The antagonistic encounters found in the Gospel narratives reflect problems of the later church in its dealings with contemporary Jewish religious authorities rather than with the confrontations between the Pharisees and Jesus fifty to sixty years earlier.

The author of the Gospel of Mark groups five episodes together in order to illustrate the growing controversy between Jesus, on the one hand, and scribes and Pharisees, on the other (Mark 2:1-3:6).[17] These stories are brought together for dramatic affect as a means of attacking the Oral Law and those who uphold it. The specific time or place of occurrence is not given nor is it clear how they relate to each other except that they are conflict stories between those religious leaders who uphold the Oral Law and Mark's Jesus who dismisses it. This theme of conflict, not chronological sequence set in the time frame of Jesus' career, is what determined their inclusion. The conflict escalates with each successive story. In the first story, Jesus' adversaries keep their thoughts to themselves. In the second, they complain to the disciples about Jesus. In the third and fourth stories, they express their disapproval of the disciples' behavior directly to Jesus. In the fifth story, they say nothing, but afterwards conspire to "destroy" him.

Mark's Jesus says to a paralytic, "Your sins are forgiven." Some scribes hearing this are said to have thought to themselves, "Why does this man speak that way? He is blaspheming. Who can forgive sins but God alone?" (Mark 2:7).[18] In another incident, the scribes and Pharisees complained to Jesus' disciples because he was "eating and drinking with tax collectors and sinners" (Mark 2:16). On another occasion Jesus is asked (by who is not specified), "Why do John's disciples and the disciples of the Pharisees[19] fast, but your disciples do not fast?" (Mark 2:18). On a Sabbath, Jesus is questioned as to why his disciples picked grain on the Sabbath, "And it came about that he was passing through the grainfields on the Sabbath, and his disciples began to make their way along while picking the heads of grain. And the Pharisees were saying to him, 'See here, why are they doing what is not lawful on the Sabbath?'" (Mark 2:24).[20] On another Sabbath, it is said that Jesus entered a synagogue and there healed a man with a withered hand, merely by speaking to him. "And the Pharisees went out and immediately began taking counsel with the Herodians against him, as to how they might destroy him" (Mark 3:6).[21]

As part of the anti-Jewish bent of the early church, Mark and/or the pre-Marcan tradition developed this series of stories in which Jesus criticized the Oral Law and was in turn criticized by Jews who upheld that law. The author of Mark wants to give the impression that the Pharisees were seeking to persecute Jesus from very early in his public career. The level of confrontation is steadily and dramatically increased. In each episode Jesus' answers, or his prior statements, confute his adversaries and provide the arguments used by the church in its ongoing struggle with Judaism.

Did these episodes occur as described in the Gospel of Mark or were they manufactured, perhaps using sayings of Jesus as passed down through Christian tradition? Certainly, it is possible that there were conflicting opinions between scribes and Pharisees on the one hand and Jesus and his disciples on the other. But were these stories recorded by the author of Mark based on actual confrontations between these two groups or were they based on later conflicts between the early Christian community and the "disciples of the Pharisees," that is, the rabbis of the latter part of the first century? In either case, this material was developed in such a way as to attack Jewish leaders and Judaism. The purpose was to show Christians (especially those who adhered to the Oral Law) that Jesus, himself, denied the validity of the Oral Law. The author of Mark cites accounts where Jesus and his disciples are at odds with the Oral Law and as such disregard it. In the end, the Marcan author adds that the Pharisees decide to "destroy" Jesus.

Thus, although Sadducees play a prominent and decisive role in the Marcan depiction of the final events leading to Jesus execution they are not alone in seeking Jesus' death. His intention is to show that deadly opposition to Jesus came from the Pharisees (and later the rabbis) as well. In essence, the presence, in the Gospel, of Jesus' alleged conflicts with the Pharisees results from a twofold plan. First, there is the author's goal of shifting the culpability for Jesus' death from the Romans to the Jews and thereby depoliticizing his intentions. Second, it is also the author's aim to rewrite into Jesus' lifetime, the religious conflict of the early church with the rabbis in the second half of the first century.

Mark 7:1-23 presents another attack on both the Written and Oral Laws. Verses 2-4, 11 make it evident that this Gospel was written for a predominantly Gentile audience. The author of Mark clarifies terms and issues unfamiliar to his readers. He explains the Jewish customs in regard to ceremonial washing and the technical term *qorban*, "offering [to God]." The content of these verses has no connection with the preceding narratives and it is impossible to determine when or where the alleged incident took place. However, Mark's inclusion of the discussion concerning defilement is instructive. It stands as the prelude to a narrative in which Jesus extends his "grace" to Gentiles.[22]

Mark's Jesus, seeking to discredit the Pharisees, accuses them of hypocrisy and of negating the law of God, of following instead an invalid tradition of their own making. Jesus then says:

> You nicely set aside the commandments of God, in order that you may keep your own tradition. For Moses said, "Honor your father and your mother"; and, "He who speaks evil of father or mother, let him surely die." But you say, "If a man says to his father or his mother, anything of mine you might have been helped by is Corban (that is, given to God)," you no longer permit him to do anything for his father or his mother; thus invalidating the word of God by your tradition which you have handed down; and you do many things such as that. (Mark 7:9-13)

According to Jesus' explanation, this allegedly is a manmade Pharisaic tradition: that a man who had devoted all his property to God is, in effect, prohibited by them from providing for his parents. But, Mark's Jesus was not well versed in the laws of the Torah. There it is written: "But any devoted thing which a man may devote to the Lord of all that he has, whether of man or beast, or of the field of his possession, shall not be sold, nor redeemed; every devoted thing is most holy to the Lord" (Leviticus 27:28). Jesus' quarrel is not with the Pharisees, but with the word of God as stated in the Torah.

Jesus is criticizing the Pharisees for their obedience to God's commandments, not for following a pharisaical rule. His attack is totally unjustified and is merely another part of the early Christian polemic directed against obedience to God's commandments to Israel. Moreover, if an individual declared his property or money to be dedicated to the Temple as a means of evading giving assistance to his needy parents most everyone, especially Pharisees, would have denounced the misuse of the Torah's precepts (cf. Mishnah *Nedarim* 9:1: "[I]n a matter [for example, to withhold their livelihood from them] between one and his father and his mother they [the Sages] may find a way out for him [to nullify his vow] by reason of the honor due his father and his mother.").

In another verbal assault on the Torah, Mark's Jesus strikes at the very heart of the continued existence of the Jewish people. Mark's Jesus declares that people are defiled not by taking in something that is outside, but by letting out something that is inside:

> And calling the multitude to him again, he began saying to them: "Listen to me, all of you, and understand. There is nothing from outside the man which going into him can defile him; but the things which proceed out of the man are what defile the man . . . ." And he said to them [the disciples]: " . . . Are you not aware that whatever goes into the man from outside cannot defile him, because it does not go into his heart, but into his stomach, and goes out into the latrine?" Thus he declared all foods clean.[23] (Mark 7:14-15, 18-19)

Mark's Jesus negates the validity of the biblical principle that there is a distinction between ritually clean and unclean foods, a distinction that is clearly spelled out in the Torah itself (Leviticus 10:10, 11:2-47; Deuteronomy 14:3-21). Jesus says: "There is nothing from outside the man which going into him can defile him; but the things which proceed out of the man are what defile the man." This negation of the distinction between permitted and prohibited foods is of great significance. With this pronouncement, Mark's Jesus presumptuously demolishes a basic biblical precept.

It has been claimed that what Mark's Jesus is stressing in his assertion is that there are many immoral things proceeding from within a person that defile him (Mark 7:20-23). This feeble attempt at denying the fact that Jesus' statement, as quoted above, refers to the dietary laws of the Torah is in vain. The author of Mark is very explicit in declaring that Jesus meant specifically the nullification of the dietary laws of clean and unclean food. This, the evangelist emphasizes with a parenthetical comment. Following his citation of Jesus' statement: " . . . whatever goes into the man from outside cannot defile him, because it does not go into his heart, but into his stomach, and goes out into the latrine," the author of Mark adds an interpretive gloss: "Thus he declared all foods clean." Whether the author is reproducing an actual saying of Jesus is doubtful, but he certainly was expressing the antinomian view of, at least, a segment of the early church (Luke 11:41; Acts 10:15, 11:9; Romans 14:14; Colossians 2:16). Although Mark's Jesus did not grant outright permission to eat unclean species, he did give his tacit approval. By denying the distinction between clean and unclean food, Mark's Jesus repudiated the dietary laws and paved the way for his followers to declare invalid an important feature of God's Torah to Israel. This nullification of the food laws is most significant. The food laws were a major distinction separating the Jewish people from Gentiles and were a topic of deep concern in the early church.

The parallel passage in Matthew 15:1-20 does not include the reference to cleansing all food. The author of Matthew changes Mark 7 so that Jesus is made to attack not the food laws found in the Torah but the purification laws of rabbinic tradition. Matthew 15:12-14 distinguishes between what he considers the laws of God and those of men. The Marcan explanation that Jesus declared all foods clean (Mark 7:19b) is omitted and replaced by, "These are the things which defile the man; but to eat with unwashed hands does not defile the man" (Matthew 15:20). This verse interprets what Jesus supposedly said as being opposed to the purification traditions of the Pharisees.

In relating this episode, the author of Mark wishes to stress the division between Judaism and Christianity. Thus, Mark's Jesus opens a breach between his teachings and Judaism, which leaves no room for reconciliation; he despises Jewish law. Jesus' goal is now to undermine not only the Oral Law but the Written Law as well. He uses the confrontation with the scribes and Pharisees as an opportunity to irretrievably separate himself from fundamental biblical commandments. In so doing, Mark's Jesus categorically rejects the authority of the Torah. The author of Mark is now ready to describe for his Gentile audience the confidence a non-Jewish woman placed in Jesus and the success it brought her (Mark 7:25-30).[24]

The appearance of this controversy over the validity of the Written and Oral Law and the faith shown by a Gentile woman is crucial to the author of Mark's anti-Judaic polemic. The question of how to admit Gentiles into the church depended, in part, upon the decisions that were taken with regard to these laws. The author of Mark is continuing a pattern established by his predecessors. Paul and his supporters favored ending any distinction between Jewish and Gentile followers of Jesus. To accomplish this Paul resolved to undermine the Torah; Mark follows suit.

The early church vacillated in its attitude toward the food laws and did not resolve this issue without great controversy (Galatians 2:11-17, Romans 14:14, Colossians 2:20-22). There were both Jewish and Gentile Christians who believed in the necessity of observing the Jewish dietary laws. They had to be convinced otherwise. That there were those in the early church that opposed the nullification of the Torah is seen, for example, in

Acts 15:5[25] and Galatians 2:11-12.[26] It is interesting that the Jerusalem Church Council's decision as to the extent Gentiles needed to observe Jewish dietary restrictions was recorded as a personal decision on the part of James and not as a divine decree: "Therefore it is *my* judgment that we do not trouble those who are turning to God from among the Gentiles" (Acts 15:19).

Paul had attacked these laws with the specific intent of undermining the decision of the Jerusalem based apostles to have Gentile Christians "abstain from things sacrificed to idols and from blood and from things strangled" (Acts 15:29). In his opinion, even these restrictions were too much. Paul's antinomian comments were directed equally to born-Jewish Christians and Gentile Christians as he sought to do away with any distinctions between them. Paul writes: "I know and am convinced in the Lord Jesus that nothing is unclean in itself; but to him who thinks anything to be unclean, to him it is unclean. For if because of food your brother is hurt, you are no longer walking according to love. Do not destroy with your food him for whom Christ died" (Romans 14:14-15); "Therefore let no one judge you in regard to food or drink or in respect to a festival or a new moon or a Sabbath day" (Colossians 2:16); and "If you have died with Christ . . . why . . . do you submit yourself to decrees, such as, 'Do not handle, do not taste, do not touch!' (which all refer to things destined to perish by being consumed)—in accordance with the commandments and teachings of men?" (Colossians 2:20-22).

The author of Acts also attacks the prohibition against eating certain foods. While in a trance, he claims, Peter is ordered by a voice to eat unclean creatures. He is told, "What God has cleansed you must not call unclean" (Acts 10:15).[27] The author of Acts, is silent as to whether the other apostles took this trance to be a mandate for allowing all born-Jewish Christians to abandon the dietary laws. However, according to this text, the dietary laws were now abrogated explicitly by an ethereal voice as earlier they had been abrogated implicitly by Mark's Jesus. The abrogation of the food laws also implied the desire for acceptance of Gentiles within the church.

The thrice-repeated vision that Peter supposedly received in Joppa, with its admonition, "What God has cleansed you must not call unclean," reflected the acceptance by, at least, part of the church of the Pauline viewpoint that the food laws had fulfilled their function and were now to be abolished (Acts 10:9-16, 11:2-10, 15:7-29). This alleged revelation to Peter has close parallels in vocabulary to the language of defilement found in Mark's attack on the food laws. It is more than likely that the author of Acts fashioned his description of Peter's vision with the Marcan narrative in mind. In Mark 7:1-23, Mark's Jesus calls into question the validity of not only the Oral Law but also the whole ritual system of the Written Law as well. "Thus he declared all foods clean" is the Marcan author's message to his Christian readers: the food laws were nullified, signifying nullification of all of the Torah. Some of his audience may have been Judaizers who he wanted to convince that they should abandon observance of Jewish ritual. The author's parenthetical observation attributes the act of nullification of the food laws to Jesus, himself. By citing Christianity's highest authority, the author of Mark hopes to end all intra-church controversy in favor of nullification. The author of Acts seeks to reemphasize that nullification.

Despite the heated controversy over the dietary laws recorded in Paul's letters, he never mentions that Jesus abrogated them. In his arguments against the Judaizers in the church, he never once refers to anything that Jesus was reported to have said. If Jesus, even implicitly, had abrogated the dietary laws during his public career, apparently neither his own disciples nor Paul knew of it. It also appears that the supposedly risen Jesus, in the forty day period prior to his alleged ascension (Acts 1:3), said nothing to the disciples concerning the abrogation of the dietary laws. It is first mentioned some forty years after Jesus' death. The Marcan passage declaring all foods clean reflects the church's controversy over the Torah generally, and the laws of kashrut, particularly, in the period after Jesus' death.

The significance of the anti-dietary law pronouncements has wider dimensions than just ending an intra-church controversy.

What lay behind this attack on the dietary laws was the need to show the election of the church, consisting of Jews and Gentiles who accepted belief in Jesus, as the new Israel. Several New Testament authors used the dietary laws for this purpose in a twofold manner. First, to show that since there is no longer a distinction between "clean" and "unclean" foods, these laws were no longer applicable. Second, to expand this notion to show that there was no longer a distinction between Jews and Gentiles in God's sight. Thus, the author of Acts records that Peter "went to uncircumcised men and ate with them" (Acts 11:3) because of what he has been supposedly taught by God: "And he [Peter] said to them, 'You yourselves know how unlawful it is for a man who is a Jew to associate with a foreigner or to visit him;[28] and God has shown me that I should not call any man unholy or unclean'" (Acts 10:28); "I most certainly understand that God is not one to show partiality, but in every nation the man who fears Him and does what is right, is welcome to Him" (Acts 10:34); and, "If God therefore gave to them the same gift as to us also after believing in the Lord Jesus Christ, who was I that I could stand in God's way?" (Acts 11:17). As a result of Peter's lobbying, it is reported that the apostles in Jerusalem accepted Gentiles as equals, "And when they heard this, they quieted down, and glorified God, saying, 'Well then, God has granted to the Gentiles also the repentance that leads to life'" (Acts 11:18). This elaborate attack on the dietary laws was part of an attempt to end the controversy over acceptance of Gentiles into the church in favor of their being accepted. At the same time, the intention was to end any further observance of the laws of the Torah by Christians. Whoever first drew the analogy between "unclean food" and "unclean Gentiles" is not known but it is obvious that this comparison became a widespread means of arguing the issue. It was, in essence, sanctioning the Pauline doctrine that there was no longer any distinction between Israel and the nations. The nullification of this significant set of commandments was symbolic of the Pauline nullification of all of the Torah. The faith of the Gentile woman (Mark 7:25-30) and its recognition by Jesus sets the course for the church to follow. The author of Mark is advancing the cause of those who declared there was no longer a need for the Torah or the Jewish people; only belief in Jesus mattered. Thus, the ultimate conclusion the New Testament reaches is that the Jewish people, having refused to accept Jesus, are no longer in God's favor and their law is superfluous. God has now turned to the Gentiles.

The author of Mark subscribed to the Pauline teaching that only some Jews are chosen to be saved while the majority are condemned (Romans 11:7). It was that author's intention to show his Gentile readers that they had now inherited God's favor which had once been the province of the Jewish people, as a whole. The Marcan author believes that it was part of the divine plan to reject the Jewish people. Accordingly, Jesus preached in parables specifically so that his Jewish audience should *not* understand his message, reject him, and demand his death. To justify Jesus' use of parables in this way, the author of Mark turns to the Hebrew Scriptures: "Go, and tell this people: Hear, indeed, but do not understand; see, indeed, but do not perceive. Make the heart of the people fat, and make their ears heavy, and shut their eyes; lest they, seeing with their eyes, and hearing with their ears, and understanding with their heart, return and be healed" (Isaiah 6:9-10). In the Isaian context, the nation has sinned to a point where punishment becomes inevitable. The compiler of Chronicles describes how, prior to the first exile, the nation sinned, "until there was no remedy" (2 Chronicles 36:16). God's mercy could no longer be exercised because the nation persisted in continuing its evil ways. Thus, the nation deprived itself of the ability to repent. Because of the people's sins, the punishment of exile was decreed upon them. How long will they not be able to repent? The answer is given in Isaiah 6:11-12: "Until cities be desolate without inhabitants and houses without man, and the land becomes utterly desolate. And the Lord has removed men far away, and there is a great forsaking in the midst of the land." That is, they will not repent until after they go into exile. The subsequent biblical record shows that during their exile the people recognized the extent of their sins, repented, and were forgiven. Thus, the punishment of exile did not mean God's total abandonment of Israel. In this case, God's punishment was physical and in this world. National punishment is ordained to occur. However, once that punishment is administered the people may return to God and be forgiven. That is, Divine retribution can lead to repentance and reconciliation with God; there is no eternal breach between God and Israel. As we shall see, the author of Mark uses verse 9 and the end of verse 10 out of context, in order to show his readers that Israel, as a nation, is eternally forsaken by God.

Belief in Jesus as the Messiah (exactly what that means varies with each denomination and sect of Christianity) is central to all forms of Christianity. Mark's Jesus expresses this centrality with the declaration: "He who has believed and has been baptized shall be saved; but he who has disbelieved shall be condemned" (Mark 16:16).[29] Accordingly, only those who believe in Jesus have "salvation," that is, an eternal relationship with God. Jesus supposedly came to earth in human form in order to affect a permanent means by which mankind can attain this relationship. But, Jesus' goal, in reaching out to humanity, with a new spiritual order, is not all-inclusive.

Mark's Jesus says that he uses parables as a means of creating a situation by which the majority of Jews will be excluded from attaining "salvation." His parables are meant to prevent Jews (the people he addressed) from understanding his message or being forgiven by God. For example, Jesus presents the parable of *The Sower and the Seed* to a Jewish audience (Mark 4:1-9; see also Matthew 13:3-9). This parable, he admits to his twelve disciples, is incomprehensible without an explanation (Mark 4:13-20).[30] This explanation Jesus only gives to his disciples in private. "To you," he says, "has been given the secret [*mysterion*] of the kingdom of God; but those who are outside get everything in parables so *that* [*hina*] while seeing, they may see and not perceive; and while hearing, they may hear and not understand; lest they return again and be forgiven" (Mark 4:11-12). Yet, it is not only the masses who do not understand the parables, the disciples themselves find them incomprehensible, "And Jesus said to them, 'Do you not understand this parable? And how will you understand all the parables?'" (Mark 4:13). The Matthean parallel to verse 12 reads: "Therefore, I speak to them in parables; *because* [*hoti*] while seeing they do not see, and while hearing they do not hear, nor do they understand" (Matthew 13:13). There is an important difference in the respective versions of Jesus' statement as they appear in Mark and Matthew. The difference results from the use of the Greek participles, *hina* and *hoti*. The author of Mark has Jesus withhold his message from the Jews "so that" (*hina*) they would not understand; as such, the Jews are destined by Jesus, himself, to reject him. The author of Matthew has Jesus withhold his message "because" (*hoti*) the Jews were unable to understand due to a deliberate refusal on their part to listen and comprehend. Mark's Jesus uses parables to deliberately prevent the Jews from understanding him. Matthew's Jesus uses parables to punish the Jews because they have made themselves incapable of understanding. In either case, Jesus' use of parables with hidden meanings contradicts the statement that Jesus is supposed to have made before the high priest. "Jesus answered him, 'I have spoken openly to the world; I always taught in a synagogue, and in the Temple, where all the Jews come together; and I spoke nothing in secret'" (John 18:20).

In accordance with Mark 16:16, rejection of Jesus brings the punishment of eternal separation from God. However, in this parable of *The Sower and the Seed*, Mark's Jesus withholds the ability of Jews generally to believe in him. Thereby, in conformity with his new spiritual order, Jesus creates the inevitability of God's eternal rejection of the Jewish people. Mark's Gospel shows its Gentile readers that the Jews as a nation are without any hope; they are not even given the opportunity to believe in Jesus. The Jews are so unworthy of salvation that comprehension of Jesus' message is divinely withheld from them; they are spiritually abandoned. Herein lies the difference between the complete Isaian message as originally promulgated (Isaiah 6:9-13) and its New Testament distortion (Mark 4:11-12). The Isaian verses do not preclude spiritual rejuvenation for God's chosen people, following punishment for their sins. There is no eternal punishment of the entire nation. A portion of the nation might be destroyed, but an identifiable remnant of Israel always survives, and not as lone individuals but as part of the corporate nation. As used by Mark's Jesus, the meaning of Isaiah's verses are warped. Jesus refers to these verses as somehow justifying his use of incomprehensible parables. The purpose of these parables is to prevent Jews from understanding his message. Thus, in the context of the New Testament concept of salvation where only belief in Jesus can bring about salvation, his ultimate objective is to damn Israel with eternal punishment, a permanent, unchangeable condition. This is not the intent of the Isaian text. Isaiah's words give hope to Israel as a nation. They affirm that repentance brings God's grace and that a remnant of the nation will survive (Isaiah 6:13). Jesus' words give nothing but unabashed condemnation, without any chance for Israel, the national entity, to understand and repent in the future. But, of course, this was the author of Mark's intention. The essential message conveyed to the Gentile readers of this parable is that God has rejected Israel as a nation. Individual Jews may become Christians, but Israel as a nation has lost its special status in God's providence.

Mark's attack on the Jews sets the tone for future Gospels. Taking every opportunity he can, the Marcan author distances Jesus from Jews and Judaism. Virtually every suggestion that Jesus was involved, in any way, in the Jewish resistance against Roman occupation is obscured. Mark's Jesus is not involved in contemporary political concerns. The only exception is his supposed endorsing of tax payments to Rome (Mark 12:14-17). In taking this pro-Roman position, Mark's Jesus sets himself apart from the Jewish rebels who refused to pay taxes to Rome and revolted against its governance. The author of Mark produced a document, which met the needs of the Christian community in Rome. Among his accomplishments was providing this community with a face-saving explanation of why Jesus had been crucified by the Romans for sedition. Simply put, the Jews rejected Jesus and compelled the Romans to execute him. In contrast to this Jewish rejection, a

Roman centurion who participated in the execution of Jesus is portrayed as saying, "Truly this man was a son of God!" (Mark 15:39).

The Marcan author set the precedent for transmitting the traditions concerning Jesus, as they supposedly relate to Jews, Judaism, and the political situation in Judea and Galilee. He shows Jesus' alienation from Jewish heritage at the same time as he demonstrates loyalty to Rome; he assures the Romans that Jesus' kingdom is spiritual rather than political and universal rather than nationalistic. His literary work became a model for establishing the anti-Jewish thrust that would to be found in future Gospels. The Marcan anti-Jewish attitudes are intensified in the Gospels of Matthew and Luke. Following Mark's example, the accusations leveled against the Jews in the other Gospels became more blatant, until they reach the point where the alleged complicity of the Jewish people in the death of Jesus was treated as a genetic inheritance (Matthew 27:25; see also John 8:44). The Jewish people would become the bearers of guilt for all the acts of murder perpetrated against the righteous of mankind (Matthew 23:34-35, Luke 11:49-50). In effect, they are represented as the archvillains of history.

Notes

[1] The author of Mark has Jesus express his feeling concerning the paying of taxes to Rome on the produce of the Land of Israel in Pauline terms. Paul writes:

> Let every person be in subjection to the governing authorities. For there is no authority except from God, and those which exist are established by God. Therefore he who resists authority has opposed the ordinance of God; and they who have opposed will receive condemnation upon themselves. For rulers are not a cause of fear for good behavior, but for evil. Do you want to have no fear of authority? Do what is good, and you will have praise from the same; for it

> is a minister of God to you for good . . . . For because of this you also pay taxes, for rulers are servants of God . . . . Render to all what is due them: tax to whom tax is due; custom to whom custom; fear to whom fear; honor to whom honor. (Romans 13:1-7)

According to this Pauline principle, all temporal authorities are to be considered as though they were carrying out God's will. This disregards the fact that many "governing authorities" behave in a manner that could not conceivably meet with God's approval.

2. In Judea taxes went directly to Rome, while in Galilee taxes were paid to Herod Antipas, who, in turn, paid tribute to Rome.

3. Subject nations under the imperial system paid tribute to Rome and in return, they were protected from invasion. All too often, the payments were burdensome and were carried by the lower classes. Roman officials and their native cronies enriched themselves in the process of tax collecting. The Roman Senate farmed tax collection to the highest bidder. These individuals, in turn, delegated their power to others, the one condition being that they should raise as much money as possible.

The Jews especially despised native tax collectors because they were both dishonest and working for the detested Romans. The Jews never recognized Roman rule in the Land of Israel as legitimate, and looked upon the tax collectors as accomplices of robbers, not the servants of a legitimate government.

Philo describes the Roman who, around the year 40 C.E. was in charge of tax collection in Judea. "Capito," he writes, "is the tax-collector for Judea and cherishes a spite against the population. When he came there he was a poor man but by his rapacity and peculation he has amassed much wealth in various forms" (*On the Embassy to Gaius* XXX. 199). Capito collected far more than he had to remit to Rome and thereby enriched himself.

4. Three men in the New Testament are called *Herodes*: Herod the Great, Herod Antipas, and Herod Agrippa I. The New Testament does not differentiate between them neither by use of descriptions, "the Great," nor by appellations, "Antipas," or "Agrippa." It refers to each respectively solely by the name Herod.

Herod Agrippa I was given the title of king by Gaius Caligula (*Jewish War* II. 9. 6 [181]). This title was affirmed by the next emperor, Claudius, who added to Agrippa's domain all the lands that had been ruled by his grandfather King Herod the Great, namely Judea and Samaria (*Jewish War* II. 11. 2 [215], *Jewish Antiquities* XIX. 5. 1 [274]). Herod Agrippa I ruled from 41 C.E. until his death in 44 C.E.

5. Tacitus records that the populace of Judea and Syria petitioned Rome in 17 C.E. for a reduction in the taxes they were compelled to pay (Tacitus, *Histories* 2. 42. 5).

6. Under the imperial system some subject nations were semi-independent client states that were allowed limited independence under local rulers. Others were ruled by a Roman governor who used local leaders for day-to-day governance. From subject rulers Rome expected undivided loyalty and cooperation, payment of tribute, defense of borders, and the maintenance of public order. In return, Rome promised protection in case of invasion. Within his realm, a ruler was permitted to do whatever he desired, as long as the main conditions were fulfilled. Abuses of power by Roman administrators and client rulers and their appointees often led to dissatisfaction on the part of the general populace.

At various times during the period between 63 B.C.E. and 70 C.E. Rome governed Galilee and Judea through a client king, ethnarch, or tetrarch, or through a governor who, in turn, made use of local aristocrats, particularly the high priest. During the late twenties and early thirties of the first century of the Common Era, Herod the Great's son, Herod Antipas, was the semi-independent client tetrarch of Galilee and Perea (regions northwest and east of the Jordan River respectively); Pilate was the governor of Judea (which included the geographical regions of Judea, Samaria, and Idumea, located west and southwest of the Jordan River); and Caiaphas was the high priest in Jerusalem with limited governmental responsibilities. Under Roman rule, there was much room for abuse and dissatisfaction in Galilee and Judea.

7. Perhaps inspiration for the formation of the Zealot party derives from 1 Maccabees 2:27-30:

> Then Mattathias went through the city shouting, "Let

everyone who is zealous for the law and who stands by the covenant follow after me!" Thereupon he fled to the mountains with his sons, leaving behind in the city all their possessions. Many who sought to live according to righteousness and religious custom went out into the desert to settle there, they and their wives and their cattle, because misfortunes pressed so hard on them.

[8] See B.F. Westcott and F.G.A. Hort, *Introduction to the New Testament in the Original Greek*, Peabody, Mass.: Hendrickson Publishers, 1988, p. 12.

[9] The Hebrew name *Yehuda*, "Judah," is rendered as *Ioudas*, "Judas," in the Septuagint. Thus, "Judas," is etymologically related to the word "Jew" (Hebrew, *Yehudi*; Greek, *Ioudaios*). Several New Testament characters have the name Judas. Sometimes this name is altered in the New Testament to "Jude." The conflicting stories about Judas' death (Matthew 27:5, Acts 1:18) and the fact that there is no mention of him in Paul's writings, suggest that the character of Judas, as presented in the Gospels, is an early Christian creation that developed independent of Paul, but was included in the Gospels (For an in-depth study of the Judas myth see, Hyam Maccoby, *Judas Iscariot and the Myth of Jewish Evil*, New York: The Free Press, 1992).

[10] Codex Bezae has the variant reading *Skariotes* for Matthew 10:4.

[11] *Jewish War* II. 13. 3 [254].

[12] Cf. Galatians 1:14, Acts 21:20; see also Acts 22:3, 2 Maccabees 4:2, *Jewish Antiquities* XII. 6. 2 [271].

[13] It is not clear who the "Herodians" were. However, the term probably refers to the Essenes. They may have had the nickname "Herodians" (possibly derogatory). Josephus tells us that Herod the Great showed special kindness toward the Essenes, "having a higher opinion of them than was consistent with their merely human natures" (*Jewish Antiquities* XV. 10. 5 [372-379].

[14] According to all four Gospels, it was customary at Passover (explicitly stated in John, implicitly stated in the Synoptic Gospels) for the Roman authorities to release a prisoner chosen by the Jews (Matthew 27:15, Mark 15:6-8, Luke 23:17 [inserted in some manuscripts], John 18:39a). However, this custom is not found in some of the best textual manuscripts of Luke (P75 [Chester Beatty Papyrus], codices Vaticanus, Alexandrinus, Sahidic [Coptic]). Scholarly opinion is divided on the question of the historicity of this custom.

Some question whether this custom ever existed while others accept its historicity but question whether it was a custom introduced by the Romans or a Jewish custom that the Romans honored. Despite claims to the contrary, it should be noted that there is nothing in Mishnah *Pesaḥim* 8:6 ("They slaughter [viz., a paschal lamb] for one who they promised to release [from prison on the eve of Passover]") that presupposes some kind of regular festival amnesty.

Some scholars also doubt the historicity of Barabbas, who is intimately connected in the Gospels with the practice of this alleged custom. "Bar Abba" means "son of Abba," that is, "son of the Father." Some manuscripts give his full name as Jesus Barabbas (literally, "Jesus son of the Father").

The greatest challenge to the authenticity of this custom is the skepticism that the Roman authorities would commit themselves to honor a custom that would require them to release someone who they considered a threat to their continued governance.

15. According to the Marcan version of the story, the son is killed inside the vineyard and his body is then thrown outside of it (12:8). The Matthean version (21:39) and the Lucan version (20:15) describe the son as first cast out of the vineyard, and then slain outside it. This is a reference to the slaying of Jesus outside the city (John 19:17, Hebrews 13:12 f.). The Gospels of Matthew and Luke "corrected" this story to conform to the sequence of events in the passion narrative.

16. This may also be the reason the author of Mark does not include a genealogy to prove Davidic descent as we find in the respective Gospels of Matthew and Luke.

17. The Gospels were all written after 70 C.E., at a time when the church's major Jewish opponents were Pharisees rather than Sadducees or priests. This has led some scholars to suggest that the controversy between Jesus and the Pharisees presented in the New Testament is frequently no more than a literary device. Accordingly, certain of Jesus' teachings did not appear originally within the context of a controversy. They were supplied with a controversy setting in order to provide a more vivid scene for the teachings and to demonstrate how such teachings could be presented in the church's ongoing

polemic with the Pharisees/rabbis. Jesus, historically, was not involved with these polemics.

18. In this story the accusation is said to be that Jesus arrogated to himself a prerogative of God by declaring the man forgiven for his sins (Mark 2:9-11). Claiming that a man's sins are forgiven never constituted blasphemy in Jewish law. The Marcan text does not have Jesus say, "I forgive your sins" but rather "your sins are forgiven." This need not mean anything more than that God forgives them and that Jesus believes himself to be God's spokesman on earth. As such, he may have been considered arrogant in claiming to know what God would or would not do but that is not blasphemy. If he maintained that he, himself, was God, he would have been considered a madman. The charge of blasphemy, as designated by the Torah, is unlikely to have been contemplated by the scribes in this episode.

Verse 10, is usually placed within the quotation starting in verse 9, in order to indicate that it was said by Mark's Jesus:

> "Which is easier to say to a paralytic, 'Your sins are forgiven'; or to say, 'Arise, and take up your pallet and walk?' But in order that you may know that the Son of Man has authority on earth to forgive sins," he said to the paralytic, "I say to you, rise, take up your pallet and go home."

Verse 10 is more appropriately a parenthetical comment made by the author of Mark. Therefore, the passage should be written as follows:

> "Which is easier, to say to the paralytic, 'Your sins are forgiven'; or to say, 'Arise and take up your pallet and walk?' (But in order that you may know that the Son of Man has authority on earth to forgive sins, he said to the paralytic) I say to you, rise, take up your pallet and go home."

The narrative then claims that the paralytic, "arose and immediately took up the pallet and went out in the sight of all" (verse 12a). The parenthetical insertion marks a transition from the earlier pre-Gospel tradition. It evolves from, "Your sins are forgiven," without Jesus claiming that he, himself, does the forgiving, to the claim made on behalf of Jesus by the author of Mark, "that the Son of Man has authority on earth to forgive sins." Even so, the Marcan Jesus is not part of a triune god. He is, for the author of Mark, God's chosen vehicle who has his authority from God, but he is not said to be God.

[19] The phrase, "the disciples of the Pharisees," is probably an anachronism referring to the rabbis. A confrontation from a later period involving Christians and rabbis is placed in an older context and setting suitable for the Marcan author's needs.

[20] In this story, the sudden appearance of Pharisees in the grainfield on the Sabbath is suspiciously convenient for the author of Mark's purposes.

[21] The Pharisees have gathered to watch, ready to accuse Jesus of Sabbath violation (Mark 3:2), but Jesus' chiding, "Is it lawful on the Sabbath to do good or to harm, to save a life or to kill?" (Mark 3:4), silences them before they can say anything to him. The Marcan Jesus then heals the withered hand by saying to the man, "stretch out your hand" (Mark 3:5). The impression is given that the Pharisees were about to accuse Jesus of Sabbath law violation when his words left them speechless. But, why should they say anything or object to what he did? No violation of Sabbath law took place. There is no Sabbath law that makes speaking a command to be healed unlawful. Someone might object had Jesus touched the hand in any way, but talking is not a violation of the Sabbath. It is doubtful that the Pharisees sought to destroy him because of this incident as maintained by the Marcan author's comment, "And the Pharisees went out and immediately began taking counsel with the Herodians against him, as to how they might destroy him" (Mark 3:6). The author of Luke adds two more cases of Jesus challenging the Sabbath injunctions in the Oral Law by healing on the Sabbath. To *The Man With the Withered Hand* (Luke 6:6-11) he adds *The Woman Bent Over* (Luke 13:10-17) and *The Man With Dropsy* (Luke 14:1-6).

[22] Christianity, after the crucifixion, very soon moved out of its original Jewish milieu into Syria, into Asia Minor, into Greece, into Egypt and into the Italian peninsula. In these regions it found a civilization whose language was Greek and whose culture and religion were Hellenistic. It was to the Hellenized ethnic groups of these regions that early Christianity, from Paul onward, was preached. The teachings of nascent Christianity had to be reworked and rendered in a way that would find acceptance among people for whom its Jewish-based content was alien. Thus, initially, the followers of Jesus had

demanded that only people who first became Jewish could become Christians. But, this hindered missionary efforts, so the Jewish phase was discarded. It was now agreed that Gentiles could become Christians without first accepting Judaism.

23. This pronouncement by Mark's Jesus stands in stark contrast to Jewish faithfulness to God. Jews suffered death rather than violate the Law of God governing unclean foods. "But many in Israel," says the First Book of Maccabees, "were determined and resolved in their hearts not to eat anything unclean; they preferred to die rather than to be defiled with unclean food or to profane the holy covenant; and they did die. Terrible affliction was upon Israel" (1 Maccabees 1:62-63). In Jesus' time, Jews had to endure the mockery of many of their pagan neighbors because they did not eat swine's flesh. Indeed, this kind of abuse has been common throughout the centuries.

24. A story of healing that allegedly took place in the Decapolis region follows this episode with the Syrophoenician woman (Mark 7:31-37). This region contained a large Gentile population but it cannot be determined from the text if the crowd or the individual in need of help were Gentiles. From the context, it would appear the author's intention was to depict those involved here with Jesus as Gentiles.

25. "But certain ones of the sect of the Pharisees who had believed, stood up, saying, 'It is necessary to circumcise them, and to direct them to observe the Law of Moses'" (Acts 15:5).

26. "But when Cephas came to Antioch, I opposed him to his face, because he stood condemned. For prior to the coming of certain men from James, he used to eat with the Gentiles; but when they came, he began to withdraw and hold himself aloof, fearing the party of the circumcision" (Galatians 2:11-12).

27. The Greek adjective, *koinos*, literally means "common." In this verse it is more precisely rendered as "unclean." In Romans 14:14, where it occurs three times, it is rendered "unclean." In 1 Maccabees 1:47, 62 the adjective means "ritually unclean."

28. Although social mores may have discouraged mingling of Jews with non-Jews there are no prohibitions in Jewish law against eating with non-Jews. The sectarian Book of Jubilees stresses the strict separation of Jews from the Gentiles (15.31). B.T. *Shabbat* 17b forbids the use of Gentile wine, bread, and oil, but does not forbid eating kosher food with them.

[29] Some scholars believe that Mark 16:9-20 is a later addition to the Gospel of Mark.

[30] Normally, a parable is meant to clarify something obscure. In rabbinic literature, parables are often used to clarify a message so that the common people could better understand it. Jesus uses parables, not to make understanding his message easier, but to make it impossible for Jews, in general, to understand his meaning.

6.
THE GOSPEL OF MATTHEW

The Romans had destroyed Jerusalem in 70 C.E., a number of years before the Gospel of Matthew was written. The Temple service could no longer be maintained. The worship of God by the offering of sacrifices had ceased. In response to this new situation, the Christians and the Pharisees/rabbis were each claiming to be the rightful heirs to the religion of the Jewish Scriptures, which, since the Temple had been destroyed, could no longer be practiced as before. The Christians believed that the Temple was destroyed because Jesus was the fulfillment of the Scriptures; the Pharisees/rabbis believed that the Torah was eternal and survived the Temple destruction as it had the previous Temple destruction, the Selucid defilement of the Temple, and life in the Temple-deficient Diaspora.

The author of Matthew[1] is determined to show a smooth transition from the Jewish Scriptures to his Gospel narrative. He provides his readers with so-called scriptural proofs to show that with the birth of Jesus and his subsequent public activity the biblical promises to Israel have been fulfilled.[2] To note this, he uses variations of the formula, "Now all this took place that what was spoken by the Lord through the prophet might be fulfilled" (Matthew 1:22). Scriptural allusions, as well as scriptural quotations, played a formative role in the development of this imaginative and often contentious volume. Biblical usage notwithstanding, the Gospel of Matthew is a highly inflammatory anti-Judaic work. The purpose of the author's attack is to support his claim that the followers of Jesus are the rightful heirs of Israel's tradition. He informs his audience that divine election has passed from the Jewish people to the church.

Many Christian commentators maintain that the author of Matthew was Jewish, and that he wrote his Gospel especially for the Jewish people. This raises the question as to how the author of Matthew could ever hope to convince the Jewish people that Jesus was the promised Messiah when he has written an anti-Jewish work? Therefore, before investigating the anti-Jewish character of the Gospel of Matthew it is important to identify its original audience and the reasons why the author of Matthew addressed his Gospel to it. Knowing for whom and why this Gospel was originally written helps to explain the direction and intensity of its anti-Jewish content. It is equally important to keep in mind that despite the setting of the Gospel of Matthew in Galilee and Judea and its use of biblical texts, the nature of its sectarian teachings had to make it unacceptable to the greater Jewish community.[3]

The assumption that the Gospel of Matthew was written for the Jews (c. 75-80 C.E.) is too broad a generalization. The evidence presented by the writings of the church fathers indicates that the Gospel of Matthew was directed at a very specific Jewish audience. Eusebius quoted Origen (185?-254? C.E.) as writing in reference to the Gospels, "The first is written according to Matthew, the same that was once a publican, but afterwards an apostle of Jesus Christ, who having published it for the Jewish converts, wrote it in Hebrew."[4] Jerome (340?-420 C.E.) wrote that Matthew "composed a Gospel of Christ in Judea in the Hebrew language and characters, for the benefit of those of the circumcision who had believed."[5] Apparently, if this information is correct, the author of Matthew was writing to strengthen the faith of those Jews who already believed Jesus was the Messiah. One way he did this was by reviling Jews who did not believe in Jesus generally and the Jewish leadership in particular. The anti-Jewish sentiments expressed in this Gospel show that Matthew's work was not intended for the general Jewish population. It was meant for born-Jewish Christians who were already embittered by the refusal of other Jews to recognize the legitimacy of their claim that Jesus was the Messiah. Yet, surely, a work that extols Gentiles for accepting Jesus as Messiah was not written solely for born-Jewish Christians.[6]

The possibility that the author of Matthew, himself, may have been Jewish and that his Gospel shows a familiarity with Jewish sources and tradition in no way alters the fact that he claims exclusively for Jewish and Gentile followers of Jesus all the biblical promises and privileges originally given to Israel. The Jews who do not believe in Jesus are to lose their biblical prerogatives, be killed, and suffer eternal damnation. God will now turn to outsiders to accept what the Jews rejected. The role of the Jews as God's people is over. The true Israel replaces them. Hence, in response to the Gentile centurion's[7] expression of faith (Matthew 8:5-9) a surprised Jesus declares, "Truly I say to you, I have not found such great faith with anyone in Israel [some manuscripts read, "not even in Israel"]" (Matthew 8:10). That is, superlative faith of the degree displayed by the centurion surpasses anything found among the Jewish people. Jesus then promises "that many shall come from east and west, and recline at table with Abraham, and Isaac, and Jacob, in the kingdom of heaven; but the sons of the kingdom shall be cast out into the outer darkness; in that place there shall be weeping and gnashing of teeth" (Matthew 8:11-12).[8] In the parable of *The Vineyard* (Matthew 21:33-43) the Jews lose their position as God's people. Matthew's Jesus states, "Therefore I tell you, the kingdom of God will be taken away from you and given to a people [*ethnei* [9]] producing the fruits of it" (Matthew 21:43). In the parable of *The Great Supper* (also called *The Great Banquet* or *The Marriage Feast*) Israel is again condemned. Matthew's Jesus declares, "The king was angry and he sent his troops and destroyed those murderers and set their city on fire" (Matthew 22:7). In the total imagery of these parables, God, the King, will send the Romans to kill the Jews and destroy Jerusalem. Thus, God will punish all the Jews who do not believe in Jesus for their lack of faith. He will then give the "kingdom of God" to the church that will carry out His will.[10]

The contrast between Gentile acceptance and Jewish rejection of Jesus is much more pronounced in Matthew than in Mark. When a Gentile woman pleads with Jesus to chase a demon out of her daughter Mark's Jesus replies, "Let the children first be fed, for it is not right to take the children's bread and throw it to the dogs." In turn, she answered, "Yes, Lord, but even the dogs under the table feed on the children's crumbs." Jesus replies, "Because of this answer go your way, the demon has gone out of your daughter" (Mark 7:24-30). The Matthean account elaborates the story. In this version the disciples urge Jesus to send the woman away, Jesus says he "was sent only to the lost sheep of the house of Israel" and when she answers him, he replies that the woman's "faith is great" (Matthew 15:21-28). This story recalls the statement concerning the centurion, "I have not found such great faith with anyone in Israel" (Matthew 8:10). Both stories emphasize the view that Gentiles have greater faith than Israelites. The Matthean elaboration is a commentary on the acceptance of Gentiles into the church and the rejection of Israel. By writing that the disciples urged Jesus to send the woman away the author of Matthew wishes to show that there had been opposition from some Jewish Christians toward the admission of Gentiles into the church. The intent of the remark attributed to Jesus is to show that exclusion was only a temporary situation. According to the evangelist, Jesus' remark shows that he was initially sent only to the Jewish people, who were given the first opportunity to accept him, but, as was obvious in the author's day, they rejected Jesus. Therefore, in stating that the woman's "faith is great" he declares the ascendance of the Gentiles to a position equal to that once held by the Jewish people. This is in agreement with the Pauline concept that the Jewish rejection opened opportunity for Gentile salvation (Romans 11:11-25).

The author of Matthew provides a further illustration of Gentile faith and Jewish disbelief to support his allegation that God has turned from Israel toward the Gentiles. After Jesus' death the evangelist has Gentile affirmation of Jesus as a "son of God" in the form of a statement by the centurion keeping guard at the crucifixion (Matthew 27:54). This is contrasted with alleged Jewish machinations seeking to prevent messianic manifestations after Jesus' death (Matthew 27:62-64). Matthew's strong anti-Jewish prejudices have him maintain that the malevolence of the Jewish authorities, the representatives of the people, toward Jesus continued even after his death. This story line compliments the period following Jesus' birth when the Gentile magi came and worshiped "he who has been born King of the Jews" (Matthew 2:2, 11), while the Jewish king Herod was seeking his death (Matthew 2:16, 20).

In the episode where Jesus is questioned concerning paying taxes to Caesar, Mark writes, "And they sent some of the Pharisees and Herodians to him, in order to trap him in a statement" (Mark 12:13). The antecedent for the "they" are "the chief priests, and scribes, and elders" of Mark 11:27. The author of Luke writes, "And they watched him, and sent spies who pretended to be righteous, in order that they might catch him in some statement, so as to deliver him up to the rule and the authority of the governor" (Luke 20:20). There, too, the antecedent of "they" are the "scribes and the chief priests" (Luke 20:19). But, the author of Matthew sees an opportunity to specifically attack the Pharisees, the contemporary Jewish leadership. His version of the payment of taxes to Caesar episode reads, "Then the Pharisees went and counseled together how they might trap him in what he said. And they sent their disciples to him, along with the Herodians . . ." (Matthew 22:15-16). The Matthean text makes a significant alteration in the Marcan story. Matthew's version has the instigation of the attempt to entrap Jesus made by the Pharisees rather than by the chief priests, scribes, and elders. By accusing the Pharisees, the author of Matthew is striking not only at them but also at all who follow their interpretation of the Law as well. The Matthean antagonism between Jesus and the Pharisees, in all likelihood, reflects the later situation of the church after 70 C.E. The Judaism of the Pharisees survived the destruction of the Temple, and this Judaism presented the challenge to Christianity when and where the Gospel of Matthew was being written. The author of Matthew considered the Pharisees/

rabbis his closest and most serious rivals and so he maligned them more than any other group.[11]

Unlike Mark's Jesus (Mark 7:14-15, 18-19), Matthew's Jesus does not undertake a frontal assault on the Law, the Torah. His Jesus maintains that the Law is to be kept and taught until it is fulfilled.

> Do you think that I came to abolish the Law or the Prophets; I did not come to abolish; but to fulfill. For truly I say to you, until heaven and earth pass away, not the smallest letter or stroke shall pass away from the Law, until all is accomplished. Whoever then annuls one of the least of these commandments, and so teaches others, shall be called least in the kingdom of heaven; but whoever keeps and teaches them, he shall be called great in the kingdom of heaven. (Matthew 5:17-19)

Is Matthew teaching doctrines at odds with Paul's teachings concerning the negation of the Law? If not, how does Matthew envision the Law being "accomplished" by Jesus? Unless the author of Matthew's Gospel is at odds with the Pauline doctrine, his readers must have already understood the Law as being fulfilled in Jesus. Paul declared, "For Christ is the end of the Law for righteousness to everyone that believes" (Romans 10:4). The same sentiment is expressed by the author of Hebrews, "In that he says, 'a new covenant,' he has made the first obsolete. Now that which is made obsolete and growing old is near to vanishing away" (Hebrews 8:13).[12] The Matthean text places this already familiar concept into a saying by Jesus. As with Mark's Jesus, so Matthew's Jesus is informing his readers that the observance of the Law is at an end. But, in the Gospel of Matthew the Law is not simply annulled, it is fulfilled. In some inexplicable way, one individual, Jesus, supposedly fulfills the Law for all Jews and for all time.[13] In this passage, Jesus' assault on the continued existence of the Jewish people and Judaism is in basic agreement with that of Marcan teachings. Except here, Jesus does not negate Judaism outright, rather he "accomplishes" its purpose through a mythical fulfillment. In either case, the result is the same. The Matthean message is that there is no longer a need for the Law, the Torah, or for that matter a Jewish people. The interdependence of Law and peoplehood is at an end; their function is fulfilled. Jesus and the church replace them respectively.

It may be that the author of Matthew considered himself and his followers Jews. However, the question is not only how he viewed his particular community, but also how he viewed those Jews who did not accept Jesus. The Matthean author considered Jesus' Jewish followers to be the true "remnant" of the fleshly people of Israel; they are now part of the larger spiritual Israel, the church. In his effort to keep the Jewish converts away from the Jewish moorings of their past, he resorted to making disparaging and offensive remarks and accusations against Jews who did not believe in Jesus. This author attempts to substantiate the position that Jewish Christians, not those Jews who follow Pharisaic teachings, were the true successors to the religion of the Jewish Scriptures. Thus, the Pharisees and their converts are not children of Abraham but "child[ren] of hell" (Matthew 23:15). The conflict between Matthew's community and Jews generally may have initially occurred from a position within Judaism. Like the Qumran community who also denounce Jews outside their own movement, the Matthean Jewish Christians believed that they, not their opponents were the legitimate heirs to the Abrahamic covenant. But, unlike the Qumran community, the Matthean Jewish Christians included Gentiles within their community to form a new entity and explicitly state that Gentiles such as these displace Jews who do not accept the community's beliefs. This is unprecedented and a distinct nullification of Jewish continuance as a people.

As we see, the author of Matthew shows particular animosity toward the Pharisees. Written in a time of increasing competition and conflict between Christians and Pharisees/rabbis criticism of the latter may be found throughout this Gospel. The Pharisees are portrayed as the opponents of Jesus. They seek, to impose their man-made traditions on Jesus and on others (Matthew 12:1-2, 9-12; 15:1-2). Because Jesus opposes their teachings, they plot against him (Matthew 12:14). They seek to trap Jesus by asking for a sign from him (Matthew 16:1) or by engaging him in controversial questions (Matthew 19:3, 22:15-16, 22:34-36). Matthew's Pharisees are hypocrites who do not practice what they teach (Matthew 23:3-4). Their prayers are said for public recognition and not from piety (Matthew 23:5-7). They pay particular attention to minor matters of the law but disregard the important matters of justice, mercy, and faith (Matthew 23:23).

Matthew 23:2-3, which speaks of the Pharisees as those who "sit on Moses' seat" and who are to be obeyed does not contradict Matthew's general attitude toward Pharisaism. The Pharisees/rabbis were consolidating their control over the Jewish community at the time this Gospel was written, and the passage acknowledges that historical reality. The Pharisees represent the Law; they are its teachers. Matthew's intention is not to attack the Law in this passage for that would alienate at least part of his audience before he gets to the primary thrust of his message. His focus is on undercutting the Pharisees as interpreters of the Law by attacking their personal integrity. Therefore, he says "do and observe" what the Pharisees tell you, but not according to their interpretation of Jewish law as they practice it. The author of Matthew attacks the scribes and the Pharisees in an attempt to invalidate these Jewish leaders and all those that follow them. In their place, he seeks to validate himself and his mixed Jewish and Gentile community as the true Israel who alone has a proper understanding of God's will, which is that presented by Matthew's Jesus.

In intensifying the conflict directed against those Jews who did not accept Jesus, Matthew introduced a particularly vicious theme of accusation into his narrative, the blood libel. This accusation has caused untold persecution and slaughter of Jews and appears intermittently throughout the Gospel. For example, the author of Matthew ultimately places the blame for the death of John the Baptist directly on the whole Jewish people. Initially, Matthew ascribes the death of John directly to Herod Antipas,

"He [Herod Antipas] sent and had John beheaded in the prison" (Matthew 14:10). Later, when Jesus identifies John as actually being Elijah, Matthew chooses Jesus' words to indict all the Jews in the death of John. This is done in anticipation of blaming them for Jesus' own death: "But I say to you that Elijah already came, and they did not recognize him, but did to him whatever they wished. So also the Son of Man is going to suffer at their hands. Then the disciples understood that he had spoken to them about John the Baptist" (Matthew 17:12-13).[14] In verse 12, to whom does the personal pronoun "they" and the possessive pronoun "their" refer? Identification is aided by the claim that these same people would kill, "the Son of Man," that is, Jesus. Blame for Jesus' death is linked to the whole Jewish people through a spurious self-indictment: "His blood be upon us and our children" (Matthew 27:25). One should not be surprised by the alleged bloodthirstiness of the Jews for the author of Matthew has already informed his readers that the Jews are the killers of the righteous (Matthew 23:35-36). Thus, in the context of Matthew's recurrent blood libel motif raised against the Jewish people, it is clear that it is the Jews as a whole, not simply Herod Antipas, who are charged with the murder of John.

The Gospel of Matthew is characterized by an ingrained anti-Jewishness, which intensifies that already found in the Gospel of Mark. The author of Matthew gives the impression that, even when the Jews perform an act of philanthropy or prayer, it is wrongly motivated. They are hypocrites and act only for show (Matthew 6:1-18). Matthew, chapter 23, presents an even starker illustration of the evangelist's animosity toward the Jewish people. Matthew's Jesus begins with a scathing denunciation of the scribes and Pharisees and concludes with the horrendous burden of guilt that he imposes upon the entire Jewish people. They are now to be considered responsible for all the shedding of righteous blood from the very dawn of humanity. In verses 1 through 33, Matthew's Jesus is attacking the scribes and Pharisees. They are called "hypocrites" and "blind guides" seven times. He then castigates them as "serpents," "brood of vipers," and "sons of hell." These imprecations are intended to counter any thought that the Pharisees are virtuous, sincere, God-fearing people and not Satan's earthly representatives. They are corrupt murderers, uninterested in justice and mercy. The Pharisees are indiscriminately accused of being the "sons of those who murdered the prophets" (verse 31). That is, their Jewish ancestors, before there was even a Pharisaic party, killed the prophets, and they, despite all appearances to the contrary, are no better.

The context shows that Matthew's Jesus ends his direct attack on the scribes and Pharisees by declaring, "You serpents, you brood of vipers, how shall you escape the judgment of hell?" (Matthew 23:33). This is a transitional condemnation leading to the author of Matthew's primary focus of attack. Beginning at verses 34-35, the evangelist's attack is no longer directed specifically at the scribes and Pharisees. A sudden, subtle shift takes place: "Wherefore, behold, I send to you prophets and wise men, and scribes: and some of them you shall kill and crucify; and some of them you shall scourge in your synagogues, and persecute from city to city; that upon you may come all the righteous blood shed upon the earth, from the blood of righteous Abel to the blood of Zechariah son of Barachiah, whom you slew between the Temple and the altar."[15]

A superficial reading of the text may lead one to believe verses 34-35 refer to the scribes and Pharisees, but this is not so. Who is actually being condemned and is to suffer for spilling "all the righteous blood," is clearly revealed in the verse (36) that follows immediately after the condemnation: "Truly I say to you, all these things shall come upon this generation." Matthew's Jesus is not speaking of the scribes and Pharisees alone but of the entire Jewish people (see also Luke 11:49-51). They became responsible for "all the righteous blood shed upon the earth," especially for the righteous blood of Jesus. Moreover, the phrase "this generation" does not confine punishment to Jesus' Jewish contemporaries alone. This is seen by the inclusion of all future Jewish generations in the statement, "His blood be upon us and our children" (Matthew 27:25).[16]

The Gospel of Matthew has Jesus turn his wrath against "this generation," that is, the nation as a whole.[17] But what is the nation of Israel being condemned for—individual sins, national sins, or sinful acts committed by part of the nation which reflect upon and must be borne by the whole nation? The astounding answer is none of these! Matthew's Jesus condemns the Jewish people for sins in which Israel had not participated. Matthew's Jesus goes so far as to condemn the entire nation for murders that were committed even before the birth of Abraham, the father of the Jewish people. According to Jesus, the Jewish people are to suffer the penalty for the murder of every righteous victim since the dawn of history. All the Jewish people who did not follow Jesus are meant, not just certain factions within the nation. This is emphasized when Jesus couples his remarks with a characterization of their spiritual center as a place of murder: "O Jerusalem, Jerusalem, who kills the prophets and stones those who are sent to her![18] . . . Behold, your house is being left to you desolate" (Matthew 23:37-38; see also Luke 13:34-35). Jerusalem is not the spiritual center of the Pharisees alone, but is representative of all Jews and their religious tradition. Thus, except for those Jews who accept Jesus, the Jews are considered inherently murderers and the Temple, the earthly dwelling place of God's presence, is to be left empty and in ruins (as it was when Matthew wrote).

Some Christian commentators say that the phrase "this generation," used by both Matthew's and Luke's Jesus, meant only the scribes and Pharisees and not all Jews. But, this does not rectify the basic injustice of the libel. Was the Gospels' Jesus justified in blaming the scribes and Pharisees, for wrongs neither they nor their ancestors committed? It is simply unreasonable to hold either the scribes or Pharisees or their ancestors responsible for all the murders of the righteous committed from Abel onwards. The fact is that it is an unjust condemnation whether applied to the entire nation or to particular groups within the nation, such as the scribes and Pharisees. But, as we have seen, the author of Matthew had an even sinister intention. Compounding the injustice, the condemnation by Matthew's Jesus was not meant to refer merely to past generations or to "this generation," but to all future Jewish generations as well. There is no reason to think that the "guilt" of "this generation" for the spilling of the blood of all the righteous of the world from even before Abraham would be confined to "this generation" alone. Indeed, how much more so did the author believe was the guilt of future Jewish generations for the death of Jesus? In contrast, neither God nor His prophets ever explicitly or implicitly faulted Israel in such an unreasonably sweeping way as Matthew's Jesus. Is it any wonder that Jews have been blamed for the world's ills when Jesus is said to have condemned them for "all the righteous blood shed upon the earth," since the slaying of Abel? Abel was slain by his brother, Cain (Genesis 4:8), before the Jewish people came into existence. Why are the Jews to bear responsibility for this act? Placing the responsibility for the death of Abel on the Jews puts them into the role of Cain, despised by all creation.

There have been some modern suggestions that Jesus' attack was not an indictment of all Pharisees or directed against Jews and Judaism as a whole. It is maintained that Jesus' comments concerning the Pharisees resulted from the conflicts he was personally involved in with some of them. Therefore, it is supposed that those Pharisees with whom he took issue did not represent all Pharisees. It is pointed out that Jesus acknowledges that the scribes and the Pharisees sit on the throne of Moses and therefore everything they teach should be followed (Matthew 23:2-3). However, on careful examination of the passage we see that Matthew's Jesus accuses the Pharisees of not doing themselves what they demand, of laying heavy burdens on the shoulders of others, and of acting piously only in order to be greeted with respect in the marketplace (Matthew 23:4-7).[19] As narrated in the Gospel of Matthew, Jesus' acrimonious remarks are not directed at a minority of persons within the Pharisaic party, but at all Pharisees.

It has been said, "Matthew's specific criticism of the scribes and Pharisees are deeply rooted in contemporaneous Jewish tradition. Pharisees were reproached as hypocrites in rabbinic sources as well as in Matthew."[20] However, there is a crucial difference in approach between the Gospel of Matthew and the rabbinic sources. The acrimonious remarks found in the Matthean Gospel are not directed at a minority of Pharisees as in rabbinic sources, but at all Pharisees and, indeed, at all Jews.

Whatever Jesus' original words may have been (presuming there is a kernel of truth to the incident) or to whom they were specifically addressed, the fact is that, as recorded in the Gospels, they go beyond condemning hypocrisy and the dichotomy between preaching and practice. His criticisms and condemnations are meant to be part of an all-out attack, not only on all Pharisees but also on Jews and Judaism as a whole. The Gospel's Jesus makes no differentiation between various types of Pharisees. The attempt to label them all as fanatical, hypocritical, or insensitive legalists is historically inaccurate but serves a polemical purpose. The Matthean community is in conflict with the Pharisees/rabbis and the author's concern is with giving a positive presentation of Jesus while deprecating the Pharisees. Therefore, the Gospel's caricature of the Pharisees is meant to highlight the conflict; it is not simply disparaging but also incomplete and disproportionate. As a result, it is incorrect to equate his indiscriminate anti-Pharisaic denunciations with the criticisms of some Pharisees as found in the Talmud.[21] The Talmudic criticism, records rabbinic displeasure with the behavior of some who did not live up to the ideals of the group. It is by no means a censure of all Pharisees. Moreover, it is addressed solely to Jews and is for the edification of the community of Israel. Jesus' condemnations were recorded in the Gospels and are directed at a mixed audience of Jews and Gentiles who had become Christians. The Matthean Jesus' purpose is to censure the general Jewish community. There is no interest in differentiating between sincere and insincere Pharisees; there is only an interest in condemning all Jews who do not believe in Jesus.

In verse 15, the Matthean author demonizes the Jewish religious leadership: "Woe to you, scribes and Pharisees, hypocrites! For you cross sea and land to make a single convert, and you make the new convert twice as much a child of hell as yourselves." Although he attributes the denunciation to Jesus, it testifies to the author's own frustration with a situation contemporary with himself. Much to his chagrin, Jewish proselytizing efforts, in the post-war years, continue to successfully compete with Christianity for Gentile converts. Although the author of Matthew considered Judaism spiritually dead, it was, in fact, very much alive as proved by its vitality, its proselytizing, and its teachings. Judaism challenged the very foundations of Christianity's claims. Christians argued that God had rejected the Jews for rejecting Jesus and felt threatened when Gentiles chose to become proselytes to Judaism and not to Christianity.[22] In response, the author denounces the "scribes and Pharisees," but it is Judaism and the Jewish people, as a whole, who are meant. This is evident throughout the Matthean Gospel. The Pharisees symbolize those Jews who are in competition with the Matthean community. Their negative portrayal is motivated primarily by the needs of the church, not by the actual dealings of Pharisees with any historical Jesus.

The author of Matthew does not deny the fundamental legitimacy of Israel or its laws. To do so would be to destroy the basis of his claims to the church's legitimacy. What he does is claim that the church is the continuance of faithful Israel and upholder of the authentic divine law. He seeks to undermine the legitimacy of contemporary Jewish authorities by attacking their integrity and the accuracy of their interpretation of Jewish law and divine will. He exaggerates any accusations leveled against the Jewish authorities in an attempt to invalidate those leaders and their teachings within the Jewish community. These leaders he contends, have broken the line of succession passing down the true understanding of Jewish law and divine will. That knowledge is now in the possession of the church. In the end, those who persist in following these Jewish authorities are charged with responsibility for the killing of the righteous of all generations and invoke upon themselves God's judgment of retribution. This leaves the reader with a basic unresolved problem in New Testament studies. How could the same writings contain the Sermon on the Mount, with its commandment to love one's enemies (Matthew 5:44) and the animus shown toward the Jewish people, generally, and their religious leadership, in particular? Even to claim that the author of Matthew limited his accusations to the leaders who opposed Jesus and did not attack the whole Jewish people does not adequately justify his attack. The fact is that the Matthean attack *cannot* be reconciled with the call to love one's enemies attributed to Jesus.

The Matthean denunciations appealed to the anti-Judaic tendencies prevalent in some quarters of the early church even where Christian communal composition included individuals of Jewish ancestry. It was the author's intention to increase Christian animosity toward Jews who did not follow Jesus. He targets Jewish leadership for special treatment, but does not neglect his attack on Jews generally. This is in conformity with a general Gospel principle concerning the Jewish people. In the Gospels, Jewish leaders have a representative role. Whatever is foretold concerning them was to also refer to all Jewish contemporaries of Jesus and to all Jews of later times who continued to disbelieve Christian claims.

The Matthean description of events surrounding the crucifixion intensifies the Marcan portrayal of a collective Jewish antagonism toward Jesus. The author of Matthew describes as hostile "the sons of Israel" (Matthew 27:9), "the Jews" (Matthew 28:15), and "all the people" (Matthew 27:25). Matthew 27:9 is particularly noteworthy since it involves a non-existent quotation supposedly taken from the Book of Jeremiah: "Then that which was spoken through Jeremiah the prophet was fulfilled, saying, 'And they took the thirty pieces of silver, the price of the one whose price had been set by the sons of Israel.'"

The author of Matthew surpasses the author of Mark in targeting all Jewish people who do not accept Jesus. The author of Mark, followed by the author of Matthew, writes that the leaders ("chief priests," in Mark; "chief priests and elders," in Matthew) persuaded the crowd to ask for the release of Barabbas. According to Mark's version, "the chief priests stirred up the crowd to ask him [Pilate] to release Barabbas for them instead" (Mark 15:11). The Matthean version states that "the chief priests and the elders persuaded the crowd to ask for Barabbas, and to put Jesus to death" (Matthew 27:20). The author of Matthew makes two significant additions to the Marcan narrative. First, he introduces "the elders" into the text. Secondly, he emphasizes that not only did "the chief priests and the elders" persuade the Jewish crowd to ask for the release of Barabbas but also, most significantly, these "chief priests and elders" specifically urged the crowd to request that Jesus be put to death.

Matthew's underlying anti-Jewish motivation is ever present. Thus he refers to Barabbas simply as "a notorious prisoner" (Matthew 27:16), omitting his connection with an insurrectionist movement directed against Rome.[23] This description makes the preference of the crowd for Barabbas over the peaceable Jesus all the more heinous for the Matthean audience.

In contrast to the enmity shown by the author of Matthew toward the Jews is the benign approach he shows in describing the Roman role in the execution of Jesus. This author does a masterful job of relieving the Romans of culpability in his death. Pilate is portrayed as attempting to maneuver the release of Jesus by giving the "crowd" a choice between Barabbas and Jesus (Matthew 27:17). He does this out of his own sense of justice, "For he knew that because of envy they had delivered him up" (Matthew 27:18), as well as in deference to his wife's recognition that Jesus is a "righteous man" (Matthew 27:19). He is thwarted in his effort by "the chief priests and the elders" who sway the crowd against the popular Jesus (Matthew 27:20). In his futile effort to obtain the release of Jesus, Pilate, once again, asks the crowd to make a decision as to which prisoner should be released (Matthew 27:21). The Jewish leaders' persuasion undermines Pilate's ploy. Pilate then calls upon the Jewish crowd to determine Jesus' punishment. The decision of "all" is to "let him be crucified" (Matthew 27:22). Pilate attempts a third time, to gain freedom for Jesus with the plea, "Why, what evil has he done?" (Matthew 27:23). Pilate's appeal is met once more with, "Let him be crucified!" (Matthew 27:23). Realizing the futility of his efforts to release the innocent prisoner and that "a riot was starting," Pilate withdraws from responsibility for the unjust death of Jesus. To symbolize this "he took water and washed his hands before the crowd, saying, 'I am innocent of this man's blood; see to that yourselves'" (Matthew 27:24). In so doing, Pilate separates himself from the Jewish people's unjust killing of Jesus.[24] But, the episode is fictitious. Would the priests have dared to incite the crowd in Pilate's very presence, to go against his clear intentions?

It is unlikely that a man of Pilate's position and character would enter a dialogue with a crowd of subject people in the way described in the Gospel accounts. The narrative presupposes that Pilate is faced with a choice of releasing one out of two condemned prisoners, so that if one is released, the other must be executed. At the time of Pilate's alleged verbal interchange with the crowd, Jesus has not yet been condemned. There is nothing to prevent Pilate, if he believed that Jesus was innocent, from releasing him and granting an amnesty to Barabbas as well. This is especially noteworthy since the Gospels' Pilate knows that Barabbas is more dangerous than Jesus is.

Matthew's Pilate expresses his frustration at not being able to release the innocent Jesus because of Jewish insistence that he be executed. He uses biblical symbolism. Taking water he "washed his hands in front of the multitude" (Matthew 27:24) to symbolize his innocence (cf. Deuteronomy 21:6, Psalms 26:6). As he washes his hands of Jesus' blood he says to the crowd, "I am innocent of this man's blood, see to it yourselves" (Matthew 27:24), a statement based on David's remark, "I and my kingdom are guiltless before the Lord forever from the blood of Abner the son of Ner. Let it be on the head of Joab, and upon all his father's house . . ." (2 Samuel 3:28-29). The Jewish crowd's response, "his blood be upon us and our children," is based on the verses used by Matthew's Pilate. The Matthean Pilate's declaration of his innocence of the blood of Jesus is meant to relieve him of his part in the death. Jewish connivance is at the root of his ill-advised condemnation of Jesus, he is aware of this, and expresses his remorse at what he is forced to do. Throughout, the story is a fabrication and a parody, attributing to Pilate a course of action simply out of character, dangerous to his status and impolitic.

The author of Matthew was not content with merely relieving Pilate of condemnation for ordering Jesus' death and placing the blame on the Jewish people of all generations. The Roman soldiers who taunted Jesus and then carried out the actual sentence of crucifixion must somehow be exonerated as well. The Gospel of Matthew relates that the Roman soldiers readily take to the cruel process leading in the end to execution. After humiliating Jesus they unhesitatingly lead him away to crucify him (Matthew 27:27-31; see also Mark 15:16-20) complying with the demand of the Jewish people that he be crucified (Matthew 27:22-23). The soldiers follow their orders without question, apparently treating this prisoner with a cruelty no different than that meted out to countless other victims of execution by crucifixion. However, on allegedly witnessing strange happenings occurring at Jesus' death they become "very frightened" and confess that "Truly this was a son of God" (Matthew 27:54).[25] This sudden profession of faith in Jesus' divine sonship demonstrates their astounding insight. Significantly, the unrepentant Jews have just brought upon themselves divine retribution but these soldiers now become the first of the Gentiles to recognize the unique essence of Jesus.[26]

Pilate is described as being outmaneuvered and manipulated by the Jewish leaders in their successful quest to have Jesus crucified.[27] Pilate did not undergo a demonstrative realization that Jesus was a "son of God." However, he stands closer to his soldiers, who have confessed such faith in Jesus, than to the Jewish people who take upon themselves and all future Jewish generations the guilt for murdering Jesus. This dramatic Gentile profession of faith in Jesus stands in sharp contrast to that Jewish national rejection. Although the Roman soldiers crucified Jesus, they now become the first individuals to be "saved by the power of the cross." The Jews, on the other hand, by invoking "his blood" upon themselves and their future Jewish generations stand condemned for not accepting the supposedly "atoning blood of Jesus." "All the [Jewish] people" are said to accept responsibility for putting Jesus to death. Divine retribution, therefore, falls most heavily, not on the Gentiles whose power, Matthew maintains, was wrongly manipulated to carry out the execution, but on "all the [Jewish] people," of all generations. In Matthean thought, it is the Jews of all future generations who by refusing to accept Jesus, in essence, reiterate their fathers' exclamation, "His blood be upon us and our children" (Matthew 27:25).

One cannot ignore the historical events of the late first century that helped shape Matthew's narrative. The Gospel of Matthew was written a few years after, what was to the Jews, the disastrous end of the Roman-Jewish War. To Christians, the destruction of Jerusalem and its Temple signified that divine punishment was visited upon the Jewish people for the death of Jesus.[28] "His blood be upon us and our children" signifies not only Jewish culpability in Jesus' day. It foreshadows the culpability of Matthew's Jewish contemporaries and all future generations that do not accept Jesus and his teachings.

Matthew 27:25 is an explicit extension of guilt to the entire nation of Israel, and they alone for the death of Jesus. By the inclusion of this verse in the narrative, the author of Matthew shows his hatred of those Jewish people who did not accept Jesus. He designed the exclamation, "And all the people answered and said, 'His blood be upon us and our children'" as the centerpiece of his anti-Jewish polemic. This author compounds the Marcan hatred of the Jewish people by his careful choice of words in recording the actions of the alleged crowd standing outside the judgment hall. The Matthean version of this fictive event uses the Greek word *laos*, "people," "nation" (Matthew 27:25; see also Luke 23:13), in place of the Marcan word *ochlos* "crowd," "multitude" (Mark 15:11). In Mark 15:13 the *crowd* "shouted back, 'Crucify him,'" in Matthew 27:22 the *people* "all said, 'Let him be crucified.'" The "all" in Matthew's version prepares the reader for "all the people" [*pas ho laos*] in 27:25 who will take on themselves and their descendants the responsibility for Jesus' blood. In the literary formulation of the narrative, the "people" demanding Jesus' death are the representative of "all" the Jewish people as a whole.

Having established a climate of universal Jewish guilt for the death of Jesus the author of Matthew 27:25 refers to the "crowd" of 27:24 as "all the people." In this way, he further insures that the blame for Jesus' death is not limited to a negligible crowd but, rather, is placed on the entire Jewish people. He reports that "all the [Jewish] people" outside the judgment hall allegedly exclaimed: "His blood be upon us and our children." These words are an anti-Jewish polemic devised for use against Jews who did not accept Jesus. The intent of this conveniently contrived verse is to show that "all" the Jews wholeheartedly accepted responsibility for the death of Jesus and that their children inherit that responsibility. No attempt is made to differentiate between this particular crowd and the rest of the Jewish people who, for the most part, never even heard of Jesus. All of Matthew's viciousness and animosity toward those Jews who did not accept Jesus' messianic pretensions are summed up in this verse. The Jewish people are depicted as brazenly taking guilt upon themselves for the execution of Jesus. The author of Matthew would have his readers believe that a Jewish crowd of unknown size congregates in the middle of the night to take upon itself and future generations and by implication all Jews, everywhere, culpability for the crucifixion of Jesus. This verse with its fictitious crowd is the most glaring of New Testament anti-Jewish passages. Its introduction into the narrative serves to magnify the alleged culpability of the Jewish people in every generation for the death of Jesus. Matthew 27:25 served as the foundation for the myth of deicide. From the time that the self-condemnation found in Matthew 27:25 was first formulated, Christians understood it to mean that "all the [Jewish] people" accepted a binding responsibility for the execution of Jesus. This was the author's intent: the Jews, not only of that generation but also of all time, are to be considered guilty and should be punished. Only those Jews who convert to Christianity are forgiven their supposed sin.

Christian author, John Paul Heil interconnects Matthew's two most vicious accusations, that is, the Jewish people are responsible for all the righteous blood shed throughout history and that they are all responsible for the execution of Jesus. Heil reiterates the traditional Christian understanding that "With the words 'his blood be upon us and our children,' the 'whole people' of Israel accepts full responsibility for the death of the innocent Jesus, their true Christ (27:25)."[29] He reiterates the Matthean allegation that the entire Jewish people accepted responsibility for the death of Jesus:

> ... "all the people" (*laos*), representative of the entire covenant people of Israel (1:21; 2:6; 4:16, 23; 13:15; 15:8; 26:5), now solemnly accept full responsibility for the shedding of Jesus' blood: "His blood be upon us and upon our children!" (27:25; see 1 [sic, should be 2] Sam 1:16; 2 [sic, should be 1] Kgs 2:33; Jer 26:15). By boldly invoking the innocent "blood" (*haima*) of the "righteous man" (*dikaio*, 27:19) Jesus, whom they regard as a "prophet" (21:11, 46), "upon us" (*eph' hemas*) and "upon our children," the Jewish people are fulfilling Jesus' prediction (23:35) that "upon you [*eph' hymas*] may come all the righteous blood (*haima dikaion*) shed upon earth, from the blood of Abel, the righteous one [*dikaiou*], to the blood of Zechariah" (a prophet). They even extend to future generations Jesus' warning that "all these things will come upon this generation" (*epi ten genean tauten*, 23:36), as they invoke his blood "upon our children" (*epi ta tekna hemon*).[30]

He then goes on to say:

> When the whole Jewish people invoked upon themselves and their children the "innocent" (27:4) and "righteous" (27:19) blood of the "prophet" (21:11, 46) Jesus (27:25), they began to fulfill Jesus' prediction that upon them would come the guilt for all the "righteous blood" shed upon earth, from the blood of Abel, the "righteous one," to the blood of Zechariah, a prophet (23:35), because they shed the blood of Jesus just as they, like their ancestors (23:30), shed the blood of the "righteous ones" (23:29), "prophets," "wise men," and "scribes" that God sends them (23:34). The "tombs" (*mnemeia*) from which the holy ones are raised and come out (27:52-53) include the "tombs" (*mnemeia*) the Jewish leaders built and adorned for the "righteous ones"

and "prophets" whom they murdered (23:29). The resurrection of the "holy ones" signifies God's vindication for the Jewish people's unjust killing not only of his righteous ones, prophets, wise men, and scribes numbered among the "holy ones" but also of Jesus, his prophet and suffering righteous one.[31]

How convenient the Matthean contrivance of a Jewish crowd shouting, "His blood be upon us and our children!" It became a duty to make sure that in the name of God, this request be granted, not only to those allegedly present in the crowd but also, to all Jewish people, everywhere and for all time. Through the church's persecution of the Jews, God is made to grant the last prayer request of collective Israel before the Law goes out of practical existence with the death of Jesus. No longer would God hear Israel's prayers for they are not made to Jesus who now controls the universe (Matthew 28:18).

Perhaps, accusations concerning inherited responsibility for the death of Jesus did not originate with the author of Matthew. However, while it may be maintained that this story was transmitted to him by a source unknown to the other Gospel authors it is more than likely that he himself created the account as part of his overall plan to defame Jews who rejected Christian claims concerning Jesus. His concern was to remind his readers and especially born-Jewish Christians of the guilt of those Jews and their descendants who did not accept Jesus as their savior. Of the Gospels, Matthew alone has "all the people" accept full and explicit responsibility for Jesus' execution on behalf of both themselves and their descendants. Surely, the other Gospel authors would have used this fictive tale if it were part of the general Christian tradition. This story, whatever its ultimate origin, is by its very nature a fabrication. In that verse, it is not the Jewish people who are speaking, but the author of Matthew, a virulent enemy of those Jewish people who did not accept Jesus. The anti-Jewish overtones in the Matthean narrative are designed to intensify the guilt of the Jews in the minds of the audience. In the words of one Christian scholar, "[Matthew 27:25] has done more than any other sentence in the New Testament to feed the fires of anti-Semitism"[32]

What is the historicity of this Jewish self-condemnation episode and its application to all Jews for all time? Examine what this crowd is supposed to have declared. The verse does not say; "his blood be upon us and our children [if he is not guilty]" but "his blood be upon us and our children [unconditionally]." Why would people voluntarily take guilt upon their children as well as upon themselves? It is incredulous to think that in a society where oaths were taken quite seriously that individuals would make such a declaration involving themselves and their children, let alone that an entire crowd simultaneously uttered these words in the middle of the night. And what night was this? According to the Synoptic Gospels, it was the *seder* night. This was not a night when persons would gather to form a background chorus for a demand that a Roman governor, a symbol of oppression and slavery, should execute a fellow Jew. It was the night for remembering the exodus from Egypt by eating the paschal lamb in the company of others (Exodus 12:4) and for instructing successive generations in the origins and significance of the festival (Exodus 12:26-27). The author of Matthew has a proclivity for alluding to biblical references in creating his tale. He distorts the *seder* association with others in order to partake of the paschal lamb and its accompanying instructional objective of passing Jewish heritage from one generation to the next. In his mind, it turns into the passing on of a curse to one's own Jewish children. The author of Matthew creates a travesty of the celebration. The Jews gather together to have Jesus, the so-called paschal lamb, sacrificed. As the blood of the first paschal lamb saved the Jews from the wrath of God, the blood of the final paschal lamb brings a self-imposed curse upon the Jews, which they now pass on as an inheritance to their children.

Presuming there was a crowd standing before Pilate demanding the crucifixion of Jesus, can any but the most prejudiced indiscriminately blame all Jews who were in Jerusalem that night? Sadly, this is exactly what has happened. The author of Acts records that Paul was just such an accuser, "For those who live in Jerusalem, and their rulers, recognizing neither him nor the utterances of the prophets which are read every Sabbath, fulfilled these by condemning him. And though they found no ground for putting him to death, they asked Pilate that he be executed" (Acts 13:27-28). Indeed, not only were all inhabitants of Jerusalem blamed but the Jewish communities of the Diaspora, not even aware of Jesus' existence, and all Jews of later generations were held guilty as well. It is Paul, of all the New Testament authors, who first groups all Jews of all generations and locations together and condemns them for all eternity (1 Thessalonians 2:14-16).

Some Christians use historical reality to soften the Matthean message. Accordingly, since it is obvious that "all the [Jewish] people" could not have been gathered together in a given locale in Jerusalem on the night prior to Jesus' crucifixion, responsibility could only apply to the relatively few who were present. All such approaches overlook that Matthew's dramatic and theological intent was to generalize the totality of Jewish involvement in order to widen the scope of Jewish culpability. Consequently, a suggestion of historical limitation is irrelevant to the meaning of the text. Matthew's generalization of responsibility makes meaningless any limitations placed upon "all the [Jewish] people" due to geographic locale or time. "All the people" take upon themselves, their Jewish contemporaries (wherever they may be located), and all future generations the responsibility for condemning Jesus to death. Still other Christians would argue that the episode is without historical basis and since this Jewish self-condemnation never occurred, the text has no real significance. This viewpoint ignores the fact that the episode represents an evangelist's teaching in the 70's of the first century, reflecting still earlier pre-Gospel condemnatory notions, and that this tale adversely influenced generations of "believers" to oppress and kill Jews. To the Jewish people, the author's intent has great significance!

When it comes to Jewish people, who do not believe in Jesus, the evangelist's intentions are lethal. What he does with the story of Judas' interaction with the priests is indicative of the intensity of his hatred of those Jews who do not accept Jesus. Judas Iscariot is portrayed by this author as repenting his betrayal of Jesus: "Then when Judas, who had betrayed him, saw that he had been condemned, felt remorse and returned the thirty silver pieces to the chief priests and the elders, saying: 'I sinned when I betrayed righteous blood.' But they said: 'What is that to us? See to that yourself!' And he threw the silver pieces into the Temple and departed, and went off and hanged himself" (Matthew 27:3-5). In his remorse, Judas attempts to return the thirty silver pieces to the Jewish officials, but they refuse to accept them. He then throws the silver pieces down, goes out, and commits suicide. The Marcan version mentions that the chief priests "promised to give him [Judas] money" for betraying Jesus (Mark 14:10-11); no further information is given. The author of Acts mentions that "this man [Judas] acquired a field with the price of his wickedness; and falling headlong, he burst open in the middle and all his intestines were poured out. And it became known to all who were living in Jerusalem; so that in their language that field was called Hakeldama, that is, Field of Blood" (Acts 1:18-19). According to this tradition, Judas felt no remorse whatsoever, did not return the money, and certainly did not commit suicide. He lived at least long enough to use the money he received to purchase a parcel of land. His subsequent death is attributed to a violent fall while on his property.

In the Book of Acts, Judas keeps the money, buys a field with it, and because of his death on that property it becomes known as the "Field of Blood." However, the author of Matthew, with his knack for finding imaginary prophetic fulfillment in Gospel episodes, tells a different story. Judas is said to have returned the money he received for betraying Jesus, and the "chief priests and elders" used that money to buy a potter's field as a burial place for strangers. This field, allegedly bought with blood money and used for burials, became known as the "Field of Blood" (Matthew 27:3-8).[33] These actions supposedly fulfilled a prophecy that the author of Matthew attributes to Jeremiah. "And they took the thirty pieces of silver, the price of the one whose price had been set by the sons of Israel; and they gave them for the Potter's Field, as the Lord directed me" (Matthew 27:9-10). This citation is erroneous. There is no such statement to be found in either the Masoretic or Septuagint versions of the Book of Jeremiah. The quotation is actually the author of Matthew's own creation, based apparently, on Zechariah 11:12-13, which mentions throwing thirty pieces of silver into the Temple. The Matthean error may have come about because Jeremiah at one point tells a parable about a potter and his clay (Jeremiah 18:1-6) and at another point speaks about buying a field for silver (Jeremiah 32:6-9).

The author of Matthew finds in Zechariah's text an opportunity to insert a spurious phrase in order to once more attack the Jewish people with the charge of being responsible for the death of Jesus. The Matthean text, incorrectly attributed to Jeremiah, rephrases Zechariah's words. The prophet states, "So they weighed for my wages thirty pieces of silver. And the Lord said to me: 'Cast it into the treasury, the goodly price that I was prized at of them.' And I took the thirty pieces of silver, and cast them into the treasury, in the house of the Lord" (Zechariah 11:12-13). Matthew's text reads, "the goodly price that I was prized of *the sons of Israel*." He changes Zechariah's unidentified "them" into "the sons of Israel," that is, not specific individuals but "the Jews," in general. In making it a biblical prophecy of a Gospel passion event, the Matthean author continues his theme of placing culpability for Jesus' death upon *all* Jews.

The Matthean mendacity bestows upon all Jews, unless they make a profession of faith to Jesus, a collective guilt in the death of Jesus. To those who take the author of Matthew at his word and follow New Testament doctrine, every Jew has crucified Jesus and can only be forgiven this imaginary sin by submitting to baptism.[34]

Notes

[1] Eusebius (260?-340? C.E.) quoted Papias, Bishop of Hierapolis (c. 140 C.E.) as writing, "So then Matthew, indeed, in the Hebrew language put together the *Logia* in writing; but as to their interpretation, each man dealt

with it as he was able" (Eusebius, *Ecclesiastical History*, 3. 39. 16). Papias' statement is ambiguous: "Matthew *synetaxeto* [composed? Compiled? Arranged?] the *Logia* [sayings? Gospel?] in *hebraidi dialekto* [the Hebrew (Aramaic) language?, the Hebrew (Aramaic) style?], and each man *hermeneusen* [interpreted? translated? transmitted?] it as he was able [but, what was being "interpreted" and by whom?]." Papias ascribes to Matthew the collecting and recording of the *Logia*, that is, most likely, the sayings of Jesus. The *Logia* formed part of the pre-Gospel material from which the Gospels were compiled. This does not mean that the Matthew mentioned by Papias was the author of the Gospel of Matthew in its present form.

[2] The author of Matthew uses the Septuagint, or a related recession, for his biblical citations. The Septuagint (or simply LXX) is a Greek rendering of the Hebrew Scriptures. Its origin dates back to the third century B.C.E. Greek translation of the first five books of the Bible, the Torah. The rest of the Scriptures were added subsequently. The name derives from the Latin, *septuaginta*, "seventy," the traditional number of the first translators.

The Greek speaking Jews used the Septuagint, and it was on this rendering that the Christian missionaries based their efforts to read Christian doctrine into the Jewish Scriptures. Free renderings and occasional inaccuracies flawed the Septuagint. Aquila of Pontus, a Greek convert to Judaism, prepared a new Greek translation of the Hebrew Bible for Jews. Aquila's translation, which was prepared between 125 and 128 C.E. was more literal than the Septuagint and adhered more closely to Jewish tradition. Greek speaking Jews adopted it because it was a more accurate rendering than the Septuagint. Christians continued to use the Septuagint. In its present form, it represents the textual recession influenced by Christian scholars, especially Origen.

[3] An important contribution to the study of the Gospel of Matthew is Anthony J. Saldarini's volume, *Matthew's Christian-Jewish Community* (Chicago: University of Chicago Press, 1994). In this account, Matthew's Christian Jewish community is a Jewish group that deviated from the larger Jewish community.

[4] Eusebius, 6. 25. 4.

5   Jerome, *Letters* [*Epistulae*] 20. 5; Eusebius, 3. 24. 6. Some scholars have argued that when the church fathers said "Hebrew" they really meant "Aramaic." To illustrate this, we should note John 19:13. There the author uses the word *hebraisti*, which literally means "in Hebrew" to indicate the linguistic origin of *Gabbatha*. However, *Gabbatha* is Aramaic.

6   If the church fathers are correct in stating that the Gospel of Matthew was written originally in "Hebrew" (that is, Aramaic), this would make the Greek version of Matthew either a totally different document or a translation and a possible modification of an earlier version of this Gospel. Thus, it does not necessary follow that the "Hebrew" Book of Matthew is the same exact work as the Greek volume now referred to as the Book of Matthew. One scholar, George Howard, has found what may be an early Hebrew version of the Gospel of Matthew embedded in a fourteenth century Hebrew manuscript. The treatise, *Even Boḥan* ("The Touchstone"), was written in Spain, by Shem-Tov Shaprut. Forced by Christian theologians and born-Jewish apostates to Christianity to debate the merits of Judaism verses Christianity, Jews in Europe, during the Middle Ages, wrote polemic works. The *Even Boḥan* is Shem-Tov's polemical treatise against Christianity. As with many of these polemical works, Shem-Tov's *Even Boḥan* contains a Hebrew text of a Gospel. Until Howard's study of this work, it was thought that this Hebrew rendering of Matthew is a fourteenth century Hebrew translation of the Greek, or its Latin version. Although there are notable differences between the Greek and Hebrew texts he believes the similarities in arrangement and wording of the Hebrew and Greek texts of Matthew show that one text served as a model for the other. There is no evidence as to which came first, the Greek or the Hebrew, but Howard maintains that both works were originals, neither a translation (George Howard, *The Gospel of Matthew According to a Primitive Hebrew Text*, Macon, Ga.: Mercer University Press, 1987).

7   A *centurion* was the Roman captain of a hundred soldiers.

8   In the Lucan version of the episode (Luke 7:1-10) Luke's Jesus "said to the multitude that was following him, 'I say to you, not even in Israel have I found such great faith'" (Luke 7:9).

9   In the Septuagint, the plural *ethne* is often used to designate non-Jewish nations or peoples. The Greeks had a similar ethnocentric usage for *ethne* as a designation for non-Greek nations or peoples. It is probable that in the

context of the verse, Matthew uses *ethnei* to signify the church, that is, Jewish and Gentile followers of Jesus.

10. One Christian commentator, Malcolm Lowe, does not believe that supersessionist statements appeared in the original Matthean text. He maintains that "wherever we find the phrases or statements that . . . have no parallel in other canonical books (or appear there in a different context and with different significance), then those phrases and statements also lack proved apostolic authority." "Precisely such," Lowe states, "are the statements in which our Greek Matthew transfers the election from the Jewish people to the church." (Malcolm Lowe, "Real and Imagined Anti-Jewish Elements in the Synoptic Gospels and Acts," *Journal of Ecumenical Studies* [Spring 1987], p. 283)

11. Sectarianism and outbreaks of strife resulting from that sectarianism marked the Second Temple period. Yet, the vast majority of Jewish laws and practices were shared by Torah-observing Jews of the Second Temple period. This common Judaism makes it incorrect to speak of there being "many Judaisms" during this period. It is best to speak of the "movements" within the Judaism of that time. In the post-war period and probably earlier the great majority of Jewish people united around the consensus of Pharisaic-rabbinic Judaism, which came to serve as the foundation for the Judaism of today. Despite their many differences, the various branches of contemporary Judaism owe their spiritual roots and religious form to Pharisaic teachings. Thus, any continued simplistic denigration of the Pharisees and their teachings is an attack at the very core of contemporary Judaism.

12. In stark contrast to these statements, the Jewish Scriptures state: "The works of His hands are truth and justice; and His precepts are sure. They are established forever and ever, they are done in truth and uprightness" (Psalms 111:7-8); "The grass withers, the flower fades; but the word of our God shall stand forever" (Isaiah 40:8). The Scriptures convey the message that God's enactments are eternally valid and immutable.

13. It is to the Jews alone that God gave the commandments of the Law. Gentiles were never required to obey the commandments given specifically to Israel.

14. For his part, John the Baptist denied that he was Elijah: "And they asked him [John the Baptist], 'What then? Are you Elijah?' and he said, 'I am not'" (John 1:21a).

15. It was Zechariah, the son of Jehoiada the priest, who was slain by the altar (2 Chronicles 24:20-21). Any claim that Zechariah, the son of Jehoiada the priest, and Zechariah, the son of Berechiah (Zechariah 1:1), are identical has no biblical basis. Zechariah, the son of Jehoiada, was slain in the days of Joash, king of Judah (ca. 840 B.C.E.), while the prophet Zechariah, the son of Berechiah, did not prophesy until the second year of Darius (ca. 520 B.C.E.), which followed the return from the Babylonian captivity. However, the Scriptures do not indicate when, where, or how Zechariah, the son of Berechiah, died. There is no reason to believe that Zechariah, the son of Berechiah, the son of Iddo, died in the manner described. As for the death described in Matthew, it was suffered by another person, the above mentioned, Zechariah, the son of Jehoiada. In narrating this incident, Luke only mentions the name of Zechariah without specifying who his father was (Luke 11:51).

16. In the literal text, "The blood of him upon us and upon the children of us," there is no verb. Grammatically there is no problem in supplying the verb "be" in translation.

17. *Genea*, commonly translated "generation," refers, as Thayer notes, to "the whole multitude of men living at the same time . . . [and is] used especially of the Jewish race living at one and the same period" (Joseph Henry Thayer, *A Greek-English Lexicon of the New Testament*, Grand Rapids, Mich.: Zondervan, 1979, p. 112).

The implication of translating *genea* incorrectly as "people," or "race" in conformity with some Christian exegetes has contributed to Christian anti-Jewish feelings throughout the centuries. "Truly I say to you, all these things shall come upon this generation" (Matthew 23:36) limits the condemnation to the entire Jewish people of Jesus' day. Matthew's Jesus denounces his Jewish contemporaries as a "wicked and adulterous generation" (Matthew 16:4) and as a "faithless and perverse generation" (Matthew 17:17). By substituting "people" or "race "for" generation," these phrases become a condemnation of the Jewish people of *all* generations. Thus, " . . . all these things shall come upon this people" who are "a wicked and adulterous people" and are also a "faithless and perverse race." No time limitation is found in this rendering of Matthew 23:36. Undoubtedly, the author of Matthew believed in this eternal condemnation of the Jews, but he does not say it explicitly in the immediate context. In the Gospel of Matthew, the punishment for the murdered righteous, going back to the very dawn of history, is not confined to that one generation of Jews, but applies to both previous and future generations as well. However, the author's condemnation of all future generations of Jews who reject Jesus is implicit in verse 36. It is explicitly found in Matthew 27:25, "And all the people answered and said, "His blood be upon us and our children!" Verse 36 acts to bridge the accusation and connect previous, present, and future generations together in being guilty of murder.

[18] Very few instances of the killing of prophets are found in the Hebrew Scriptures.

[19] The author of Matthew depicts the Pharisees as "hypocrites" and "blind guides." But, what about the character of the Matthean Jesus? Matthew's Jesus instructs his audience, giving advice he himself never followed: "Rejoice, and be glad, for your reward in heaven is great, for so they persecuted the prophets who were before you" (Matthew 5:12; cf. Matthew 26:37-38, "He . . . began to be grieved and distressed. . . . 'My soul is deeply grieved, to the point of death . . . .' "); "Do not resist him that is wicked; but whoever slaps you on your right check, turn to him the other also" (Matthew 5:39; cf. John 18:22-23, " . . . [O]ne of the officers . . . gave Jesus a blow . . . Jesus answered . . . '[W]hy do you strike me?'"); "But I say to you, love your enemies, and pray for those who persecute you" (Matthew 5:44; cf. Matthew 26:24, " . . . [W]oe to that man through whom the Son of Man is betrayed! It would have been good for that man if he had not been born."). Elsewhere, the author of Matthew describes Jesus, using a passage from Isaiah (42:2-3), as one who "will not quarrel, nor cry out, nor will anyone hear his voice in the streets, a battered reed he will not break off, and a smoldering reed he will not break off, and a smoldering wick he will not put out" (Matthew 12:19-20; cf. Luke 19:27, "But these enemies of mine, who did not want me to reign over them, bring them here, and slay them in my presence."). We see continual contradiction.

[20] Moshe Weinfeld, "The Jewish Roots of Matthew's Vitriol," *Bible Review* 13:5 (October 1997), p. 31. See also Moshe Weinfeld, "The Charge of Hypocrisy in Matthew 23 and in Jewish Sources," *The New Testament and Christian-Jewish Dialogue: Studies in Honor of David Flusser*, ed. M. Lowe,

Immanuel 24/25 (1990), pp. 52-58; Anthony Saldarini, "Understanding Matthew's Vitriol, *Bible Review* 13:2 (April 1997), pp. 32-39, 44-45.

[21] Mishnah *Sotah* 3:4, B.T. *Sotah* 22b. The Talmud identifies itself with the Pharisees (see, e.g. Mishnah *Yadayim* 4:6-8; *Niddah* 33b). When the rabbis of the Talmud criticize certain types of Pharisees and their practices, which is precisely what is being done in *Sotah*, it is clear that it is not referring to all or most Pharisees. However, when Matthew's Jesus denounces the Pharisees there is no reason to believe from the context that his remarks are restricted to criticizing a limited group.

[22] Even after Christianity became the state religion of the Roman Empire, Judaism remained a threat to Christian credibility. Despite the promulgation of imperial laws to curtail conversion to Judaism, it still was able to attract a sizeable number of proselytes. Origen, in referring to the success of Jewish proselytizing, writes that " . . . [T]he Jew said . . . they were scattered in the dispersion and smitten, that as a result of the scattering of the Jews among the other nations many might become proselytes . . . . (Origen, *Contra Celsus* I. 55)

[23] If the insurrection Barabbas was involved in (Mark 15:7) was directed against the priesthood, the chief priests would not have sought his release (Mark 15:11). In Judea, they were the only other governmental authority besides that of the Romans.

[24] It is no wonder that the Coptic Church venerates Pilate as a saint. Saint Pilate's day is June 25. The Greek Church has honored Pilate's wife on October 27. Pilate's image has met with less favor in the Western Church than in the Eastern Churches.

[25] The Gospel of Mark confines this confession to the centurion alone (Mark 15:39); Luke has no such confession (Luke 23:47).

[26] Presuming historicity for this episode, what would pagans mean by the phrase, *huios theou* (Mark 15:39), alternately *theou huios* (Matthew 27:54), "a son of God," "son of a god," "God's son"? Did they make a miraculous profession of faith as understood by later Christian theology or were they thinking in terms of pagan mythology? The doctrine of Jesus as literally and exclusively the "Son of God" is a theological development that arose sometime after the crucifixion.

[27] In 1964, the Christian theologian, Wolfhart Pannenberg, expressed this as follows: "The Jews had him killed—the Romans appear only as the ones

carrying out the sentence, so to speak" (Wolfhart Pannenberg, *Jesus—God and Man*, Tran. Lewis L. Wilkins and Duane A. Priebe, Philadelphia: Westminster Press, 1968; orig.—*Grundzüge der Christologie*, Gütersloh: Gütersloher Verlagshaus Gerd Mohn, 1964, pp. 246-247)

[28] After the destruction of Jerusalem and the Temple the various Jewish Christian and Gentile Christian sects increased their missionary efforts directed at Jews. Christians viewed the destruction as verification of God's condemnation of the Jews for the crucifixion of Jesus. The destruction of Jerusalem and especially the Temple seemed to them to be confirmation of their faith. Christians also saw the Temple's destruction as a major vindication of Christianity's ascendancy over Judaism. Therefore, when the Emperor Julian (331-363) issued a number of edicts limiting Christian privileges he was despised but did not become known as "Julian the Apostate" until he announced his plans to allow the rebuilding of the Temple. This announcement infuriated Christians since they considered the destruction of the Temple as proof that they, not the Jews, were God's Chosen People. In addition, they believed it showed Jesus to be a true prophet for it is claimed that he had specifically predicted the razing of the Temple (Mark 13:2, Matthew 24:2, Luke 21:6; cf. Mark 14:58, 15:29; John 2:19).

[29] John Paul Heil, *The Death and Resurrection of Jesus: A Narrative-Critical Reading of Matthew 26-28*, Minneapolis: Fortress Press, 1991, p. 8.

[30] Heil, p. 76.

[31] Heil, pp. 85-86.

[32] Gerald G. O'Collins, "Anti-Semitism in the Gospels," *Theological Studies* 26 (June 1965), p. 663.

[33] The respective Matthean and Lucan versions of Judas' death pose a problem concerning the ownership of the property. In the Matthean version, Judas returns the money; the priests buy the field, and this property receives its name from its use as a burial plot. The author of Acts applies Psalms 69:26 (verse 25 in some versions) to the death of Judas as owner of the "Field of Blood." "For it is written in the book of Psalms, 'Let his homestead be made desolate, and let no man dwell in it'" (Acts 1:20). Thus, the Lucan narrative, in which Judas is the purchaser and owner of the field, is at odds with the Matthean account, in which the Jewish authorities, not Judas, purchase and own the field.

[34] Wolfhart Pannenberg argued "that the intention of the law continues to be decisive for Jesus' rejection." He then concluded:

That means that every Jew who was faithful to the law would have had to act in the same way or similarly had he been in the position of the Jewish authorities. In the light of Jesus' resurrection not only the circle of his judges but in principle every Jew who lives under the authority of and is bound to the law thereby is shown to be a blasphemer. The death penalty borne by Jesus is the punishment deserved by the whole people to the extent that it is bound to the authority of the law. (Pannenberg, *Jesus-God and Man*, p. 260)

According to Pannenberg, all Jews "faithful to the law," if they were present at the time, would have condemned Jesus. Therefore, in every generation they are held liable for the death of Jesus. Moreover, to be faithful to the Law is to be a blasphemer deserving of death. As he explains this New Testament notion the renouncing of the Law and the acceptance of Jesus as one's Lord and Savior is the only way to avert this condemnation.

7.
THE GOSPEL OF LUKE AND THE BOOK OF ACTS

It is generally agreed among New Testament scholars that the two books known as the Gospel of Luke and the Acts of the Apostles respectively were written by the same author (Luke, c. 80-85 and Acts, c. 90-95).[1] This author continued to press the attack against Jews and Judaism that began early within the pre-Gospel Christian community. The author of Luke-Acts sees his anti-Judaic mission clearly: defame the Jews who do not accept Jesus, exonerate the Roman of any guilt for the crucifixion, and show that the Gentiles are the new Israel—the people of God. To this end, he incorporates material from a number of sources in the service of his literary and theological purposes. These sources include tales either borrowed from Samaritan Christianity or of his own manufacture. In Luke 10:29-37, it is the Samaritan who is the good neighbor, not the priest or Levite.[2] In Luke 17:11-19, it is a Samaritan, a "foreigner," who "turned back to give glory to God," not the Jews. In both instances, the behavior of a Samaritan is commended and used to highlight Jewish failings. Descriptions of Jewish lack of compassion and faithlessness are the norm in Luke-Acts.

Similar to what we find in Matthew 23:34-36, the Lucan Jesus declares:

> Woe to you! For you build the tombs of the prophets, and it was your fathers who killed them. Consequently, you are

witnesses and approved the deeds of your fathers; because it was they who killed them, and you build their tombs. For this reason also the Wisdom of God said, "I will send to them prophets and apostles, and some of them they will kill and some they will persecute; in order that the blood of all the prophets, shed since the foundation of the world, may be charged against this generation, from the blood of Abel to the blood of Zechariah, who perished between the altar and the House of God, yes, I tell you, it shall be charged against this generation" (Luke 11:47-51).

Luke's Jesus denounces the Jewish people. How does he come to this judgment? They "build the tombs of the prophets." Their "fathers" are accused of killing the prophets and the Jewish people, by building the tombs of the prophets, become, thereby, "witnesses" who "approved the deeds" of their ancestors. This twisted logic is compounded in the following verses with Jesus' accusations leading to further condemnation of the Jewish people. Obviously, in verse 49, when Luke's Jesus declares that "the Wisdom of God said, 'I will send them prophets and apostles, and some of them they will kill and some they will persecute,'" and then in verses 50 and 51 he speaks of "this generation" he is also speaking of all the Jewish people. His remarks are not just directed at the Pharisees or "those versed in the Law" (Luke 11:45). As Matthew's Jesus so Luke's Jesus condemns the Jewish people for "the blood of all the prophets, shed since the foundation of the world," that is, even before Abraham was born.

In the parable of *The Great Banquet* (Luke 14:15-24) Luke's Jesus further illustrates the New Testament notion that the Jews have lost God's favor and that their place in history has been taken by the Gentiles who have accepted Jesus. A man sends his servant to first invite certain distinguished guests to a great banquet. However, they all find excuses not to attend. In his anger, the man orders his servant to go out into the city and invite the poor, the crippled, the blind, and the lame; they fill the banquet room. "For I tell you," declares the man, "none of those men who were invited shall taste of my dinner" (verse 24). In the imagery of this parable, God, through His servant, Jesus (or a prophet), invites the people of Israel to partake of the kingdom of God. They reject this offer and in His wrath, God disowns them and orders Jesus to turn to the Gentiles who will accept the offer.

Not to be outdone by his predecessors, the author of Luke contributes a parable with a vicious anti-Jewish theme to the New Testament's overall anti-Judaic attack. Luke, chapter 19, attributes a parable to Jesus the theme of which has caused unspeakable anti-Jewish persecution.

> He [Jesus] went on to tell a parable, because he was near Jerusalem, and they supposed that the kingdom of God was going to appear immediately. He said therefore, "A certain nobleman went to a distant country to receive a kingdom for himself, and then return. And he called ten of his slaves, and gave them ten minas, and said to them, 'Do business with this until I come back.' But his citizens hated him, and sent a delegation after him, saying, 'We do not want this man to reign over us.' And it came about that when he returned, after receiving the kingdom, he ordered that these slaves, to whom he had given the money, be called to him in order that he might know what business they had done. And the first appeared, saying, 'Master, your mina has made ten minas more.' And he said to him, 'Well done, good slave, because you have been faithful in a very little thing, be in authority over ten cities.' And the second came, saying, 'Your mina, master, has made five minas.' And he said to him also, 'And you are to be over five cities.' And another came, saying, 'Master, behold your mina, which I kept put away in a handkerchief; for I was afraid of you, because you are an exacting man; you take up what you did not lay down, and reap what you did not sow.' He said to him, 'By your own words I will judge you, you worthless slave. Did you know that I am an exacting man, taking up what I did not lay down, and reaping what I did not sow? Then why did you

not put the money in the bank, and having come, I would have collected it with interest?' And he said to the bystanders, 'Take the mina away from him, and give it to the one who has ten minas.' And they said to him, 'Master, he has ten minas.' I tell you that to everyone who has shall more be given, but from the one who does not have, even what he does have shall be taken away. But these enemies of mine, who did not want me to reign over them, bring them here, and slay them in my presence." (Luke 19:11-27)

This parable, in particular verses 14 and 27, addresses the problem the nascent Christian community faced as a result of the continuing Jewish rejection of Jesus' alleged lordship. Rejection was considered a challenge to the church's claims concerning the meaning of Jesus' death and the implications of his supposed resurrection. In addition, the author of Luke wrote at a time when the delay in Jesus' return was a disturbing factor in the minds of Christians. He sought to address their concerns by presenting a parable, which places a second coming sometime in the indefinite future.

Although Christian commentators have attempted to harmonize the various sections of this parable, its disjointedness shows that originally there were two parables that at some point in time were combined into one. Verse 14 of this chapter breaks the continuity of the story by introducing rebellious citizens into the parable. The main story is resumed in verse 15. The rebellious citizens do not reappear until verse 27. Verses 13, 15-26 originally appeared in a separate parable that we may assume also mentioned a "nobleman" who "went to a distant country" and then returned (verse 12). A clearer understanding of what originally constituted the other parable before it was modified is found by reading verses 12, 14, and 27 as a separate parable introduced by verse 11.

> He [Jesus] went on to tell a parable, because he was near Jerusalem, and they supposed that the kingdom of God was going to appear immediately. He said therefore, "A certain

nobleman went to a distant county to receive a kingdom for himself, and then return. But his citizens hated him, and sent a delegation after him, saying, 'We do not want this man to reign over us.' But these enemies of mine, who did not want me to reign over them, bring them here, and slay them in my presence."

In the total imagery of the parable, Jesus is the nobleman who went to a distant country (heaven) to receive a kingdom (rather absurd if he is God) before returning. The parable continues with a strange episode in which those who hate the nobleman/Jesus sent a delegation after him (to heaven) to protest having him rule over them. As his parable is directed toward the Jewish people who constituted his audience (verses 1-11), these enemy-citizens represent the Jews who reject Jesus as king. In verse 14, they were called citizens; in verse 27, through their rebellious refusal to accept the nobleman's kingship, they are now considered enemies. Therefore, Jesus (represented by the king in the parable) decrees a time of judgment on the unfaithful and disobedient. Echoing the warning of the Matthean Jesus, "He who is not with me is against me" (Matthew 12:30), the Lucan Jesus demands of his followers that those who reject his rule be immediately destroyed before him. Luke's Jesus declares, "But those enemies of mine, who did not want me to reign over them, bring them here, and slay them in my presence." The timing of the return of the nobleman/Jesus is before the judging of the "slaves," but does not come before implementing the demand of verse 27. There is nothing in the context in which verse 27 is found that shows it refers to a future event associated with a second coming of Jesus. In verse 26, the nobleman/Jesus speaks of the rewards of the faithful followers and punishments of the not so faithful followers as being in the future (after the second coming): "I tell you that to everyone who has shall more be given, but from the one who does not have, even what he does have shall be taken away." This is not the case in verse 27. The text does not say, "you shall slay them in my presence" but "slay them in my presence." Unlike verse 26, it is written in the present tense and calls for immediate fulfillment. Thus, in the context of the passage, the murderous rampage of verse 27 comes before any alleged second coming by Jesus.

The intent of Jesus' words was not lost on subsequent generations of his followers. They could not but interpret this parable as a call for judgment upon the Jewish people for rejecting Jesus. This was made all the more poignant as this commandment came from Jesus himself. The destruction to be carried out upon those who refuse to accept Jesus is the *bloody commission*, the sanction for slaughter of all who refuse the cross.[3] The tragic results of what is taught in this parable are recorded in the history of subsequent encounters of the Jewish people with those who followed Jesus' dictum. Why do the Jews suffer oppression at the hands of his followers? This Gospel passage answers, "The Jews suffer persecution because of their refusal to accept Jesus as the Messiah."

In leading up to the events of the passion narrative, Luke is relentless in his attack on the Jewish authorities. The author of Mark 12:13 (followed by Matthew 22:15) writes, "And they sent some of the Pharisees and Herodians to him, in order to trap him in a statement." In the Lucan expansion of this text, the author intensifies certain dimensions of the story. He exaggerates the involvement of the Jewish authorities, in order to underscore their guilt in the death of Jesus. Thus, he writes, "And they watched him and sent spies who pretended to be righteous, in order that they might catch him in some statement, so as to deliver him up to the rule and the authority of the governor" (Luke 20:20). The intensity of his attack on the Jewish authorities never diminishes. His overall charge is that the issue of responsibility for the death of Jesus rests upon all Jews who do not accept Jesus as the Messiah.

The Lucan account of the arrest of Jesus differs from the episode as recorded in Mark and Matthew. Mark and Matthew do not describe the composition of the "crowd" that arrested Jesus. Mark says they came "from the chief priests and scribes and the elders" (Mark 14:43). Alternately, Matthew says they came "from the chief priests and the elders of the people" (Matthew 26:47). The "crowd" that Judas is said to lead in the Lucan narrative of this event does not come from, but, rather includes "the chief priests and officers of the Temple and elders" (Luke 22:52). According to the Gospel of Luke, instead of leaving the apprehension and arrest to a "crowd" of unknown composition as in the Gospels of Mark and Matthew or to soldiers, as in the Gospel of John (cf. John 18:3, 12), these Jewish religious leaders personally join in the arrest. At a time when other Jews are celebrating the exodus from Egypt, the Jewish religious leaders are portrayed as neglecting their religious duties to play at being policemen. The author of Luke goes out of his way to cite personal involvement by Jewish religious leaders in the apprehension and arrest of Jesus. But, the allegation that the chief priests, officers of the Temple, and elders personally took part in the actual arrest is a malevolent accusation not even supported by the other Gospels. It serves as a reminder of the mendacious nature of this author's work. All three Synoptic Gospels carefully omit any reference to Roman involvement in the arrest (cf. John 18:3, 12) and attribute the entire arrest event, from arrangement to apprehension, solely to the Jewish religious authorities. But, the author of Luke sees an opportunity to increase enmity toward the Jewish leaders by having them also personally involved in the actual apprehension and arrest.

The evangelists often target Jewish leadership for special attack while not mentioning the common people. However, concentrating their attack on the leaders, rather than on the common people, does not mean that they do not also hold all Jews responsible for Jesus' execution. For example, the author of the Gospel of Luke reiterates the charge of the Jewish leadership's responsibility in the death of Jesus. True to form, he carefully evades any direct reference to Roman involvement. The author of Luke quotes Cleopas, a follower of Jesus, as saying that "the chief priests and our rulers delivered him up to the sentence of death, and crucified him" (Luke 24:20). There is no explicit mention of Jews in general being culpable. However, the author makes up for his omission elsewhere. In other contexts, within his Gospel and in Acts, the author continues the process of placing the blame for Jesus' death directly on the entire Jewish people; the speeches he records in the name of Stephen and Peter in Acts condemn all Jews indiscriminately for killing Jesus. In all cases, Pilate and the Romans are exonerated and "the people" are implicated. Thus, this author writes:

> And Pilate summoned the chief priests and the rulers and the people, and said to them, "You brought this man to me as one who incites the people to rebellion, and behold, having examined him before you, I have found no guilt in this man regarding the charges which you make against him. No, nor has Herod, for he sent him back to us; and behold, nothing deserving death has been done by him. I will therefore chastise him and release him." [Now he was obliged to release to them at the feast one prisoner.][4] But they cried out all together, saying, "Away with this man, and release for us Barabbas!" He was one who had been thrown in prison for a certain insurrection made in the city, and for murder. And Pilate, wanting to release Jesus, addressed them again, but they kept on calling out, saying, "Crucify, crucify him!" (Luke 23:13-21)

This passage is a deliberate Lucan attempt to make the Jewish people collectively responsible for the crucifixion.[5] The author of Luke places responsibility for instigating Jesus' execution solely on "the chief priests and the rulers and the people" who he alleges demand that Jesus be crucified (Luke 23:13). It is not one group of Jews that brought Jesus to Pilate and accused him but, essentially, all of them. Thus, Pilate says, "You brought this man to me as one who incites the people to rebellion," that is, all of you, chief priests, rulers, and *people*. Pilate is portrayed as attempting to save Jesus from execution. He is said to have called "the chief priests and the rulers and the people" together. But, despite Pilate's protestations "they" (the Jewish chief priests, rulers, and people), demand that Jesus be taken out and crucified. Thus, personal and collective guilt is again laid upon the whole Jewish people.

The author of Luke writes with the intention of demonstrating why Christianity should be considered favorably by Rome. The Lucan narrative has Pilate state: "I will therefore chastise him and release him" (Luke 23:16). The word "chastise" (*paideusas*) is different from the term used in the Marcan and Matthean accounts to describe the flogging of Jesus (*phragellosas*, Mark 15:15; Matthew 27:26). In the context of this verse, it means, "punish." The thought conveyed is that Pilate considered Jesus innocent and therefore is saying, "I will let him go with a mild whipping."

In Luke 23:22, the author of Luke writes in defense of Pilate, "And he [Pilate] said to them the third time, 'Why, what evil has this man done?'" He emphasizes that it is the "third time" that Pilate spoke on Jesus' behalf (see also verses 15 and 20). In addition, the author of Luke omits the incident (Mark 15:17-20) of the Roman soldiers' mockery (cf. verse 11 where it is Herod Antipas and his soldiers who mock Jesus). He clearly emphasizes (verses 24-25) that Pilate acted in accordance with the Jewish crowd's wishes. Jesus is delivered to the "demand" (verse 24) of the crowd and is "turned over . . . to their will" (verse 25). The verb "to crucify" (*stauroo*) is not specifically used in Luke 23:25 as it is in Mark 15:15 and Matthew 27:26. The Lucan form ("but he turned Jesus over to their will") is the more precise in the sense that it makes quite explicit the concern shown by all three Synoptic Gospels to express that Pilate was under relentless pressure from the Jews to convict Jesus. Thus, the real cause of the injustice of the crucifixion was the ill will of the Jews. The Greek verbal form *thelete* ("Do you will?") is used by Pilate when questioning the Jewish crowd (stirred up against Jesus by the Jewish leaders—Mark 15:11) in Mark 15:9 (see also Matthew 27:17, 21), but not in the Lucan parallel. But the author of Luke makes up for this by introducing the substantival form *thelemati* ("will") as the penultimate word of his trial narrative (Luke 23:25). This is part of the author's plan to stress the political innocence of the Romans in the responsibility for the death of Jesus. In place of Roman culpability is the stress placed on the Jews. They are accused of being completely at fault with regard to the death of Jesus.

The author of Luke does not describe Pilate as washing his hands of responsibility for Jesus' sentence to be crucified (cf. Matthew 27:24), he does not mention the Jews' acceptance of responsibility for Jesus' death (cf. Matthew 27:25), and he says nothing of Pilate's wishing to "satisfy" the people (cf. Mark 15:15). As part of his attack on the Jewish people, he directs attention from Pilate to the people. He does this by ending the Greek sentence that is now Luke 23:23, not with the verb (as in the English rendering), but with a remark that it was solely at the insistence of the Jews that Jesus was executed: *hai phonai auton*, "their voice" (literally "the voices of them").

The Lucan version of events surrounding the crucifixion emphasizes a collective guilt of all segments of the Jewish community. It reads as though Pilate only pronounced the death sentence on the innocent Jesus (Luke 23:14) in order to satisfy the demand of "the chief priests and the rulers and the people" that Jesus be crucified. Apparently, he then handed Jesus over to the Jews, who bring him to the place of execution and crucify him.

> But they were insistent, with loud voices asking that he be crucified. And their voices began to prevail. And Pilate pronounced sentence that their demand should be granted. And he released the man they were asking for who had been thrown into prison for insurrection and murder, but he turned Jesus over to their will. And when they led him away, they laid hold of one Simon, a Cyrenian, coming in from the country, and placed on him the cross to carry behind Jesus. (Luke 23:23-26)

According to the Lucan account, Pilate decides that "their demand should be granted" (Luke 23:24) and so "he turned Jesus over to their will" (Luke 23:25) to be crucified. The "their" in both verses 24 and 25 has its antecedent in "the chief priests and the rulers and the people" of Luke 23:13. The Jews appearing in Luke 23:13 are the last mentioned antecedents for any "they" appearing in the episode prior to the execution itself, that is, up to and including Luke 23:30-31. As a result, "And Pilate pronounced sentence that their demand should be granted. And he released the man they were asking for who had been thrown into prison for insurrection and murder, but he turned Jesus over to their will" (Luke 23:24-25) is Luke's clarification of the extent of Jewish responsibility. In Luke 23:26, "And when they led him away, they laid hold of one Simon, a Cyrenian," the "they" lead Jesus off to be crucified. The Lucan account is not explicitly stating that "the chief priests and the rulers and the people" physically crucified Jesus. It is not suggesting outright that Jews crucified Jesus in the sense of physically nailing him to the cross but it leaves that impression. Hovering over the episode is the accusation that Jewish participation in the crucifixion is such that they have primary responsibility for it in being its instigators; Pilate is coerced into condemning him and "the [Roman] soldiers" are not mentioned until verse 36. Thus, the author of Luke-Acts writes, that the "house of Israel" (Acts 2:36) or the "men of Israel" (Acts 3:12-15) are the "you" who "crucified" Jesus or "put to death the prince of life" and the "they" who put Jesus "to death by hanging him on a cross" (Acts 10:39). However, they had him put to death by using "godless men," that is, the pagan Roman soldiers[6] who were men without the Law (Acts 2:23). The Romans carry out the physical execution. But, in order to emphasize his accusation of Jewish primary responsibility, the author of Luke writes, "the chief priests and our rulers delivered him up to the sentence of death, and crucified him" (Luke 24:20).

It is only by comparison of the Lucan version with the other Gospels that one can see that it is actually the Gentile soldiers who took Jesus and crucified him, not the Jews. The Lucan text, the self-acclaimed definitive Gospel (Luke 1:3-4), is purposely left ambiguous. In his rewriting of the Marcan account the author of Luke omits the scourging of Jesus found in Mark 15:15 and the entire mocking scene found in Mark 15:16-20a and continues with Mark 15:20b. The Marcan account also has a "they" ("they led him out to crucify him"—Mark 15:20b); but there is no ambiguity in Mark because of the presence of the Roman soldiers in the preceding verses. These are the verses deleted in the Lucan account. The author of Luke knew his deletion of a crucial part of the Marcan passage now meant that "they" in his version of the episode has lost its original Marcan antecedent (the soldiers). It now has grammatically a new Lucan antecedent (the chief priests, the rulers, and the people) from thirteen verses earlier. The author's goal is to leave the impression that it is the Jews, not the Gentile soldiers, who actually take Jesus from Pilate and crucify him. Anxious to offset the centrality of the Roman role in the crucifixion the author of Luke omits the Roman scourging although it meant that Jesus' own prophecy that he would be scourged (Luke 18:33) remained unfilled in the Lucan Gospel. In the Gospel of Mark, the mockery of Jesus follows the scourging and was done by "soldiers" who then take him out to be crucified: "And the soldiers took him away into the palace (that is, the Praetorium), and they called together the whole cohort. And they dressed him up in purple, and after weaving a crown of thorns, they put it on him; and they began to acclaim him, 'Hail, King of the Jews.' And they kept beating his head with a reed, and spitting at him, and kneeling and bowing before him. And after they had mocked him, they took the purple off him, and put his garments on him. And they led him out to crucify him" (Mark 15:16-20). The Lucan version narrates that Jesus was mocked while in the custody of the Sanhedrin (Luke 22:63-65) and before Herod Antipas (Luke 23:11).[7] However, it does not mention a mockery of Jesus by what are apparently Roman soldiers until Luke 23:36 (the word "Roman" is not mentioned in the Greek text).

In the Marcan narrative the antecedent of "they" is clearly the "soldiers" mentioned in verse 16, but this is not the case in the Gospel of Luke. What occurs in the Lucan narrative is not a case of careless use of antecedents. The author was well aware of what he was doing. The grammatical sense of what the author of Luke wrote was exactly what he intended to convey. The Lucan audience would have understood 23:26 ("they led him away [to the place where they crucified him]") to mean that the Jews crucified Jesus (whether by their own hands or those of others), in accordance with the antecedent of verse 13. Although they may have understood this to have been accomplished through the agency of the Roman authorities it is all due to a Jewish conspiracy and a direct Jewish demand for Jesus to be killed. The ambiguous pronoun, "they," of verse 26 served to call audience attention back to verse 13 for a reminder of where the author felt guilt was to be placed. The author of Luke cannot completely deny that there were Roman soldiers involved in the crucifixion, but he first mentions them only after Jesus is already on the cross (Luke 23:36). Elsewhere, the author indicates that there was Gentile complicity in the killing of Jesus (Luke 18:32-33, Acts 4:25-27). But, it is the Jews who bear the greater guilt.

It is left to a later interpolator to clarify that the soldiers' part in the crucifixion was forgiven. After all, they were merely "godless men" (Acts 2:23) who, unlike the Jews, did not know better. In verse 34, the first part of which is not found in the earliest manuscripts of Luke, Jesus asks God to forgive his executioners. "But Jesus was saying, 'Father forgive them; for they do not know what they are doing.'[8] And they cast lots, dividing up his garments among themselves" (Luke 23:34). The referent of "them" and "they" is not identified directly. Identification of "them" and "they," in verse 34a is not established by a reference to an antecedent preceding that verse. It is to be identified with the "they" described in the postposition, that is, "they . . . [who] cast lots dividing up his garments among themselves" (verse 34b). A comparison with the parallel Johannine description of the execution scene shows the object of Jesus' request for forgiveness is the soldiers who physically affixed him to the cross. "The soldiers therefore, when they had crucified Jesus, took his outer garments and made four parts, a part to every soldier and also the tunic; now the tunic was seamless, woven in one piece. They said therefore to one another, 'Let us not tear it, but cast lots for it, to decide whose it shall be; that the Scripture might be fulfilled, They divided my outer garments among them, and for my clothing they cast lots.'[9] Therefore the soldiers did these things . . ." (John 19:23-25). By comparison with the Johannine narrative we (unlike the initial Lucan audience which did not have verse 34a in their text or the Gospel of John as a reference) can see that the "they" of Luke 23:34b refers to "soldiers." Therefore, the "they" who physically crucify Jesus, "And when they came to the place called The Skull, there they crucified him" (Luke 23:33) also refers to the soldiers.

The author of Luke never directly presents the Roman soldiers as responsible for the physical action of nailing Jesus to the cross. Verse 36, the only reference to soldiers being present at the crucifixion merely mentions that "the soldiers also mocked him, coming up to him, offering him sour wine." There is no explicit indication that they were Roman soldiers or that they were there in an official capacity as executioners. The only indication of a Roman military presence is the author of Luke's statement that "when the centurion [a Roman military rank] saw what had happened, he began praising God, saying, 'Certainly this man was righteous'" (Luke 23:47). The individual who added verse 34a had access to John 19:23-25 (written years after the Gospel of Luke) with its reference to soldiers. He saw in it an opportunity to continue the Lucan process of blaming the Jews and neutralizing any accusations of Roman guilt. Thus, he inserted the request for *forgiveness due to ignorance* clause on behalf of the Roman soldiers. Since the original Lucan format was maliciously left ambiguous in order to increase Jewish culpability, the addition of verse 34a has caused confusion. Some readers of the episode assume that the Jews are included in the forgiveness. However, contextually, there is a definite exclusion of the Jews from this plea for forgiveness. The interpolator never intended that his addition should be read to include forgiveness for the Jews. Instead, his words serve to emphasize the alleged guilt of the Jews, contrasting the forgiving Jesus with the merciless Jews.

Jesus' alleged request for God to grant forgiveness was confined to those casting lots for his garments, that is, the soldiers. As usual, Jesus did not personally forgive anyone. Jesus told God to forgive, but he himself never forgave anyone who he felt wronged him personally. As noted above, Luke 23:34a does not appear in the earliest manuscripts of the Gospel of Luke and shows signs of being an interpolation. Its function is to grant the naive unbelieving Gentiles, who were present and actually participated in the crucifixion, divine forgiveness. These Gentiles are exonerated for the disingenuous Jews misused them. By inference, all Gentiles are exonerated whether believers in Jesus or not. However, at no time is even one Jew who did not believe in Jesus, even if he took no part in the crucifixion, forgiven. A careful reading of the Gospels shows that Luke 23:34a is not in consonance with their overall presentation of Jesus' true feelings concerning those who do not believe in him.

According to the *textus receptus*, Jesus requests the "Father" to grant unconditional forgiveness to "them." Jesus places no stipulation on his request; no profession of faith in Jesus is called for, prior to a grant of forgiveness. Jesus asked for forgiveness because those for whom he prayed did not know what they were doing. Apparently, he considered the soldiers to be undergoing their task in a robot-like manner unconcerned with critically evaluating what they were doing. Unconcerned with guilt or innocence or in his person, the Roman soldiers were carrying out an order to execute the prisoner in a dispassionate and perfunctory manner. Even mockery of the prisoner was part of the crucifixion process. Therefore, Jesus allegedly requests that their actions be forgiven.

The very notion that anyone should be forgiven "for they do not know what they are doing" (or that persecutors should be blessed rather than cursed) is contrary to overall New Testament teaching and brings the question of the authenticity of verse 34a into further doubt. As we have seen above, verse 34a speaks of bestowing unconditional forgiveness solely on the soldiers for they do not know better in crucifying Jesus. This is inconsistent with the New Testament concept of forgiveness whereby unconditional forgiveness is only given to one who accepts Jesus. For example, the author of Acts also identifies the Jews and their rulers as acting in ignorance when they executed Jesus. "And now, brethren, I know that you acted in ignorance, just as your rulers did also" (Acts 3:17). Does this mean that the Jews are forgiven "for they do not know what they are doing"? Are they held blameless, because of ignorance? Not at all! There is no simple granting of forgiveness for the alleged participation of the Jews in the crucifixion. Forgiveness can only come, as the full text indicates, with acceptance of Jesus. "Repent therefore and return, that your sins may be wiped away, in order that times of refreshing may come from the presence of the Lord; and that he may send Jesus, the Christ appointed for you" (Acts 3:19-20). Luke 23:34a with its unconditional forgiveness of the unrepentant Roman soldiers is fundamentally at odds with the Christian concept that one must believe in Jesus in order for one's sins to be forgiven. In Luke, there is no profession of faith by the soldiers or the centurion alone following Jesus' death. The closest we come to that is when the centurion praises God and acknowledges a belief in Jesus' innocence (Luke 23:47). But, praising God or believing Jesus to be innocent as charged (or even believing Jesus is "a son of God") is not the same as a profession of belief in him as a personal savior.

Could Jesus have preached political revolt or hated anyone when he spoke words of forgiveness and non-resistance to wickedness? Did he not say, "Love your enemies" (Matthew 5:44, Luke 6:27), "Do not resist him that is wicked; but whoever slaps you on your right cheek, turn to him the other also" (Matthew 5:39) and, alternately, "To him that strikes you on the cheek, offer the other also" (Luke 6:29)? These verses are taken as representative of the extraordinary forgiveness taught and exercised by Jesus himself. However, the sublime dictum to "turn the other cheek" was not practiced by Jesus himself. According to the Gospels, Jesus preached turning the other cheek, loving one's neighbor and praying for them, and forgiving those who wrong you. When did Jesus manifest such behavior in his personal relationships, during his lifetime, for others to emulate? Was it his cursing of the Pharisees (Matthew 23), his threat of violent retribution on cities that rejected his message (Matthew 11:20-24, Luke 10:13-15), or his condemnation to death of Jews who would not accept him (Luke 19:27)? The fact of the matter is that he himself never turned the other cheek; Jesus never forgave anyone who rejected his claims. He responded to his opponents, not with passive resistance, but by answering criticism with criticism, and by reviling and threatening his adversaries (for example, Matthew 23).

It is clear from the Gospels that Jesus never forgave anyone who wronged or criticized him. At best, he only forgave those who wronged others. Whenever an opportunity to personally forgive others presented itself, he always declined. For example, "he [Jesus] began to reproach the cities in which most of his miracles were done, because they did not repent. 'Woe to you, Chorazin! Woe to you Bethsaida! . . . Nevertheless I say to you, it shall be more tolerable for Tyre and Sidon in the day of judgment, then for you. And you, Capernaum, will not be exalted to heaven, will you? You shall descend to Hades; for if the miracles had occurred in Sodom which occurred in you, it would have remained to this day. Nevertheless I say to you that it shall be more tolerable for the land of Sodom in the day of judgment, than for you'" (Matthew 11:20-24, Luke 10:13-15). Instead of forgiving Judas for betraying him he said: "But woe to that man through whom the Son of Man is betrayed! It would have been good for that man if he had not been born" (Matthew 26:24). In John 18:22-23, we find that Jesus, when beaten by an officer, instead of offering quietly his other cheek argues with him:

> But having said these things, one of the officers standing by gave Jesus a slap, saying: "Is that the way you answer the high priest?" Jesus answered him: "If I have spoken wrongly, bear witness concerning the wrong; but if rightly, why do you hit me?"

For his part, Paul, that great follower of Jesus, did not submit meekly to the high priest Ananias' order that he be smitten on the mouth:

> And the High Priest Ananias commanded those standing

beside him to strike him on the mouth. Then Paul said to him: "God is going to strike you, you whitewashed wall. And do you sit to judge me according to the Law, and in violation of the Law order me to be struck? (Acts 23:2-3)

Paul did not offer his other cheek in compliance with Jesus' command. Instead, he swore at Ananias in direct contradiction of another of Jesus' alleged commandments: "Bless those who curse you, pray for those who mistreat you" (Luke 6:28), and his own statement: "Bless those who persecute you; bless, and do not curse" (Romans 12:14).

One function of the Book of Acts is to show that opposition to Christianity, both in Judea and other places in the Empire, came not from the Romans but from the Jews, who sought to misrepresent the new faith (Acts 13:50; 14:2, 19; 17:5, 13; 18:12 ff; 24:1 ff.). What is more, the author of Acts sets out to create a strong sense, in the reader, that there is a collective Jewish responsibility for Jesus' death. Sole blame for Jesus' execution is placed on the Jewish people of all segments of society. Going beyond the accusation of Jewish involvement in the death of Jesus are those texts from Acts which portray the Jews as either primarily responsible for the death of Jesus or as actually having killed him. Peter is quoted as saying, "Men of Israel, listen to these words: Jesus the Nazarene, a man attested to you by God with miracles and wonders and signs which God performed through him in your midst, just as you yourselves know—this man, delivered up by the predetermined plan and foreknowledge of God, you nailed to a cross by the hands of godless men and put him to death" (Acts 2:22-23). Once more it is the "men of Israel" who nailed Jesus to the cross. The Romans (not identified as such in the text), "the hands of godless men," are simply the instrument used by the Jews to carry out the deed. A few verses later Peter allegedly says, "Therefore let all the house of Israel know for certain that God has made him both Lord and Christ—this Jesus whom you crucified" (Acts 2:36).

As recorded in Acts, there is no doubt in Peter's mind that it is the Jews, as a whole, and they alone that are to bear the entire burden of guilt for Jesus' execution. Peter says, it is *you* men of Israel who "delivered up, and disowned [Jesus] in the presence of Pilate, when he had decided to release him. But you disowned the holy and righteous one, and asked for a murderer to be granted to you, but put to death the prince of life, the one whom God raised from the dead, to which we are witnesses" (Acts 3:13-15). Their only hope, Peter says, is to accept Jesus (Acts 3:19).

The theme of *all* the Jews bearing the responsibility for the crucifixion of Jesus is ingrained in the literary structure of Acts.[10] Thus, we find: "Let it be known to all of you, and to all the people of Israel, that . . . Jesus Christ the Nazarene, whom you crucified . . . (Acts 4:10); "The God of our fathers raised up Jesus, whom you had put to death by hanging him on a cross" (Acts 5:30); "And we are witnesses of all the things he did both in the land of the Jews and in Jerusalem. And they also put him to death by hanging him on a cross" (Acts 10:39); "For those who live in Jerusalem, and their rulers, recognizing neither him nor the utterances of the prophets which are read every Sabbath, fulfilled these by condemning him. And though they found no ground for putting him to death, they asked Pilate that he be executed (Acts 13:27-28); "For truly in this city there were gathered together against Your holy servant Jesus, whom You did anoint, both Herod and Pontius Pilate, along with the nations and the peoples of Israel, to do whatever Your hand and Your purpose predestined to occur" (Acts 4:27-28). Although Pilate and the nations are implicated in the death of Jesus, overall they remain background figures doing the bidding of the Jews. Herod,[11] who is a Jew, is mentioned in this passage because the author had previously involved him in his account of the trial narrative (Luke 23:7-12). It should be noted that none of the other evangelists mention any involvement by Herod in the alleged events surrounding the crucifixion. Moreover, according to Acts 4:27-28, the exact conditions of Jesus' suffering and death were supposedly "predestined to occur" (as, for example, in the Christian interpretation of Psalm 22 and Isaiah 53). The implication is that the Jews, as a national entity, were given no free will choice concerning Jesus. Hence, there was no opportunity for Jewish national acceptance of Jesus or for deviating from the exact sentence administered to him. So, what is the extent of Jewish culpability in the "predestined" death of Jesus?

In a further attempt to condemn the Jewish people in the eyes of his readers the author of Acts distorts the circumstances surrounding Paul's escape from Damascus.[12] Paul writes that "the ethnarch of Aretas the [Nabatean] king" was waiting to apprehend him outside Damascus, and so he "was let down in a basket through the wall" (2 Corinthians 11:32-33). The Lucan author's version of the same episode appears in Acts 9:23-25: " . . . [T]he Jews plotted together to do away with him, but their plot became known to Saul. And they were also watching the gates day and night so that they might put him to death; but his disciples took him by night, and let him down through the wall, lowering him in a basket." According to this version, it is the Jews who are waiting to apprehend Paul, not King Aretas' ethnarch. It is quite obvious that despite the author of Acts' attempt to implicate "the Jews," in this episode, Paul's own account makes no mention of Jews being involved in this attempt to capture him.

In a second distortion of Paul's missionary activity the author of Luke claims a further Jewish attempt on Paul's life. He claims that after leaving Damascus, Paul went to Jerusalem where the Jews once more attempted to kill him. Paul himself maintains that he did not return to Jerusalem after his conversion until he had spent three years in Arabia, and even then he stayed privately with Peter and spoke to no other apostle except James. Then he went to Syria and Cilicia where he began preaching (Galatians 1:18-24). On the contrary, Acts 9:26-30 maintains that when Paul left Damascus he came to Jerusalem where Barnabas brought him to the apostles and told them of his conversion. According to Acts, Paul preached openly in Jerusalem until Hellenistic Jews sought to kill him; then he left for Tarsus (which is in Cilicia).[13] It is highly unlikely that Paul would omit an attempt on his life by Jews in Jerusalem and that he had to flee as a result of their actions.

In order to malign the Jews, the author of Acts also distorts a third episode in Paul's career. This involves the question of alleged Jewish persecution of Christianity in Thessalonica. Acts relates that Paul was very successful in converting Thessalonian Gentiles, as well as Jews (Acts 17:4). Consequently, "the Jews, becoming jealous and taking along some wicked men from the market place, formed a mob and set the city in an uproar" (Acts 17:5). They then attacked the Christians (Acts 17:5-6). The Jews who are "persuaded" by Paul are referred to as "them," those who are not are called "the Jews." In 1 Thessalonians 2:14-16, Paul tells a different story. Thessalonian Christians are persecuted, but they suffer at the hands of their fellow Gentile Thessalonians. There is no mention of Jewish involvement. Paul compares the persecution of the Thessalonian Christians "at the hands of . . . [their] own countrymen" to that persecution suffered by the Judean "churches of God" at the hands of the Jews. Unlike the author of Acts, Paul attributes the persecution of the Thessalonian Christians solely to their "countrymen." If there were a Jewish instigation or participation in this persecution of Thessalonian Christians, Paul would not have hesitated to mention it. He would call them Jews, not "countrymen."

Stephen's speech in Acts, chapter seven, is used to portray the Jews of all generations as hostile to God's will and of not keeping God's law. In a theme found in a number of New Testament contexts, they are accused of being killers of the prophets and Jesus. "You men who are stiffnecked and uncircumcised in heart and ears are always resisting the Holy Spirit; you are doing just as your fathers did. Which one of the prophets did your fathers not persecute? And they killed those who had previously announced the coming of the righteous one, whose betrayers and murderers you have now become; you who received the law as ordained by angels, and yet did not keep it" (Acts 7:51-53). Stephen's speech is used to set the stage for the receptive Gentiles replacing the stubborn Jews in God's favor and becoming the inheritors of the divine promises to Israel. This theme reverberates throughout the Book of Acts. Thus, when the Jews of Pisidian Antioch contradict Paul's message they are told by Paul and Barnabas, "It was necessary that the word of God should be spoken to you first; since you repudiate it, and judge yourselves unworthy of eternal life, behold, we are turning to the Gentiles" (Acts 13:46). And when the Jews of Corinth "resisted and blasphemed" his message, Paul declared, "Your blood be upon your own heads! I am clean. From now on I shall go to the Gentiles" (Acts 18:6). These verses complement Paul's final statement, as recorded at the end of the Book of Acts. There, Paul states: "Let it be known to you [Jews], then, that this salvation of God has been sent to the Gentiles. They will listen" (Acts 28:28). The Jews are pictured as outcasts whose place in God's scheme of things has been supplanted by the Gentiles.

Notes

[1] It is believed that originally these two volumes circulated together as one complete and independent work. The author of Luke considered his work to be a definitive study, with no need for the reader to cross-reference with similar works. Thus, he writes that "it seemed fitting for me . . . having investigated everything carefully from the beginning, to write it out for you in consecutive order . . . so that you might know the exact truth about the things you have been taught" (Luke 1:3-4). Acts now stands as a sequel to the four Gospels. It purports to describe the growth and development of the church in the approximately thirty years following the death of Jesus.

[2] The man attacked by robbers "was going down from Jerusalem." This shows that he was a Jew. For the story to have a dramatic impact the two individuals who do not help the victim (the priest and Levite) would also have to be Jewish and Jews of rank in order to fully contrast their behavior toward a fellow Jew with that of the Samaritan.

[3] Over the centuries much of Christianity's worldwide growth has been through intimidating and terrorizing people who have come under the dominion of Christian rulers and clergy. There are those who readily accept the Christian message, those who convert for personal gain, those who out of unbearable

fear for their lives accept baptism with regret, those who are forcibly baptized against their will, and those who refuse baptism and are brutalized and murdered. The various denominations of Christianity that increased their adherents in this way were well aware of the overall insincerity of most first generation converts. The clergy's goal, however, was the indoctrination of the young and future generations. With notable exceptions, most descendants of those intimidated and terrorized into baptism soon became loyal adherents of one form of Christianity or another.

4 Some manuscripts insert the bracketed verse 17.

5 In Luke 23:13, Codex Bezae has the reading "*all* the people" making Luke's description correspond to Matthew 27:25, where all the people answer, "His blood be upon us and our children."

6 The Roman soldiers stationed in Judea were often not ethnically Roman and were often of local Gentile origin.

7 Luke 23:6-12 is the only passage in the Gospels to report a trial before Herod Antipas, the tetrarch of Galilee. There are those who argue for the authenticity of this passage, but they offer no satisfactory explanation of how three trials (Jewish, Herodian, and Roman) could all take place within the space of a few nighttime and early morning hours. It is improbable that the episode ever occurred. Why did the evangelist insert this story? There is an opinion that he inserted the alleged episode in order to demonstrate that Herod Antipas, as well as Pilate, was convinced of Jesus' innocence. Still others are of the opinion that this story was introduced to involve a secular Jewish ruler in the condemnation of Jesus.

8 The idea for the interpolation of verse 34a may have come from the prayer the author of Luke-Acts attributes to Stephen as he is being stoned to death, "Lord do not hold this sin against them!" (Acts 7:60).

9 This verse explicitly states that the pagan soldiers knew and quoted from the Hebrew Scriptures.

10 "All" is used with the meaning that all Israel is held culpable for the execution of Jesus to the exclusion of those Jews who accept Jesus. Luke 23:48 describes the sorrow of "all the multitudes who came together" to witness the crucifixion. Historically, it is not unlikely that many of the Jews among the "multitudes" observing the crucifixion were distraught at seeing a fellow Jew being put to death by the Roman authorities for fomenting rebellion against their governance. This did not make them believers in the Lucan Jesus' claims.

[11] That is, Herod Antipas.
[12] It should be noted that the Paulinism of the Book of Acts is not the Paulinism of the Pauline letters.
[13] Acts 9:30 gives the name of the city, Tarsus, while Galatians 1:21 gives the name of the larger district, Cilicia, in which the city is located.

8.
THE GOSPEL OF JOHN

The anti-Jewish enmity expressed by the evangelists reaches its most noxious form in the Gospel of John. This Gospel is considered by many to be the most anti-Jewish of the four. It contains some of the harshest anti-Judaic statements and characterizations in the New Testament.[1] As with the Synoptic Gospels, the Fourth Gospel does not address the fundamental issues underlying the confrontation between Jesus and the Roman authorities. Like his predecessors, the author of John shows a decided interest in downplaying Roman involvement and represents the confrontation as between Jesus and Judaism and the Jewish people at large.

Written toward the end of the first century of the Common Era, when relations between Jews and Christians had deteriorated to the breaking point, this Gospel bears the mark of the time in which it was written. The controversies in this Gospel reflect more the antagonisms at the close of the first century of the Common Era than those contemporaneous with Jesus.[2] A recurring theme is the hostility of "the Jews" to Jesus and to the early Christian movement. Jews are unbelievers (6:41-52, 8:25, 8:48-57, 10:19-21, 12:37). Jews persecute Jesus and those who believe in him (7:13, 8:37, 10:31). The author of John frequently combines these themes: Jews both disbelieve and they persecute those who do believe (5:10-18, 9:18-23). Jews question and misunderstand Jesus' words (2:18-21, 6:52, 7:35, 8:22), they murmur at him (6:41), and they desire to kill him (5:16, 18; 7:1).

Moreover, the Gospel of John shows the influence of Samaritan Christianity. Samaritans who became Christians brought with them ideas that helped shape the Johannine community's attitude toward non-Christian Jews and Judaism. This, combined with the developing Christological claims of the Johannine Christians, results in a virulent hostility toward Jews and Judaism.

Christian tradition says the author of the Gospel of John was a Jew. A perusal of the relevant texts shows that the Johannine author and, indeed, John's Jesus both harbor vehement anti-Judaic feelings. But, what of the alleged Jewish antecedents of the author of John? For that, one need but look to the hatred spewed by some Jewish converts to Christianity in later centuries. The bitter suffering they brought upon the Jewish people gives an indication of the intense hatred harbored by individuals of this stamp. In reality, we cannot determine with any certainty the origin of the initial author of this Gospel. The author of this proto-Johannine document was either a Samaritan oriented sectarian Jew who had become a Christian, a Jewish-born Christian missionary to the Samaritans, or a Samaritan convert to Christianity. The author of the final redaction was more than likely not a Jew.

The Fourth Gospel includes numerous anti-Jewish comments and often employs the phrase "the Jews," *hoi Ioudaioi*, disparagingly. "The Jews" is used in John seventy-one times as compared to a total of sixteen occurrences in the Synoptics (Mark, six; Matthew, five; Luke, five).[3] Some uses of the term "the Jews" are neutral in meaning, such as in designating a geographical area (John 3:22), a religious festival (John 2:13, 7:2), a religious custom (John 19:42), when it speaks about individuals as Jews to separate them from non-Jews (John 4:9), or when it is used as part of a title (John 18:33, 19:3). However, these uses of the term "the Jews" are not typical Johannine usage. The overwhelming majority of the seventy-one occurrences of *hoi Ioudaioi* in the Gospel of John are expressions of an anti-Judaic polemic.[4] When used of the Jewish people as a whole, the Jewish inhabitants of Judea or Galilee, or the Jewish religious leaders (the chief priests, the scribes, and the Pharisees) the majority of uses of the term are negative. The evangelist consistently applied the term "the Jews" with the expectation that it would give the Christian reader and listener a most contemptuous feeling toward the Jewish people. History shows that he was right.[5]

The Johannine Gospel is characterized by an all-pervasive anti-Judaic hatred. Those branded as enemies of Jesus are simply labeled "the Jews." This identification is so complete that the author disregards the facts that Jesus himself and his disciples were also Jews.[6] More than the other Gospels, the Book of John demonizes the Jews. Its author portrays the Jews as a collective earthly embodiment of the powers of satanic evil. This Gospel insists that the Jews do not know God (John 5:38-47; 7:28; 8:19, 47; 15:18-25; 16:1-3). It is alleged that their denial of "the son" is a denial of "the Father" (John 5:23). Jesus becomes an otherworldly visitor who has nothing in common with "the Jews" among whom he lives.

The singular role of the Jewish people in the divine scheme of history is nullified. For the author of this Gospel, the Jewish people are no longer God's people. "The Jews" become the theological symbol of all that is evil and debased; they are the devil's children. Symbolically, the relationship between the Jews and Satan is expressed in the person of Judas (Hebrew, *Yehuda*, "Judah"). In the Johannine sequence of events leading to Jesus' execution Judas is possessed by Satan (John 13:27). After this, the reader is told that Judas himself is "a devil" (John 6:70). But, this is not surprising since the description applies to Jews in general (John 8:44). In the Gospel of John, not only is Judas a devil, but all Jews (who do not believe in Jesus) are the devil's offspring; therefore any evil can be expected of them because they do the devil's bidding. True worshipers of God are now only those who believe in Jesus. The author of John is reiterating what was in his day already established as church teaching on supersessionism. The Christian church had replaced the Jewish people as God's chosen people; the church was the true Israel, its members the true Israelites. The Johannine belief agrees with Paul's statement, found at the conclusion of the Book of Acts, "Let it be known to you therefore, that this salvation of God has been sent to the Gentiles; they will also listen" (Acts 28:28).

Some commentators claim that John's derogatory use of the term "the Jews" never involved the Jewish people as such. They maintain that wherever the term "the Jews" is employed it is best understood to mean "the other Jews" or "some of the Jews," or "a few of the Jewish leaders," or "the Jewish leaders (but not the entire people)." Seldom, they insist, does it refer to the nation as a whole. However, this contention is not supported by the text of the Johannine Gospel. The author of John intentionally creates a pejorative meaning for the phrase "the Jews" inclusive of all Jews.[7] Thus, he writes:

> The Jews were looking for him [Jesus] at the feast, and saying, "Where is he?" And there was much muttering about him among the people. While some said, "He is a good man," others said, "No, he is leading the people astray." Yet for fear of the Jews no one spoke openly of him. (John 7:11-13)

The dominant note of this passage is the enmity of "the Jews" against Jesus. The conclusion of this passage, "Yet for fear of the Jews no one spoke openly of him," gives the reader no indication that all of the people participating in this putative discussion were Jews. This passage illustrates some of the mechanics of Johannine anti-Judaic propaganda and the methods by which its advocates sought to influence readers' (and hearers') thoughts and emotions. From the text, it is impossible to distinguish among the various Jewish groups involved even if the author had intended such distinctions. Few readers would think of distinguishing among them and would read the passage as:

> The Jews were looking for him [Jesus] at the feast, and saying, "Where is he?" And there was much muttering about him among the [Jewish] people. While some [of the Jews] said, "He is a good man," others [of the Jews] said, "No, he

is leading the [Jewish] people astray." Yet for fear of [Jesus' enemies among] the Jews no[t] one [of these Jews] spoke openly of him.

The author of John chose his anti-Jewish phraseology here and elsewhere in the Gospel, with the predetermined aim of inciting his audience against "the Jews." It is virtually impossible, simply by reading this passage, to distinguish between "the Jews" who were Jesus' enemies and the rest of the Jewish people. The author of John does not aim for his audience to make such a differentiation. There is no intention of leaving it up to the audience's ability to discern any such differences between the various participants or the roles they played. These anti-Jewish ambiguities were designed to condemn all Jews. Had the author of John wished to specifically attack *the Jewish leaders* he could easily have written those few words rather than the more general *the Jews*. All indications are that the author of John chose his words with deliberation and aimed to defame "the Jews."[8] The Fourth Gospel singles out "the Jews," without any qualifiers, as Jesus' killers and the enemies of God.

Some New Testament commentators maintain that the usual rendering of *hoi Ioudaioi*, in John, as "the Jews" is incorrect. They allege that the primary meaning of *hoi Ioudaioi* derives from a geographical identification; that they are people from *Ioudaia*, that is, "the Judeans." They claim that there is no anti-Jewish attitude in the Gospel of John at all; it is at the most anti-Judean. Thus, they conclude that "the Jews" is a mistranslation because it is inconsistent with rendering *Ioudaia* as "Judea." However, assigning every mention of *hoi Ioudaioi* to a strictly geographical meaning purposefully overlooks the polemical and theological purpose behind the use of "the Jews" in the text. H*oi Ioudaioi* in the Gospel of John is not connected to a geographical entity. It is a polemic with a distinct theological symbolism. "The Jews" are the devil's surrogates, the theological representatives of satanic hostility to God's revelation. The Johannine use of "the Jews" denotes all that is sinful in the world. It makes "the Jews," as a people, the ultimate embodiment of evil. The fact remains that no matter how one endeavors to explain away the use of the term "the Jews," in the Gospel of John, this is precisely the term its author used. And certainly, the Jews have paid a price for the malevolent way they are portrayed in this document.

It has been suggested that the use of the term, "the Jews," reflects hostility between the respective Jewish inhabitants of Galilee and Judea. Therefore, it is assumed that the hostility shown toward Jesus and his disciples echoes the general tension between Galileans and Judeans. Accordingly, it is argued that the Galileans frequently referred to their antagonists as "Judeans," *Yahudim*, that is, "Jews." But, if the Gospels, and especially the Gospel of John, are supposed to reflect a mutual antagonism between the Jewish inhabitants of the two regions, the point is lost. Aside from superficial remarks, such as, "Surely, the Christ is not going to come from Galilee, is he? Has not the Scripture said that the Christ comes from the offspring of David, and from Bethlehem, the village where David was?" (John 7:41-42)[9] and "Search, and see that no prophet arises out of Galilee" (John 7:52), no meaningful differentiation can be made between Galileans and Judeans based on regional hostility.

Some commentators reason that *hoi Ioudaioi* cannot be a negative reference to the entire Jewish people. Such a view, they maintain, would make no sense given the fact that Jesus and his disciples are themselves Jews. But, this superficial reading of the Johannine texts totally disregards Samaritan influence. Starting in the early pre-Gospel period, the term, "the Jews," began to mean for Christians of Jewish origin (for example, Paul in 1 Thessalonians 2:14-15[10]) the same as it meant to Samaritans and Gentiles, that is, *the Jews, as distinct from us*.

The origin of the Gospel of John has usually been associated with the Gentile Christian community of Ephesus. However, its appearance and final redaction in the Gentile churches of the Roman province of Asia does not preclude the inclusion of material derived from several diverse sources. In this case, there is extensive internal Gospel evidence to suggest Samaria (the Samaritan Christian church) was where many Johannine traditions or a prototype Johannine Gospel developed. Indeed, the overall connection of this Gospel with Samaritan Christianity has been established by a number of scholars.[11] Samaritan Christianity, seemingly barely touched upon in the Johannine narrative, plays a pivotal role in shaping this Fourth Gospel. It is essential to understand Samaritan Christianity's influence upon the development of Johannine anti-Judaic tradition. The presence and influence of Samaritans in the Johannine community explains, in part, the antagonism and the spirit of rejection of "the Jews" found in the Gospel of John.[12]

The Johannine anti-Judaic tradition was shaped in a Christian community heavily influenced by Samaritanism and seeking to gain Samaritan converts.[13] It built upon Jewish rejection of Jesus while attempting to establish a case for Samaritan acceptance of Jesus. As described in this Gospel, "the Jews" are overwhelmingly hostile to Jesus. Alternatively, the Samaritans who he encounters are friendly and open to his message, and accept his teachings wholeheartedly.[14] At one point in his narrative the author of John may also be claiming that in the course of his public career Jesus took refuge among the Samaritans: "So from that day on they planned together to kill him. Jesus therefore no longer continued to walk publicly among the Jews, but went away from there to the country near the wilderness, into a city called Ephraim; and there he stayed with the disciples" (John 11:53-54). There is no city of Ephraim, but the very name suggests Samaria.[15]

Some Samaritans who accepted Jesus as the *Taheb*, the Moses-like prophet, apparently were influential in the Johannine community and brought with them their usual anti-Jewish prejudices. These are reflected in the pejoratives found in the Gospel of John. The story of Jesus' discussion with the Samaritan woman and the subsequent positive reception he receives from Samaritans (John 4:39-42) stand in contrast to his encounters with "the Jews." There is no record, in the Fourth Gospel, of Samaritan hostility to Jesus or to the belief in him, although these had to have existed. In point of fact, there is nothing negative to be found in the Gospel of John about any Samaritans who do not accept Jesus (cf. John 4:39-42).[16]

When John's Jesus says to a Samaritan woman that "You worship that which you do not know; we worship that which we know, for salvation is from the Jews" (John 4:22), he is not denying that the Jews of the past had a unique relationship with God. What the author wishes to establish is that the Jews no longer possess that relationship. They were the protectors of God's entire word, the Hebrew Scriptures (not just the Torah, which the Samaritans accepted). For John's Jesus, "Salvation is from the Jews" does not refer to the Jewish people per se. It refers to the concept of salvation found in the Hebrew Scriptures given by God to the Jews, but which they rejected. The Jewish people are no longer in possession of the biblical record because the relationship established in the Hebrew Scriptures between the Jews and God is now nullified. The Hebrew Scriptures and the salvation to which they bore witness are no longer "from the Jews." They are now part of the inheritance of the true Israel. Thus, his Jesus says, "But an hour is coming, and is now, when the true worshiper shall worship the Father in spirit and truth, for such people the Father seeks to be his worshipers" (John 4:23). According to the author, this search by God for true worshipers is not confined to Jews alone. This is shown by the evangelist's assertion that many Samaritans also believed in Jesus (John 4:39-42).[17]

The episode involving the Samaritan woman is representative of the Jewish proto-Christian missionary presentation of Jesus to the Samaritans. These missionaries did not confine their source material to the Pentateuch alone but utilized the prophetic books as well. This passage reflects that usage. The Samaritan knowledge of God's will is incomplete; they only have the Torah portion of Scripture. Consequently, John's Jesus says, "You worship that which you do not know." Samaritans have the right idea in expecting a savior likened to Moses. But, they do not have the full understanding that the prophetic portion of Scriptures provides. The Jews did have this knowledge. Therefore, John's Jesus, connecting with those that he considers knowledgeable and accepting God's will, says, "we worship that which we know." This is the missionary's reference to those who have the knowledge and act positively upon it. Thus, Philip, one such individual, says to Nathanael: "We have found him of whom Moses in the Law and also the Prophets wrote, Jesus of Nazareth, the son of Joseph" (John 1:45). In so far as Philip's "we" group is representative, "salvation is from the Jews." But, *the Jews* did not follow through on this knowledge and did not acknowledge that the Law and the Prophets spoke of Jesus. This brought on a totally new order of things.

In the Gospel of John, Jesus is rejected by the great majority of Jews, but accepted by some (John 1:11-12). The terms "Galilean" and "Israelite" are used to describe the followers of Jesus who were of Jewish background. The "Galileans" are those Jews who welcome Jesus, "having seen all the things that he did in Jerusalem at the feast; for they themselves also went to the feast" (John 4:45). Nicodemus, a member of the Sanhedrin, speaks out on Jesus' behalf, in the presence of the other "rulers of the Jews." In return, they accuse him of behaving like a "Galilean" (John 7:52).

To bolster his claim that Jesus was favorably received in Galilee the author of John manipulates pre-Gospel tradition to suit his needs. For example, the Synoptic Gospels explain Jesus' use of the saying, "A prophet is not without honor except in his own country and among his own relatives and in his own household" (Mark 6:4, Matthew 13:57, Luke 4:24—"no prophet is welcome in his own country") as a reference to his rejection in Nazareth, which is situated in Galilee. But, the author of John explains Jesus' use of this saying ("a prophet has no honor in his own country"—John 4:44) in reference to his rejection in Judea (John 4:44-45). This author claims that after Jesus left Judea for Galilee (John 4:3) he passed through Samaria (John 4:4) where he was well received (John 4:39-40). From there he went into Galilee where the Galileans also "received him" favorably (John 4:45)—just as the Samaritans had previously done. Therefore, the author of John's citation of this saying must be a reference to Jesus' stay in Judea. Although, in the Synoptic Gospels, Galilee is Jesus' *patris*, his "own country," where he is rejected. In John, Jesus' *patris*, the place where he is rejected, is Judea. This points to a conflict in gospel tradition. Moreover, while, the Fourth Gospel depicts Jesus as being favorably received in Galilee, in the Synoptic Gospels, Jesus cursing the Galilean towns of Chorazin, Bethsaida, and Capernaum (Matthew 11:20-24, Luke 10:13-15) for not believing in him brings us to question the extent of his popularity in Galilee.

Nathanael, who may or may not have been a Galilean Jew (he may have been a Samaritan) is, in any case, not identified as a Jew, but as a "true Israelite" ("That man is a true Israelite. There is no guile in him"—John 1:47) who recognizes Israel's king: "Rabbi, you are the Son of God; you are the King of Israel" (John 1:49). "Israelite," was a term that would be looked upon with particular favor by Samaritans. They considered themselves descendants of Ephraim and Manasseh, the remnant of the northern kingdom of Israel, and distinct from Jews. John's use of the terms, "Galilean" and "Israelite," suggests that he also intended to emphasize these distinctions. For the Johannine author, Jews who believe in Jesus were not to be confused with non-believing-in-Jesus-Jews; therefore, the use of such terms as "Galilean" and "Israelite."

The episode involving Nathanael is derived from Samaritan Christian sources.[18] It drew on the past: northern kingdom (Israel) versus southern kingdom (Judah). There were two types of Israelites—"true Israelites" and those who called themselves Israelites but were not really Israel, that is, the Jews. Apparently, in proto-Samaritan Christianity, Jews could become "true Israelites" on becoming followers of Jesus—however, only if they did so within the norms of Samaritanism rather than Judaism.[19] As we have seen above, when Jesus first encountered Nathanael, he described Nathanael, not as a Jew, but as a "true Israelite" in whom there was no guile (John 1:47). Nathanael responded: "Rabbi, you are the Son of God, you are the King of Israel." This couplet is important for understanding the difference in the way the terms "Israel" and "the Jews" are used in the Gospel of John. Why the phrase "the king of Israel" and not "the king of the Jews"? For the modern reader, the difference may appear insignificant. But, in its contemporary setting, the distinction had a real deep meaning.

In the Gospel of John, Jesus is regularly referred to as the Son of God, used in Nathanael's parallelism synonymously as "the King of Israel." From Jesus' response (verse 50), we see that the title met with his approval. Nathanael, the "true Israelite," after acknowledging Jesus to be the king of Israel, was promised that he would see "the heavens open up and the angels going up and down upon the Son of Man" (John 1:51). This is a scene reminiscent of Jacob's vision at Bethel in Samaria (Genesis 28:12). Samaritan tradition refers to Mount Gerizim as *Beit El*, the house of God.[20] Thus, a connection is made between true Israelites and the true place of worship. This would be most meaningful to Samaritans who would surely make the connection.

The mention of kingship in Jesus' encounter with Nathanael stands in stark contrast with the mention of kingship in his encounter with Pilate. When Pilate asks, "Are you king of the Jews?" (John 18:33) Jesus disassociates himself from "the Jews," but does not deny that he is a king: "My kingdom is not of this world. If my kingdom were of this world, then my servants would be fighting, that I might not be delivered up to the Jews; but as it is, my kingdom is not of this realm" (John 18:36).[21] The author of John does not deny the tradition that Jesus had been crucified as king of the Jews (John 19:19). But, John's Jesus does not accept this title nor do the rulers of the Jews (John 19:20-22). Thus, as used in these respective passages, "Israel" and "the Jews" are not synonymous terms.

According to the Gospel of John, Jesus' messianic entry into Jerusalem was met by a crowd shouting, "Hosanna! Blessed be he who comes in the name of the Lord, even the king of Israel!" (John 12:13). The parallels to this entry in the Synoptic Gospels contain significant differences in wording. The Marcan version states: "Hosanna! Blessed be he who comes in the name of the Lord! Blessed be the coming kingdom of our father David! Hosanna in the highest!" (Mark 11:9-10). The Matthean version states: "Hosanna to the son of David! Blessed be he who comes in the name of the Lord! Hosanna in the highest!" (Matthew 21:9).[22] Where the Matthean version had the crowd call Jesus the son of David, the Marcan version did not call Jesus "son of David but spoke of "our father David," and the Johannine version of the messianic entry calls him "king of Israel." In Romans 1:3, Paul acknowledged Jesus to be the son of David. The author of Mark was very careful to disassociate Jesus from the title, "son of David." Here too, the Johannine Gospel not only does not mention this Judaic designation, it states that some of Jesus' opponents understood him to be of Galilean origin and therefore assumed that he was neither "the Christ" nor a descendant of David (John 7:41-42).

The initial Johannine author came from the anti-Jewish Samaritan Christian church. The Samaritan component was of limited interest to the later redactors of the Johannine Gospel, who reedited and prepared it for a Gentile audience. As the Gospel material took its final form, the Samaritan derivation paled until it was barely visible. What became important was the anti-Judaic expression contributed by Samaritan Christianity, not the source of any hostile remark. The conflict in the Gospel of John became a clash between the "true Israel" and "Judaism." A true Jew (Israelite) and becoming a Christian (of whatever background) would now be defined as the same thing. "Those who say they are Jews and are not" (Revelation 2:9) were those who follow Judaism.

The Gospel of John claims that "the Jews" accused Jesus of being a Samaritan and possessed by a demon. This Gospel records four occasions when Jesus was accused of being demon possessed (John 7:20, 8:48-49, 8:52, 10:20). However, it is only in John 8:48-49 that he is accused of being both a Samaritan and demon possessed: "The Jews answered him, 'Do we not say rightly that you are a Samaritan and have a demon?' Jesus answered, 'I do not have a demon; but I honor my Father, and you dishonor me.'" This answer has a significant omission. John's Jesus explicitly denies being demon possessed but ignores completely the allegation of being a Samaritan. In the passage as a whole, Jesus challenges the claim of the Jews that they have exclusive right to the promises made to Abraham and his descendants. Thus, Jesus says, "If you are Abraham's children, do the deeds of Abraham" (John 8:39) and "He who is of God hears the words of God; for this reason you do not hear them, because you are not of God" (John 8:47). This is similar to the Samaritan position concerning the Jewish claim to being the people of God.

Jesus was not a Samaritan, but in all likelihood this episode evolved in pre-Gospel Samaritan Christian circles and reflects a missionary desire to win Samaritans over to Christianity. This hint at assent by silence was more conducive to missionary work among Samaritans than an indignant denial would have been. Consequently, the story line does not have Jesus deny the accusation of being a Samaritan. Overall, he is presented in the Johannine pre-Gospel material as friendly to the Samaritans and as accepted by them (John 4). By not denying the accusation of being a Samaritan, the Johannine Jesus exhibits further proof of his friendship. By questioning the Jewish claim to being Abraham's heirs and the people of God he becomes to the Samaritans, in essence, one of their own.

The Gospel of John shows a positive attitude toward Samaritans and toward certain Galileans/Israelites, that is, Jews who accepted Jesus. The Johannine Gospel incorporated Samaritan Christian pre-Gospel material that supposedly described Jesus' interaction with Jews during his public career. Apparently, as expressed in the pre-Gospel story line, Jesus was not rejected by Jews to be accepted by Gentiles, but accepted by Israelites (that is, from a Samaritan viewpoint, in its broadest interpretation, some Samaritans and some Jews) and persecuted and rejected by "the Jews" generally. The Samaritan Christians incorporated this anti-Jewish propaganda, derived from non-Christian Samaritan antagonism toward Jews and Judaism, as part of their missionary program among Samaritans. But, the attitude expressed had a special utility for the redactor of the Fourth Gospel who adapted the Samaritan Christian pre-Gospel (or proto-Gospel) traditions of antagonism directed at Jews to reinforce his own message to Gentiles. As used in the *textus receptus* of this Gospel, the Johannine anti-Judaic attack is used politically to place blame for the death of Jesus on those Jews who do not follow him and to exonerate the Romans of ultimate culpability for Jesus' execution. Religiously, it seeks to gain Gentile converts by showing that the evil Jews were no longer the people of God;

their place was now taken by those from all nations who would believe in Jesus.

Many of the Johannine anti-Jewish arguments were rehearsed in the Synoptic Gospels. Nevertheless, much of its anti-Jewish approach is derived from Samaritan Christian missionary propaganda. The origin and intensity of the anti-Jewish Johannine tradition specific to the Fourth Gospel is to be found among Christians of Samaritan background. The anti-Jewish Johannine tradition, with its emphasis on "the Jews" as inherently evil, took formative shape in the Christian church in Samaria.[23] As the work known today as the Gospel of John developed (out of a Samaritan proto-Johannine Gospel), it incorporated Samaritan anti-Judaic expressions which had been used in the Samaritan Christian church, adapting them to the specific needs of evangelizing Gentiles.

Yet, there are elements in the Gospel of John, which have no parallel with, and, indeed, run counter to Samaritanism and Judaism respectively. This shows that there were traditions that developed in the church independent of former communal ties and that there were additional outside influences upon this Gospel as well. But, there is little doubt that the several redactors of John, whatever their respective origins, were deeply influenced by Samaritan Christian anti-Jewish teachings. These they found convenient to exploit in presenting Christianity to Gentile Christians and pagans in Ephesus.

What we call the "author of the Gospel of John" shows a particular interest in promulgating the belief that Jews who become followers of Jesus are disassociated from the rest of the Jewish people. To show that the Jewish followers of Jesus are not to consider themselves physically part of the Jewish national unit we look at an incident that is said to have taken place during Jesus' lifetime. The Johannine author writes: "His parents said this because they were afraid of the Jews; for the Jews had already agreed, that if anyone should confess him [Jesus] to be the Christ, he should be put out of the synagogue" (John 9:22). This is an anachronism. Exclusion of Jesus' followers from the synagogue never happened in the time of Jesus. This accusation is unsupported in the Synoptic

Gospels. (Later, Peter and Paul preached in the Temple and Paul preached in the Diaspora synagogues). Surely, the other evangelists would have included such incidents, had they heard of them. There is little doubt that such incidents of expulsion, if they had occurred in Jesus' day, would have circulated throughout the Christian communities and would have been incorporated into a number of New Testament texts other than the Gospel of John. In all, the author of John writes of three instances as if such an exclusion was indeed the case (John 9:22, 12:42, 16:2). The term *aposunagogos* "excluded from the synagogue" occurs only in these Johannine texts of the New Testament. The author is most likely responding to the exclusion of Jewish Christians of the Johannine community from the synagogue in the last decades of the first century. But, there is nothing to indicate that exclusion of Jewish Christians from the synagogue was a general rule at this time, although some of them probably already held beliefs that warranted excommunication.[24] Excommunication was the inevitable consequence of the ever growing theological differences between normative Judaism and the several Jewish Christian groups. There was also the problem of the blurring of the lines between Christians who were of Jewish ancestry and Christians of Gentile ancestry. Within a few centuries, those Christian groups whose members claimed to be descended from the first Jewish followers of Jesus were but an historical memory.

The practice of excommunication, itself, may be induced from the insertion of the *birkat ha-minim*, "benediction against the heretics," incorporated into the *Shemoneh Esrei*, about 90 C.E.[25] However, the New Testament evidence that there was a policy of exclusion of Jewish Christians is best explained on the local level. Action was not taken against them solely because they believed Jesus was the Messiah. The anachronism found at John 9:22 (see also John 16:2) alleging excommunication of Jesus' followers during his lifetime sanitizes the fact that this Johannine Christian community included Jews who had accepted various doctrines outside the norm of common Jewish belief.

The author of the Gospel of John mandates a Christian

separation from Jews and Judaism. John's Jesus speaks as if he were not a Jew. The author treats the Jews as if they are an alien people, having no connection with Jesus or his disciples. His phraseology shows detachment, as when he writes that "there was a feast of the Jews; and Jesus went up to Jerusalem" (John 5:1) and "Now the Passover of the Jews was at hand" (John 2:13, 6:4, 11:55).[26] He speaks in the third person of the religious rules of the Jews concerning purification (John 2:6), of a religious festival of the Jews (John 5:1), of the Festival of Tabernacles of the Jews (John 7:2), of the Day of Preparation of the Jews (John 19:42), and of the way in which Jews prepare a body for burial (John 19:40).

The author of John also wants to separate Jesus from the Jewish people and from Judaism. It is true that twice Jesus is called a Jew: by the Samaritan woman (John 4:9) and by Pilate (John 18:35). But in both instances, the term is used in its sense of "person of Judah," in contrast to a Samaritan and the Roman. The same applies in John 4:22, where Jesus responds to the Samaritan woman, "You [Samaritans] worship that which you do not know; we [Jews] worship that which we know, for salvation is from the Jews." These references must be understood from the perspective of John 1:11. There, Jesus is identified as a Jew, in the statement that he came to "his own country," but "his own people" did not receive him. Overall, the Gospel of John shows Jesus as no longer being a part of "the Jews." They reject him and he, in turn, rejects them because of their denying his claims. In his further dealings with them, Jesus appears as no longer a member of the Jewish people or its religion but speaks to the Jews as if he were a non-Jew. From its inception, the Fourth Gospel was never about a Jew, as such. As we shall now see, Jesus' Jewish connection is severed in every meaningful way.

The Johannine author's animosity reaches a particularly vicious level in the contrived dialogue of John 8. Hearing Jesus speak in the Temple, some Jews believe in him (John 8:30). To them, John's Jesus says that belief in him is the only way to truth and freedom (John 8:31-32). This subsection (verses 30-32) stands in contrast to verse 45, "But, because I speak the truth, you do not believe me." Verse 45 shows that the section of condemnation could not have been addressed to "the Jews who had believed in him" (verses 30-32). With that part of his audience who do not believe in him, Jesus continues a bitter dialogue. In John 8:32, Jesus says to those in the audience who accept him, "You shall know the truth, and the truth shall make you free." The audience, in general, misunderstands the direction of his statement and thinks he is speaking to the whole group. Therefore, they say to Jesus in verse 33 that as descendants of Abraham (*sperma*, literally, "seed," but also "offspring." "descendants") they have never been slaves.[27] In verse 37, John's Jesus acknowledges that the Jews are *sperma Abraam*, but in the following verses the author of John makes a crucial distinction between what he considers inferior physical descent and superior "spiritual" descent. "If you are of Abraham's children," Jesus says, "do the deeds of Abraham" (verse 39). The implication is that if the Jews are children of Abraham they should be doing his works, but by rejecting Jesus, the Jews show that they cannot be his children (verses 37, 40). A contrast is made between *sperma* ("descendants," that is, Torah-observant Jews) and *tekna* ("children" that is, the followers of Jesus). *Sperma* and *tekna* are not simply variant terms, each has a specific meaning. *Sperma* represents the external Law-observant followers of Judaism who have lost favor with God, while *tekna* represents those who have truly inwardly accepted the teachings of Jesus. The Jews are the physical descendants of Abraham, but not truly his children. John's Jesus makes a distinction between the deeds of the Jews and those of Abraham. The Jews do not do the deeds of Abraham and are therefore not his children. Instead, they must be doing the works of their real (still undetermined) father. In verse 41, the Jews assert that they have "one Father, God." In verse 42, Jesus rejects this claim, because they do not love him who was sent by God. In verse 43, Jesus alleges that the Jews do not understand him because they cannot hear him. The reason for this is explained in verses 44-47. As already mentioned, the author of John regards Jews who do not accept Jesus as their Messiah as degenerates and the most evil of all people; they are the very children of the devil.[28] Thus, John's Jesus addresses this Jewish crowd in the Temple as follows:

> You are of your father the devil, and you want to do the desires of your father. He was a murderer from the beginning and does not stand in the truth, because there is no truth in him. Whenever he speaks a lie, he speaks from his own nature; for he is a liar, and the father of lies.... He who is of God hears the words of God; for this reason you do not hear them, because you are not of God. (John 8:44-47)[29]

"The Jews" are controlled by and obedient to their father, the devil. Verse 44 is the most inflammatory statement about the Jews to be found in the Gospel of John. Jesus asserts, "you are of your father the devil." The Jews are separated from all that is good and holy. Divine sonship is denied them, Abrahamic sonship is refuted, and demonic sonship is attributed to them. Thus, the Jews are the devil's minions and allied with the demonic world. It is not their rejection of Jesus that links the Jews with the devil, but it is because they are already associated with the devil that they reject Jesus. Is there any question as to the meaning of this passage? The statements, "you are of the devil" and "you are not of God" do not lend themselves to a variety of interpretations. The author of the Gospel of John preaches absolute condemnation of the Jewish people. He encourages his audience to see Jews as unfaithful and Judaism as invalid and both as part of the forces of evil and darkness.

John's Jesus declares that the Jews never were the children of God, that they never believed or obeyed Him, that they have the devil as their father, and are of the devil. Having demonized the entire Jewish nation, Jesus now proceeds to disassociate himself from the Jewish people by stating that he was before Abraham (John 8:58) and thus is unrelated to "the Jews," being in existence before the progenitor of the nation. By speaking of "your Law" (John 8:17, 10:34) John's Jesus disassociates himself from the nation's law code[30] even while Matthew's Jesus claims to fulfill it (Matthew 5:17). Significantly, Jesus' remarks in John 8:17 ("Even in your Law it has been written, that the testimony of two men is true.") and 10:34 ("Has it not been written in your Law, 'I said you are gods'?") refer respectively to Deuteronomy 19:15 and Psalms 82:6, not to the Oral Law. Thus, "your Law" refers to the Mosaic Law and this is the law from which John's Jesus disassociates himself. Even when described as teaching within the totally Jewish milieu of the synagogue and the Temple, John's Jesus is portrayed as detached from "the Jews." This adds to the mood of anti-Jewish bias set by John's Gospel. It follows that, within the total framework of the Gospel of John, those Jews who accept Jesus cease to be Jews.

The author of John maintains that the Jews of the late first century could no longer be considered the children of Abraham. The Johannine Jesus says to those claiming Abrahamic descent, "If you are Abraham's children, do the deeds of Abraham.... You are of your father the devil, and you want to do the desires of your father" (John 8:39b, 44a). John thus echoes Paul's principle that mere physical descent from Abraham does not place an unbeliever among Abraham's spiritual offspring (Romans 9:6-8; Galatians 3:6-9, 4:21-31). The Jews of John's time who did not accept Jesus were no longer within the covenant. There is no explicit statement of supersession in John and no explanation of how it is that Christians have replaced Jews in the covenant, but there is no doubt that the author of the Gospel believed this to be the case. He did not so much argue for supersession as assume it. Salvation may have been from the Jews (John 4:22), but the Jews disbelieved and so separated themselves from God.

An expression of the Johannine author's antagonism toward the Jewish leadership of his own day is shown in his relatively frequent mention of the Pharisees as a distinct group (John 7:32, 47-48; 9:13, 15, 40; 11:46; 12:19). More than describing their influential role among the people at the time of Jesus his remarks are actually a response to their strengthened claims to leadership following the catastrophe of 70 C.E. His greatest hatred, however, is always directed toward the Jewish people for their continued disbelief in Jesus. For example, those who accuse Jesus before Pilate are no longer only the chief priests and the elders but also include "the Jews" in general (John 18:31, 19:7). When John's Jesus says to the non-Jew, Pilate, "If my kingdom were of this world, then my servants would be fighting, that I might not be delivered up to the Jews" (John 18:36), the target is the enemies of Jesus but does the author of John want us to believe that Pilate understood Jesus' words to mean specifically the Jewish leaders? Does the author of John expect his readers to understand that only the Jewish leaders are meant or did he intend that the phrase "the Jews" should be taken to mean the people as a whole? The verbal exchange between Pilate and Jesus is very telling. Pilate exclaims, "I am not a Jew, am I? *Your own nation* and the chief priests *delivered you up to me*" (John 18:35). In his response, Jesus places a different emphasis on events. "If my kingdom were of this world, then my servants would be fighting, that I might not be *delivered up to the Jews*" (John 18:36). The author of John, writing with the forethought of inflaming his audience, deliberately uses this contrived discussion between Jesus and Pilate to attack those Jewish people who did not follow Jesus. He uses the term "nation" to describe those who, with the chief priests, handed Jesus over to Pilate. For his part, the Johannine Jesus emphasizes that he was "delivered up to the Jews" not to Pilate, the Roman. These verses are a reminder that it is the Jews, not the Romans, who are to be held collectively guilty for Jesus' execution. It is not the Jewish authorities alone who the author of John condemns but the entire nation of Israel.

Some commentators maintain that John made use of the phrase "the Jews" as a literary device to eliminate the constant repetition of the words "high priests and Pharisees," but, in point of fact, it is the phrase "the Jews" which is used. These commentators expect the reader to be aware of the author's intention from merely reading the text. Yet, one may wonder whether brevity was the reason for this choice of words. When the author of John writes concerning the man blind from birth, it is the Pharisees who question the man (John 9:15-17), but it becomes "the Jews" who "did not believe" (verse 18). It is then reported that the former blind man's parents "feared the Jews" (John 9:22). Was there a need to substitute the term "the Jews" instead of "the Pharisees" in order to eliminate repetition? The purpose of the change was neither to eliminate repetition, nor for the sake of brevity, nor to give an understanding that the reader would know that "the Jews" did not refer to the entire people. It was a means, by simply inserting the term *the Jews* at a critical point in the story, of condemning the entire people of Israel.

In some of the Johannine conflict stories, the opponents of Jesus are identified as "Pharisees" at the beginning of the passage, but as the hostility intensifies, they become *hoi Ioudaioi* (John 9:13, 18 ff; 8:13, 22 ff.). What this change of phraseology does is provide a derogatory context for the word "Jew." In this way, the author extends the condemnation beyond the religious authorities to involve the whole Jewish people. An additional example that "the Jews" cannot simply be identified with the religious authorities is also seen in passages in which there is a similar change from *ochlos*, "crowd," to *hoi Ioudaioi*, "the Jews." In John 6:30 a non-belligerent "crowd" (6:24) asks for a sign so they "may see and believe," but by verse 41 (cf. 52), the "crowd" has become hostile and so is referred to as "the Jews." In the passion narrative, the "crowd" is always *hoi Ioudaioi* and it is always hostile. In substituting "the Jews" for the "crowd," the author of John accuses the whole Jewish people, and not just the authorities, for their hostility toward Jesus. The Johannine author is not interested in individual identities nor group affiliations. In fact, through his usage of "the Jews" he intentionally obliterates all identities and group affiliations and expresses indiscriminate hostility toward all Jews—those of Jesus' time, of his own time, and of future generations. For the author of John, the opponents of Jesus and of Christianity are all "the Jews" of all times and all places.

In truth, there is no convincing way of rendering the Johannine term *hoi Ioudaioi* as anything else than "the Jews," the physical Jewish people, whatever the context. It is "the Jews," the Jewish people actually and not as a theological abstraction that the Johannine author considers condemned, superseded, and supplanted by the new Israel, the church.

This author seeks to create an overwhelming aversion to the Jewish people and Judaism. Consequently, there pervades the

Gospel of John a constant harangue relentlessly directed against "the Jews," that is, the entire nation of Israel, and not toward any specific faction. For example, in order to demonstrate that "the Jews" are the persecutors of Jesus and oppressors of the church, the author of John writes:

> The man went away, and told the Jews that it was Jesus who had made him well. And for this reason the Jews were persecuting Jesus, because he was doing these things on the Sabbath. But he answered them, "My Father is working until now, and I myself am working." For this cause therefore the Jews were seeking all the more to kill him, because he not only was breaking the Sabbath, but also was calling God his own Father, making himself equal with God. (John 5:15-18)

> The Jews therefore were grumbling about him, because he said, "I am the bread that came down out of heaven." (John 6:41)

> But when his brothers had gone up to the feast, then he himself also went up, not publicly, but as it were, in secret. The Jews therefore were seeking him at the feast, and were saying, "Where is he?" And there was much grumbling among the multitudes concerning him; some were saying, "He is a good man"; others were saying, "No, on the contrary, he leads the multitude astray." Yet no one was speaking openly of him for fear of the Jews. (John 7:10-13)

> The Jews took up stones again to stone him. (John 10:31)

> So from that day on they planned together to kill him. Jesus therefore no longer continued to walk publicly among the Jews, but went away from there to the country near the wilderness, into a city called Ephraim; and there he stayed with the disciples. (John 11:53-54)

> As a result of this, Pilate made efforts to release him, but the Jews cried out, saying, "If you release this man, you are no friend of Caesar; every one who makes himself out to be a king opposes Caesar" (John 19:12)

> When therefore it was evening, on that day, the first day of the week, and when the doors were shut where the disciples were, for fear of the Jews, Jesus came and stood in their midst, and said to them, "Peace be with you." (John 20:19)

Passages such as these show the true target of the Johannine author's malevolence.

The author of John places Jesus' takeover of the Temple courtyard at the beginning of his public activity (John 2:14-15, cf. Mark 11:15-16, Matthew 21:12, Luke 19:45). Apparently, this restructuring of the chronological order of events in the life of Jesus is done to lessen the significance of the episode as a reason for his apprehension. In his depiction of events, the Johannine author does not want the Jewish authorities to use the Temple attack as a pretext for having Jesus arrested. This could lead to the question: What would be the Roman interest in Jesus' violent action? Placing the episode at the beginning of Jesus' public activity deflects its possible importance as a reason for his arrest years later. To explain his eventual arrest, the story of Lazarus (mentioned in no other Gospel) is introduced toward the end of Jesus' life as a means of explaining why the Jewish authorities sought his death and eventually had him executed:

> And when he had said these things, he cried out with a loud voice, "Lazarus, come forth." He who had died came forth, bound hand and foot with wrappings; and his face was wrapped around with a cloth. Jesus said to them, "Unbind him, and let him go." Many therefore of the Jews, who had come to Mary and beheld what he had done, believed in him. But some of them went away to the Pharisees, and told

> them the things that Jesus had done. Therefore the chief priests and the Pharisees convened a council, and were saying, "What are we doing? For this man is performing many signs. If we let him go on like this, all men will believe in him, and the Romans will come and take away both our place and our nation." But a certain one of them, Caiaphas, who was high priest that year, said to them, "You know nothing at all, nor do you take into account that it is expedient for you that one man should die for the people, and that the whole nation should not perish." . . . So from that day on they planned together to kill him. (John 11:43-53)

Fear is expressed for the safety of the nation, "If we let him [Jesus] go on like this" and his following increases, "the Romans will come and take away both our place and our nation." Caiaphas advises that "it is expedient for you that one man should die for the people, and that the whole nation should not perish" (see also John 18:14). The author of John (or a later interpolator) inserts his own commentary into the text. "Now this he did not say on his own initiative; but being high priest that year, he prophesied that Jesus was going to die for the nation; and not for the nation only, but that he might also gather together into one the children of God who are scattered abroad" (John 11:51-52). He attributes to the high priest a prophecy that Jesus died not only for the sake of the nation of Israel, but for all "the children of God": this results in the creation of the church.

It is maintained that the Jewish authorities sought Jesus' death out of fear of the repercussions, which would follow if the masses supported him. This support is said to be a result of his allegedly raising Lazarus from the dead. The reasons given in favor of apprehending Jesus are based on the Jewish leaders' personal fear for their religio-political position and their general fear for the nation's well-being. If they did not stop Jesus, Roman punishment of the Jewish people was inevitable. But, why would the Romans get involved if the masses were simply following a charismatic religious preacher who had nothing negative to say about them?

According to the Gospel of John, the Romans are not recorded as having made any demands concerning the apprehension of Jesus. Thus, the Romans are removed as an interested party seeking Jesus' life; this leaves only the "chief priests," the "Pharisees," and the "nation" as seeking his death. But, it is precisely this cover-up that exposes the extent of Roman interest and involvement. What the author of the Fourth Gospel describes as the high priest's fears only makes sense if there was a seditious element to Jesus' teachings and actions which was directed at the Romans. Disorder would result in decisive action by the Romans. Therefore, there is no reason why the high priest should not have regarded Jesus as a danger to the nation.

The behavior of the Jewish authorities suggested by the Johannine Gospel becomes intelligible only when it is recognized that they exercised authority by the grace of the Romans. It is only natural that the Jewish authorities should be sensitive to the inevitable consequences of the unrest Jesus was causing. They would be anxious to spare the people the suffering that a confrontation with the Romans would bring. The precautionary measures the Jewish authorities were said to take were inspired by the fear that Jesus' actions would provoke Roman reprisals against the people as a whole. Clearly, the Roman authorities were in control of the polity. The Jewish authorities were ever mindful of the pervasive power of their Roman overlords.

True to form, the author of John does not admit that the Romans sought to arrest Jesus, even though, in the end, it is a large contingent of their troops that apprehend him (John 18:12). Instead, he says the Jews planned to kill Jesus (John 11:53). He has the Jewish authorities anticipate Roman actions. But, again we must ask why would the Romans care about a benign Jewish religious preacher? Did not Pilate, himself, realize that the Jews had accused Jesus "out of envy" (Mark 15:10, Matthew 27:18)? Considering Jesus' subversive displays, a different picture appears. According to the Gospel of John, great consternation was shown by the Jewish authorities because the Romans must have demanded or were about to demand Jewish assistance in the apprehension and arrest of this specific rebel (John 11:47-50). Whether or not to hand over a fellow Jew to heathen authorities or have the nation suffer the consequences of noncompliance was the dilemma that needed to be dealt with. The author of John distorts this predicament in his narrative.

The author of the Gospel of John was careful not to mention the word "Roman" in describing those who arrested Jesus. However, a large-scale Roman presence can be deduced from the use of the Greek word *speira*, regularly used to render the Roman military term *cohors*, "cohort" (a cohort consisted of three hundred to six hundred men). The Johannine author indirectly indicates that the Romans were not only present but took a prominent role in apprehending Jesus. This is unlike the story found in the Synoptic Gospels, which gives no indication at all that there were Romans present. However, the evangelist emphasizes direct Jewish involvement. In particular, the Gospel of John is the only Gospel to explicitly involve the Pharisees in Jesus' arrest. It alone maintains that present at the arrest were "officers [*huperetas*] from the chief priests and the Pharisees" (John 18:3). It may be that the high priest, whose appointment and power were dependent upon the Roman administration, willingly or unwillingly, sent along "officers," or "servants." It is unclear who the "officers" or "servants" of the Pharisees were. In any case, Jewish involvement is blown out of proportion in comparison to that of the Romans. Yet, according to this same Gospel, it is a Roman cohort (*speira*), led by a Roman military officer (*chiliarchos*), that arrests Jesus (John 18:12); it is Pilate who condemns Jesus (John 19:16); it is Pilate who writes the charge of sedition on the cross (John 19:19); it is the Roman soldiers who crucify Jesus (John 19:23); it is Pilate alone who can give permission to remove the body from the cross for proper burial (John 19:38). It is the Roman imperial administration of Judea that sought Jesus' death and executed him.

Although, according to the Johannine account, Judas and Jewish officers (servants) accompanied Roman troops to arrest Jesus, the Roman administrative process was in control of the situation from beginning to end. A Roman *chiliarchos* could not have participated in a planned arrest without being ordered to do so by the Roman governor. Some argue that the author of John was referring to a Jewish force rather than a Roman one. However, he clearly distinguishes Roman troops from those sent by "the chief priests and the Pharisees" (John 18:3) or "of the Jews" (John 18:12) by using Roman military terminology. This shows the cohort is not Jewish or under the command of Jewish authorities.[31] The presence of the Roman troops, under a Roman commander, is a clear intimation that we are dealing here with a political rather than a religious offense. Romans would not have involved themselves in searching out a purely religious offender, since it was the general policy and the practice of the Roman authorities to respect local and especially Jewish autonomy in all cultural and religious affairs. Clearly, the Jesus movement was considered politically subversive. So, it was not in the best interests of nascent Christianity to blame Rome. They found a simple expedient: blame it on the Jews. Thus, the origin of the canard that it was the Jews who manipulated Roman concern over potential rebels and victimized Pilate with threats of denouncing him to the emperor. This falsehood is recorded in the New Testament as part of the general attack upon the Jews. And so, it helped establish the basis for Christian contempt and abuse of the Jews as an inherently evil people, the very children of Satan.

Of course, we must allow for a certain amount of Johannine exaggeration in order to show that it was the Jewish leaders, the representatives of the people, and not the Romans, who initiated the plan to kill Jesus and actively sought his death. Therefore, when Pilate asked, "What accusations do you bring against this man?" (John 18:29) they answered, "If this man were not an evildoer, we would not have delivered him to you" (John 18:30). Pilate, then, shows lack of interest in the case: "Take him yourselves, and judge him according to your law. The Jews said to him, 'We are not permitted to put anyone to death'" (John 18:31). Would the Jewish authorities remind a Roman prefect of the limitations of their legal powers, and would a Roman prefect need any such reminder? The passage reveals the religio-political intentions of the evangelist. The implication of this verbal exchange is that an individual whom the Jews consider an "evildoer" turns out to be someone who Pilate considers harmless. To the point, Pilate questions Jesus about a claim that he is "the king of the Jews" (John 18:33-37) although there is no mention of this accusation by the Jews. He finds Jesus not guilty (John 18:38, 19:4), scourges him (John 19:1), and then wants to let him go (John 19:4). In answer to a continued demand for his crucifixion Pilate says, "Take him yourselves, and crucify him, for I find no guilt in him" (John 19:6). The Jews respond, "We have a law, and by that law he ought to die because he made himself out to be the Son of God" (John 19:7). Pilate now learns that the actual charge leveled by "the Jews" against Jesus is his claim to be God's Son.[32] This is an issue that is of no interest to the Romans, but is inserted into the narrative in order to create a smokescreen around Pilate's real concern. Finally, by questioning Pilate's loyalty to the emperor (John 19:12), "the Jews" force him to give in to their demand and he reluctantly sentences Jesus to death. All four Gospels agree that the charge published at the execution was the claim that Jesus was the king of the Jews (Matthew 27:37, Mark 15:26, Luke 23:38, John 19:19). This is, indeed, what Pilate questioned Jesus about and for what he was condemned.

In relating Jesus' trial before Pilate the author of John wants to show that Jews who do not accept Jesus have forfeited all rights to being called the people of God. To accomplish this end he inserts a statement into his account similar in purpose to the fictive Matthean self-condemnation, "His blood be upon us and our children" (Matthew 27:25). He writes, "The chief priests answered, 'We have no king but Caesar'" (John 19:15b). This phrase, "We have no king but Caesar," is supposedly expressed by the chief priests *in their representative role* as spokesmen for "the Jews."

The message of Matthew 27:25 is that the acceptance by the Jewish crowd of the responsibility for Jesus' death confirms that God is taking away the kingdom from them. "Therefore I say to you, the kingdom of God will be taken away from you, and be given to a nation producing the fruit of it" (Matthew 21:43). There is a similar confirmation in John's account. "He who is of God hears the words of God; for this reason you do not hear them, because you are not of God" (John 8:47). John 19:15b is a product of Johannine creativity. This is another example of a Gospel reporting fictive events in order to show Christian supersession over "the Jews." The context is meant to give the impression that the statement is historical, but it is an impression that is not true. The explicit Jewish affirmation of loyalty to the emperor at the implicit expense of loyalty to God is a Johannine theological device. It is not necessary to show that the author of John, himself, composed this statement; the statement itself is patently false in what is supposed to be its most significant meaning. Its denigrating theological implications—the Jewish people abandoning God and, in turn, being abandoned by God—are proved false by history. Despite what the author of John affirms, there was no rejection of God's promises by the Jewish people, only the rejection of a false messiah, Jesus. Jesus failed to bring about the visible messianic signs like regathering the scattered exiles of Israel, universal peace, and prosperity.

Superficially, the effect of the statement, "We have no king but Caesar" may not seem as damaging to the Jewish people as the more infamous Matthean verse. However, its theological impact in shaping centuries of Christian thinking and attitudes toward the Jewish people, has been just as detrimental. Represented here are not Jews rejecting nationalistic movements and rebellions, Jews who preferred Roman rule to internecine struggles among Jews; rather Jews who reject God and his "son." This episode culminates the Johannine representation of Jewish attitudes toward Jesus first stated at the beginning of the Gospel, "He came to his own, and those who were his own did not receive him" (John 1:11).

The purpose in attributing a profession of loyalty to the emperor by the priests is not to address a political reality, but to nullify a theme that is found throughout God's relationship with the people of Israel. Isaiah 26:13 declares, "O Lord our God, other lords beside You have had dominion over us; only concerning You will we mention Your name." The eleventh benediction of the *Shemoneh*

Esrei, implores, "Reign over us, You, Lord, alone." The hymn, *Nishmat kawl chai*, proclaims, "Beside You, we have no king, redeemer, or savior." God's spiritual kingship need not exclude the reality of simultaneous earthly subjection to foreign rule; but the author of the Gospel of John is not interested in simply recording Jewish political loyalties. In Johannine phraseology, "We have no king but Caesar" is meant to express a Jewish rejection of God's spiritual rule through his messianic king. To the author of John, it is an inner loss of faith in the primacy of the rule of God that is manifest in the outward rejection of Jesus. Thus, the implication of this statement is nothing less than the total national abandonment of the messianic hope of Israel. According to the author of John, it is not Jesus alone who the Jews are rejecting; any claimant to the messianic office is excluded on the basis of the phrase, "We have no king but Caesar." Their repudiation of Jesus in the name of loyalty to the emperor, John goes on to say, entails their repudiation of not only the kingdom of God, but all that God promised Israel, and, indeed, the repudiation of God Himself. In turn, they are rejected of God. Their estrangement is complete. There is now a new heir to God's promise, the church.

To whom did Pilate turn Jesus over for crucifixion? John 19:16 states, "And so he then delivered him up to them to be crucified," the closest antecedent for "to them" is the "chief priests" at the end of John 19:15: "Pilate said to them, 'Shall I crucify your king?' The chief priests answered, 'We have no king but Caesar.'" A perusal of the Johannine passion narrative indicates that Roman soldiers executed Jesus. However, the reference back to the "chief priests" is not simply the result of an unclear writing style. The author's intent is to emphasize who is ultimately responsible for the crucifixion. It is only in John 19:23 that the text says, "The soldiers therefore, when they had crucified Jesus . . . ." The Johannine community knew that the Roman soldiers did the crucifying and the author of the Gospel of John is not interested in convincing them otherwise. But the emphasis of his message is on the culpability of the representatives of the Jewish people, the "chief priests," representing the national mood. The attack is more explicit in Luke's passion narrative. The antecedent for those to whom Pilate "turned Jesus over to their will" (Luke 23:25) is described as being "the chief priests and the rulers and the people" (Luke 23:13). The soldiers did the actual deed of crucifying Jesus but any culpability for their role is greatly modified. In the Johannine Gospel, as well, the chief priests and the nation of Israel have the greater sin; Pilate and his soldiers have a lesser sin. In their modified role the Romans are merely the instruments of the "the Jews:"

> The Jews therefore, because it was the day of preparation, so that the bodies should not remain on the cross on the Sabbath (for that Sabbath was a high day), asked Pilate that their legs be broken, and that they might be taken away. The soldiers therefore came, and broke the legs of the first man, and of the other man who was crucified with him; but coming to Jesus, when they saw that he was already dead, they did not break his legs; but one of the soldiers pierced his side with a spear, and immediately there came out blood and water. (John 19:31-34)

The soldiers' putative involvement, as narrated in these verses, is in order to fulfill Scripture. "For these things came to pass, that the Scripture might be fulfilled, 'Not a bone of him shall be broken.' And again another Scripture says, 'They shall look on him whom they pierced'" (John 19:36-37).

Why did the author of John, the most anti-Jewish of the Gospel authors, preserve traditions that implicate the Romans in the action against Jesus? The Johannine author's intention is strictly theological. There is a desire to remove the theological blame for the crucifixion as far as possible from the imperial authorities and to fix it firmly on the Jewish people by implicating the Jewish leadership. The evangelist's narrative establishes the notion of the ultimate responsibility of "the Jews" for the death of Jesus (John 19:1-16). A situation is described in which the Romans were compelled to execute Jesus at the insistence of "the Jews." According to the Fourth Gospel, Pilate's authority to execute Jesus was derived from "above" (John 19:11) but he was coerced into the deed by the Jewish rulers. The Jews, in the Johannine narrative, were acting as conscious agents of the devil while Pilate acted as the unconscious agent of God. Therefore, Pilate's authority over Jesus was given from above. The greater responsibility and the greater sin are thus placed on those who had delivered Jesus and demanded his execution (John 19:11-15). Jesus' comment, "he who delivered me to you has the greater sin," indicts Judas, but the implications of his words do not stop there. Judas' deed was but one part of the process by which Jesus' "own nation and the chief priests" handed him over to Pilate (John 18:30-31, 35). Therefore, according to the author of John, all Jews are held accountable for Jesus' crucifixion. The Romans executed Jesus, he claims, only because "the Jews" were forbidden by the Roman rulers from executing anyone (John 18:31). Anxious to have Jesus put to death, "the Jews" coerced Pilate into carrying out the deed against his will (John 19:12). As such, the Jews bear the greater burden of responsibility for Jesus' execution.

In spreading an aversion of Jews, the overall impression the author of the Fourth Gospel deliberately seeks to form is that Jews and Judaism are evil. As a result of the influence that this Gospel has had on Christendom and its attitude toward the Jewish people, its author shares in the responsibility for what has subsequently befallen the Jews by the hands of those influenced by the Gospel of John's anti-Judaism.

Notes

[1] See Eldon Jay Epp, "Anti-Semitism and the Popularity of the Fourth Gospel in Christianity." *Central Conference of American Rabbis Journal* 22 (Fall 1975), pp.35-57. Epp's conclusion is "that the Fourth Gospel, more than any other book in the canonical body of Christian writings, is responsible for the frequent anti-Semitic expressions by Christians during the past eighteen or nineteen centuries" (p. 35).

2. Epps remarks: "The sweeping anti-Jewish feelings expressed in the Fourth Gospel are not . . . historical with respect to Jesus and Jesus' time, though they are historical with respect to the Johannine author and his time; unfortunately, these anti-Jewish views have since been misunderstood by millions of Gentile Christians as representative both of Jesus' time and of Jesus' own attitude" (p. 52).

3. The plural term "the Jews" occurs 170 times in the New Testament. There are an additional twenty-five occurrences of the term in the singular, for a total of 195. The occurrences in all four Gospels total eighty-seven. Eighty occurrences are found in the Book of Acts and twenty-eight in the remaining New Testament writings.

4. The hostile uses of the term "the Jews" stand out prominently. Wayne Meeks comments: " . . . [It] is undeniable that in the Fourth Gospel 'the Jews' is generally used in an alien, even hostile sense, particularly in the notes, evidently by the hand of the evangelist, that 'the Jews persecuted Jesus' or 'sought to kill him,' and in the repeated phrase 'because of the fear of the Jews' (7:13, 9:22, 19:38, 20:19)." (Wayne Meeks, "'Am I a Jew?': Johannine Christianity and Judaism," in Jacob Neusner, Ed., *Christianity, Judaism and Other Greco-Roman Cults*, Leiden: E. J. Brill, vol. 1, 1975, p. 181) For a discussion of the various nuances of *hoi Ioudaioi*, see Reginald Fuller, "The 'Jews' in the Fourth Gospel," *Dialog* 16 (Winter 1977), p. 32. According to Fuller there are five different nuances of *hoi Ioudaioi*, three of which are neutral, one which functions both neutrally and polemically, and one (the focus of his article) which always functions polemically. See also Robert Bratcher. "'The Jews' in the Gospel of John," *The Bible Translator* 26 (1975), p. 409.

5. It has been said that the Gospel of John is an anti-Semitic document. A. Roy Eckardt observes: "The Gospel of John again and again makes indiscriminate, hostile judgments against '*the* Jews' as Jews, and this is what is meant by anti-Semitism. The article '*the*' is as decisive as the word 'Jews' or more so" (A. Roy Eckhardt, "The Nemesis of Christian Anti-Semitism," *Journal of Church and State* [Spring 1971], p. 233).

6. Rudolf Bultmann comments: "The Jews are spoken of as an alien people . . . ; Jesus himself speaks to them as a stranger and correspondingly, those in whom the stirrings of faith or of the search for Jesus are to be found are to be distinguished from 'the Jews,' even if they are themselves Jews (7:19, 8:17,

10:34)." (Rudolf Bultmann, *The Gospel of John*, Philadelphia: Westminster Press, 1971 [English translation], p. 86)

7   Raymond Brown has written that the Johannine author's attitude toward "the Jews" encompasses all Jews collectively and that it cannot be reduced to some smaller Jewish group such as the "Jewish authorities" or the "Judeans" (Raymond Brown, *The Community of the Beloved Disciple*, New York: Paulist Press, 1979, p. 41). Brown is of the opinion that the author's antipathy to the Jews may have arisen from many factors, including the presence of Samaritans among the early Johannine community, the role that some of the religious authorities played in the death of Jesus, and the expulsion of Christians from some synagogues toward the end of the century (*Ibid*. pp. 40-43). According to Brown, the acceptance into the Johannine community of a group of anti-Temple Jews and Samaritan converts who influenced the groups particular Christology led to the community's expulsion from the larger Jewish community. The theology of these newcomers, Brown believes, was based not on a Davidic but on a Mosaic background. It understood Jesus in terms of "descent from above" and "pre-existence." Therefore, they alleged that Jesus had been with God, had seen God, and had brought down God's words to the people (cf. John 3:13, 31; 5:20; 6:46; 7:16; 6:32-35). Brown remarks: "The acceptance of the second group catalyzed the development of a high, pre-existence Christology, which led to debates with Jews who thought that the Johannine community was abandoning Jewish monotheism by making a second God out of Jesus (Brown, *Community*, p. 166). The reaction of the local Jewish leadership to this new Christology, Brown concludes, was to expel the Johannine Christians from the synagogue.

Brown suggests that the hostile Johannine usage of "the Jews" may have been "borrowed from the Samaritans on whose lips (as non-Jews) it would have been quite natural." He notes that the hostility in John's Gospel immediately increases after John 4 (p. 40). This section of the Gospel alleges a friendly encounter between Jesus and Samaritans. (See pp. 43 ff. for a brief overview of Samaritan theology). The Christology of the Gospel of John reflects a polemic with Samaritanism that was later incorporated into a polemic with "the Jews."

8   Reginald Fuller maintains that the Johannine author made a threefold polemical alteration in his pre-Gospel tradition: he changed the designation

of Jesus' opponents to "the Jews"; he reinterpreted the issues between Jesus and his opponents "in explicitly Christological terms"; and he gave the hostility between them an "unprecedented and unparalleled bitterness" (Reginald Fuller, "The 'Jews' in the Fourth Gospel," *Dialog* 16 [Winter 1977] p. 35)

9. The Johannine representation of Jesus as a Messiah is non-Davidic in nature. In the Gospel of John, Jesus, "the Christ," is not a royal figure of the house of David. There is no Davidic connection made and the term "son of David" does not occur at all. The only mention of the name David occurs in words put in the mouth of some of the crowd who raise the question about "the Christ" coming from Galilee. But, the author does not press a case for Jesus being the Messiah based on Davidic descent or birth in Bethlehem. There is nothing whatsoever in the Gospel of John that would lead the reader to suppose that Jesus was born in Bethlehem. Jesus is from Galilee, a fact that this Gospel has made clear from the beginning.

10. Paul may already have assimilated this negative use of the term into his own preachings (1 Thessalonians 2:14-15).

11. There are a number of studies relating the Gospel of John to Samaria and the Samaritans, and to the form of Christianity which developed in the pre-Gospel period in Samaria. Examples are: John Bowman, "The Fourth Gospel and the Samaritans," *Bulletin of the John Rylands Library*, 40 (1958), pp. 298-308; George W. Buchanan, "The Samaritan Origin of the Gospel of John," *Religions in Antiquity: Essays in Memory of E.R. Goodenough*, Ed., Jacob Neusner, Leiden: E.J. Brill, 1968, pp. 149-175; Edwin D. Freed, "Samaritan Influence in the Gospel of John," *Catholic Biblical Quarterly*, 30 (1968), pp. 580-597; Edwin D. Freed, "Did John Write the Gospel of John Partly to Win Samaritan Converts?" *Novum Testamentum*, 12 (1970), pp. 241-256; Wayne E. Meeks, "Galilee and Judea in the Fourth Gospel," *Journal of Biblical Literature*, 85 (1966), pp. 159-169; James D. Purvis, "The Fourth Gospel and the Samaritans," *Novum Testamentum*, 17 (1975), pp.161-198; Charles H.H. Scobie, The Origins and Development of Samaritan Christianity," *New Testament Studies*, 19 (1972-73), pp. 390-414.

12. John 4:5-42 describes the positive acceptance Jesus allegedly found among the Samaritans. In John 4:25 the woman expresses the Samaritans' messianic expectation as defined in Deuteronomy 18:15-18. She says to Jesus, "I know that Messiah is coming (he who is called Christ); when that one comes, he will declare all things to us." Jesus responds, "I who speak to you am he"

(John 4:26). The usual Jewish term "Messiah" is put in the mouth of the Samaritan woman. (Jesus readily accepted the messianic title from this Samaritan woman, but he is equivocal before Pilate when the Roman governor asked if he was "king of the Jews" [John 18:33-37].) Do Samaritan proselytizing considerations influence this dialogue with its Davidic intimation? Samaritans did not accept the Davidic monarchy; therefore, the Samaritan woman must have meant by "Messiah" someone other than the anointed king of the House of David. The author of John substitutes *Messias* for the word a Samaritan would use, namely, *Taheb*. The *Taheb* (or, *Shaheb*), the "Restorer," is another Moses whose task is to restore true belief in God and the true worship of God. The belief in the coming of the *Taheb* is based on the promise found in the Samaritan tenth commandment and on Deuteronomy 18:15 and 18. As with Moses, he is to be a prophet who will come out of the tribe of Levi. For the Samaritans there could be no prophet after Moses except the one like him that was promised. (Much of the information concerning the *Taheb* comes from very late sources. What is clear is that the Mosaic prophet concept of Deuteronomy forms the core belief. This much is early, however, while other features may be the result of Jewish and/or Christian influence.) In the Gospel of John, several times Jesus is revealed as "the prophet" who was expected (so 6:14, cf. 4:19, 9:17, "a prophet"), while also identifying him with the "Christ" (7:40-41). The Johannine story reflects the missionary work of Philip and other proto-Christians among the Samaritans (Acts 8:5-25). The Christian church that developed in Samaria must have argued that Jesus was the *Taheb*, the expected prophet. But, instead of reconstituting worship on Mount Gerizim as the Samaritans believed would happen (See, John Macdonald, *The Theology of the Samaritans*, Philadelphia: The Westminster Press, 1964, p. 365.) Jesus had declared that no temple, whether on Mount Gerizim or Jerusalem, was necessary to worship God (John 4:21).

13. Passages in the Gospels and Acts which place the disciples in either Jerusalem or Galilee in the postresurrection period may show that a more or less distinct Galilean-Samaritan center developed with its own theological outlook alongside the Jerusalem center. Such differentiation would explain many aspects of the Johannine theology and Stephen's speech (Acts 7).

14. According to the Gospel of John, the Samaritans ask Jesus to stay with them. He consents to stay for two days. "And many more [Samaritans] believed

because of his word; and they were saying . . . '[W]e believe for we have heard for ourselves and know that this one is indeed the savior of the world'" (John 4:41-42). "Savior" is a title ascribed to Moses (and therefore to the eschatological prophet, the *Taheb*) by Samaritan teaching (See, Macdonald, *The Theology of the Samaritans*, pp. 147-222.) as well as Acts 7.

15. Josephus writes that Samaria was a traditional haven for Jews who had been at odds with Judaism. Perhaps, what he said of an earlier time (late third century B.C.E.) still applied in the formative years of Christianity: "And, whenever anyone was accused by the people of Jerusalem of eating unclean food or violating the Sabbath or committing any other such sin, he would flee to the Shechemites [that is, Samaritans], saying that he had been unjustly expelled [variant, "accused"]." (*Jewish Antiquities* XI. 8. 7 [346].)

16. The only explicit statement in the Gospels that may be construed as showing a negative feeling toward Samaritans, by the author himself or the Jesus he is presenting in his narrative, is found in the Gospel of Matthew. The Matthean Jesus instructs the twelve disciples, saying, " . . . [D]o not enter any city of the Samaritans" (Matthew 10:5). In the Gospel of Luke, there is a more favorable attitude shown toward Samaritans. Jesus "set his face to go to Jerusalem; and he sent messengers on ahead of him. And they went, and entered a village of the Samaritans, to make arrangements for him. And they did not receive him, because he was journeying with his face toward Jerusalem" (Luke 9:51-53). The author of Luke is careful to show that the Samaritan villagers rejected Jesus and his disciples solely because they were going to Jerusalem. They do not reject his person or message. Thus, Jesus' reaction to Samaritan rejection is different than that shown toward Jewish rejection. He expresses a negative reaction toward Jewish "cities" which reject him (Luke 10:10-15) for whom "it will be more tolerable in that day for Sodom, than for that city" (verse 12) and who "will be brought down to Hades" (verse 15). But, "when his disciples James and John" say to him, "Lord do you want us to command fire to come down from heaven and consume them [the Samaritan villagers]?" he "rebuked them [James and John]" (Luke 9:54-55). Jesus and his disciples then "went on to another village" (verse 56). The impression is that it was another Samaritan village, one more receptive. In this way, the author of Luke shows a contrast between Jewish faithlessness and the more receptive Samaritan attitude toward Jesus. The negativity shown by some Samaritans toward Jesus results from cultic differences (that

is, by Samaritan rejection of Jerusalem as a religious center) but not hostility to Jesus himself.

17 Apparently, Christian communities differed as to whom Jesus included in the term, "house of Israel." Used in the Gospel of Matthew, it includes the Jewish inhabitants of Judea and Galilee, but excludes the Samaritan population of Samaria: "Those twelve Jesus sent out after instructing them, saying, 'Do not go in the way of the Gentiles, and do not enter any city of the Samaritans; but rather go to the lost sheep of the house of Israel'" (Matthew 10:5-6).

18 It is Philip (John 1:43-48, 6:5-7, 12:21-22, 14:8-9), who first tells Nathanael of Jesus: "Philip found Nathanael, and said to him, 'We have found him whom Moses in the Law [a reference to Deuteronomy 18:15, 18] and also the Prophets wrote, Jesus of Nazareth, the son of Joseph'" (John 1:45). There is no mention of this Jesus being of Davidic descent. The "son of Joseph," in all likelihood, serves to establish a connection between Jesus and the Samaritans through some sort of common descent. Jesus is the son of Joseph, and so are the Samaritans the sons of Joseph, through Ephraim and Manasseh.

It may be that Samaritan Christianity was, in part, rooted in the preaching of John the Baptist. According to John 3, "John also was baptizing in Aenon ["Spring"] near Salim . . . and they [people] were coming and were being baptized" (John 3:23). If Salim and Aenon are located in Samaria as some believe, it shows that John had a limited following in that region. Some may later have been attracted to Samaritan proto-Christianity.

In its formative period the Samaritan Christian community was probably connected with Stephen and Philip (cf. Acts 7-8). There are a number of similarities between Samaritan teachings and the teachings found in John and in Stephen's speech. Most notable is their negative attitude toward a Davidic Messiah and their favorable treatment of northern Israelite tradition at the expense of Judahite tradition.

19 One such group, of which Stephen was a member, settled among the proto-Jewish Christian community of Jerusalem and were referred to as "Hebrews."
20 Macdonald, *The Theology of the Samaritans*, pp. 328-330.
21 Perhaps, as originally promulgated in Samaritan Christian tradition, Jesus' "realm" was in this world albeit in Samaria, not in Judah. Then the change to

a "kingdom not of this realm" would be due to the politico-theological needs of a later redactor.

22 The Lucan version states: "Blessed is the king who comes in the name of the Lord; peace in heaven and glory in the highest!" (Luke 19:38).

23 Samaria may have been the territory entrusted to the apostle John in that distribution of responsibilities which assigned Paul and Barnabbas to the Gentiles and James, Peter, and John to the circumcised" (Galatians 2:7-9). "Circumcised" could refer to Samaritans as well as Jews.

24 See Asher Finkel, "Yavneh's Liturgy and Early Christianity," *Journal of Ecumenical Studies*, 1981, pp. 231-250.

25 *Shemoneh Esrei*, "Eighteen [Benedictions]," is the principal Jewish prayer (also known as *tefillah*, "prayer," or *amidah*, "standing"). The *Bet Din* (rabbinical court) in Yavneh, under the leadership of the *Nasi*, Rabban Gamaliel II, inserted a nineteenth benediction directed against the sectaries (*birkat ha-minim*). This occurred some time after the destruction of the Second Temple. *Minim* is a Hebrew designation for adherents of any type of sectarian Judaism. Heretics endangered the spiritual continuity of Israel. There was a need to prevent them from leading Jewish worship and introducing heretical ideas into the prayers. It was a period in which heretical Jewish sectaries, not clearly differentiated from their fellow Jews, took advantage of the chaos in Jewish life following the Temple's destruction. They attempted to persuade Jews to join their respective groups. The rabbis saw this sectarian splintering as a threat to the survival of the Jewish people.

26 A Samaritan might express himself in this manner concerning dates of festivals set in accordance with Jewish calendric reckoning.

27 Either this supposed Jewish crowd is ignorant of Israel's experience with slavery in Egypt or the author of this Gospel tale is.

28 The word translated "devil," is from the Greek, *diabolos*, literally "slanderer." In the New Testament, it is used synonymously with the word "Satan," which is a transliteration of the Hebrew word *Satan*, literally "adversary," "accuser."

29 Commenting on the impact of this passage Geza Vermes writes, "Here is the origin of the Christian tendency to demonize the Jews, the source of all mediaeval and much modern religious anti-Judaism, which directly or indirectly led to the Holocaust." (Geza Vermes, *The Religion of Jesus the Jew*, Minneapolis, Mn.: Fortress Press, 1993, p. 213)

30 Using the expression "your law" is characteristic of Gentiles when referring to Jewish Law (See John 18:31 for Pilate and Acts 18:15 for Gallio.).

31 There are occasions in Josephus' works where he uses Roman military terms for non-Roman troops (*Jewish Wars* II. 1. 3 [11]; *Jewish Antiquities* XVII. 9. 3 [215]) but that is not the case here. The Johannine distinction between the two groups shows that the arresting party is divided into Roman and Jewish contingents. The Roman troops were not Jewish, but were most likely not ethnic Romans either.

32 The Johannine narrative gives no indication that Pilate was familiar with the case against Jesus prior to his being brought before him by the Jewish authorities. Thus, "Pilate therefore went out to them, and said, 'What accusation do you bring against this man?'" (John 18:29). Yet, he disregards their accusations and questions Jesus about his claim to being a king. Pilate would not be concerned about someone claiming to be a god's son. Gods visiting earth in human guise and siring children by human females was a familiar claim in Hellenistic religion (See Paul's and Barnabas' reception at Lystra: "And when the multitudes saw what Paul had done, they raised their voice, saying in the Lycaonian language, 'The gods have become like men and have come down to us.' And they began calling Barnabas, Zeus, and Paul, Hermes, because he was the chief speaker"—Acts 14:11-12.).

9.
THE BOOK OF REVELATION

In the Book of Revelation, there are seven letters to seven churches supposedly written by the heavenly Jesus. They appear as Revelation 2:1 through 3:22. In each letter, the angel (messenger) of the specific church is addressed and, in turn, the church members are told that Jesus knows who they are and he knows the level of their spirituality. We are concerned here with letters two (2:8-11) and six (3:7-13).

In Revelation 2:9, Jesus is said to have written, "I know your tribulation and your poverty (but you are rich), and the blasphemy by those who say they are Jews and are not, but are a synagogue of Satan." In Revelation 3:9, Jesus is said to have written, "Behold, I will cause those of the synagogue of Satan, who say that they are Jews, and are not, but lie—behold, I will make them to come and bow down at your feet, and to know that I have loved you." Jews who do not accept Christianity are characterized as worshipers of Satan, hence, the expression "synagogue of Satan."

According to Paul's definition of a "true" Jew, "he is not a Jew who is one outwardly; neither is circumcision that which is outward in the flesh; but he is a Jew who is one inwardly; and circumcision is that which is of the heart, by the spirit, not by the letter; and his praise is not from men, but from God" (Romans 2:28-29). That is, the Pauline notion of a "true" Jew refers to Jews and Gentiles who follow Paul's concept of submission to belief in Jesus, not adherence to the Torah. Jews by birth or choice who do not believe in Jesus as Lord and Savior are classified as Jews of the "flesh" not "true" spiritual Jews. The author of Revelation declares that Jews of the "flesh" who do not become "true" Jews (that is, Christians) worship Satan and are destined to someday be subdued and will come to bow down at the feet of Jesus' beloved church. Is it any wonder that the expression "synagogue of Satan" in combination with John 8:44, where "the Jews" are characterized as descended from Satan, helped produce a portrait of the "evil" Jew whose deeds on behalf of Satan took on ominous proportions? Is it any wonder that the church and its faithful followers sought to hasten the day when Jesus would fulfill his promise to "make them [the synagogue of Satan] come and bow down at your feet" (3:9) by their persecution of the Jews?

10.
WHAT HAPPENED TO THE DISCIPLES FOLLOWING THE DEATH OF JESUS?

PART 1

Jesus, toward the end of his life, left his native Galilee and journeyed to Jerusalem for the Passover festival. There, in the final week of his life, he drew attention to himself through the manner of his entry into the city and the scene he caused on the Temple Mount. What transpired following these two incidents is obscured by Christian theological and political concerns. But, it is apparent that the Romans moved against him and demanded assistance from the chief priests who were in charge of maintaining order. Arrested around the time of the Passover festival,[1] allegedly tried before the Sanhedrin,[2] or perhaps only interrogated by a high priest,[3] Jesus, it is said, was handed over to Pilate by the Jewish authorities. He crucified him for sedition, following a Roman trial.

But, what happened to Jesus' disciples following the crucifixion? The sole source for the information concerning the disciples in this period is the highly edited fragmentary account found in the *Book of Acts of the Apostles*. Acts is a religio-political apologetic work of the mid-80s of the first century, not a true history of the church. In this context of the postcrucifixion period, the Romans are not even mentioned by name. Their role in the death of Jesus is glossed over. It is the Jews, and the Jews alone who are accused of being responsible for Jesus' death.

The reliability of Acts as an historical documentation of the early church is questionable. Unfortunately, it is only this book that claims to provide a continuous record for the Jerusalem proto-Christian community in the years following the crucifixion of Jesus. Consequently, there is little to compare to this recognizably faulty record. We, out of necessity, must work with it. In the aftermath of the first Roman-Jewish War, which left Jerusalem desolate, the Gentile church mythologized the original community of Jesus' followers associated with that city. The description of its teachings following the death of Jesus was adjusted to agree with the emerging Gentile church. Whether the antebellum Jerusalem church actually gave up its overt bellicose views or sublimated its true intentions in order to save itself from Roman ire is not clear. There are indications that, at least, some of Jesus' disciples and their followers never completely gave up on the idea of seizing religio-political power.

The author of Acts does not give a true picture of the Jerusalem church and probably did not know much to begin with. What may be said with some certainty is that there existed a Jewish sect that acknowledged Jesus as Messiah. From them, later Gentile Christianity derived some of its beliefs and practices. It had no notion of virginal conception nor a trinitarian doctrine. It simply saw Jesus as a man sent and endowed by God to be the Messiah. They proclaimed their dead leader was alive in heaven and directing events on earth in the capacity of the Messiah they claimed him to be. At this point in time, they were still within the Jewish fold despite their sectarian teachings. By the first quarter of the second century, they absorbed some beliefs from Gentile Christianity while still adhering to some aspects of the Torah. This brought about a separation between themselves and the main body of the Jewish people. Their syncretic practices also caused a break with Gentile Christianity and they were soon viewed as heretical by the mainstream Gentile dominated church.[4]

What developed under the influence of the Gentile church was the birth of a new religion distinct from Judaism. Overall, the nature of what is called Jewish Christianity and the identity of its adherents are problems in the history of early Christianity. Groups identified by patristic writers of the third and fourth centuries as Jewish Christians also included sects of Gentile Judaizers. Which sects, if any, were descendants of Jesus' early Jewish followers are unclear. Within a few centuries, they all disappeared.

According to the Book of Acts' tendentious retelling of the aftermath of the crucifixion, neither the Roman nor Jewish authorities sought to apprehend Jesus' followers. It is maintained that they did not flee, but remained in Jerusalem (Luke 24:47-53, Acts 1:4). By contrast, the other Gospels place the disciples in Galilee shortly after the crucifixion (Mark 16:7, 15; Matthew 28:10, 16, 19; John 21:1). If, for the sake of argument, one accepts Acts' description of events, there are a number of questions that need to be raised.

Why was there no attempt by either Jews or Romans to pursue and detain any of Jesus' disciples immediately following the crucifixion? Why were they allowed freedom of movement and assembly? Perhaps Pilate and/or the Jewish authorities thought that without their erstwhile leader the group would quickly dissolve. Or, perhaps the answer lies in a variant tradition recorded in the Gospel of John that Jesus agreed to surrender, but called upon his would-be captors to allow his followers to go free: "Again therefore he [Jesus] asked them, 'Whom do you seek?' And they said, 'Jesus the Nazarene.' Jesus answered, 'I told you that I am he; if therefore you seek me, let these go their way'" (John 18:7-8). This variant tradition explains why the disciples were not arrested with Jesus. This is more than likely the Johannine authors own imaginative contribution to explain why the disciples were not also seized immediately or hunted down afterward. However, its contention must be considered.

Surely, when the arresting party was given its orders, the person, claims, and actions of Jesus himself were not the only concern; the disciples were his closest followers and assisted him in the announcement of his kingship: "And as he was approaching, near the descent of the Mount of Olives, the whole multitude of the disciples began to praise God joyfully with a loud voice for all the miracles which they had seen" (Luke 19:37). Moreover, that they could be violent in their own right, is seen from Peter's sword attack on the high priest's servant (John 18:10). This incident follows immediately after John's Jesus has lain down the condition that his disciples are to be allowed to go free before he surrenders. For whatever reason, there is no attempt to seize the servant's attacker, despite the violent assault. Only Jesus is arrested. The Romans are satisfied to crucify Jesus alone. This occurred at the Passover season, a potentially volatile time, and suggests that Pilate wanted to make an example through swift cruel punishment. Having accomplished his goal, Pilate may have decided there was no further need to pursue the rest of the fugitive band.

If, as the Gospels state, Pilate really thought Jesus was innocent, then one can easily infer he was not interested in pursuing Jesus' followers. Yet, the Gospels claim "the Jews" viciously opposed Jesus and his teachings. Would they not also be concerned that his followers could present a potential problem? Would they not pressure Pilate to pursue these enemies of Caesar, as well, and finish the task? Were the Jewish authorities afraid of the people they had allegedly deftly manipulated on Passover eve? If so, why did they not silence the disciples surreptitiously, if outright confrontation was impossible? It might be contended that the Jewish authorities also expected the dissolution of the group once their leader was removed from the scene. In the short run, this might have been their assumption. However, according to Luke-Acts, the disciples continued to proclaim Jesus as Messiah right there in Jerusalem, but now added resurrection, salvation, and belief in Jesus. Under these circumstances, why is it that the Jewish leaders did not immediately act against them? This lack of action is especially surprising when we consider that on Pentecost, alone (approximately fifty days after the crucifixion), it is claimed that three thousand individuals were baptized in Jerusalem: "So then, those who had received his word were baptized; and there were added that day about three thousand souls" (Acts 2:41). The baptizing of three thousand individuals in one day, in Jerusalem, must have created quit a commotion. There were many *mikvaot*, "ritual baths," available in Jerusalem, but this baptizing "in the name of Jesus" would surely draw the negative attention of the authorities.

The lack of action by the Jewish authorities toward Jesus' followers, for some time after his death, is explicable only if they were never enthusiastic about apprehending him or them in the first place. On the other hand, Pilate's actions are understandable if he was concerned with apprehending Jesus for political reasons. He ordered Jesus' execution because Jesus declared himself king of the Jews. Pilate must have seen Jesus as a religious fanatic and would-be king who posed a particular threat. Through his words and actions, he was stirring up anti-Roman feelings among the Passover pilgrims who might easily get out of control. This was of great concern to Pilate. Jesus had no sizable following, but could have expected to raise an army from among the Passover pilgrims. They would become the human agents of God's planned intervention, their aim to overthrow Roman governance of Judea. Once Pilate swiftly dealt with this troublemaker, he probably did not consider those who assisted Jesus in his Temple attack to be a serious threat. Reminding them of what seditionists could expect, Pilate made his brutal point to the pilgrim throngs. Having done this, he chose not to pursue the matter by attempting to apprehend those who followed Jesus. They were most likely considered rendered impotent without their charismatic leader. It is even conceivable that Pilate had made a concession to the religious authorities in exchange for their help in subduing this seditionist. Consequently, Pilate did not pursue the disciples or unleash the usual Roman practice of indiscriminant slaughter of the populace.

According to Mark 14:50 and Matthew 26:56, Jesus' disciples fled when Jesus was arrested. The Lucan version does not say anything about them fleeing, but does say they were prepared to resist the arresting party (Luke 22:49). The Gospel of John maintains that rather than fleeing, the disciples were allowed to go free because Jesus negotiated their freedom (John 18:8). In any case, Jesus' followers were not pursued; the eleven disciples fled or were let go at the time of Jesus' arrest. There is no mention of any attempt to arrest Jesus' followers. The closest one comes to such a claim is when, following the crucifixion, the disciples have the doors of the place where they were staying shut "for fear of the Jews" (John 20:19). Yet, there was nothing to fear; the Jews do not seek them out. In fact, nothing is said about any plans to arrest Jesus' followers.

If they so desired, the authorities could have found cause to arrest Jesus' followers. The disciples were known to have consorted with a convicted seditionist and could have been arrested on suspicion of grave robbing. Yet, according to the Gospels and Acts, neither the Jewish nor Roman authorities used either of these charges as a pretext for arresting them. It is claimed that the guards allegedly watching Jesus' place of burial came to Pilate with the story that the disciples stole the body (Matthew 28:11-15). Nevertheless, the disciples were not arrested and tortured by the Romans to elicit confessions.[5] Perhaps Paul's words, spoken years later, explain why the Romans did nothing: "We preach Christ crucified, to Jews a stumbling block, and to Gentiles foolishness" (1 Corinthians 1:23). Pilate, on hearing that the crucified seditionist's followers were claiming Jesus was resurrected and that he then ascended to a heavenly throne, there to await the time of his return to earth in order to establish an earthly kingdom, would have dismissed the report as foolishness. Laughable and harmless, so long as the disciples left their claim as being spiritual and not temporal.

Why did neither the Jews nor the Romans attempt to arrest the disciples if they thought that Jesus and his teachings were dangerous? Is it because the author of Luke-Acts has fabricated his story? Only the author of Luke-Acts has the disciples remaining in Jerusalem after the crucifixion (Luke 24:47-53, Acts 1:4; cf. Mark 16:7, 15; Matthew 28:10, 16, 19; John 21:1). He writes that Jesus' followers did not leave Jerusalem following Jesus' execution. Instead, they established a small community of those who believed him to be the Messiah and remained in the city to await his return and the establishment of the kingdom of God. If they did leave Jerusalem and return to Galilee, as mentioned by the other evangelists, there is no information available on when and how they returned and established themselves in the city.

It is most likely that following their disavowing complicity in Jesus' sedition (Mark 14:66-71, Matthew 26:69-74, Luke 22:57-60, John 18:15-17) the disciples fled in fear of arrest. They are not present at his execution nor do they bury him. Most of the twelve disciples are never heard of again as individuals except in later legends devised to explain their absence from the Book of Acts. Except for listing their names as being present in the "upper room" (Acts 1:13), the author of Luke-Acts, who maintains the twelve disciples did not leave Jerusalem following Jesus' crucifixion, does not mention most of them again. Their fate is unknown.

Sometime after the death of Jesus, a few of the disciples are said to be in Jerusalem. Later, the proto-Christian community came under the leadership of James, the brother of Jesus. His early connection to the Jesus movement is unclear. However, the first mention of his presence (by a fleeing Peter), "Report these things to James and the brethren" (Acts 12:17), shows that he was an important figure in the group. He was probably chosen to lead the sect because he was the brother of Jesus. Acts of the Apostles tells us very little about only a few of the Apostles. It concentrates its efforts on Paul and his missionary work. Acts does not even mention that James is the brother of Jesus!

Christians in the late first century were trying to give the impression that the kingdom to be established by Jesus is not to be established by earthly means like the kingdoms of the world. John 18:36 ("My kingdom is not of this world") is meant to show the Romans that Christians were not political revolutionaries intent on overthrowing the Roman Empire. This verse reflects the Christian apologists' concern in the post-70 period to disassociate Christians from any suspicion of political messianism (cf. Matthew 26:52-53). Yet, in the 30's and 40's of the first century C.E. did all the disciples abandon thoughts of a violent overthrow of Roman hegemony over the Land of Israel? No definitive answer can be given. Jesus' own insurrection is covered-up by the author of Luke-Acts and it is more than likely that he simply extended his disingenuous description of events to the postcrucifixion period as well. Whatever its historical validity, it appears from the Book of Acts that the Jerusalem based post-crucifixion Jesus movement adopted a new policy shortly after the collapse of Jesus' insurrection: There would be no physical confrontation with Rome. They maintained that the executed Jesus had been resurrected and now dwells in heaven and would soon return to bring about the kingdom of God. Their armed participation was not needed.

The author of Acts records that shortly after the crucifixion Jesus' followers preached openly and no action, whatsoever, was taken against them. The church's first recorded postresurrection public debut is said to be on *Shavuot* ("Pentecost"), the "Feast of Weeks" (Acts 2:1ff.). In the weeks that followed, the proto-Christian movement met regularly on the Temple grounds. There, it is claimed, they publicly worshiped and preached and gained new converts every day (Acts 2:46-47). Apparently, in constant expectation of Jesus' return, the proto-Christian community suspended their direct political agitation against Rome. Instead, they concentrated their condemnation on the priestly authorities, while at the same time sought to increase the numbers of their adherents (Acts 5:12-42). Within a short time, we are told, they made more converts than Jesus ever did during his lifetime. About three thousand Jews are said to have joined the Jesus movement at the behest of Peter's first sermon. The author of Acts reports, "So then, those who had received his word were baptized; and there were added that day about three thousand souls" (Acts 2:41). In the days following Peter's first sermon, it is claimed that individuals joined the group on a daily basis (Acts 2:47). Following Peter's second major sermon, the number of Jews added to the church brought the total to about five thousand converts (Acts 4:4). It is maintained that the church population in Jerusalem exploded. The author of Acts writes, "And all the more believers in the Lord, multitudes of men and women, were constantly added" (Acts 5:14) and that "the number of disciples continued to increase greatly in

Jerusalem" (Acts 6:7). The number of new adherents is most likely exaggerated. Nevertheless, even if one takes the figures given seriously it should also be realized that many of those who joined did not retain their sectarian identity once they saw the fruitlessness of the movement's messianic expectations. Whatever the actual number of new recruits each of these converts were Jews; still the authorities take no decisive steps to end this challenge to their leadership! According to Acts, the apostles' message was not spread in secret. Yet, it is said that the apostles continued their public work at Jerusalem with relatively little interference from the Jewish authorities.

The apostles preached that Jesus was resurrected from the dead. But, the Saducean authorities that opposed this teaching are slow to react. It is only several months after the crucifixion that "the priests and the captain of the Temple and the Sadducees" are said to have become increasingly hostile, especially toward the apostles, Peter and John, "being greatly disturbed because they [the disciples] were teaching the people and proclaiming in Jesus the resurrection from the dead" (Acts 4:1-2; see also Acts 4:33, 5:30). The Saducean authorities feel themselves increasingly on the defensive. Thus, although the high priest allegedly says to the apostles, "We gave you strict orders not to continue teaching in this name," he adds, "behold, you have filled Jerusalem with your teaching, and intend to bring this man's blood upon us" (Acts 5:28). The Sadducees were specifically opposed to the content of apostolic preaching. It accused them of murder and gave validity to the doctrine of resurrection from the dead. Nevertheless, the Saducean objection appears not to have been directed at their general right to preach. This apparently remained unrestricted. As a result, the author of Acts writes that "the word of God kept on spreading; and the number of the disciples continued to increase greatly in Jerusalem, and a great many of the priests were becoming obedient to the faith" (Acts 6:7). We see that the Sadducees and the priestly authorities objected to the accusation that they were responsible for Jesus' death (Acts 4:10). However, as narrated in Acts, their greatest concern seems to be the apostles' preaching of the doctrine of resurrection. The religious conflict that developed between the proto-Christians and the Saducean priestly hierarchy over the concept of resurrection was of no concern to Pilate. Pilate had completed his duty of eliminating a threat to the peace of the province; he had no further interest in Jesus' followers, as long as they kept the peace.

The Sadducees denied the reality of an afterlife, claiming it was unscriptural.[6] Years later, Paul uses the controversy between the Pharisees and Sadducees, over belief in resurrection, as a means to escape punishment by the Sanhedrin:

> But perceiving that one party were Sadducees and the other Pharisees, Paul began crying out in the Council, "Brethren, I am a Pharisee, a son of Pharisees; I am on trial for the hope and resurrection of the dead!" And as he said this, there arose a dissension between the Pharisees and Sadducees; and the assembly was divided. For the Sadducees say that there is no resurrection, nor an angel, nor a spirit; but the Pharisees acknowledge them all. And there arose a great uproar; and some of the scribes of the Pharisaic party stood up and began to argue heatedly, saying, "We find nothing wrong with this man; suppose a spirit or an angel has spoken to him?" And as a great dissension was developing, the [Roman] commander was afraid Paul would be torn to pieces by them and ordered the troops to go down and take him away from them by force, and bring him into the barracks. (Acts 23:6-10)

Paul's statement was a half-truth for there was certainly more objectionable material in his teachings. However, this episode provides circumstantial evidence that initially most, if not all, opposition to proto-Christian preaching was from Saducean opposition to the centrality of the doctrine of resurrection in their beliefs. As we shall see, opposition to the teachings of the Jesus movement increased with the addition to the proto-Christian community of Jews who held that the Torah should be interpreted allegorically. They introduced into the church ideas antithetical to the Torah. Such notions were unacceptable to the vast majority of Jews including those more normative Jewish members of the church (Acts 15:5, Galatians 2:12). As acceptance of non-Torah ideas spread within the church, Jewish opposition increased as well.

In an age accustomed to Roman brutality, the moderate response of the Jewish authorities toward the challenge of the Jesus movement stands in stark contrast. According to the Book of Acts, the post-resurrection Jesus movement, residing in Jerusalem, held a deep-seated antagonism toward their fellow Jews. These proto-Christians save all their vituperation for those Jews who do not accept Jesus as Messiah. The postcrucifixion apostolic accusations leveled at the Jewish people, generally, and their leaders, in particular, accuse them of having Jesus executed. In their initial historicity, these accusations may have been due to the disciples' anger that the Jewish authorities did not do enough to save Jesus or that some assisted in his capture. But as these accusations stand in the text we must ask why the Jewish leaders did not deal with the problem of proto-Christian preaching about Jesus with the same zeal they supposedly showed in their opposition to Jesus himself? Months went by before they used even mild punishment against the apostles. We find that Peter and John were charged with preaching about the risen Jesus and were brought before the Sanhedrin. They were warned not to preach in Jesus' name and released (Acts 4:17-18). Later, having previously warned them, they were flogged and released by the Sanhedrin (Acts 5:40). But, what were the objections the Jewish leaders had against the apostles? According to the author of Acts, they objected to the apostles "giving witness to the resurrection of the Lord Jesus" (Acts 4:33) and to the apostles claim that "God . . . raised up Jesus, whom you had put to death . . . [and] exalted . . . [him] to His right hand as a Prince and a Savior, to grant repentance to Israel, and forgiveness of sins" (Acts 5:30-31). Thus, two points troubled the Jewish leaders: First, that the apostles claimed that Jesus was allegedly raised up from the dead and exalted by God and second, the apostles' accusation that the Jews killed Jesus. When several extremist factions arose within the Jesus movement, the encounter intensified.

Apparently, for some time following the death of Jesus, the apostles had free reign to preach publicly, even in the Temple, without reprisal. In particular, no mention is made of any preaching restrictions being placed on the apostles during the so-called "great persecution" itself (Acts 8:1). Based on what Acts reports, the disciples were making thousands of converts: "And the Lord was adding to their number day by day those who were being saved" (Acts 2:47). It is plain to see that within a few months of Jesus' death the authorities were going to have even more trouble on his account now that he was dead than they had before his death. Yet, the Jewish authorities do scarcely anything! Is this a bizarre situation? Indeed, as noted above, the first time Peter and John were arrested by the Sadducees it is because they were "proclaiming in Jesus the resurrection from the dead" (Acts 4:1-2) a doctrine the Sadducees opposed regardless of who taught it or who it is claimed was raised. Then, although Peter and John have just made five thousand converts (Acts 4:4) they are let go with a warning: "But in order that it may not spread any further among the people, let us warn them to speak no more to any man in this name. And when they had summoned them, they commanded them not to speak or teach at all in the name of Jesus" (Acts 4:17-18). That's it? The Jewish leaders see the small band of Jesus' followers become a mass movement right before their eyes and they virtually do nothing. Where is the plotting and scheming they allegedly used to bring down Jesus? The report in Acts 5:13 that "None of the rest dared to associate with them [the apostles]; however, the people held them in high esteem," is an incomprehensible statement considering the claims made by the author of Acts. It certainly does not imply fear of joining the church as is made clear by the verse immediately following: "And all the more believers in the Lord, multitudes of men and women, were constantly added" (Acts 5:14).

What Acts tells us is even more incomprehensible in light of what the Gospels tell us about the Jews and the Jewish leadership in particular. In the aftermath of the crucifixion, the Jewish authorities did not pursue or persecute the disciples. They did not attempt to prevent Jesus' disciples from continuing their preaching for a considerable length of time after his death. When they did make some attempt to suppress them it was far from vigorous. It is said that the Sanhedrin was "intending to slay them [the disciples]" (Acts 5:33), but then its members are easily convinced by "a certain Pharisee named Gamaliel . . . respected by all the people" (Acts 5:34) not to kill them; instead they were flogged and let go (Acts 5:33-40).[7] If there is any truth to the description of events as found in Acts there is but one explanation for this lack of vigorous response, one that cannot be admitted to by those who uphold Christian theology: The impetus for apprehending and executing Jesus came from the Romans, not the Jews. Early antagonism directed at the disciples was based on Saducean opposition to the emphasis placed on what was claimed to be an actual resurrection experience; later antagonism was more widespread and directed at those who preached deviations from commonly held Judaism.

We need to understand who actually was involved in the confrontation between the Jewish authorities and the proto-Christian movement in Jerusalem. When the "great persecution" came against the church the author of Acts does not say the entire proto-Christian community was targeted (Acts 8:1). The comment that "they were all scattered" (Acts 8:1) evidently refers to only certain members of the church. The apostles, who earlier were said to have been threatened with death by the Jewish authorities, remained free and presumably those who held to the same beliefs as these leaders were also spared repression. This is implied in the words "those who were scattered because of the persecution that arose in connection with Stephen" (Acts 11:19). The phraseology "those who were scattered" shows that not all of the group were scattered. Moreover, the verse suggests that those who were scattered had similar views to those held by Stephen. Looking at the broader picture, we can conclude that the Jewish authorities and people had no interest in wanting to see Jesus or his disciples killed. But, that does not mean that the Romans did not coerce some of the Jewish authorities into aiding them in apprehending Jesus.

The relevant New Testament documents are, in part, political apologetics. Consequently, there is scant information on the Roman interest in Jesus' activities during his public career and none on their interest in his followers' activities, after his execution. In the aftermath of Jesus' death, the Romans may have believed the group was hopelessly scattered and simply lost interest in them. Perhaps, the Romans took some action unrecorded in the Gospels or Acts. As the author of Acts describes events, there is no immediate reaction by either the Jews or the Romans; the followers of Jesus simply remain in Jerusalem. Any problems the proto-Christian community eventually encounters are from the Jewish authorities. We can only assume that when the Romans hear of them next the group has transformed itself. They revere the crucified Jesus but now proclaim themselves to be disinterested in an earthly kingdom and proclaim that this was also the teaching of Jesus. There is a reinterpretation of things he said and eventually sayings are attributed to him that were designed to show that he never was a threat to Roman rule. Thus, he is supposed to have said to Pilate, "My kingdom is not of this world. If my kingdom were of this world, my servants would fight, that I might not be handed over to the Jews; but as it is, my kingdom is not of this realm" (John 18:36). Apparently, the author of Acts' silence on the relationship between the proto-Christian community and the Roman authorities is meant to indicate that this transformation met with Roman approval.

With Jesus' death, his followers looked to a miraculous second coming at which time he was to restore the kingdom of Israel. It is only after Jesus' death that the tale developed that during his lifetime he did not take actions leading to religio-political salvation because he was motivated purely by a spiritual concept of salvation. Under such circumstances, the overthrow of Roman rule was irrelevant. Yet, the first followers of Jesus had hoped that a resurrected Jesus would soon return from heaven in order to fulfill the messianic office by restoring the kingdom of Israel.

The author of Acts gives a sketchy mythological description of the proto-Christian movement's transformation from a revolutionary group into a spiritual fraternity. He records two early memories of what the original followers of Jesus expected him to accomplish. In the earlier part of his work, this author wrote, "But we were hoping that it was he who was going to redeem Israel" (Luke 24:21). As expressed in this verse, the kingdom is understood to have a temporal quality. The speaker is forlorn because of Jesus' failure to physically redeem Israel. Later, the author reports Jesus' followers as saying, "Lord, will you at this time restore the kingdom of Israel?" (Acts 1:6). (This was the expectation that got Jesus killed.) The answer to the question articulates one example of the spiritualized redefinition of this expectation. (We have already seen the Johannine expression of this spiritualized redefinition of the coming of God's kingdom in John 18:36.):

> He said to them, "It is not for you to know times or seasons which the Father has placed in His own jurisdiction; but you shall receive power when the holy spirit has come upon you; and you shall be my witnesses both in Jerusalem, and in all Judea and Samaria, and even to the remotest part of the earth." And after he had said these things he was lifted up while they were looking on, and a cloud received him out of their sight. And as they were gazing intently into the sky while he was departing, behold, two men in white clothing stood beside them; and they also said; "Men of Galilee, why do you stand looking into the sky? This Jesus, who has been taken up from you into heaven, will come in just the same way as you have watched him go into heaven."
> (Acts 1:7-11)

Developing pre-Gospel Christianity sought to conceal the historical state of affairs by distorting the original context in which certain of Jesus' statements and actions occurred. In his redefined form, the earthly Jesus is portrayed as politically benign. His message of the imminence of the kingdom of God is disassociated from any thought of establishing a worldly kingdom. The Christian message is clear: The Romans were misguided into thinking Jesus was seditious; his anger was directed only at the spiritually corrupt

Jewish leadership and people. According to the author of Acts, the allegedly resurrected Jesus is asked, "Lord, will you at this time restore the kingdom of Israel?" (Acts 1:6), that is, are you now going to overthrow Roman rule of the Land of Israel and renew the earthly kingdom of David? In his reply, an important political transformation takes place. The earthly political aim of Jesus' quick return and ascension to the throne in order to govern an independent Jewish people is squelched. The author of Acts has Jesus answer, "It is not for you to know times or seasons which the Father has placed in His own jurisdiction" (Acts 1:7).[8] Events will occur in God's own time. In the meantime, the Romans are reassured that Jesus did not intend to overthrow Roman rule of the Land of Israel and restore the temporal kingdom of Israel, for if this were the Father's will, it would have been done already. The author of Acts does not answer the question of when Jesus will return, but, no doubt, expects a future second coming at which time Jesus is expected to establish his kingdom. The reestablishment of the earthly kingdom of Israel, so thoroughly connected with the arrival of the true Messiah, is put off to some indeterminate future date. Meanwhile, Jesus' followers are to be his worldwide "witnesses" in preparation for his return. With Jesus' alleged ascension, the Jewish term "Messiah" undergoes a change from an earthly religio-political title to a Christian heavenly soteriological title, "Christ."

In summation, as described in Acts, when the proto-Christians resurface, they have discarded Jesus' radical political agenda. They proclaim their message to be solely spiritual and are anxious to stress that Jesus had been opposed to violence and preached love and forgiveness. The group suppresses or reinterprets all its dead leader's volatile phraseology in the spiritual sense that will later be reflected in the respective Gospel narratives. The proto-Christians of Acts become models of indifference to the presence of the Roman authorities. Consequently, the Roman authorities were apparently neutralized and no longer interested in them as a political threat. But, there was no such indifference or simple silence on the part of the proto-Christian movement of the Book of Acts toward the Jews.

Two more confrontations between church members and Jewish authorities recorded in the Book of Acts, along with one from the works of Josephus, need to be mentioned. When Herod Agrippa I seized "some who belonged to the church," put James, the brother of John, to death (44 C.E.) and arrested Peter the specific reason for his actions are not given: "Now about that time Herod the king laid hands on some who belonged to the church, in order to mistreat them. And he had James the brother of John put to death with a sword. And when he saw that it pleased the Jews, he proceeded to arrest Peter also. Now it was during the days of the Feast of Unleavened Bread. . . . [Peter is allegedly released miraculously.] And when Peter came to himself, he said, 'Now I know for sure that the Lord has sent forth his angel and rescued me from the hand of Herod and from all that the people of the Jews were expecting'" (Acts 12:1-3, 11). Why did Herod Agrippa want "to mistreat" certain members of the church? How factual is the remark that "it pleased the Jews" to have such things done to the apostles? What were "the people of the Jews" expecting Herod Agrippa to do with Peter? According to the passage, Herod Agrippa did not go after the whole church, but only after certain of its members. What brought on the confrontation? As the text appears in the Book of Acts, there is more emphasis on anti-Jewish accusations than on mentioning the root causes of Herod Agrippa's actions.

The source of the confrontation may have been a religio-political dispute resulting from Herod Agrippa's appointment as king. Herod Agrippa's reign was the first time, since the rule of his grandfather, Herod the Great, over a half-century earlier, that a Jewish king was in charge of the whole Jewish homeland. During the period of Herod Agrippa's reign, there was no direct Roman rule in the regions under his control. Could it be that certain church members emboldened by the absence of direct Roman rule again caused a violent religio-political disturbance around the time of the Passover festival? Did they believe that only the head of the church should rule, as king of the Jews, until Jesus returns? Were Herod Agrippa's fears of a religious or of a political nature? Perhaps his actions against "some who belonged to the church" were only directed at those in the church that spoke out against the Temple and the Law. More likely, they made treasonable political statements about the king that the author of Acts conceals from his audience. The Book of Acts is silent on the matter; it does not even give a Christian explanation for Herod Agrippa's initial action.

In later years, when Paul is assaulted, in Jerusalem, it is by Jews from the Diaspora who have previously heard his antinomian preaching and know him well. James and the sect he oversees remain undisturbed, but Paul is another matter. He is taken into custody. Appearing before the Roman governor, the Jewish authorities are said to justify Paul's arrest: "For we have found this man a real pest and a fellow who stirs up dissension among all the Jews throughout the world, and a ringleader of the sect of the Nazarenes. And he even tried to desecrate the Temple; and then we arrested him" (Acts 24:5-6). By contrast, the violent death of James, the brother of Jesus, is met with a different reaction. According to Josephus, in 62 C.E., the high priest, Ananus, had James tried before the Sanhedrin for having transgressed the law and executed. The exact charges against James are not known. A high priest and a Sanhedrin are involved in this episode, but it provides no insight into the role of the priesthood and Sanhedrin of thirty years earlier in the Roman apprehension and execution of Jesus. When the animus between Jesus' Jerusalem centered followers and Ananus developed is not stated nor is there any clear delineation of the content of the hostility. According to Acts, proto-Christian accusations that the priesthood was involved in the death of Jesus were made soon after his death. One may speculate that this and developing beliefs about Jesus (especially his supposed resurrection) must have contributed to a growing tension between the Jerusalem church and the high priest. But, Ananus chose to end whatever disagreement he had with James by using capital punishment. This extreme measure was greatly disapproved of by non-Christian Jews and protests were made to the Emperor. "Those of the inhabitants of the city who were considered the most fair-minded and who were strict in observance of the law were offended at this [action by Ananus]."[9] Their protests, Josephus continues, led to Ananus being removed from the high priesthood. So we see, that the alleged blanket persecutions of the early church by Jews are greatly exaggerated.

According to the author of Acts, Jews in the Diaspora were on occasion the instigators of Gentile persecution of Christians. Jews are alleged to have instigated action against Jewish Christian missionaries by poisoning the mind of the populace (Acts 13:50), stirring up the rabble to attack missionaries (Acts 17:5), bringing Christians before Gentile tribunals on charges of having broken Gentile law (Acts 17:6 f., 18:13), and inciting Gentiles to bring Christians into court on such charges (Acts 17:5-7). Jews may have been involved in each of these kinds of action; however, we have no way of knowing the truth of the author's accusations. We know that we cannot rely on Acts, which has exaggerated the situation in other incidents where it blames Jews for persecution of Christians (cf. Acts 9:23-25 with 2 Corinthians 11:32-33; cf. Acts 9:26-30 with Galatians 1:18-24; cf. Acts 17:5-6 with 1 Thessalonians 2:14-16). Furthermore, it cannot be assumed that wherever Christians went Jews, invariably incited Gentiles to act against them. The author of Acts also mentions two incidents in which Gentiles took hostile action against Christians without any Jewish instigation (Acts 16:19-24, 19:23-41).

Despite controversy, which was often acrimonious and bitter, Jewish followers of Jesus were still counted as part of the community of Israel. It is only when they adopted distinctive non-biblical beliefs that they were rejected. The Jewish Christians in time were unacceptable to both Gentile Christians and Jews, regarded as heretics from the church by the former and as apostates from Israel by the latter. How far these Jewish Christians, now divided into several groups, had strayed from the beliefs of earlier Jewish followers of Jesus is difficult to determine. It is not even known if they were in a direct line from the original group of Jesus' followers. But, it is known that certain doctrines of some of these groups were not new inventions but survivals of older traditions that were at odds with newer doctrines that had become fundamental to what became known as mainstream Christianity.

There are indications in Acts that Gamaliel's pronouncement before an earlier Sanhedrin, whether actually made or not, encapsulates the general Jewish attitude toward the first century proto-Christian community of Jerusalem which followed the teachings of the apostles: "And so in the present case, I say to you, stay away from these men and let them alone, for if this plan or action should be of men, it will be overthrown; but if it is of God, you will not be able to overthrow them; or else you may even be found fighting against God" (Acts 5:38-39). The presumption may have been that when they would see that Jesus did not return as expected these transgressors would abandon their misguided beliefs.[10] The author of Acts, writing in the post-war period, attributes to Gamaliel his own comment which is directed more against those who followed the apostles than at the "unbelieving" Jews. He shuns any open criticism of any of the several proto-Christian groups that developed following the crucifixion, but artfully introduces his disdain for that part of the church that kept closest to common Judaism. The author of Acts writes, "And so in the present case" (verse 38a), as a reference to the apostles and their followers. He intends to differentiate between what the apostles taught and what the Hellenistic branch of the church was teaching. It is the author's judgment on the post-war disposition of the Jerusalem church: "for if this plan or action should be of men, it will be overthrown." It is precisely the Jerusalem church that disappears after 70 C.E. Indeed, by the second century the Jewish-born Christians were reduced to a marginalized minority within the church. It is the Gentile church, from which all present-day Christian groups are descended, that the author has in mind when he cites, "but if it is of God, you will not be able to overthrow them; or else you may even be found fighting against God."[11]

Much of the portrayal of the postcrucifixion period, as found in Acts, has been shaped by the generally Gentile Christian anti-Judaic religio-political climate in which the author of Acts wrote. Therefore, the material found in Acts is not historical merely as described; any underlying facts have been heavily reshaped. Although the author of Acts wished to give the impression that its contents were completely historical, such an impression is unfounded. He says nothing of the plan of the emperor Gaius Caligula (37-41 C.E.) to have a statue of himself set up in the Temple at Jerusalem. One would think that it would have had a profound effect on the members of the Jerusalem church.[12] Moreover, when recounting the fourteen year interval between the death of Herod Agrippa I (44 C.E.) and Paul's last visit to Jerusalem (58 C.E.) the author says virtually nothing about the Jerusalem church.

Despite the distorted material found in Acts, one is able to discern evidence that neither the Jewish authorities nor Jews, generally, were intent on persecuting or killing Jesus' followers. The accusation originated in the hostility toward those Jews who did not accept Jesus and because of a perceived need to show the Romans that Jesus and his disciples had not preached sedition. As the story line developed, it became contended that Jesus was the victim of a Jewish conspiracy. The process of making false accusation against the Jews continued with the charge that their persecution persisted after Jesus' death, but now was directed at his followers. A careful perusal of the evidence shows this was not the case. Accusations that the church had undergone widespread continuous harassment or persecution in Jerusalem at the hands of hostile Jewish authorities or populace are simply without foundation. Indications are that the followers of Jesus were generally free to express their views openly and frequently did so. Following the death of Jesus, the majority of Jews in Judea did not agree with the proto-Christian assessment of Jesus, but did not seek to impose their will through violence, even after thirty years of proto-Christian preaching.[13]

PART 2

Soon after its establishment, the Jerusalem church consisted, in part, of "Hellenistic" Jews and "Hebrews" (Acts 6:1-5). A third group consisted of the native-born Jews, mostly Aramaic speaking Jews. Who were the members of these respective groups? The term

Hellenistai, "Hellenists," means more than simply "Greek-speaking Jews." Daily interaction of native-born Jews in the Land of Israel with resident Diaspora-born Jews or visiting Jews from the Diaspora and non-Jewish inhabitants residing in the Jewish homeland often necessitated familiarity with the vernacular Greek (*koine*), especially by the merchant classes. Inscriptional evidence indicates that in the first century C.E. many Jews in Judea were trilingual, speaking Aramaic, Hebrew, and Greek, although Aramaic was the dominant language.

In the Diaspora, Jews were directly exposed to Hellenistic culture and the influence of Hellenism on them varied. Establishing communities in cities and towns for social, occupational, and religious reasons, they for the most part resisted compromise with religious syncretism. Nevertheless, there were incidents where attraction to certain aspects of Hellenism led to deviations from the basic norms of Judaism. Even within the areas comprising Judea, Samaria, and Galilee, there was a large number of Hellenized Jews. It is these Jews of the Diaspora and the Land of Israel, with their variegated Jewish commitment and belief, who are referred to as "Hellenists." As such, it is best to render *Hellenistai*, as "Hellenized Jews." "Greek-speaking Jews," is simply an inadequate description. *Hellenistai*, as used in Acts 6:1, refers to Jews whose cultural and linguistic background was Greek, but who had joined the church. When exactly these Hellenistic Jews first entered the proto-Christian church is a matter of conjecture. In any case, a significant number of these proto-Christian Hellenists may have been originally attracted to the new movement because they saw in it a vehicle by which to fulfill their preconversion syncretic interpretation of Judaism.[14]

The term *Hebraioi*, "Hebrews," as used in Acts 6:1, in all likelihood refers to a group of Jews (perhaps also Greek speaking) who, before becoming followers of Jesus, had come to share many Samaritan notions, especially their rejection of the Jerusalem Temple. It is best to understand the definition of "Hebrews" as Samaritan influenced Jews rather than a group of Samaritans actually taking up residence in Jerusalem. A reference to a group of people, the term "Hebrews" is found three times in the New

Testament (Acts 6:1, 2 Corinthians 11:22, Philippians 3:5). Josephus writes that the Samaritans called themselves "Hebrews"[15] and this term was apparently applied to Samaritan influenced Jews as well (at least, in the Jewish proto-Christian community). In contrast, the Jews of the first century did not generally call themselves "Hebrews," nor did the Gentiles call them "Hebrews."

Tensions between the Hellenist and Hebrew followers of Jesus developed over the daily food allocation made to poor members of the Jerusalem church. The Hellenist widows were said to be at a disadvantage in comparison to the Hebrew widows. The apostles, representative of the native-born Jews, called on the parties involved to select seven men to administer the food allocation. All seven have Greek names. Stephen was one of them (Acts 6:1-5). Are we to presume, based on their Greek names, that they were all Jewish Hellenists? The author of Acts does not call these administrators "Hellenists," but because the seven all have Greek names it is usually assumed that they were all from the "Hellenist" faction. But, it is hard to imagine that only Hellenist Jews were chosen for these administrative positions. This would give the "Hebrews" no say concerning food distribution. We cannot infer that they were Jewish Hellenists simply based on their names or rule out the use of Greek names by non-Hellenists. Certainly, there were native-born Jews who also bore Greek name[16] and there are indications that Samaritans often bore Greek names as well.[17] From the list of administrators, we can only infer that some of them were Jewish Hellenists. The rest were Samaritan influenced Jews, nicknamed "Hebrews," because of their inclination toward Samaritan theological notions. The "Hellenists" came from a kind of sectarian Judaism that held some sectarian beliefs in common with the "Hebrews." They were therefore grouped together. The Hellenist-Hebrew group within the church may have been allied in their opposition to the Jerusalem Temple and its ritual. Because of their different pre-conversion religious perspectives they shared some notions, but differed on others. These individuals were drawn to Jerusalem because it was the center of the church and the place where the imminent return of Jesus was to occur. As the narrative unfolds, Stephen suddenly appears in the role, not of a food administrator, but, of a preacher with a provocative teaching (Acts 6:14).

To understand why the Hebrews of Acts 6:1 are identified as Samaritan influenced Jewish Christians we must look at Stephen's speech as recorded in Acts 7:2-51, and the context in which it is found. The views he is recorded as expressing appear to have originated under the influence of Samaritan tradition. Stephen's speech, made while he was supposedly "full of the Holy Spirit" (Acts 7:55), shows a distinct use of Samaritan sources and a stress on Samaritan interpretation. The speech reflects traditions that are at variance with those found in the Masoretic text and the Septuagint. However, these traditions show evidence of dependence on Samaritan theology and thereby suggest a Samaritan influence in the formulation of the speech. Therefore, if Stephen's speech is any indication of belief, there was a strongly pro-Samaritan viewpoint to be found among certain members of the Jerusalem proto-Christian community.

Stephen was influenced by the Samaritan Torah textual tradition, dependent on Samaritan interpretations, and held beliefs in common with the Samaritans concerning the Jerusalem Temple. Although Stephen expresses such views, it is doubtful that he was a Samaritan. In all likelihood, he was a Jew who had adopted Samaritan teachings either while living in proximity to the border with Samaria or by association with Samaritans in the Diaspora. There may have been such a Jewish sect of like-minded individuals to which Stephen belonged prior to his conversion. As we shall see, the speech shows evidence of being influenced by Samaritan theology and tendentiousness. But, it must be kept in mind that the Samaritanism centered at Mount Gerizim was only one example of the Samaritan religion's expression. Samaritan proto-Christianity probably drew its initial followers from a sectarian group of Samaritans. It probably was paralleled by a like-minded Jewish sect from which Stephen and the other Samaritanized "Hebrews" eventually emerged.[18]

The actual circumstances in which the accusations leveled

against Stephen were made cannot be ascertained with any certainty. In focusing on the episode, as recorded by the author of Acts, we must take into consideration the extent of that author's editorial activity. It may be that he combined the ideas contained in this speech, the product of the church's missionary work in Samaria, with a report of the martyrdom of one such missionary, Stephen, at the hands of Jews or possibly even Samaritans. Despite the lack of any information that would reveal something of Stephen's background, his speech, as recorded in Acts, does show his connection to Samaritan biblical exegesis. There are a number of variations of biblical quotations or allusions in Acts 7 that are not found in either the Masoretic text or Septuagint, but are supported by the Samaritan Torah version.

Acts 7:4 states that God brought Abraham from Haran to Canaan "after his father died." This contradicts both the Masoretic text and Septuagint. According to the Masoretic and Septuagint texts (Genesis 11:32), Abraham's father, Terah, was seventy when Abraham was born (Genesis 11:26), and he died in Haran at the age of 205 (Genesis 11:32). Abraham was seventy-five when he moved from Haran (Genesis 12:4). At that time, Terah was 145 years old and still had sixty years before his death. Thus, he lived for sixty years following Abraham's departure from Haran. Stephen claims that Abraham left after his father's death (Acts 7:4) following the same chronology as the Samaritan Torah text. The Samaritan Torah followed by the Samaritan Targum gives Terah's age at death as 145 years, not 205 years, as found in the Masoretic and Septuagint texts.[19] The claim that Abraham did not leave Haran until his father was dead is asserted also by Philo.[20] This suggests that this interpretation was also accepted in some Hellenistic Jewish circles. Thus, the author of Stephen's speech could have used the Samaritan Torah version or another variant text. It is also possible to account for the variation as the plain sense reading of the biblical narration. One has to read the dates very carefully in Genesis 11:32-12:1 in order to get the true sense of the narrative. By itself, this occurrence would seem a mere coincidence but its significance grows in conjunction with other texts.

Stephen relates that God declared to Moses, "I am the God of your fathers, the God of Abraham and Isaac and of Jacob" (Acts 7:32); this is based on Exodus 3:6. The Masoretic and Septuagint texts read, "I am the God of your father," in the singular. Both the Samaritan Torah version and the Samaritan Targum give the plural, "fathers," a reading that conforms grammatically to the text. The plural is also to be found in other repetitions of the formula in both the Masoretic text and the Septuagint (for example, Exodus 3:15). As a result, Acts 7:32 is in agreement with the Samaritan reading as against the Masoretic text and Septuagint. This again does not show conclusively that Acts follows the Samaritan tradition. It is possible that the similarity is due to changes that were simply made by the author of Stephen's speech or by a later copyist to achieve grammatical harmony.

Stephen's speech follows the narrative outlined in Genesis and Exodus. The section on Moses describes events in the Book of Exodus: the burning bush, the exodus, the giving of the Law, and the golden calf. However, in Acts 7:37 the orderly sequence is interrupted by the insertion of a text similar to that from Deuteronomy 18:15, concerning God raising up a prophet like Moses. Significantly, immediately following Exodus 20:17 of the Samaritan Torah text there is a passage composed from verses in Deuteronomy and called by the Samaritans the tenth commandment. This passage is not found in either the Masoretic or Septuagint texts. It contains, in part, the promise of the future prophet from Deuteronomy 18:18. The word order of the quotation in Acts 7:37 is slightly closer to the text of Deuteronomy 18:18 than to that of Deuteronomy 18:15. (Deuteronomy 18:15 and 18:18 are almost identical, the main difference is who is speaking). Apparently, the author of Stephen's speech used a text of Exodus that contained an insertion from Deuteronomy corresponding to that found in the Samaritan Torah version.

Acts 7:5 reads: "Yet He [God] gave him [Abraham] no inheritance [*kleronomian*] in it [Seir], not even a foot's length." This is ostensibly from Deuteronomy 2:5b, yet the noun "inheritance" is not found in the parallel position in the Masoretic,

Targum, or Septuagint texts of this verse. In these texts, the word "inheritance" is found only in 2:5c. In the Samaritan text, however, *y-r-sh-h*, "inheritance," also appears in 2:5b.

There are a number of instances where Samaritan traditions are used or alluded to in Stephen's speech. In one such instance, Shechem, the Samaritan religious center—their alternative to Jerusalem—is given added significance. Stephen makes Abraham the purchaser of a piece of ground at Shechem, in effect, transferring the burial place of the patriarchs from Hebron in Judea to Shechem in Samaria. The Masoretic text (and the Septuagint Version) identifies Hebron as the location of the burial cave (Machpelah) which Abraham purchased from Ephron the Hittite (Genesis 23:1-20) and where Abraham, Isaac, and Jacob were buried (Genesis 49:29-32). However, Stephen locates the burial cave of "Jacob . . . and our fathers" in Shechem, bought from "the sons of Hamor [Gr. *Emmor*]" by Abraham (Acts 7:15-16). By claiming that Jacob and his sons were buried in a tomb that Abraham bought in Shechem, he infers that Abraham and Isaac were likewise buried there (cf. MT Genesis 49:29-32). The Jewish Scriptures state that Jacob was buried at Hebron, in the cave of Machpelah, which Abraham had purchased from Ephron the Hittite for four hundred silver shekels (Genesis 23:16, 49:29-33, 50:13). Joseph was buried at Shechem, in the piece of ground which Jacob had purchased for a hundred silver shekels from the sons of Hamor (Genesis 33:19, Joshua 24:32). According to Josephus, the other sons of Jacob were buried at Hebron.[21] There is no known Samaritan Torah text or tradition that supports Stephen's assertion. Most Samaritan traditions on the burial of the Patriarchs agree with the Masoretic text and relate to Hebron. However, there are some Samaritan traditions that locate the cave of Machpelah at Gerizim.[22] The tradition to which Stephen refers can only be of Samaritan origin. It is clearly an example of a Samaritan counterclaim to that of the Jews. Living in the territory previously occupied by the Israelite tribes of Ephraim and Manasseh, Josephus reports that the ancestors of the Samaritans claimed "they are descended from Joseph"[23] and traced "their line back to Ephraim and Manasseh, the descendants of Joseph."[24] This connection with Joseph is also implied in Stephen's speech, one-fifth of which focuses on Joseph. Joseph's brothers who were "jealous" of him and "sold him into Egypt" are not even mentioned by name (Acts 7:9-18). Stephen joins the Samaritans in attempting to enhance the validity of their claims by locating the burial place of the patriarchs within their own territory. Why did he do this? One must remember that this speech and its teachings may have originated in the missionary work directed at the Samaritans. In any case, the author of Luke found it useful for his purposes.

Acts 7:7, "'And whatever nation to which they shall be in bondage I Myself will judge,' said God, 'and after that they will come out and serve Me in this place'" seems to quote Exodus 3:12. In this verse, God instructs Moses at Mount Horeb, "When you have brought forth the people out of Egypt, you shall serve God upon this mountain." However, the verse found in Acts is addressed to Abraham, not Moses, and is reminiscent of the appearances of God to Abraham at Shechem (Genesis 12:6-7) and in an unnamed location (Genesis 15:1-21). Instead of the word "mountain" Stephen uses the word "place," a typical Samaritan term for a shrine.[25] Stephen's objective is clearly to make it appear as if God instructed Abraham that Shechem (that is, Mount Gerizim) is the place where God is to be worshiped.

Stephen's speech contains characteristics that are in agreement with Samaritan traditions, interpretations, and attitudes and of a textual tradition very similar to the Samaritan Torah. The Samaritans did not accept either the Prophets or Writings. Interestingly, the overwhelming number of scriptural allusions in Acts 7 are concerned with passages in the Torah. There are a few non-Torah quotations taken from either the Prophets or Writings, but in each case the text has been selected and altered to reflect a pro-Samaritan and anti-Jewish bias. The evidence shows a strong connection between the Samaritan text of the Torah and Stephen's speech. It goes beyond textual similarities that can be attributed to the use of non-Masoretic textual traditions other than that of the Samaritans. The version of the Torah that Stephen uses has features in common with both the Septuagint and Samaritan texts, however, Stephen's use of traditions and interpretations favoring Samaritanism places him squarely within a Samaritan, not a Jewish, context.

Stephen's speech also reflects Samaritan interpretations of biblical history from Abraham to Solomon. In tracing a history of Jewish apostasy, Stephen makes reference in Acts 7:42 to worshiping "the host of heaven, as it is written in the book of the prophets." This alludes to Jeremiah 7:18 and 19:13—the prophecy that Jerusalem and its Temple will be destroyed. In Acts 7:42-43 Stephen connects this statement with a version of Amos 5:25-27 which is apparently based on the Septuagint rendering, but which contains notable variations. The changes that he makes in the text are justified neither by the Masoretic text nor the Septuagint, nor by historical reality. Both the Masoretic text and the Septuagint version of the verse from the Book of Amos foretell the Assyrian exile of the northern kingdom of Israel (from whose tribes the Samaritans claimed descent). The place of their captivity is described as "beyond Damascus" (Amos 5:27). Stephen deliberately substitutes "beyond Babylon" for "beyond Damascus" (Acts 7:43). This makes the prophecy refer rather to the southern kingdom of Judah, and connects the Jews with the idolatrous generation Amos speaks of. As Stephen tells it, the apostasy from true worship that occurred in the wilderness, at the time of the exodus from Egypt, caused the downfall of the kingdom of Judah (Acts 7:41-42).

Stephen now makes one more revision of history before getting to the heart of his attack. In Acts 7:46, Stephen states, "And David found favor in God's sight, and asked that he might find a dwelling place for the house of Jacob." This apparently alludes to Psalms 132:5, "Until I find out a place for the Lord, a dwelling-place for the Mighty One of Jacob." However, as Stephen expresses it, David shows his interest in building a "dwelling place [*skenoma*] for the house of Jacob," that is, it is David's desire to build a national capital. This contrasts with the Masoretic text of the psalm, in which David's desire is to build a national sanctuary, "a dwelling place for the Mighty One of Jacob." One should not be confused by the many modern New Testament versions of Acts 7:46 that read "God of Jacob," which is found in the Septuagint. The earliest New Testament manuscripts read "house of Jacob." Thus, Stephen declares that it was not David's intention or desire to build a temple.

In Stephen's speech, it is not the sacrificial system that he rejects, but the Jerusalem Temple.[26] The exaltation of the Tabernacle, a sanctuary common to all of Israel's ancestors, both Jew and Samaritan alike, is used to attack the Jerusalem Temple. In this speech, there is no demeaning of the Tabernacle or the ceremonial laws connected with it; Mosaic Law does not come under attack. Stephen condemns the Jewish nation from the time of Solomon on as a people who had resisted the "Holy Spirit." According to Stephen, the height of Israel's apostasy, in the biblical period, comes with the construction of the Jerusalem Temple (Acts 7:47-50). With the sanctuary on Mount Gerizim destroyed many years before, there likely developed a view among some Samaritans that God does not dwell in a temple, his throne is in heaven. Stephen uses this notion. Isaiah 66:1-2 is cited in Acts 7:49-50 with some changes in wording from both the Masoretic and Septuagint texts. "Heaven is My throne, and earth is the footstool of My feet. What kind of house will you build for Me? Says the Lord; or what place is there for My repose. Was it not My hand which made all these things?" In the context of Stephen's speech, this citation is used to question the legitimacy of the Jerusalem Temple as the "place" (*topos*) where God dwells. The fact that God is not confined to a finite space was a concept found in the commonly held Judaism of Stephen's Jewish contemporaries but he or a later redactor ignore this fact. The purpose was to condemn the Jerusalem Temple (the "house"—*oikos*), as if Jewish belief confined God to a finite space, cf. "Hear in heaven Your dwelling place" (1 Kings 8:43).

A crucial differentiation is made between Tabernacle and Temple. The Tabernacle is acceptable; it was built according to the divine specifications shown to Moses, was brought into the Land by "our fathers [that is, the Israelite nation as a whole] . . . with Joshua [from the tribe of Ephraim]," and was the only sanctuary up to the end of David's reign (Acts 7:44-45). Solomon's Temple, however, is denounced as being "made with hands" (Acts 7:48). As used in Acts 7, this phrase is applied in a negative sense and in reference to the Jerusalem Temple only, not to the Tabernacle. Stephen condemns those Jews, past and present, who continued in Solomon's footsteps: "You men who are stiffnecked and uncircumcised in heart and ears are always resisting the holy spirit; you are doing just as your fathers did" (Acts 7:51). In the speech, a distinction is made between "our fathers" and "your fathers," between the faithful Israel and the unfaithful Jews. This expressed precisely the Samaritan position—the illegitimacy of the Jerusalem Temple and those who worshiped there.[27]

Stephen's speech denigrated the Jerusalem sanctuary but said nothing concerning Mount Gerizim as the proper location for a Temple. It stands to reason that Stephen would feel the same way about a temple on Mount Gerizim (if it still stood) as he felt about the Temple in Jerusalem. However, he did not have to concern himself with Mount Gerizim as its sanctuary, also "made with hands," had long been destroyed. The Samaritans, while they continued to worship on Mount Gerizim, did not worship in a Temple. Stephen, probably expressing his pre-conversion views, yet now seeking fulfillment in Jesus, looked forward to the destruction of the Jerusalem Temple (Acts 6:14). This viewpoint certainly was helpful in presenting Christianity to Samaritans. Johannine tradition, recorded after the destruction of the Jerusalem Temple, put the same sentiment into the mouth of Jesus, but included Mount Gerizim's sanctuary as well, "Woman, believe me, an hour is coming when neither in this mountain [Gerizim], nor in Jerusalem, shall you worship the Father" (John 4:21). John 4 reflects the Christian mission to Samaria, but more than likely underwent some changes before the final redaction of the Fourth Gospel. Worship at Jerusalem and Gerizim is rejected in favor of worship in spirit, which for the author of John is through "Christ." The Johannine Jesus' words declare the inadequacy of the respective claims of both Jews and Samaritans. Now, true worship is no longer contained within a given place or nation, but is universalized. The compiler of Stephen's speech and the editors of John respectively utilized these Samaritan beliefs for their own purposes.

More than half of Stephen's speech is concerned with Moses. Moses as deliverer of Israel is emphasized (Acts 7:25, 34, 35). However, the people did not understand that he was their deliverer (Acts 7:25) and totally rejected him (Acts 7:39). Those who did not repent (that is, Judah and Benjamin) were removed "beyond Babylon" (Acts 7:43). Those who repented had the "tabernacle of testimony in the wilderness" which Joshua had brought into the Land of Israel (Acts 7:44-45). This is significant because Joshua was from the tribe of Ephraim and the Samaritans referred to their temple as the "tabernacle."[28] Thus, the Samaritans are those who truly followed Moses.

There is another consideration of a Mosaic theme. The Christology of the speech centers on the figure of the Moses-like prophet of Deuteronomy 18:15, 18 (quoted at Acts 7:37). This individual plays a minor role in Jewish messianic expectations, which looks forward to a Davidic Messiah. However, a Moses-like prophet, the Taheb, is the central figure in Samaritan eschatology.

According to the author of Acts, Stephen is brought before the Sanhedrin. His speech provokes a violent reaction from those present. As a result of his opposition to the Temple and his negative attitude toward the Law, he is summarily killed.[29] There are three accusations leveled against Stephen: blasphemy against Moses and God (Acts 6:11), speaking continuously against the Temple and the Law (*nomos*) (Acts 6:13), and asserting that Jesus would destroy the Temple and change the customs (*ethe*) which Moses had delivered (Acts 6:14). His speech before the Sanhedrin confirms that he held such views.

The first accusation states: "We have heard him speak blasphemous words against Moses and God" (Acts 6:11). What is meant by the accusation that he spoke "blasphemous words against Moses and God"? Was his audience offended because Stephen demoted Moses' role as lawgiver by asserting that he did not receive the Law directly from God, but that God dealt with him only through an angel? Did they feel God was "blasphemed" in that Stephen claimed God gave the Law through an angelic intermediary rather than by Himself (Acts 7:38,

7:53)?[30] The accusation found in Acts 6:11 is too vague as stated. The author of Acts tells his audience nothing of substance concerning the charge. But, there is good reason for believing that this accusation has been interpolated into the text just prior to the speech in order to produce an effect. The positive figure of Moses dominates the speech that follows. If Stephen spoke so prominently of Moses in this speech, surely his accusers and others have heard similar praise of Moses from Stephen prior to this time. Why then would they make an accusation many would know is false? Apparently, the author of Acts wants to show that the accusations made against Stephen were completely false and resulted from Jewish hostility. Furthermore, one should not underestimate what the author of Acts wished to accomplish with his source material. There is no explicit mention of Jerusalem or the Temple in the Torah. Thus, an attack on the Jerusalem Temple as an invalid place of worship, was an assault on Jewish religious practice, however, it was not an attack on the Torah. This suited the author of Acts' agenda. His ultimate aim is not to prove the Law wrong, but that it is no longer valid. As for the Jews and Judaism, it is the author's goal to show that they have no credibility.

The second accusation states: "This man incessantly speaks against this holy place, and the Law" (Acts 6:13). Despite the claim that this is a false charge, it finds justification in that Stephen implies that the Temple was built by Solomon without divine permission (Acts 7:46-47) and in his assertion that God does not dwell in "houses made by hands" (Acts 7:48). Therefore, it can be assumed that he declared that this "place" (the Temple) had no sanctity. The author of Acts does not record what Stephen said against the Law. Was it felt that he diminished the Law by saying it was given through an angel (Acts 7:38)? Did he imply that the Law was not worthy enough to be given by God Himself? Perhaps, this accusation gives some indication that the word "blasphemous" is used (Acts 6:11) with the meaning of being "irreverent" toward God by demeaning the Law and the Temple (cf. Acts 21:28, 25:8). But, again, the accusation, as recorded, is too vaguely stated for one to know to what it refers. Moreover, the accusations against Stephen might have included other things he said outside of the speech.

The third accusation states: "[T]his Nazarene, Jesus, will destroy this place and alter the customs which Moses handed down to us" (Acts 6:14). Stephen is said to have used the term "place," *topos* (see parallel usage in John 11:48), even though his statement is based on a saying of Jesus who is said to have used "Temple," *naos*, not "place" (cf. John 2:19, Mark 14:58). When the Jewish witnesses quoted Stephen indirectly, they qualified the term "place" by adding the adjective "holy," thus referring to the Temple as "holy place" (Acts 6:13). The first half of this accusation directly quotes Stephen. The second half of the charge is presented as an indirect quotation of Stephen. This is seen from the phrase "which Moses delivered to us" that is, to "us" Jews. The question that evolved in Christian circles was not *if* Jesus spoke of destroying the Temple, but exactly what did he say. Again, there is scant information given concerning the charge.

In order to attract converts, Christian missionaries made accommodations to the way of life of the peoples to whom they preached. Paul, in speaking of himself, states that he has "become all things to all men, that I might by all means save some" (1 Corinthians 9:22). To a lesser extent, Peter and Barnabas acted in a similar fashion, though Paul criticizes their inconsistency (Galatians 2:11-14). Perhaps Stephen, when he preached the gospel to Samaritans, likewise expressed himself in Samaritan terms. What Stephen's speech may represent is the message he or others delivered to Samaritans. According to the author of Acts, Stephen's anti-Jewish message, when preached in Jerusalem, proved fatal for him. The hostility that Stephen's radical teachings provoked among his Hellenistic Jewish audience shows that opposition to the Temple and its ritual was not generally acceptable among them.

Chronologically, the passage that is generally identified as Stephen's speech (Acts 7:2-53) post-dates Stephen. However, it serves as the setting for Stephen's martyrdom. What we have in this passage is a Samaritan Christian restating of Israelite history.

The author of Acts employed a version of biblical history that could only be derived from the missionary activity of the Samaritan Christian church—although it contains elements of general Samaritan biblical revisionism. Its selections from the Torah and non-Torah biblical scriptures are carefully chosen and redesigned to agree with Samaritan thought. Its attack on those who worshiped at the Temple in Jerusalem, that is, the Jews, fits well with the author's theological needs. It suited the author's anti-Judaic purposes to have the martyrdom of the Samaritan church's hero take place in Jerusalem, at the hands of Jews, and to be the springboard for a persecution of the church. As the story unfolds in the Book of Acts, Stephen expresses Samaritan oriented anti-Jewish and anti-Jerusalem Temple sentiments while in Jerusalem and is killed. This may, indeed, have happened. But, (if it actually occurred) was it an outburst against the followers of Jesus per se? If Jews who had come to worship at the Jerusalem Temple actually stoned Stephen it was not because of his being a follower of Jesus, but because he espoused Samaritan anti-Jewish views in Jerusalem.

As we have seen, Stephen espouses views that are supportive of the Samaritan Torah version and the Samaritan Targum. Indeed, some sectarian Jews may have held certain traditions associated with Samaritan interpretations. But, what makes the suggestion of a direct relationship between the speech credited to Stephen and Samaritanism obvious is that so much of the speech is tailored to be compatible with specifically Samaritan biblical traditions and theology. The geographic substitution in the prophecy of Amos, now shifts the meaning toward the kingdom of Judah rather than the kingdom of Israel; the change in the location of the burial places, so that the patriarchs are now all buried in Shechem (near Mount Gerizim); the interpolation of Deuteronomy 18:15, into an otherwise orderly sequence of biblical narration—all suggests a Samaritan outlook. Special note should be taken of Stephen's exaltation of Moses and his rejection of the Jerusalem Temple. Both of these are key features of Samaritan theology. Although this documentation apparently dates, at the earliest, from the third century C.E., the Samaritan exaltation of Moses appears to have been a constant tradition, which was not confined to any one period.

The author of Stephen's speech was well acquainted with the Samaritan Torah version. He favored the Samaritan biblical narrative; he identified with Samaritan feelings concerning the Jerusalem Temple; and when he used the prophetic writings, which the Samaritans did not accept, he altered them to reflect Samaritan beliefs. At no time does he explicitly attack the Torah that the Samaritans hold sacred. It is not the Torah which is denounced, but the unrepentant negative response to God's will by a certain segment of the people. These apostate people who continue the sin of Solomon by worshiping in the Jerusalem Temple are the Jews.

Stephen's speech contains a viewpoint that is at variance with the author of Acts own Christology. It is completely non-Davidic. Its messianic expectation is tied to Moses, not David. Nevertheless, with some editing, he incorporates it into Acts, because it serves his purposes. It accuses the Jews of apostasy from the true worship of God and goes on to further accusations of murder and persecution. The alleged martyrdom of Stephen helps create the illusion that the Jews carried out a bloody persecution of the early church.

PART 3

The Book of Acts mentions a Jewish repression of the nascent church following the execution of Stephen (Acts 7:56-59). "And on that day a great persecution arose against the church in Jerusalem; and they were all scattered throughout the regions of Judea and Samaria, except the apostles" (Acts 8:1). There is no doubt that the incident reflects the antagonism that developed between the Jews who did not accept Jesus and certain Jewish members of the church. But, let us be clear, belief even in an individual as the Messiah, albeit incorrect, did not, in and of itself, exclude one from the mainstream of the Jewish fold. There were more compelling reasons to be wary of these sectaries than just their belief in Jesus. The Samaritan-oriented anti-Temple statements made by those within the church like Stephen could have prompted Jewish anger. Stephen's poor relations with normative Jews, only one problem he faced, resulted from his deprecating of the sanctity of the Temple. The Jewish witnesses maintain, "We have heard him say that the Nazarene, Jesus, will destroy this place [the Temple] and alter the customs which Moses handed down to us" (Acts 6:14). Although the author of Acts calls the witnesses against Stephen "false" (Acts 6:13), his speech served only to confirm the charges brought against him. He declared, "It was Solomon who built a house for Him. However, the Most High does not dwell in houses made by hands" (Acts 7:47-48). Stephen's difference of opinion was not only with general Jewish belief. He was in conflict with apostolic beliefs as well. Stephen preached beliefs much more radical than those maintained by the apostles, especially with regard to the Jerusalem Temple.

The author of Acts attempted to hide the theological division within the early church. Nevertheless, it is clear that Stephen was a leader of a fringe group of proto-Christians who were distinguished from other followers of Jesus by their radical opposition to the Temple in Jerusalem.[31] The apostles and their followers seem to have had a more conservative attitude toward the Temple than that preached by Stephen. According to Acts, Stephen's provocative speech touched off a persecution of the church. With the exception of the apostles, it is claimed that its members were forced to flee (Acts 8:1, 4). This is a startling admission! It shows that the entire church was not forced to flee. The reaction on the wake of Stephen's death was not aimed at the apostles and their followers; it was only aimed at those proto-Christians closer to Stephen's theological views.

Stephen and those who maintained similar anti-Temple notions were predisposed to join the Jesus movement. Perhaps, it was something Jesus said about destroying the Temple. In any case, they used Jesus as a springboard for their own theological concepts and they now melded these views with his teachings. The report that "they were all scattered" evidently refers to the members of Stephen's group and others (that is, some Hellenistic

Jewish members of the church) who shared certain of that group's notions. Because of this scattering, we find another of the food administrators, Philip, proclaiming the gospel to the Samaritans with apparently great success (Acts 8:5-6, 12). The more normative Jewish members of the church remained in Jerusalem with their leaders, the apostles. The Book of Acts is silent on the reaction of the more normative wing of the church to this "persecution" but, later, the Book of Acts claims that "When the apostles in Jerusalem heard that Samaria had received the word of God [preached by "those who had been scattered"], they sent Peter and John to them, who came down and prayed for them, that they might receive holy spirit" (Acts 8:14-15). If the apostles did, indeed, send Peter and John it may show an underlying concern the apostles had about the instruction being given to the new converts. According to the author of Acts, they gave their approval to what was being taught. Any indication of conflict between the Jerusalem based church and the rise of a formal church in Samaria is carefully suppressed.

Acts 8:1-4 neither specifically identifies nor explains why only some from within the proto-Christian church and not the entire church was "persecuted." One must surmise from its proximity to the Stephen story that it had something to do with him and the teachings he expounded. The resulting dispersion raises the question, Why did some of those who left Jerusalem go to Samaria? Was it because they had Samaritan sympathies? This is strongly suggested by the contents of Stephen's speech. The mission to the Samaritans implies the acceptance of the Samaritans as Israelites, which the Samaritans themselves maintained.[32] Therefore, the mission to the Samaritans should not be conflated with outreach to Gentiles. The issues associated with Gentile Christianity's non-acceptance of the Torah, which arose later, are not applicable in this situation. Yet, the apostolic leadership must have been concerned about what those who came to Samaria were teaching the Samaritan neophytes and, therefore, sent Peter and John. The author of Acts, as he does throughout his relating of events surrounding the Stephen story, seeks to cover-up this dissension in the proto-Christian church. So, he obscures the true concerns that brought about Peter's and John's alleged visit to Samaria.

The phrase "except the apostles" (Acts 8:1) is a reference to the first generation proto-Christian communal leadership in Jerusalem. What kind of "great persecution" was this that its highest leadership, the "apostles," was not among the persecuted? Indeed, of those who fled, how endangered were they when some of them did not "scatter" far, but, "went about preaching the word" in Judea (Acts 8:4), that is, in the very region where Jerusalem is located. The conclusion to be drawn is that, if it happened at all, it was not much of a persecution. Only certain followers of Jesus are said to have found themselves in difficulty with Jews who did not accept Jesus as the Messiah. Heavy manipulative editing by the author of Acts has left an ambiguous story. Certainly, the extent of the alleged repression is left unclear. What is clear is that not only were the Hellenist-Hebrew teachings repulsive to those Jews who were not Jesus' followers but they must have been at odds with the teachings of the apostles as well. Throughout this alleged "great persecution" the apostles in Jerusalem remained unharmed. Moreover, some years later they are shown to still advocate that Jewish members of the church should bring sacrifices (specifically, sin offerings) to the Temple (Acts 21:23-26).[33] Here we have apostles, such as Peter and John, who are said to have been arrested, beaten, and threatened on account of their refusal to stop preaching in the name of Jesus (Acts 4:1-21). Yet, strangely, when the so-called great persecution occurs these same apostles and their followers are not repressed (Acts 8:1).

The possibility of the persecution narrative never having taken place has been raised. The persecution of a group in which the leaders remain untouched but where the members are forced to flee stretches credulity. Other traditions in Acts mention that the church underwent sporadic harassment, but that its membership as a whole was unmolested and continued to grow rapidly. Indirect evidence demonstrates that church factions with clearly divergent beliefs existed in Jerusalem along side of the church led by some of Jesus' disciples. That only some within the church were said to be persecuted indicates that already some formal separation existed between the more traditionally Jewish followers of the apostles and those church members with more radical views. What happened then was a persecution not of the entire church, but of this radical group alone. The radical group most likely consisted of the "Hellenist" and "Hebrew" members of the church. This is the only plausible explanation of how the apostles could have remained unmolested. The Jerusalem Jewish authorities must have distinguished between the different proto-Christian groups and found one acceptable, within certain parameters, and the others intolerable. The reasons must have been the differences in theology between the proto-Christian groups involved.

What were the theological differences that set the "Hellenists" and "Hebrews" at odds with other proto-Jewish Christians and especially against normative Jews? Again, only indirect evidence is available. Scant evidence exists which sheds light on the common points of agreement between the different gospels that the "Hellenists" and the "Hebrews" preached. Nevertheless, this slight evidence is enlightening. In particular, the narration of the arrest, trial, and death of Stephen (Acts 6:8-15, 7:54-60) and the speech of Stephen (Acts 7:2-53) contains information specifically meaningful to an understanding of the Hebrew faction of the church. It also contains some of the points of commonality they had with the Hellenistic faction. It is the Hellenistic faction of the church which was the mother of the church that survived. Soon its allegorical interpretation would give way to a law-free gospel.

In summation, only some major deviation from Jewish belief by the Hebrew faction could account for their persecution. This could have three possible causes: a belief in Jesus as the Messiah, the rejection of the Law, or the rejection of the Temple. Since the apostles were not persecuted for their belief in Jesus as the Messiah, this could not be the explanation. Being Samaritan-oriented, the Hebrew faction would be faithful to the Law as they interpreted it. This leaves rejection of the Temple as the only plausible answer. In the case of the Hellenistic faction, their pre-conversion allegorical interpretation of the Temple, sacrifice, and the Law may now have reached an intolerable stage. Perhaps, it was the notion that with the coming of Jesus, Temple, sacrifice, and the Law were all nullified. Thus, the common denominator specific to the beliefs of the allegorically oriented Hellenists and the Samaritan oriented Hebrews (but not the apostles) was rejection of the Temple. This must have been the impetus for the persecution. An explicit rejection of the Temple, expressed in their missionary propaganda, as exemplified by Stephen's Samaritan oriented speech, must have incited the persecution of those identified with that rejection. Even prior to the establishment of the church in Jerusalem, there may have been problems in that city with those who rejected the Temple. The difference now was that there was a concentrated contingent of such people who had come to Jerusalem, not because of the Temple, but, because it was the center of the proto-Christian church. They became too vocal in their views in exactly the place where one could expect strong reaction—Jerusalem. An implication of the statement that the apostles were not molested shows that there was also a division over the Temple in the earliest church. It was a split between the apostles' group on the one hand and the Hellenist-Hebrew group on the other. This raises a basic question: Did the apostles disregard Jesus' teaching or did the Hellenist-Hebrew group misinterpret and/or misrepresent Jesus' teaching in order to find confirmation for their pre-conversion beliefs?

Most of the information concerning the Hellenistic faction is gleaned from Paul's teachings following his conversion. Originally, the author of Acts maintains, Paul was supposed to apprehend Hellenist and/or Hebrew proto-Christians living in Damascus. But, Paul subsequently aligned himself with the proto-Christian Hellenists. However, he remained an antagonist of what became Samaritan (Hebrew) Christianity and those Jewish proto-Christians who closely allied with them. This was because he was opposed to certain aspects of the gospel taught by Samaritan Christians. In 2 Corinthians 11:22-23, Paul inveighs against what were more than likely Samaritan Christian missionaries: "Are they Hebrews? So am I. Are they Israelites? So am I. Are they descendants of Abraham? So am I. Are they servants of Christ? (I speak as if insane) I more so." Paul did not consider the contemporary usage of the respective appellations "Hebrews" and "Jews" as synonymous. This is seen from the continuation of Paul's words (2 Corinthians 11:24): "Five times I received from the Jews thirty-nine lashes." Thus, he differentiates between "Hebrews" and "Jews" within the same context. Similarly, in Philippians 3:5, he declares himself to be "a Hebrew of Hebrews"; that is, a better Hebrew than those who call themselves Hebrews. Samaritan communities were found throughout the eastern Mediterranean region and could even be found in Rome. The Samaritan Christian missionaries preached a gospel at odds with that preached by Paul. More than likely, their gospel message was more law-oriented than that presented by Paul.

The Book of Acts explains why Paul (Saul) was on his way to Damascus when he was converted to Christianity. It claims that he requested and received letters of recommendation from the high priest in order to arrest members of the church in Damascus (Acts 9:2). These individuals would be from the radical members of the church, Hellenist and Hebrew alike, who denounced the Temple, not those who held to a more normative Jewish belief. The beliefs held by these individuals that Paul found most repulsive are not explicitly stated. It would seem that Paul was particularly offended by certain beliefs held by the Hebrew faction, and that he continued to harbor these feelings even after his conversion. Paul was initiated into a belief in Jesus by proto-Christian Hellenistic Jews who before their conversion probably held sectarian concepts that allegorized the commandments of the Torah. They now added a belief in a resurrected messiah who they expected to fulfill all their previously held sectarian notions.

Paul's introduction into the Book of Acts' narrative turns our attention to the question of the origins of the church doctrines attributed to him. He is credited with instituting antinomian doctrines into the church. However, the evidence indicates that initially he simply expanded on ideas which were first preached by the Hellenist faction of the church in Syria and taught to him at the time of his conversion. What did the Hellenist faction of the church preach? What was the cause of its "persecution," while, at the same time, the more normative wing of the church was left unmolested? The discourse attributed to Stephen gives partial insight into the Hellenistic and Hebrew factions' generally shared attitude toward the Temple and why it led to their "persecution." On other aspects of the Law and concerning Jesus' role, these two proto-Christian groups differed from each other. This can be seen in Paul's later attitude toward the "Hebrews." This evidence suggests that the Hebrew faction of the church was more focused on adherence to the Torah, albeit in its Samaritan version. The Hellenistic faction, however, was far more radical, held to an allegorical interpretation of the Torah, and eventually began preaching a law-free gospel to both Jews and Gentiles. For the most part, the author of Acts plays down the conflicts in belief that existed between the several factions that made up the proto-Christian church.

The Book of Acts avoids explicitly stating what, in particular, caused the enmity toward the proto-Christian Jewish Hellenists and Hebrews, when no such feeling was expressed toward the more traditional proto-Christian Jews. We can surmise what the root problem was by examining the respective Jewish reactions to Stephen and Paul. The rage expressed toward Stephen and, later, toward Paul (Acts 24:5-6) concerned their negative attitudes. Stephen denigrated the Jerusalem Temple and championed Samaritan teachings while in the city of Jerusalem itself. To judge from Paul's writings, what precipitated the conflict between him and other Jews was his advocating the cessation of any literal observance of the Law.

In the first century of the Common Era, certain beliefs and practices were held in common in Judaism. Central was the belief in one God and a devotion to the way of life that He had established for Israel by Moses and subsequent prophets. The focal point of Jewish worship was the Temple, even for those who had religious differences with the Jerusalem priesthood. All views shared a basic common orthodoxy that included ideas about the election of Israel, the divine origin of the Law, repentance, atonement, and divine forgiveness. There was a widespread consensus on the duty of all Israel to keep the Law literally; however, there also existed diversity of opinion on the proper way to keep various aspects of it. Groups with their own interpretations and claims as to what was the true expression of God's will arose within Judaism. Josephus describes a number of Jewish groups whose interpretation of the Law distinguished them as distinct communities within Second Temple Judaism. He discusses the Pharisees, Sadducees, Essenes, and the followers of Judas the Galilean;[34] Philo discusses the Essenes[35] and the Therapeutae.[36] Philo also speaks of "some Jews" who were extreme allegorists, allegorizing the meaning of the commandments to such an extent that they ceased to observe them literally.[37]

This information helps us in understanding the formation of early Christian doctrine. Although Philo favored the symbolic interpretation of the Torah's commandments, he was critical of those who, because of carrying symbolism too far, neglected the actual observance of the Law. The allegorization he criticizes fits the pattern of sectarian belief that we would expect to have characterized the forerunner of the Hellenistic proto-Christian teachings. Philo stated:

> There are some who, regarding laws in their literal sense in the light of symbols of matters belonging to the intellect, are over punctilious about the latter, while treating the former with easy-going neglect . . . . It is quite true that the Seventh Day is meant to teach the powers of the Unoriginate and the non-action of created beings. But let us not for this reason abrogate the laws laid down for its observance, and light fires or till the ground or carry loads or institute proceedings in court or act as jurors or demand the restoration of deposits or recover loans, or do all else that we are permitted to do as well on days that are not festival seasons. It is true also that the Feast is a symbol of gladness of soul and of thankfulness to God, but we should not for this reason turn our backs on the general gatherings of the year's seasons. It is

> true that receiving circumcision does indeed portray the excision of pleasure and all passions, and the putting away of the impious conceit, under which the mind supposed that it was capable of begetting by its own power: but let us not on this account repeal the law laid down for circumcising. Why, we shall be ignoring the sanctity of the Temple and a thousand other things, if we are going to pay heed to nothing except what is shown us by the inner meaning of things. Nay, we should look on all these outward observances as resembling the body and their inner meanings as resembling the soul. It follows that, exactly as we have to take thought for the body, because it is the abode of the soul, so we must pay heed to the letter of the laws. If we keep and observe these, we shall gain a clearer conception of those things of which these are the Symbols; and besides that we shall not incur the censure of the many and the charges they are sure to bring against us.[38]

Apparently, certain Jewish allegorists who interpreted the Torah's laws as symbolism saw in the passion of Jesus and the subsequent claim of resurrection an allegorical device to explain their nullifying of the outward observance of the commandments. It is their incipient Christian teachings that brought on the "censure of the many" which was directed at those New Testament characters who were influenced by these ideas. Thus, the allegorists are the source of those notions that developed into Paul's antinomian pronouncements.

Philo comments that "we shall be ignoring the sanctity of the Temple and of a thousand other things, if we are going to pay heed to nothing except what is shown us by the inner meaning of things." The great majority of Jews rejected the extreme notions that nullified the commandments of the Law and, instead, participated in their common Judaism. Despite distinct differences on important issues of interpretation, most groups interacted (albeit sometimes bitterly) with each other within a framework of shared common beliefs and practices. The first generation of proto-

Christians believed in Jesus as a resurrected Messiah, but that, in itself, did not exclude them from the community of Israel. Their expulsion revolved around Jewish fidelity to Torah. Antinomian Jews who joined the church used Jesus as a peg on which to hang their own notions. When they began telling other Jews that as a result of Jesus' putatively salvific death that the Torah was abrogated, when they claimed he was an angelic being, and when they began to establish law-free Gentile churches, then all faithful Jews knew they had to separate themselves from them and to oppose this group. It is only when proto-Christians began to adopt doctrines completely unreconcilable with the Torah (such as, making Jesus into a god-like figure and accepting uncircumcised adherents into the sect) and when the church, as a whole, became gentilized, that the permanent estrangement occurred.

Jesus' initial Hellenistic followers were drawn from Jewish antinomian circles that, by appealing to allegory and symbolism, advocated the cessation of literal observance of certain aspects of the Torah. Perhaps these Hellenists were attracted to Jesus because of something he said concerning the destruction of the Temple. It was these same remarks that drew Samaritans to him as well. The Gospels of Mark and Matthew claim that Jesus was accused of (Mark 14:58, Matthew 26:61) and taunted for (Mark 15:29, Matthew 27:39-40) making a hostile statement about the Temple. Apparently the author of the Gospel of Mark, with the authors of Matthew and Acts following suit, were concerned by what Jesus' Temple destruction remark conveyed about his true intentions toward the Jewish and Roman authorities. Therefore, they brand the accusation as false (Mark 14:57-58; see also Matthew 26:59-61, Acts 6:13-14). The author of the Gospel of John finds a way out of the predicament not by denying that Jesus made such a statement, but by giving his own interpretation of what Jesus meant by it. According to the Johannine wording of this statement, Jesus said, "Destroy this Temple, and in three days I will raise it up" (John 2:19). The author of the Gospel of John comments, "But he was speaking of the temple of his body" (John 2:21).

As portrayed in Acts, all the factions of the proto-Christian church accuse the Jews of killing Jesus while they simultaneously exonerate the Romans. But, the Hellenistic and Hebrew factions display extremist views in other areas as well. They inveigh respectively against fundamental institutions of Judaism. By the Hellenists allegorizing the Law and the Hebrews denigrating the Temple and those who worship there, they laid the foundation for much of the anti-Judaic disposition of the developing Christian churches.

Notes

[1] The Gospel of Mark, followed by the Gospels of Matthew and Luke respectively, say Jesus was arrested on the first night of Passover; the Gospel of John says his arrest took place on the night before.

[2] The Gospels of Mark and Matthew cite two meetings of the Sanhedrin to judge Jesus; the Gospel of Luke describes only one.

[3] According to the Gospel of John, there was no Jewish trial, only an interrogation by the priestly authorities.

[4] See, Shlomo Pines, *The Jewish Christians of the Early Centuries of Christianity According to a New Source*, Jerusalem: Central Press, 1966.

[5] The Romans considered torture a legitimate means for arriving at the truth of an accusation.

[6] A mishnah states that "the Sadducces [some editions read *ha-minim*, "the sectarians"] perverted the truth and said there is only one world [that is, only this life and no future life]" (Mishnah *Berachot* 9:5).

[7] The historicity of this episode as presented in Acts is questionable. If this self-serving story is true, Gamaliel most likely made his speech before 35 C.E. Gamaliel is said to refer to two revolts. Theudas led the first and "After this man [i.e. Theudas] Judas of Galilee rose up in the days of the census" (Acts 5:36-37). Judas met his death (6 C.E.) when he opposed the census conducted in Judea by Quirinius (*Jewish War* II. 17. 8 [433]). The Lucan chronology would place Theudas' revolt sometime before 6 C.E. However, according to Josephus (*Jewish Antiquities* XX. 5. 1 [97-98]), a Theudas revolted sometime after Gamaliel is supposed to have made his impassioned

appeal. The revolt led by this Theudas occurred in 45 or 46 C.E. Was the Theudas mentioned by Josephus different from the Theudas cited by Gamaliel in Acts? Gamaliel's Theudas must have made some impact or else citing him, over thirty years later, would have had no effect on his audience. As such, it is unlikely that Josephus would not have mentioned this supposedly earlier Theudas as well. We may conclude that there was only one Theudas who rebelled and that he lived after Gamaliel allegedly spoke.

8   This is one more example of the breakdown in the concept of a trinitarian god held by most of Christendom. This supposed triune god of three equal persons in one being does not know what another part of itself is thinking or planning. Jesus was not equal to God. Mark's Jesus admitted that there were things that neither he nor the angels knew, but that only God knew: "But of that day or the hour no one knows, neither the angels in heaven, nor the Son, but the Father" (Mark 13:32). Furthermore, when having trouble, he displayed submission to God and prayed for help: "Father, if you are willing, remove this cup from me; yet not my will, but Yours be done" (Luke 22:42). Are these quotations from the Gospels consistent with the claim that Jesus is, in fact, one in substance and power with God?

9   *Jewish Antiquities* XX. 9. 1 [200]. We will presume for the purposes of this volume that this text in Josephus has not undergone any Christian interpolation.

10 For an excellent study of the rabbinic reaction to the early Christians see, Lawrence H. Schiffman, *Who Was a Jew? Rabbinic and Halakhic Perspectives on the Jewish-Christian Schism*, Hoboken, NJ: Ktav Publishing House, 1985.

11 By the time Acts was written Christianity had survived for five decades. The Gentile churches predominated and the Jerusalem church was no more.

12 Julius Caesar was formally deified by decree of the Senate following his death. However, the apotheosis of the reigning emperor began during the rule of his successor, Augustus. For Augustus, an assumption of divinity, the Imperial Cult, was a matter of policy to secure unification of the Empire and gain the loyalty of the provinces to Rome. Gaius Caligula was the first of the Roman emperors to take his divinity literally, instead of as an expression of loyalty by his subjects.

13 Concerning persecution of Christians in the early centuries of the Common Era, Douglas R.A. Hare remarks: "It is clear even to the most biased students

that the severest persecution suffered by Christians in the early centuries were imposed not by the Jews but by the Roman government. A number of modern scholars have maintained, however, the Roman persecution was due in no small measure to the activities of Jews . . . . The thesis of this article is that such a charge cannot be substantiated on the basis of the available evidence and ought to be dismissed" (Douglas R.A. Hare, "The Relationship Between Jewish and Gentile Persecution of Christians," *Journal of Ecumenical Studies*, 1967, pp. 446-447). "That Jews did in fact have a role in Gentile persecution," Hare continues, "need not be denied. That this was a role of primary importance, at least with respect to official persecution by the Roman government, cannot be demonstrated on the basis of available evidence" (p. 456).

[14] It should be noted that something is not necessarily Jewish because it may be practiced by certain Jews on the fringe of Judaism. Moreover, in the vast literature of what are called "Jewish books" one can find almost any idea one is looking for. One must also distinguish carefully between the materials of commonly-held Judaism and *tangential* Judaism.

[15] " . . . [T]hey said they were Hebrews . . ." (*Jewish Antiquities* XI. 8. 6 [344]). They "are called Chuthaioi [Cuthim] in the Hebrew tongue, and Samareitai [Samaritans] by the Greeks" (*Jewish Antiquities* IX. 14. 3 [290]).

[16] For example, Philip and Andrew (John 1:44).

[17] See, James D. Purvis, "The Samaritans," *The Cambridge History of Judaism*, Ed. W.D. Davies and Louis Finkelstein, Cambridge: Cambridge University Press, vol. 2, 1989, p. 604 ff.; James Alan Montgomery, *The Samaritans: The Earliest Jewish Sect*, Philadelphia: The John C. Winston Co., 1907, pp. 76-77.

[18] Purvis, in writing of John Hyrcanus' motives for destroying the Samaritan temple on Mount Gerizim (128 B.C.E.), comments that "A temple in the north, supported by a comparatively insignificant cultural-political force, would have been no great threat to the cultural or political stability of Judah; but would have been a divisive factor in the allegiance of the people of the rural areas of the north. The creation of a greater unity between Judah and the rest of Palestine would have been abetted by the removal of any other force which divided the north and south" (James D. Purvis, *The Samaritan Pentateuch and the Origin of the Samaritan Sect*, Cambridge: Harvard University Press, 1968, p. 113). It may be that in some rural areas of the north there were, during the first century C.E., Jews who had developed an ambivalent loyalty between Mount Moriah and Mount Gerizim.

19. In the pre-Christian period, the only part of the Septuagint that was authorized in a more or less fixed text was its Torah rendering. The Greek version of other books of the Bible were much more fluid. What is now commonly referred to as the Septuagint version of the Bible is the form these books eventually assumed as a result of the work of Christian scholarship (Origen in particular). Christian scribes were responsible for the preservation of the Septuagint, since the Jewish community stopped using it during the course of the second century C.E. Although originally a Jewish work, no Jewish manuscript of the Septuagint has survived, except for a handful of pre-Christian fragments discovered in recent times.

20. "No one versed in the Laws is likely to be unaware that at an earlier date Abraham migrated from Chaldea and dwelt in Haran, and that after his father's death there, he removes from that country also . . ." (Philo, *Migration of Abraham* XXXII. 177). This disagrees with the Masoretic and Septuagint texts. It may be due to Philo using a variant Greek text, or his misinterpreting, or his incorrectly recalling the relevant verses from memory.

21. "His [Joseph's] brethren also died after sojourning happily in Egypt. Their bodies were carried some time afterwards by their descendants [and their sons] to Hebron and buried there" (*Jewish Antiquities* II. 8. 2 [199]).

22. Macdonald writes that according to Samaritan belief, "Another reason for its [Mount Gerizim's] supreme place and sanctity was the fact (if it is a fact!) that the mount contained the cave of Machpelah" (Macdonald, *Theology of the Samaritans*, p. 329).

23. *Jewish Antiquities* IX. 14. 3 [291].

24. *Jewish Antiquities* XI. 8. 6 [341].

25. See Abraham Spiro, "Stephen's Samaritan Background," Appendix V in *The Acts of the Apostles* by Johannes Munck, rev. by W.F. Albright and C.S. Mann, The Anchor Bible 31; New York: Doubleday, 1967, pp. 285-300.

26. That the sacrificial system was abrogated at Jesus' death is argued in the Book of Hebrews, the work of an unknown follower of Jesus. The writer of Hebrews does not mention the Temple, but only speaks about the Tabernacle and may show Samaritan influence.

27. Purvis writes that the Samaritans, "had come to regard themselves not simply as a part of the Israelite nation, but as the true remnant of the ancient Israelite faith. Conversely, they regarded the Jews as a deviant and apostate part of the Israelite nation that had departed from the true faith of which they were

28. Macdonald records a prayer from the Samaritan liturgy that speaks of the restoration of worship on Mount Gerizim, "May God prolong your lives till the days of the Taheb, the Tabernacle (restored) and the days of favour" (Macdonald, *Theology of the Samaritans*, p. 359).

29. Some commentators have expressed the view that the author of Acts modeled the trial and death of Stephen on the trial and death of Jesus. This brings into question the historicity of the trial scene of Stephen before the Sanhedrin.

30. Stephen maintains that the Torah was given to Moses by an angel, not by God, which shows that, whatever his background, he held to a number of marginal doctrines. According to Jubilees 1:27-29 and 2:1, an angel ("angel of the presence"—there are a number of angels called by this name) spoke with Moses on Mount Sinai. The angel in Jubilees writes, not the Torah, but a history up to the establishment of the messianic kingdom (cf. Testament of Dan 6:2, Philo, *On Dreams* I. 143). Josephus writes that "we have learned the noblest of our doctrines and the holiest of our laws from the messengers [*angeloi*] sent by God" (*Jewish Antiquities* XV. 5. 3 [136]. Here, *angeloi*, does not mean "angels," but prophets or priests (cf. *Apion* 1. 37, Septuagint Malachi 2:7). In Galatians 3:19, Paul states that the Law was "ordained through angels by the hand of a mediator." Paul uses this exposition to show that the Law is inferior to the promises that God made to Abraham without any intermediary (Galatians 3:16-18).

It should be noted that the Septuagint Exodus does not have an angelic mediator but, as in the Masoretic text, the mediator is Moses. In the Septuagint the people stood far off in a state of fear (20:18) and "said to Moses, speak to us, let not God speak to us, lest we die" (20:19). This is similar to the Masoretic text, "And they [the people] said to Moses: "Speak with us, and we will hear; but let not God speak with us, lest we die"

(Exodus 20:16). God not only speaks to Moses directly but also to all the children of Israel: "And the LORD said to Moses: 'Thus you shall say to the children of Israel, You yourselves have seen that I have talked with you [plural] from heaven'" (MT Exodus 20:19).

31. Attempts have been made to find a connection between Stephen's negation of the Temple as a place of worship and the Qumran community's attitude toward the Temple. Such comparisons are fallacious. The Qumran community did not reject the Temple itself but the priests who officiated there. Therefore, there is really no relationship at all between the Temple views of Acts 7 and those of the Qumran community.

32. In the first century C.E., Jews often considered Samaritans to be renegade Israelites rather than Gentiles. This attitude is also implied in the proto-Christian mission to the Samaritans taking place before that to the Gentiles.

James D. Purvis observes that "Early Christian attitudes toward the Samaritans appear to have been . . . ambivalent. At least one New Testament writer regarded them as being other than 'the house of Israel,' although in a category somewhere between Jews and Gentiles (Matthew 10:5-6). Other New Testament writers were, however, more favorably disposed towards the people of Samaria, as is evidenced by such tests as the parable of the good Samaritan (Luke 10:25-37), the story of the Samaritan who was the only thankful leper out of ten who were cleansed (Luke 17:11-19), and the account of Jesus' revelation of his vocation to the Samaritan woman at Jacob's well (John 4:1-42). Inasmuch as these favourable reports contrast with the animus expressed toward the Samaritans in much Jewish writing, it is tempting to attribute these to some peculiar Christian attraction to these people. It would not be difficult to find reasons for this, given the success of the Christian mission in Samaria (so Luke-Acts), and given the fact that the early church found itself in an adversary relationship with the Jewish leaders, in particular the Pharisees, analogous to that of the Samaritans (so John's gospel). It is likely, however, that the early church was no more or no less ambivalent towards the Samaritans than was the Jewish community of that time." (Purvis, "The Samaritans," p. 593)

33 Each of the four men under a Nazarite vow whose expenses Paul is said to have paid in Acts 21 (on the advice of the Jerusalem Christian leadership more faithful to the Law) would have had to offer a lamb as a sin offering to end this particular vow (Numbers 6:13-14). Was this not in conflict with the concept of Jesus dying as a final sin offering?
34 *Jewish Antiquities* XVIII. 1. 2-6 [11-25].
35 Philo, *Every Good Man Is Free* XII. 75-XIII. 91.
36 Philo, *On the Contemplative Life* I. 2-XI. 90.
37 Philo, *On the Migration of Abraham* XVI. 89-93.
38 Ibid., XVI. 89-93.

11.

THE CRUCIFIXION OF THE JEWS

Glossing over the facts

As we have seen, the Roman involvement in the execution of Jesus is glossed over by the evangelists while the Jews are depicted as ultimately responsible for Jesus' death. Pontius Pilate, elsewhere known for his contemptuous attitude, his perverseness, and his brutal heavy-handed policy in governing Judea is portrayed, contrary to every other contemporary record as easily manipulated by "the Jews." The evangelists present the events as though Pilate had stood up for Jesus' acquittal, but yielded in the end to the demands of the Jews. Contrarily, it is maintained that Pilate, known for his brutal methods of crowd control, was intimidated by a Jewish mob into releasing a known anti-Roman seditionist. At the same time, he is compelled against his will to pronounce a death sentence on a loyal subject.

We find in the Gospels that before Jesus' arrival in Jerusalem, he made secret arrangements with supporters other than the twelve disciples for his entrance and stay in the city. Moreover, he was planning something, which his closest disciples were not completely informed of. Jesus' activities make it plain that he constituted a threat to public safety and order. The speed with which the authorities apprehended and executed Jesus just before Passover suggests that his actions alerted them to some plot coordinated to occur at the time of the festival. Having determined that there was an anti-Roman plot, Pilate would certainly have demanded assistance from the Jewish authorities in apprehending the ringleader. Fearing Roman reprisals, the Jewish authorities would have been compelled to assist Pilate in his apprehension of Jesus. In their efforts to deny that Jesus preached sedition it is understandable that the evangelists give no exact details of the plot, but only give information that can be interpreted in other ways. We do not know who Jesus' confederates were, or the details of what they conspired to do. But, the Gospels infer that Jesus did have a secret infrastructure. Who provided the donkey for his entrance into Jerusalem (Mark 11:2, Matthew 21:2, Luke 19:30)? Who was the man with the pitcher of water who showed the way to the upper room (Mark 14:13-14, Luke 22:10-11)? How did Jesus know where and when to send his emissaries (Mark 14:16, Luke 22:13)? Rather than see these incidents as part of a prearranged plan some Christians would rather believe these to be examples of miraculous foreknowledge on the part of Jesus. However, it is clear that Jesus had associates in and about Jerusalem with whom he coordinated plans that were not known to his twelve disciples.

Most Christian commentators have not sufficiently considered Jesus' reaction to any contemporary political events. They have also shied away from confronting the significance of remnant remembrances of the revolutionary Jesus that are scattered throughout the Gospels. Despite efforts to conceal the truth, a few illustrations of his insurrectionist pre-planning and activities do survive. When Jesus "resolutely set his face to go to Jerusalem" (Luke 9:51, 19:28) it was to make his entrance as Israel's king. This act was set to coincide with the week before the Jewish festival of freedom, the Passover. It is clear that Jesus' intention was to ride into Jerusalem on the foal of an ass, as a symbolic act to proclaim that he was the King Messiah (Mark 11:7-11, Matthew 21:7-11, Luke 19:35-38, John 12:14-15). This was in accordance with the prophecy of Zechariah 9:9 cited in Matthew 21:5[1] and John 12:15. Everything was carefully planned in advance including providing for a donkey (Mark 11:1-6, Matthew 21:1-3, Luke 19:29-35) and having his followers stir up the crowd to greet his entrance with messianic fervor: "And as he was now approaching, near the descent of the Mount of Olives, *the whole multitude of the disciples began to praise God joyfully with a loud voice for the miracles which they had seen*" (Luke 19:37). Thus, a few days prior to Jesus' arrest he and his followers staged a provocative "messianic" entrance into the city. This was immediately followed (according to the Synoptic Gospels) by a coordinated disruptive action, led by Jesus, within the Temple precinct (Mark 11:15-16, Matthew 21:12-13, Luke 19:45-46; cf. John 2:14-16). The Gospels specifically mention an attack on the moneychangers and those selling sacrificial animals.[2]

The Temple was the social, economic, and political, as well as religious center of the Jewish world. The Temple complex was quite large and protected internally by the Temple guard. The Romans could observe everything going on in the Temple compound from their vantage point in the Antonia fortress to the immediate north.[3] To prevent movement through the Temple area, even for a brief period of time, would require a show of force supported by a large group of armed followers. (They would have to face the Temple guard, a Roman cohort, the moneychangers and sacrificial animal dealers, as well as the throng of pilgrims.)

The Gospels relate that Jesus entered Jerusalem and proceeded to disrupt the peace of the Temple area in a manner which was openly defiant not only of the priestly hierarchy but of the Roman hegemony over Judea as well.[4] The Synoptic Gospels' noting that the Temple attack took place a few days before Jesus' execution might indicate that it was a primary cause in bringing about his condemnation (Mark 11:15-16, Matthew 21:12, Luke 19:45-46). In the Gospel of John, the incident occurs at the beginning of Jesus' public activity and appears to have no serious consequences (John 2:13-16). This episode, it is said, occurred just before Passover, the very time of the year the Romans considered the most volatile in Judea. Thousands of pilgrims flooded the city of Jerusalem to celebrate the festival of freedom from bondage; for this reason the Romans were especially vigilant in watching over the crowds thronging the Temple precinct.⁵ As a preventive measure the Roman governor and additional troops came to Jerusalem from Caesarea during the festivals to ensure that the pilgrim crowds did not become unruly.⁶

It is no wonder if the Temple hierarchy regarded Jesus as a threat to their leadership positions and Jewish political autonomy. The continuation of what semblance of Jewish independence still existed under Roman rule depended upon their maintenance of order and their ability to suppress revolts. Jesus' actions were not politically harmless. Jesus' carefully staged entry into Jerusalem and his Temple disruption could not go unnoticed by the Romans. To the Romans, Jesus could be nothing other than an insurrectionist.

Jesus was now putting into action what he had advocated in his preaching. Jesus' advocacy of resistance to Roman domination is expressed in "render to Caesar that which is Caesar's," that is, nothing, "and to God that which is God's," that is, everything (cf. Luke 20:25 with Haggai 2:8). Jesus declares, "he that has no sword, let him sell his garment and buy one" (Luke 22:36). This has to be done, Luke's Jesus reasons, so that he would be "reckoned with the transgressors [as supposedly in Isaiah 53:9]" (Luke 22:37). This is an artificial fulfillment of prophecy to explain why Jesus asked his disciples how many swords they possessed. When his disciples say, "Lord, here are two swords," his response is, "It is sufficient" (Luke 22:38). Jesus' satisfaction at the number of swords in the possession of his most intimate followers accords with the needs of assassins rather than those of a large armed force. This cryptic incident shows his political intrigue and not political pacifism. Did Jesus plan to create a situation whereby some of his associates would be able to carry out an assassination? Perhaps, Pilate (or the high priest) was the intended victim.

The Greek word rendered "swords," *makhairai*, is the one used for a short sword. It is the word usually used for "sword" in the New Testament (cf. Matthew 26:47). The Greek word *hromphaia* is used in the New Testament to denote a large, broad sword. The word *makhaira* is also used in the Septuagint for the double-edged sword that Ehud used in his assassination of Eglon, king of Moab (Judges 3:16-22). Such a short sword would be suitable for an assassination since it could be easily concealed under the upper garment (as apparently the disciples' weapons were concealed). Jesus' response, *hikanon estin*, "sufficient it is," was an emphatic approval. The verb is singular and the predicate's adjective is in the emphatic first position. That is, collectively two swords were enough for the purpose he had in mind. The exact nature of Jesus' plan is not recorded in the narrative, but was apparently aborted by circumstances. Modern Christian commentaries disregard the plain meaning of the text. In a forced interpretation, some maintain that Jesus' statement about buying swords is a deliberate use of irony. His answer is understood to be one of despair, that by producing swords the disciples showed that they did not understand his meaning. These commentators point to Matthew 26:52 where Jesus is quoted as having said in the Garden of Gethsemane, "Put your sword back into its place; all those who take up the sword shall perish by the sword." This supposedly shows Jesus' true feelings about the use of swords. The author of Matthew introduced this saying into the text of his Gospel as part of the ongoing process initiated by Mark to make Jesus appear as a politically non-violent individual who had no intention of resisting Roman domination. However, shortly after the Last Supper we see the use of a sword by a disciple that contradicts the admonition of the Matthean Jesus. In the Garden of Gethsemane arrest scene, where one of those coming to seize Jesus has his ear cut off, the Gospel of Mark does not describe the sword-wielder as a disciple (Mark 14:47). The Matthean narrative which never mentioned any swords in conjunction with the disciples identifies the sword-wielder as a disciple (Matthew 26:51). The Johannine narrative, which also never mentioned any swords in conjunction with the disciples, identifies the sword-wielding disciple as Peter. Only Luke, among the evangelists, offers a reason why a disciple would be carrying a sword, especially when the disciples had just come from the Last Supper (Luke 22:36, 38).

The respective authors of Mark and Matthew do not record

the sword incident. It is only found in Luke, possibly because it was too descriptive of Jesus' actual attitude toward the use of physical confrontation. But, the author of Luke also wanted to portray Jesus as submissive to Roman rule. However, he saw an opportunity for safely recording this enigmatic conversation about the need for swords by having it benignly refer to a supposed fulfillment of prophecy. By calling on his disciples to arm themselves, the author of Luke says that Jesus was merely preparing the way for his enemies to class him among criminals. This author would have his readers believe that Jesus' words are not to be taken literally. Accordingly, Jesus set the stage, as if in a play, to create the situation whereby his enemies, taking the incident literally, would be able to make this accusation. This is one more attempt to conceal Jesus' call for resistance to Roman governance. However, it is revealing. It is not farfetched to ask, Did Jesus plan to assassinate Pilate (or the high priest), but did his disciples lose their nerve at the very last minute? Is this the source of their later feelings of guilt?

According to the Gospel of Luke, the Jewish authorities said to Pilate: "We have found this man misleading our nation and forbidding to pay taxes to Caesar, saying that he himself is Christ [Messiah] a king. . . . He stirs up the people, teaching all over Judea, starting from Galilee, even as far as this place" (Luke 23:2, 5). Several references to Jesus' activities found in the Gospels show these accusations to be an accurate description of his religio-political agitation. The Lucan use of the term "Christ" ("Messiah") in its political sense of king is unique in the Gospels. It illustrates that Jesus' capital offense was a political matter rather than a religious matter. If it was a strictly religious concern Jesus would not have been taken before Pilate. Pilate had no interest in Jewish religious matters. It is likely that Luke, for political and theological reasons, took the Roman charge against Jesus and attributed it to the Jewish leaders as part of his contribution to covering up the fact that Jesus was a rebel against Roman authority. In any case, both the Jews and the Romans considered any messianic claim to refer to a temporal king. Jesus' activities, as described by the Gospels, show him to be agitating the people to resist the Roman authorities in exactly the temporal sense that the accusations describe. There was nothing otherworldly about Jesus' actions. The inscription "King of the Jews," placed on the cross to show the reason for the execution, was not Roman sardonicism. It was the accusation upon which he was found guilty.

Jesus' afflictions did not come about because of the sins of other men, but because of his provoking the Romans. One should not be befuddled by those who claim Jesus was solely concerned with spiritual matters. Despite attempts to wrench them from their historical context or obliterate them altogether, echoes of Jesus as an anti-Roman rebel resound in the Gospels. Jesus spoke to a people yearning for liberation from alien oppression. In addressing their needs, the evidence shows that the historical Jesus fused political activism with religious fervor. By arousing Roman ire, Jesus brought upon himself, not a religious, but a distinctly political death. Found guilty of sedition in claiming to be the king of the Jews, he was condemned to be executed by the usual method the Romans reserved for political rebels. In sum, why was Jesus executed? Because he challenged Roman hegemony over Judea and lost.

Jesus' encounter with Roman law did not end differently than those of other rebels. Pilate did not need the Jewish authorities to prod him into executing Jesus. Based on Jesus' own words and actions, as recorded in the Gospels, the governor had enough reason to consider him as a rebel agitator. Apparently, Jesus expected to be proclaimed king by the masses of Jewish pilgrims who had come to Jerusalem for Passover. Jesus was promoting sedition! Consequently, Jesus was arrested by the Romans as a rebel, put on trial, and executed as such. Historically, it may be that Pilate dispensed with a trial. Jesus' subversive actions, which culminated in his Temple attack, may have led to his apprehension and immediate crucifixion as a public warning. The Romans could not possibly ignore or overlook Jesus' direct and hostile challenge. In their eyes, it was nothing less than the opening confrontation in a Jewish revolt. They handled it accordingly, surely pressuring the

Jewish authorities to either turn this rebel over or suffer the consequences of Roman anger.

The fact that Jesus was executed shows that the Romans considered Jesus a dangerous seditionist. What was the nature of the perceived danger? The Gospels of Mark and Luke record that the Romans had just suppressed a Jewish insurrection (Mark 15:7, Luke 23:19). Whether Jesus was personally involved in this particular revolt is unknown, but it is entirely plausible. His actions, in the least, certainly would have made him highly suspect to the Romans. Nevertheless, the New Testament prefers to place full blame upon the Jews for Jesus' death. The problem is that the manner of execution makes placing culpability upon the Jews untenable. Moreover, the Gospel of John maintains that under the Roman administration the Jews did not have the right to pass a death sentence: "The Jews said to him [Pilate], 'We are not permitted to put anyone to death'" (John 18:31).[7] Crucifixion as the instrument of execution establishes Roman involvement. It was a Roman, not a Jewish, form of execution.[8] It was used for slaves, violent criminals, and political rebels.[9] If the Sanhedrin had sentenced Jesus to death he would have been stoned. The fact that he was crucified shows that he was tried and condemned by a Roman court. Why was Roman crucifixion the means of execution? The most common Christian answer to the question of why crucifixion was the method of execution is that the Jews rejected Jesus and forbidden by the Romans from executing anyone themselves manipulated the Romans into putting him to death. It is an answer rooted in the Gospels themselves, which claim that despite the Roman execution, the primary responsibility for his execution was Jewish.

But, which Jews did the church hold responsible for Jesus' death? Was it those in Jerusalem, Alexandria, Rome, Thessalonica, or Antioch? Was it those supposedly watching the trial? If a mob demanding the death of Jesus really existed and was not merely invented as a means of denouncing the Jews, it would have consisted of an extremely small fraction of all the Jews alive at that period. Even of the Jews living in Judea and Galilee at the time of his death, only an infinitesimal percentage would have been in the "crowd" to demand Jesus' crucifixion; and even fewer would have mocked him on the cross. Yet, the New Testament's answer to the question is that the entire Jewish people are to be blamed. The New Testament makes it clear that it accuses all Jews, in all regions, for all time. The Jews are accused despite the fact that during his lifetime the great majority of contemporary Diaspora Jewry never heard of Jesus. Indeed, how widespread was contemporary awareness within the regions where Jesus allegedly preached, that is, Judea, Galilee, and surrounding areas? Of those who heard of him, how many sought his life? It is obvious that of the estimated four to seven million Jews contemporary with Jesus in the Roman Empire only a few, if any, may have had any intention to harm him in any way. Thus, when Matthew 27:25 has "*all* the people" say, "His blood be upon us and our children," or Acts 2:36 declares, "Let *all* the house of Israel know for certain that God has made him both Lord and Christ this Jesus whom *you* crucified" we are dealing with a deliberate attempt to manipulate events so as to condemn the entire Jewish people. "All" and "you" are used in these verses with the denotion that the entire Jewish people, with the exception of those who accept Jesus, are guilty for the death of Jesus. In short, the New Testament purposely distorts and fictionalizes these events. What was produced in the Gospels and the Book of Acts is a work of historical fiction, a fictionalized story in an historical setting.

The role of the Jewish authorities

Why would the high priest and his advisors or the full Sanhedrin consider Jesus dangerous? Is it that the priests were afraid that Jesus' agitation would incite the populace against them? But, what was the possibility of that happening? The priests had Torah mandated divine authority and centuries of tradition and practice to support their institutional legitimacy. Whether the high priest was personally beloved or not, the office was deeply revered. The individual in the office was intermediary not only between the

Roman authorities and the populace, but also between God and his people. It was the high priest that, on the Day of Atonement, entered the Holy of Holies and made atonement for the sins of the people of Israel.[10] Under such circumstances, how much of a threat could Jesus be to them? Nevertheless, perhaps they still considered him a danger to their position and decided to rid themselves of him. Yet, if the priests feared popular outrage were Jesus known to be arrested, as the Gospels suggest (for example, Mark 12:12, Matthew 21:46, Luke 20:19), why did they suddenly act contrary to their best interests? Why did they make a public spectacle of their intent at Passover and then exacerbate the situation by involving Pilate? If Jesus was so popular with the people, they could have incarcerated him until after the festival when the pilgrims would depart for home. Instead, they noisily arrested him in the volatile climate of the Passover pilgrimage and marched him back into Jerusalem. Why would they agitate the masses by involving Roman soldiers? Were the Jewish authorities not concerned that their action could spark an anti-Roman outbreak among the people?

What would account for the priestly authorities assisting in Jesus' arrest? Jesus' belief in the imminent approach of the kingdom of God and the role he must play in its establishment impelled him to go up to Jerusalem for Passover, the festival of freedom from bondage. His manner of entrance into the city and his Temple attack, if historical, would have been manifestations of his announcement of the arrival of said kingdom. Such displays of messianic kingly power would have outraged Pilate. The high priest would certainly be furious at Jesus' Temple attack. But, the high priest had far more to worry about for himself and the nation. It was his responsibility to keep order among the people, especially the pilgrim throngs in and about the Temple enclosure. He was aware of the Passover crowd's restive energy. The pilgrims were ever mindful that, while celebrating their freedom from a slavery, the Land of Israel was subject to foreign rule. The high priest and the Jewish authorities for whom he was spokesman could not tolerate the problems in keeping public order caused by this upstart. But, they knew that whether the pilgrim crowd heard of Jesus or not, gave serious thought to what he said or were indifferent to his message, were his followers or detractors, he was, still to the masses, a fellow Jew. To maneuver Pilate into putting him to death could be no solution to their problems. His executing someone claiming to be the liberating king of the Jews, the Messiah, on Passover would inflame the people's passion against the Romans. It invited riots, if not revolt—the very situations they wished to prevent. The Jewish authorities surely knew this was not the time of the year to execute would-be national liberators (as Jesus' own followers saw him [Luke 24:21, Acts 1:6]). Therefore, it is impossible to think that the Jewish leaders arranged to have Jesus killed. If they did help in the apprehension, it is most likely that they were coerced into assisting the Romans in Jesus' capture and execution. Pilate saw the solution to the situation: a message of raw terror—riot and proclaim yourself a king and you will suffer the brutal consequences of defying Roman power.

As a heuristic, the Romans determined that this advocate of insurgency must be immediately apprehended. They expected full cooperation from the Jewish authorities in tracking Jesus down. But, the author of John still manages to blame the Jewish authorities for arranging to kill Jesus, although he acknowledges extensive Roman pressure upon these leaders (John 11:48, 50). According to "the chief priests and the Pharisees," who have convened the Sanhedrin specifically to deal with the situation, Jesus continued to present a problem by ".performing many signs" (verse 47). So, they fear that "If we let him go on like this, all men will believe in him, and the Romans will come and take away both our place [the Temple] and our nation [i.e. the Jews will be exiled]" (verse 48). In response, the high priest, Caiaphas, argues that it is better to put Jesus to death rather than that the whole nation perishes through Roman revenge upon the entire people. "It is expedient for you that one man should die for the people, and that the whole nation should not perish" (verse 50). Whether this statement was actually enunciated by Caiaphas or not it reflects a widely discussed problem within the Jewish community, especially following the disastrous war with Rome. What is the Jewish community-at-large to do when confronted by heathen authorities with the alternative of either delivering an individual over to their control or facing total annihilation? Two midrashic passages illustrate the problem. First, "Better one life should be risked than that all should be certain [to die]."[11] Second, "It was taught: If a company of people are threatened by heathens, 'Surrender one of you and we will kill him, and if not we will kill all of you,' they should all be killed and not to surrender one son of Israel. But if they specified a particular person, as in the case of Sheba the son of Bichri [2 Samuel 20:1], they should surrender him and should not all be killed."[12] A distinction is made between the authorities demanding that Jews choose an arbitrary victim and a demand by the authorities for a specific individual. The discussions of the problem are found in this literary work written some time after Caiaphas died, but the problem was much older than the final redaction of the Midrash (*Bereshit Rabba*).

Why should there be a fear that "if all men believe in him [Jesus]" the Roman authorities "will come and take away both our place and our nation"? Is the answer found in the Gospels' Jesus? Did the Romans concern themselves with a Jewish miracle worker who supposedly heals the sick, turns water into wine, walks on water, and has a kingdom that is not of this world? Certainly not! But, they were concerned with one who stirs up the people politically and who gave every indication that he intended his kingdom to be of this world. Jesus' remarks about withholding taxes from Caesar, his "triumphal entry" into Jerusalem with its messianic overtones, and his disruption of Temple commerce right under the watchful eyes of the Roman authorities in the Antonia fortress were not actions for which one should expect Pilate to find "no guilt in him" (John 19:6). Pilate would have been aware of Jesus' activities since his entrance into the city and would demand his immediate apprehension. He would be thoroughly knowledgeable of the charges to be raised when Jesus appeared before him. The charges were primarily of a Roman concern. Pilate was concerned about Jesus' political, not his strictly religious, activities. The Jewish authorities certainly had what to fear when

Pilate became concerned over Jesus' actions. The Gospels endeavor to keep this concern a secret by creating a web of fiction, distortion, and false accusation.

If Jesus was of little or no concern to the Roman governor, then why was a Roman cohort which consists of three hundred to six hundred soldiers and its commander sent along with the Jewish arresting party to capture Jesus (John 18:12)? Surely, that sized force would need Pilate's approval! Why did Pilate show no concern, in his interrogation, about Jesus' call for nonpayment of taxes to Caesar (Although, alternatively as found in the Synoptic Gospels, it appears as if Jesus supported the Roman tax policy—Mark 12:17, Matthew 22:21, Luke 20:25.) Why did Pilate make no mention of Jesus' triumphal entry into Jerusalem (Mark 11:7-10, Matthew 21:4-9, Luke 19:35-38, John 12:12-15)? Why did he say nothing about Jesus' Temple attack which the Synoptic Gospels report occurred earlier that week (Mark 11:15-16, Matthew 21:12, Luke 19:45)? The Gospel of John also mentions an attack, but it occurs during an earlier visit to Jerusalem (John 2:14-16). With such a record, why does Pilate believe Jesus when he says that his claim to kingship is otherworldly, an abstract kingship that is no threat to Roman governance? The truth is that Jesus was of great concern to Pilate and that concern could have very easily turned into the use of force against the Jewish people if their leaders did not assist in his apprehension. Pilate sent a cohort to apprehend Jesus (John 18:3). One simply does not send that size an arresting party[13] unless one expects armed resistance. This could be expected given the provocative and violent actions (other incidents were probably not recorded) the Gospels attribute to Jesus (e.g. Mark 11:15-16, Mark 5:13, Mark 11:13-14). The Gospel records obscure and obliterate at least some vital facts about the Roman role and concerns in the apprehending, trial, and execution of Jesus. If Pilate's concerns turned to anger because of their non-cooperation, the Jewish authorities had much to fear for the safety of their people.

Josephus provides an example from a later period that illustrates why the Jewish authorities had good reason to fear Pilate's anger. Florus, procurator of Judea from 64-66 C.E., culminated his tyrannical rule with the seizure of seventeen talents of gold from the Temple treasury. A riot ensued, and mockingly, a basket was passed around to collect coins for the relief of the "needy" procurator. Florus was furious at this insult.[14] "[He] lodged at the palace, and on the following day had a tribunal placed in front of the building and took his seat; the chief priests, the nobles, and the most eminent citizens then presented themselves before the tribunal. Florus ordered them to hand over the men who had insulted him, declaring that they themselves would feel his vengeance if they failed to produce the culprits. The leaders, in reply, declared that the people were peaceably disposed and implored pardon for the individuals who had spoken disrespectfully. It was not surprising, they said, that in so great a crowd there should be some reckless spirits and foolish youths; but to pick out the delinquents was impossible, as everyone was now penitent and would, from fear of the consequences, deny what he had done."[15] Florus' answer was to turn his troops loose on the city with unprecedented rage, ordering "the soldiers to sack the agora . . . and to kill any whom they encountered. . . . [M]any of the peaceable citizens were arrested and brought before Florus, who had them first scourged and then crucified."[16] With Pilate's past record of atrocities there is no reason to believe that the Jewish leaders had less to fear from him than what was suffered by the people a generation later in this incident under Florus.

The legal power to decide life or death for a prisoner was in the hands of the governor. This is illustrated by another incident that happened approximately thirty years later. Josephus reports that in 62 C.E. one Jesus, son of Ananias, who went about proclaiming the destruction of Jerusalem and the sanctuary was arrested and "severely chastised" by leading citizens of Jerusalem who were angered by his "ill-omened words." "Thereupon, the magistrates [*hoi archontes*], supposing . . . that the man was under some supernatural impulse, brought him before the Roman governor." "Flayed to the bone with scourges" and questioned by the governor, Albinus (62-64 C.E.), he said nothing but, "Woe to

Jerusalem!" The governor must have considered him a politically harmless religious fanatic for he pronounced Jesus, son of Ananias, a "maniac" and released him.[17] Albinus had the final say in matters of release or condemnation. Similarly, Pilate did not have to be coerced into making the decision to execute Jesus. Unlike Jesus, son of Ananias, who had done no violence and had no following, but had merely spoken words of doom, this Jesus, son of Joseph, had undertaken violent action and was considered a politically harmful religious fanatic. He had entered Jerusalem to the announcement of his kingship. He had led a physical attack in the Temple enclosure. He had a following, although, perhaps, it was not very large. So, all in all, he was not a harmless religious preacher or a madman. Bluntly, he was executed rather than merely flogged and released. Bluntly, it is not simply what Jesus said, but what he did to actualize his assertions that got him in trouble.

Much of governing Jerusalem was left to the high priest and his advisors. The Romans considered him to be in charge of Jerusalem and he was expected to maintain public order. In case of any civil disorder, the high priest was held accountable. Caiaphas' involvement in the arrest of Jesus, if any, was due to his political responsibility. It was incumbent on him to maintain the peace and to avert riots and bloodshed. To safeguard the populace, as well as himself, he would be compelled to assist Pilate in apprehending Jesus, were the demand made. Caiaphas was the high priest from 18 to 36 C.E. Appointment to the office of high priest was at the whim of the Roman government. That his tenure of office was well above the average in length shows a diplomatic and political skill. There is no direct indication in the sources as to the extent of general cooperation between Caiaphas and Pilate or his predecessor, Valerius Gratus.[18] But, it was Caiaphas who was in the vulnerable position in relation to Rome's representatives.[19]

Under the circumstances described in the Gospels there is little doubt that Jesus angered the high priest and his coterie of advisors. But, they did not seize him on their own initiative. More critical for his safety was the fact that he had aroused Roman ire. The Romans empowered the Jewish leaders with the responsibility for maintaining the domestic peace in Roman-controlled Judea. That is now what they would demand. As a causal determinant, the ire of the Roman authorities dwarfed the Jewish leadership's displeasure with Jesus' teachings and actions. The high priest, apprehensive about Pilate and anxious to minimize bloodshed, may have assisted in the arrest of Jesus. According to the Gospel of John, the high priest then turned Jesus over to the governor, after questioning him "about his disciples and his teaching" (John 18:19). Since Rome did not take kindly to those who proclaimed rival kings or kingdoms Pilate executed Jesus. Luke's revisionist history probably ascribed to the Jewish religious leaders sentiments actually expressed by the Romans: "This [man] we found subverting our nation and forbidding the paying of taxes to Caesar, and saying that he himself is Christ, a king" (Luke 23:2). This is a Roman issue, not a Jewish one. This would also account for the accusation Pilate ordered nailed to the cross, "This is Jesus, the King of the Jews" (Mark 15:26, Matthew 27:37, Luke 23:38, John 19:19). Pilate certainly did not need any Jewish prodding in making his decision to execute Jesus. In sum, it was Jesus' teaching about the kingdom, the manner of his entry into the city, his Temple disruption, and perhaps other actions the Gospel authors found advantageous not to record that caused his arrest.

Jesus: Blasphemer or seditionist?

The claim of non-involvement by the Jewish authorities or Jews generally in the death of Jesus is said by some Christian commentators to be a modern idea. Apparently, there are no ancient sources which call into question the claim that there was Jewish juridical action taken against Jesus. Often cited is a Talmudic reference that says:

> On the eve of Passover Yeshu was hanged. For forty days before the execution took place, a herald went forth and cried, "He is going forth to be stoned because he has practiced sorcery and enticed Israel to apostasy. Anyone who can say

anything in his favor, let him come forward and plead on his behalf." But since nothing was brought forward in his favor he was hanged on the eve of Passover. (T.B. *Sanhedrin* 43a)

It cannot be assumed that this passage originated contemporaneously with Jesus or that there was a direct Jewish recollection of Jesus. In fact, we have no evidence that his contemporaries transmitted anything at all about Jesus. There are two questionable citations in Josephus, which mention Jesus.[20] By the early second century, Jews considered Christians of Jewish ancestry to be heretics. In this above Talmudic citation, there seems to be some reliance on Gospel material. However, the extent to which it draws upon Christian sources (for example, the Johannine eve of Passover chronology, the charge of sorcery, and enticing to apostasy) or how (if at all) they were transmitted to what became the Talmudic citation is not clear. It may also be that this episode was conflated to elements of an incident relating to an earlier malefactor. Only the Gospel of John claims Jesus was executed on the eve of Passover; the Synoptic Gospels claim the execution took place on the first day of Passover. The Gospels say nothing about any forty-day period between Jesus' trial and execution. The Yeshu of the Talmudic citation is apparently tried, convicted, sentenced, and executed solely by a Jewish court. The Romans crucify the Jesus of the Gospels; the Yeshu of the Talmud is stoned. The dissimilarities weigh against simply uncritically equating the Yeshu of this passage with the Jesus of the Gospels.

The Gospels' respective narrations do not necessarily represent what occurred forty to seventy years before their authorship. They address late first century Christian conflicts with Jews contemporaneous with the writing of the respective Gospels. Jews of the late first century hearing Christian claims proclaiming Jesus as the Son of God, begotten of a virgin without a human father and by direct action of God's holy Spirit, and empowered to forgive sin, were aware of the common motif such beliefs had with pagan religions and mystery cults. They would have considered such allegations sacrilegious since Christians claimed that this literal sonship was associated with the God of Israel. Jesus' supposed ability to heal would be considered the work of sorcery not a gift from God. Indeed, if the New Testament contains teachings on the essence of who Jesus was, what he believed about himself, and what he taught others, then Jews would have no recourse but to consider him a false prophet who led Israelites astray and deserved to be stoned and then hanged.

According to the Talmudic citation, Yeshu was stoned for practicing sorcery and enticing Israel to apostasy. The Gospels relate that Jesus worked signs and wonders, but that the Scribes and Pharisees considered them as acts of sorcery (Mark 3:22; Matthew 9:34, 12:24). If, in later generations, it was thought that these were the charges brought against Jesus and upon which he was found guilty as charged by a Jewish court, Jews of later generations had no reason to deny involvement of Jewish authorities in the death of Jesus. Because Jesus had led them astray, the followers of Jesus had separated from the Jewish people and rejected the religious principles of Judaism. It is a given that someone accused of practicing sorcery and enticing Israel to apostasy would be apprehended, interrogated, and put on trial; if found guilty, he would be executed. Nevertheless, it cannot be said with any certainty that the Jesus of the Gospels is to be equated with the Yeshua of the Talmudic passage.

As we have seen, the Gospels of Mark and Matthew claim that the Jewish leaders charged Jesus with blasphemy. This was based on his profession of messiahship ("the Christ," "the Son of Man") and acceptance of the title "the Son of the Blessed One"/"God" (Mark 14:61-64, Matthew 26:63-65, see also, Luke 22:67-71). It is claimed that the high priest asked Jesus: "Are you the Christ, the Son of the Blessed One [Matthew: "the "Son of God"]?" (Mark 14:61, Matthew 26:63). Jesus is said to answer: "I am; and you shall see the Son of Man sitting at the right hand of Power, and coming with the clouds of heaven" (Mark 14:62, Matthew 26:64; see also Luke 22:69, 70). Mark (followed by Matthew) says that Jesus' affirmation was considered blasphemy by the high priest and that the Sanhedrin condemned him as deserving to be put to death (Mark 14:63-65, Matthew 26:65-66). The author of Luke says nothing about a charge of blasphemy. He alleges that after Jesus' declaration concerning the Son of Man and confessing that he is "the Son of God," the members of the Sanhedrin felt they had enough reason to take him to Pilate; they charge Jesus with the claim of being "the Christ," a king who misleads the nation and forbids the payment of taxes to Caesar (Luke 22:67-23:2).

What did Jesus say that the Sanhedrin could have considered as blasphemous? Was it the statement concerning the Son of Man sitting at the right hand of God (that is, the claim to some special prerogatives) or was it his confession of messiahship (that is, the claim that he was "the Christ")? These charges would be meaningless at a trial since they did not warrant a charge of blasphemy.

Did Jesus attribute to himself powers that Jews associated with God? On occasion he is said to blaspheme by attributing to himself the power to forgive sins (Mark 2:7, Matthew 9:3, Luke 5:21). In another instance, it is said, "the Jews" accused Jesus of blasphemy because, being a man, he made himself like God (John 10:30-33; cf. John 10:36). If Jesus made such claims, the Sanhedrin would not have understood his father-son relationship with God in a transcendental sense. According to biblical teaching, the Messiah was supposed to be a man and nothing more; he would not have any divine attributes. Those biblical passages that were later thought of by the church in some kind of transcendental manner (for example, Isaiah 7:14, 9:6; Psalms 2:7, 110:1; Daniel 7:13-14) were interpreted by normative Judaism in a human sense. True, there was an element of late Jewish apocalyptic literature (for example, Psalms of Solomon, Book of Enoch, 4 Esdras) which attributed a more supernatural existence to the Messiah. However, there was nothing in any of these beliefs that would lead the high priest or Sanhedrin to understand Jesus' comments as referring to a divine sonship in the sense of being of the same essence or substance as God. If the Jewish authorities had thought this was his meaning, they would have considered him insane not blasphemous. Therefore, there was no charge of blasphemy involved.

Perhaps Jews considered the deification of the human Jesus as comparable to the sin of blasphemy, the sin of cursing God (Leviticus 24:15-16). The exaltation to divine stature of a human being and the applying to that individual of biblical references reserved for God intrinsically challenge monotheistic principles. God is one in essence. Therefore, any attempt to exalt a human or an angelic being to a state equal to God's is an insult to the intrinsic nature of God. To Jews, the church's exalting of the human Jesus to the status of a divine being approaching equality with God may have been expressed as "blasphemy" (Mark 14:64). In any case, the Jewish outrage at Christian claims describing the human Jesus as a divine being appear to have found expression in Christian tradition by the use of the term "blasphemy" incorporated into the accounts of the alleged Jewish trial of Jesus.

Some scholars suggest that Jesus was condemned on the charge of being a false prophet thus complying with the Torah's requirement that the false prophet must be put to death (Deuteronomy 13:6, 18:20). The Synoptic Gospels record that after his condemnation, Jesus had been mocked as a false prophet (Mark 14:65, Matthew 26:68, Luke 22:63-65). But, being a false prophet does not fall into the category of the crime of blasphemy. And in the charge of blasphemy that the Jewish authorities are said to have brought against Jesus there is never any mention of either Deuteronomy 13:6 or 18:20 or of the crime of false prophecy.

It is most likely that the accusation of blasphemy was never made by the high priest but was a result of the Christian-myth making process. Following Jesus' execution, the early followers of Jesus sought to justify their continued belief in him by seeking support in the Hebrew Scriptures. One such supposed prooftext was Deuteronomy 21:22-23 which speaks of hanging a corpse: "And if a man shall have committed a sin whose judgment is death, he shall be put to death, and you shall hang him on a gallows. You shall not leave his body overnight on the gallows, rather you shall surely bury him on that day, for a hanging person is a curse of God . . ." (Deuteronomy 21:22-23). Since Jesus was crucified, that is, hung on a "tree," Paul extrapolated a prophetic inference from this passage. Thus, he says, "Christ redeemed us from the curse of the Law, having become a curse for us—for it is written, 'Cursed is every one who hangs on a tree'" (Galatians 3:13). The pre-Gospel tradition expanded on this alleged prooftext concerning hanging and wove a tale of an accusation by the high priest that Jesus was a blasphemer. It is more likely that the charge of blasphemy was developed from comments by postcrucifixion first century Jews who considered sacrilegious the Christological elevation of Jesus to be "the Son of God." In Christian teaching, instead of referring to one who simply followed the commandments of God this term increasingly became synonymous with divine status.

The Torah, the Written Law, expressly states that blasphemy is punishable by stoning to death. "And one who pronounces blasphemously the Name of God shall surely be put to death, the entire assembly shall surely stone him; proselyte and native alike, when he blasphemes the Name, he shall be put to death (Leviticus 24:16). It is from the Oral Law that we know that one who was stoned to death for idolatry or blasphemy was then placed on a gallows to hang for a short period. "'All that were stoned were [then] hanged'; this is the view of R. Eliezer; but the Sages say, 'No one is hanged [after being stoned], excepting the blasphemer and the idolater.'"[21] One who was executed by stoning for the sin of proclaiming idolatry or blasphemy was subsequently hanged. However, he was to be buried before nightfall because any degradation of the human body is offensive to God (cf., Leviticus 19:28). The culprit was hanged as a reminder that this Jew worshiped an idol or blasphemed against God. It is the disgrace of leaving a corpse hanging that is a "curse of God" not the executed person himself. The "curse of God" is minimized by not leaving the corpse hang overnight. Allowing the corpse to hang overnight would not bring further punishment upon the dead person, who paid the penalty specified by the Torah. However, it would bring punishment upon those Jews who, contrary to the Torah, permitted the body to remain exposed overnight. In the case of Jesus, execution was by crucifixion, that is, hanging on the "tree" while still alive, not by a prior stoning to death.

Paul misinterpreted the biblical text to mean that a crucified person was, as such, cursed: "Christ has redeemed us from the curse of the law, being made a curse for us: for it is written, 'Cursed is everyone that hangs on a tree'" (Galatians 3:13). This interpretation disregards the fact that everyone viewing the corpse of Jesus hanging would realize that he was not placed on the cross subsequent to stoning, in accordance with Jewish law, but, rather, was executed in accordance with Roman practice. Moreover, far from being considered an ignoble death, all Jews knew that crucifixion was often a hero's death, the death sentence meted out to thousands of Jewish martyrs who died fighting for freedom from Roman oppression.

The historical Jesus certainly had much in common politically with those who opposed Roman rule. He was not the peaceful otherworldly figure of Christian myth. Although execution by crucifixion was reserved for rebels, the evangelists maintain that Jesus did not challenge the political system. Jesus is shown as a preacher, teacher, and healer. But, if he had confined his preaching to non-political religious topics he would never have been crucified—a political rebel's death among the Romans. He would never have come into conflict with the secular authorities, or of either Herod (Luke 13:31) nor Pilate (Mark 15:2, Matthew 27:11, Luke 23:3, John 18:33). The Romans, in particular, were profoundly indifferent to purely doctrinal matters among the Jews. They were concerned about resistance to Roman rule not about Jewish tradition.

Jesus entered Jerusalem just prior to Passover as a messianic pretender. But, his initiative did not work out as planned. What the populace of Jerusalem would have observed was the Romans apprehending a person claiming to be king of the Jews. Thus, Jesus was not arrested as a blasphemer but as a seditious agitator. His subsequent death was due to Pilate's authority to pursue, judge, and execute whomever he wished. That Jesus was executed for sedition was the early church's embarrassing secret. It had to cover it up at all costs if it hoped to find acceptance in the Roman Empire.

The alleged trials of Jesus

The judicial proceedings against Jesus narrated in the Gospels of Mark and Matthew (who is dependent on Mark's narrative) take place at a nighttime trial. At this Sanhedrin trial there appear witnesses with testimony concerning Jesus' threat to destroy the Temple (Mark and Matthew differ significantly in what these witnesses supposedly said), there is an interrogation by the high priest, Jesus' admission that he claimed to be the Messiah and "the Son of the Blessed [God]," the high priest's statement that Jesus is guilty of blasphemy, and a condemnation by "all the chief priests and the elders and the scribes" on the religious charge of "blasphemy" (Mark 14:53-64, Matthew 26:57-65). This is followed by a description of a second legal proceeding by the Sanhedrin the next morning. The Sanhedrin then completes its trial of Jesus with the decision to hand him over to the Roman authorities. There is no condemnation to death. Jesus is then delivered to the Roman governor, Pilate, who it is alleged would have preferred to let him go (Mark 15:6-15). Matthew magnifies the Jewish responsibility at the Roman trial by adding to Mark's account the spurious declaration of the Jewish crowd, "His blood be upon us and our children!" (Matthew 27:25).

Whether or not the so-called Jewish trial episode ever took place is questionable. The Lucan version of the Jewish proceedings has no witnesses, no mention of the high priest as an interrogator, a very vague answer by Jesus to the question of whether he is the Messiah, no charge of blasphemy, and no death sentence (Luke 22:66-71). Unlike the other three Gospels, the Lucan version has the entire proceedings take place in the morning (Luke 22:66). There is no indication of a trial on the previous night and his sequence of events leaves no time for one. Following the Jewish judicial proceedings, Jesus is brought before Pilate (Luke 23:1). The author of Luke gives credence to the charge of Jewish responsibility by adding that the Jews accused Jesus of being a *political* rebel. They bring a threefold accusation of sedition against him: "misleading our nation," "forbidding paying taxes to Caesar," "and saying that he himself is Christ, a king" (Luke 23:2). When Pilate finds Jesus not guilty (Luke 23:4) the chief priests become insistent, saying, "He stirs up the people, teaching all over Judea, starting from Galilee, even as far as this place" (Luke 23:5). In this way, the author of Luke explains away how it came about that Roman crucifixion was the means of execution. He gives the actual reason for Jesus' execution, which was obvious to his contemporaries who were familiar with what criminal classifications warranted crucifixion. But, by putting the accusation in the mouth of the perfidious Jews, he brings the veracity of the charge into question. It is the chief priests, the representatives of the nation, who, the author of Luke states, insist that Pilate execute the innocent Jesus. Thus, Jesus remains guiltless, the Romans were duped, and the Jews remain culpable.

The Johannine description of the Jewish proceedings is quite different from those found in any of the Synoptic Gospels. Only the Gospel of John does not create a Sanhedrin trial narrative as a background to the supposed Jewish condemnation of Jesus. This Gospel makes no mention of the Sanhedrin or a judicial body of any kind. There is no parallelism between the Johannine content or format and the alleged Sanhedrin trial versions of the Synoptic Gospels. There are no witnesses, no Sanhedrin, no interrogation concerning threats made against the Temple, no question concerning a claim of divine sonship, no charge of blasphemy, and no sentence. The high priest who interrogates Jesus is Annas (John 18:13, 19-28), not an unidentified high priest as in Mark (Mark 14:60), and not Caiaphas, Annas' son-in-law, as in Matthew (Matthew 26:57, 62), and not the entire Sanhedrin as in Luke (Luke 22:66). Annas, after questioning "Jesus about his disciples, and about his teaching" (John 18:19) "sent him bound to Caiaphas [also called] the high priest" (John 18:24); but there is no judgment by Annas. In what follows, there is no mention of any type of proceedings taking place before Caiaphas. Jesus is then led to the Praetorium to stand in judgment before Pilate (John 18:28-29).[22] In the Synoptic Gospel accounts of the Roman trial, Jesus is virtually silent before Pilate, but, to the contrary, John's Jesus has a dialogue of some length with Pilate (John 18:33-38).

Commensurate with their pro-Roman anti-Jewish agenda the evangelists have Jesus condemned by the Sadducean High Priest, Caiaphas, for the blasphemy of claiming to be the Messiah and the Son of God (Mark 14:61-64, Matthew 26:63-65; see also Luke 22:67-71, John 19:7). The law of blasphemy (Leviticus 24:15-16) does *not* include condemnation for such claims. This episode is a fictional device to conceal the facts. The Gospel narrations are full of incidents of mutual hostility between Jesus and the Pharisees. Yet, when it comes down to his so-called Jewish trial(s), the issue is not his religious differences with the Pharisees but rather a charge of blasphemy. If Jesus was arrested for criticizing Pharisaic tradition, Caiaphas, as a Sadducee, would have most probably agreed with him. The evangelists' objective is to show Jesus as a rebel against the Jewish religion rather than a rebel against Rome. But, Jesus was not condemned for claiming to be God or the Son of God or for saying that he would sit at the right hand of God. These statements had nothing to do with the Torah's concept of blasphemy, which is confined to the sin of cursing God. Jesus was condemned by the Romans for aggressively asserting that he was the divinely designated king of the Jews, the Messiah, and therefore in violation of Roman law (Luke 23:2). To the Romans, his action was a defiance of imperial prerogative; only the emperor could appoint rulers. It is important to understand the anti-Jewish significance of the so-called Jewish trial/trials as recounted in several versions by the Gospels. The purpose of the Gospel accounts is to deliberately portray the high priest, the representative of the people, as disregarding proper legal procedures, even to the extent of employing false witnesses (Mark/Matthew). He has decided to put Jesus to death as an *a priori*.

Questions have been raised as to the differences between the Gospel accounts of the Jewish proceedings against Jesus and the mishnaic procedures for trying capital cases. The Gospels of Mark,

Matthew, and John maintain that Jesus was tried/interrogated before the Sanhedrin on the same night that he was arrested. The impossibility of a nighttime trial before the Sanhedrin, especially if one maintains the trial took place on the *seder* night, 15 Nisan, is an example of the unreliability of the trial accounts. The question of gospelic accuracy is further complicated in that there are in the Gospels, at least, three different presentations of the alleged Jewish proceedings against Jesus (Mark/Matthew, Luke, John). The scholarly debate over whether the mishnaic rules were in effect during this period and, if they were, whether they would have been followed by a Sadducean dominated Sanhedrin only obscures the obvious: there was no Jewish trial of Jesus. The Jewish high priest and his inner-circle of advisors might have conducted a private interrogation of Jesus prior to the Roman trial, but this would be a private interrogation not a formal Jewish trial before a full Sanhedrin.

Therefore, the historicity of the Synoptic Gospel narratives of Jesus' trial before the Sanhedrin is just a fabrication. But, these accounts may show how outrageous Jews considered the church's divinization of Jesus at the time the Jewish trial story was being developed.

Paul's letters provide examples in the progressive divinization of Jesus. In his Christology he altered several statements about God found in the Jewish Scriptures by now having them refer to Jesus (cf. Romans 10:13; 1 Corinthians 1:31, 2:16; 2 Corinthians 10:17). He writes, in other passages, about the supernatural and divine characteristics of an exalted Jesus (for example, Romans 8:34; 1 Corinthians 10:4, 15:47; 2 Corinthians 4:4; Philippians 2:6, 2:9-10; also Ephesians and Colossians *passim*). Once the exaltation of Jesus occurs, his divinization as an angelic being also occurs. A fundamental shift has occurred. Any connection with Judaism is being severed.

The Jews are reported to be interested in knowing whether Jesus thought he was the Messiah (Mark 14:61, Matthew 26:63, Luke 22:67). The Romans are reported to be interested in knowing whether Jesus thought he was king of the Jews (Luke 23:3, John

18:33). In none of the trial episodes are the issues of contention between Jesus and the members of the Sanhedrin concerned with his behavior and teachings that were contrary to the Written and Oral Laws (for example, Mark 7:1-23). Disagreements concerning Jesus' and his disciples' behavior and teachings contrary to the Law play a prominent role in the confrontations taking place prior to his arrest. Yet, they have no place at his so-called Jewish trials. In addition, the Gospels' Pilate does not probe nor cross-examine Jesus very deeply concerning the charge of claiming to be king of the Jews. Yet, this is the charge of most concern to the Romans. The Johannine Jesus does not deny the title before Pilate but spiritualizes the concept. "My kingdom is not of this world. If my kingdom were of this world, then my servants would be fighting, that I might not be delivered up to the Jews; but as it is, my kingdom is not of this realm" (John 18:36). Pilate accepts this interpretation and seeks to free Jesus. In essence, he therefore drops the accusation that he carried out seditious activity that was a threat to Roman rule. The Gospel's Pilate condemns Jesus ostensibly to placate the Jews. Nevertheless, he inscribes the charge of "king of the Jews" on the cross as the accusation because of which Jesus is condemned. Jesus was crucified on a charge of sedition against Rome involving his claim to being "king of the Jews" and because of certain acts involved in promoting that claim. The title need not mean the anointed king of the house of David. Pilate probably thought of it simply as a claim to being a Jewish king. The wording of the inscription on the cross varies in each Gospel. However, all have the four words "The King of the Jews," a title not mentioned in reporting on his public career:

> Mark 15:26: "The King of the Jews."
> Matthew 27:37: "This is Jesus, the King of the Jews."
> Luke 23:38: "The King of the Jews this [man]."
> John 19:19: "Jesus the Nazarene, the King of the Jews."

If there is an historical basis for the inscription, only one version could be correct.[23]

Answering opponents

Some Christian commentators have suggested that the New Testament's vilifying and demonizing of Jewish opponents and projecting on them all they considered evil was a common method of answering opponents in first century Judaism. They portray first century Judaism as divided into multiple antagonistic sects; some describe them as variant "Judaisms." The fact is, the number of sectarian groups, their size, influence, and the full extent of mutual antagonism is not known. Although there was no one unified Jewish community with one leadership guiding the faithful the multiple "Judaisms," caricature ignores the commonality between groups. Among the great majority of the people identifying themselves as Jews, there were no conflicting days for slaughtering the paschal lamb or celebrating the Sabbath and festivals, no disagreements on the necessity of actual observance of Torah, nor on the election of Israel. This is not to say that conflicting interpretations of Jewish law did not exist. Often cited are the impassioned predictions of punishment made by the dissident Jewish group at Qumran against those who did not follow their interpretation of Torah observance. But, the New Testament denigration of Jews and Judaism contained significant departures when compared to sectarian polemics among Jewish groups.

In its origins, the movement formed by the followers of Jesus interacted with other Jewish groups within the greater commonality of Jewish belief. Their polemical attacks against those they accused of complicity in the death of their leader certainly aroused mutual acrimony. But, what we see fully developed in the final redaction of the Pauline letters, the Gospels, and the Book of Acts is no longer a familial disagreement among various factions of Jews as to the proper observance of Torah. What emerges in Christianity is not a Jewish movement, but one that is decidedly Gentile no matter what its antecedents. Totally at odds with the general Jewish community, the Christianity represented by the New Testament argued for the nullification of the fundamental laws of Torah and the national existence of the Jewish people. Its "spiritual Israel," consisting of Jews and Gentiles, was a formation outside the Jewish community and had no interest in the continuance of the Jewish people.

The New Testament authors wrote from a perspective that was spiritually outside the community of Israel. Herein lies the difference between the Christian polemical attack on Jews and Judaism and inter-communal polemical strife among Jewish groups. Even an insular Jewish group as that represented by the Qumran community saw itself as the remnant of physical Israel and sought to carry out the literal observance of Torah as interpreted by the group's leaders. In its polemics, it railed against Jews outside its community arguing for what it considered proper fidelity to Torah. But, this group and those with whom they disagreed still had much in common. Certainly, they never countenanced the notion that a messianic figure could "fulfill" the Torah's commandments, making its observance no longer necessary. Moreover, no other Jewish group outside the followers of Jesus created a movement that went outside of Judaism into the Gentile world to create a new religion which had among its central tenets the notion that it had supplanted the religion from which it originated. Once this occurred, Christians were no longer concerned with feuding brothers sharing certain commonalties, but with opposing hated strangers. It is at this point where the content of Christian rejection of Jews and Judaism sowed the seeds of crusades, inquisitions, and pogroms.

Some Christian commentators consider the New Testament's attack on the Jews quite mild. Yet, how mild is the *bloody commission*, a statement that calls for the death of all who do not accept Jesus (Luke 19:27), or a denunciation that places upon the Jews guilt for all the righteous blood ever shed upon the earth (Matthew 23:35, Luke 11:50-51), or a spurious self-condemnation whereby the Jewish people supposedly take upon themselves and their offspring an eternal blame for the death of Jesus (Matthew 27:25), or a declaration that the Jews are the children of the devil (John 8:44), and that the Jews are a "synagogue of Satan" (Revelation 2:9, 3:9)? The New Testament was written by-and-large for Gentiles and institutionalized an anti-Judaic theme for an alien audience. It distorted and fictionalized events in order to portray the Jews, all Jews who do not accept Jesus, as evil and responsible for his death. Therefore, it would be a mistake to assume that the New Testament polemic against the Jews was simply an intrafamily devise used by some Jews to win other Jews to belief in Jesus. The New Testament's denunciations go beyond a family dispute, beyond a mere difference of opinions among Jews, beyond community.

Although Jesus was supposedly "delivered up by the predetermined plan and foreknowledge of God" (Acts 2:23), the emphasis of the author of Acts is on Jewish culpability and Roman subservience to Jewish coercion. Thus, he has Peter declare that "you [Jews] nailed [Jesus] to a cross by the hands of godless men [pagan Roman soldiers] and put him to death" (Acts 2:23), "this Jesus whom you crucified" (Acts 2:36), "whom you delivered up, and disowned in the presence of Pilate when he had decided to release him" (Acts 3:13). In agreement with these accusations, Matthew's Jesus, "began to show his disciples that he must go to Jerusalem, and suffer many things from the elders and chief priests and scribes, and be killed" (Matthew 16:21). More pointedly, he then declares, "Behold, we are going to Jerusalem, and the Son of Man will be delivered up to the chief priests and scribes, and they will condemn him to death, and will deliver him up to the Gentiles to mock and scourge and crucify . . ." (Matthew 20:18-19). The purpose of these statements is to condemn the Jewish people, generally, and their religious leaders, specifically, for Jesus' execution. For the authors of the New Testament, it was the Jews and not the Romans who must be blamed for the death of Jesus. The Jews would have personally killed Jesus if they were empowered to do so. Therefore, it is claimed that although the Romans actually executed him, the Jewish people as a national entity are responsible. The author of John summarizes the doctrine that the Jews are guilty and the Romans are exonerated. He has Pilate say, "I am not a Jew, am I? Your own nation and the chief priests delivered you to me; what have you done?" (John 18:35). Then, after interrogating him, Pilate "said to them, 'I find no guilt in him'" (John 18:38b).

Questioning the Gospels' omission of the Roman governmental interest in having Jesus executed is not an attempt to diminish any guilt of the Jewish people in Jesus' death. The point is that there never was any Jewish culpability, only false condemnations of the Jewish people. Some Jews may have been involved in Jesus' arrest, conviction, or sentencing, but this is very different from the New Testament accusation that all Jews, everywhere, and for all time are responsible for his execution.

The function of the prophetic office

On the matter of individual verses national responsibility there is a major difference between the Jesus of the New Testament and the prophets of Israel. As is well known, the function of the prophetic office was *not* primarily to foretell future events. The prophets served as a voice for God, proclaiming God's righteousness to Israel and calling for adherence to the Torah and repentance from sinful behavior. In so doing, they often severely chastised the Israelites. Accordingly, Moses addresses the children of Israel with the words: "You have been rebellious against the Lord from the day that I knew you" (Deuteronomy 9:24). Hosea admonishes his people living in the northern kingdom of Israel, where idolatry was rampant, saying:

> Hear the word of the Lord, you children of Israel, for the Lord has a controversy with the inhabitants of the land, because there is no truth, nor mercy, nor knowledge of God in the land. By swearing and lying, and killing and stealing, and committing adultery. They break all bounds, and blood touches blood. (Hosea 4:1-2)

In the same vein Isaiah declares to the inhabitants of the kingdom of Judah:

> Ah, sinful nation, a people laden with iniquity, a seed of evildoers, corrupt children. They have forsaken the Lord,

they have provoked the Holy One of Israel to anger, they drew backwards. (Isaiah 1:4)

Similarly, Jeremiah delivers this message:

> Since the day that your fathers came forth out of the land of Egypt unto this day; and though I have sent to you all My servants the prophets, daily rising up early and sending them: Yet they hearkened not to Me, nor inclined their ear, but made their neck stiff; they did worse than their fathers. (Jeremiah 7:25-26)

Ezekiel follows suit:

> But the house of Israel will not hearken to you: for they will not hearken to Me: for all the house of Israel are impudent and stubborn hearted. (Ezekiel 3:7)

Often the prophets denounced the shortcomings of the nation as a whole although there was always a faithful remnant which never strayed from proper behavior and worship of God even in the northern kingdom of Israel (see 1 Kings 19:18). The prophets often addressed the people, no matter what the degree of individual sinfulness, as a united whole and chastised them all as a collective body. Nevertheless, there is no doubt that they remained integrally part of their people.

When an Isaiah or a Jeremiah castigates his people, he does not infer that they are indeed all degenerate and Godforsaken. The prophet demands so much because he trusts the essential righteousness of the people, and the people as expressions of their own conscience, preserve his words. But, when external enemies take the same words out of context, they add up to a verdict of condemnation.

While denouncing sin, calling for repentance, and offering God's forgiveness, the prophets, unlike Jesus, never condemned the nation or a group within the nation to suffer for the crimes of someone outside the nation. Unlike the Hebrew prophets who identified with their people, the Jesus presented in the Gospels has willfully disassociated himself from the Jewish people (John 8:17, 10:34). Yes, the prophets castigated Israel as a nation even if not all the people were guilty, but they never condemned them to suffer for all the righteous blood ever shed. The prophets often hyperbolized when they spoke of the shortcomings of the nation of Israel as a whole. They chastised them as a collective body for the sins of the few, but they never accused them all for the murder of a specific individual; they always charged the culprit directly (for example, 1 Kings 21:1-19). The Jesus of the Gospels does otherwise. In the Gospels of Matthew and Luke respectively, Jesus' invectives represent an attack on the Jews and Judaism by an outsider. The Jesus of these two Gospels disassociates himself from the Jewish people and condemns the entire people, not for what may be classified as their own sins, but for the shedding of all the righteous blood from Abel onwards (Matthew 23:35, Luke 11:50-51). The Gospels' Jesus irrationally denounced the entire Jewish people for murders neither they nor their fathers committed. He holds them liable for sins which they could have had no part because they were committed even before the birth of Abraham, the progenitor of the nation of Israel. What the prophets had condemned did not necessarily apply to all the people but at least could be attributed to part of the nation. What Jesus condemned could not be properly applied to any part of the nation.

Some modern Christian commentators explain that the harsh New Testament passages directed toward the Jews are prophetic-type warnings, not judgments. That they were directed in the main against specific leaders and authorities, not against the whole Jewish population then living and *certainly* not against the Jews of today. That it was only later generations of "uninformed and misguided Christians" who, it is claimed, misused these passages by projecting their denouncements upon the entire Jewish people.

It is these later generations who they allege transformed prophetic criticism into an anti-Jewish condemnation, a self-fulfilling prophecy. However, these authors sidestep an essential point: the difference between a so-called prophetic-critique and anti-Judaism lies in the relation of the critic to the Torah and people of Israel. A perusal of the Gospel of John provides examples of this thought. Unlike the prophets of Israel, the Johannine Jesus is portrayed as no longer a member of the Jewish people. As one standing outside the Jewish people, Jesus' alleged prophetic pronouncements are nothing more than bitter anti-Judaic condemnations that serve no constructive purpose. They will only become the seedbeds for destructive accusations and mayhem.

The prophetic descriptions of the shortcomings of Israel found in the Hebrew Scriptures were accepted by the people as God's word and were included in Jewish sacred tradition. The prophets spoke to Israel about Israelites and their words were recorded by Israelites for Israelites. They were not addressing themselves to a non-Israelite audience. Faithfully calling for self-examination, the prophets rebuked the children of Israel, but loved their people passionately, expressing a deep love for Israel. They do not convey a consistent attitude that they are speaking about an alien group even when they reproach their people severely. While the prophets identified positively with their people and with the Torah of Israel, the Jesus portrayed in all four Gospels chose not to do so. The prophets castigated with love; the Gospels' Jesus castigated in hatred. The entire anti-Jewish tenor of the New Testament is not in the prophetic tradition of seeing all Israel as responsible, one for the other. That tradition never spoke of Israel as if it were an alien people and certainly no prophet disassociated himself from the Torah. The New Testament tradition creates a totally different atmosphere. Directed toward a non-Jewish audience, it disassociates Jesus from both Israel and the Torah. In the New Testament, the "old Israel" is to whither away, to be replaced by the church, the "new Israel." The church is the inheritor of God's promises to the patriarchs.

New Testament disassociation of Jesus from the Jews and Judaism

The contents of Jesus' original pronouncements are a matter of conjecture. It may be that they were not to be taken as anti-Jewish but solely as a critique spoken by a Jew among Jews. However, as redacted in the Gospels and directed at a mostly Gentile audience, they take on an anti-Judaic form. They have been heard ever since as anti-Jewish diatribes pronounced by Jesus. Unlike the Hebrew Scriptures, which were compiled by Jews for Jews, the New Testament was compiled for a predominantly non-Jewish audience. Its purpose was to instruct those people who had become Christians in the teachings of Jesus and the meaning of events surrounding his death, as interpreted by the church. These people harbored animosity toward those Jews who did not convert.

When statements of reproach about someone or something are written in order to be read by persons other than those admonished the purpose of such statements is not meant to be instructive to the subject of the rebuke. When these statements are inaccurate or outright fabrications, a sinister motive can be even more suspected. What we see in the Gospels is a Jesus who does not speak to the Jewish people as much as he speaks against them. This is part of the New Testament's disassociation of Jesus from the Jewish people and Judaism. Even before the Gospels were written, the Gentile Christian churches founded by Paul constituted, of their own volition, a religious movement outside the Jewish community. This disassociation from the Jewish people and Judaism is already present in the earliest recorded accusation that *the Jews* were responsible for the death of Jesus. In Paul's first letter to the Thessalonians, in which he blames *the Jews* for the death of Jesus and for hindering the spread of the gospel message to the Gentiles, he was addressing a Gentile Christian audience (1 Thessalonians 2:15-16). Paul does not address the people denounced; it is not an intrafamily quarrel. The fact that the denunciation of the Jews is presented to a Gentile audience shows that Paul placed himself outside the community of Israel. His remarks were delivered to Gentiles to bolster their faith that they were the "new Israel." Jews who did not accept Jesus were cut off from God. This points to a basic reason for the rift that quickly developed between Judaism and Christianity. While the very earliest controversies with Jesus' followers may be considered as an intra-Jewish phenomenon that situation soon changed. The Christian attack on Judaism quickly moved from being a controversy within Jewish parameters and soon stood, in its essential theological thrust, outside the scope of Jewish intrafamily experience. As we have noted, there are attempts to dismiss the anti-Jewish polemics within the New Testament by reducing them to "expressions of a family quarrel." This ignores the historical truth that within the New Testament period and the New Testament documents the conflict already broke the bounds of the Jewish family.

An influential group of early church leaders saw the future of the movement to be among the Gentiles. Therefore, the New Testament is addressed to Gentiles; it rejects the Jews as the people of God. In place of the Jewish people, the church stands as the new Israel. The New Testament in its final redaction is the product of a Gentile church. Gentile dominated Christianity eventually obtained the religious, political, and military support of the Roman Empire. With that support one branch of the church was able to advance its interests and persecute its opponents—Jews, dissident Christians, and pagans. All the present-day Christian denominations and sects are spiritual descendants of Gentile Christianity. All forms of Jewish Christianity, descended from the Jewish proto-Christian community, disappeared within a few generations.

Is the New Testament a Jewish Book?

To maintain, as some Christians have, that it is not at all easy to find a book more Jewish than the New Testament shows defective reasoning if not insincerity. The New Testament texts that embody its animosity toward Jews and Judaism are often explained away or are subsumed by appealing to some sort of indistinct fundamental Jewishness of the New Testament. The Jewish environment, in which certain New Testament characters lived and in which the seminal events of Christian origins occurred, does not make the New Testament either a Jewish or pro-Jewish document. Jews and Judaism are portrayed negatively and used to contrast and underscore the supposed superiority of New Testament doctrines. The geographical setting for the Gospels and part of Acts is the Land of Israel; the rest of the New Testament takes place mostly in Asia Minor. It is, in large measure, a work of historical fiction.

By the time the various New Testament books were written, the overwhelming majority of the church was Gentile and it was to them that these works were directed. The political and theological perspective that the New Testament expresses is decidedly anti-Judaic and very much a product of conditions which occurred years after the death of Jesus. The original intra-Jewish dispute became subsidiary to the major theme of separating Jesus from the Jewish people both politically and theologically. As cited, one cannot disregard how Jesus is disassociated from the satanic Jews (John 8:44), the manner in which *all* Jews are held responsible for the murder of the righteous who lived even before Abraham (Matthew 23:35), how *all* Jews are responsible for the death of Jesus (Acts 2:36), how *all* future generations stand accused of participating in that execution (Matthew 27:25), and how Jesus called for the slaying of those who did not believe in him (Luke 19:27). These attacks are the work of adversaries outside the Judaic system.

In the New Testament, Jews who do not accept Jesus are condemned. The targets of the New Testament attack are variously identified as Pharisees, Sadducees, scribes, elders, priests, high priests, the people, or simply as "the Jews." In addition, Jewish law is dissected. Pre-Jesus Judaism is appropriated and the New Testament authors take from it anything they find useful for their purposes. Everything else is condemned as obsolete (Hebrews 8:13); Judaism ceases to exist. Christianity becomes the natural and necessary culmination of the relevant Jewish history. The New Testament proclaims Judaism and its adherents unnecessary and obsolete. Thus, "Salvation is from the Jews" (John 4:22) refers to the past, but is no longer true for the present and future once Jesus arrives on the scene.

Notes

¹ The Synoptic Gospels inform us that, in fulfillment of prophecy, Jesus sent two of his disciples to get the animal he was to ride into Jerusalem (Mark 11:2-7, Matthew 21:2-7, Luke 19:30-35). At variance with this, the author of the Gospel of John states that Jesus found the animal all by himself: "And Jesus, finding a young ass, sat on it; as it is written: 'Fear not, daughter of Zion; behold, your King comes sitting on a she-ass's colt'" (John 12:14-15).

The Gospel narratives present the reader with still another mystery. Did Jesus enter Jerusalem riding on one animal, as Mark, Luke, and John tell it, or on two, as Matthew relates?

> [Jesus said] to them: "Go into the village opposite you, and immediately you will find a she-ass and a colt with her; untie them, and bring them to me. And if anyone says something to you, you shall say, 'The Lord needs them'; and immediately he will send them." Now this took place that what was spoken through the prophet might be fulfilled, saying: "Say to the daughter of Zion, behold your King is coming to you, and mounted upon a she-ass, and upon a colt, the foal of a beast of burden." And the disciples went and did as Jesus had directed them, and brought the she-ass and the colt, and put upon them their garments, and he sat upon them. (Matthew 21:2-7)

Matthew, in his eagerness to use Zechariah 9:9 as an example of how Jesus fulfilled prophecy, misses the point that biblical poetry makes frequent use of synonymous parallelism. Reading Zechariah correctly, we see that the prophet is not speaking of someone riding two animals. As is common in biblical poetry, which is based on parallel structure, the repetition of an idea or fact does not indicate its duplication in reality. Parallelism is a poetic device to create a thought rhythm and is not to be taken literally as a repetition in fact. The prophet's statement, "riding upon an ass, even upon a colt the foal of a she-ass," describes the same event in different words. Matthew sought compliance with a prophecy that did not exist. The evangelist assumes that two different animals are involved and so has the disciples bring two, a she-ass and its colt. He writes: "Behold your King is coming to you, gentle, and mounted upon a she-ass, and upon a colt, the foal of a beast of burden. And the disciples . . . put upon them their garments, and he sat upon them."

According to Matthew, Jesus came to Jerusalem riding astride both animals, one being male and the other female. The garments of Jesus' disciples covered each animal. Contrary to Matthew's record, Zechariah mentions only the riding of one male animal. Although more subdued in their claim, the other Gospels give us no reason to believe they are based on traditions any more trustworthy than Matthew's. These narratives, describing Jesus' entry into Jerusalem, are suggested by Zechariah's prophecy. Using such methodology, it is no wonder that the New Testament is able to make so many claims of prophetic fulfillment by Jesus. Christians must accept these alleged fulfillments of prophecy on unquestioning faith alone; they lack any basis in historical fact.

2   The Mishnah tells us why the moneychangers were in the Temple: "On the fifteenth thereof [Adar] they set up moneychanger's tables in the provinces; on the twenty-fifth they set them up in the Temple; when they had set them up in the Temple they began to accept pledges [from those who had not paid the tax in species] and, in exchange, supply the required half-shekel]. From whom did they take pledges? Levites and Israelites, proselytes and freed slaves, but not from women, slaves, and minors . . . (Mishnah *Shekalim* 1:3). Moneychangers at the Temple offered a convenience for pilgrims and were essential for the collection of the half-shekel Temple tax. Jews were not allowed by the Romans to issue their own coins, and Roman coins bore images of their deified rulers and gods which Jews considered sacrilegious claims of rule and divinity. Jews needed to exchange this type of coinage for coins devoid of idolatrous images with which they could pay their half shekel Temple tax and buy their animal sacrifices. People could acquire the proper coinage anywhere, but apparently, many preferred this central location for the exchange of currency. The tax, paid by all eligible Israelites, rich and poor alike, served through the coming year to provide the public daily whole-

offerings in the name of the community of Israel (Exodus 30:15-16). These daily whole-offerings paid for from the communal funds provided by every Israelite equally served all of the people individually and collectively, as their atonement for sin. Thus, the half-shekel allowed all Israelites to participate in the provision of the whole offering, which accomplished an atonement for sin on behalf of the people of Israel as a whole. "For public offerings appease and effect atonement between Israel and their father in heaven" (Tosefta *Shekalim* 1:2). The moneychangers' services made possible this involvement of every Israelite in the daily atonement sacrifice. In addition, a convenient area was provided where people could buy sacrificial animals, because if pilgrims transported their sacrifices for some distance they might become blemished and thus prohibited for sacrificial purposes.

3. The Antonia fortress located at the northwest corner of the Temple served as quarters for a Roman cohort, thus giving the soldiers easy access to the Temple Mount if they so desired: "For if the Temple was situated as a fortress over the city, Antonia dominated the Temple; and those who were in that post dominated all three" (*Jewish Wars* V. 5. 8 [244-245]). It was there that the Romans kept the robe which the high priest wore when he offered sacrifice (*Jewish Antiquities* XV. 11. 4 [403]).

4. Many Christian commentators call this incident the "cleansing of the Temple." The actions of overturning and scourging appear more to symbolize destruction rather than acts of "cleaning."

5. Josephus describes the situation. "The usual crowd had assembled at Jerusalem for the feast of unleavened bread, and the Roman cohort had taken up its position on the roof of the portico of the temple; for a body of men in arms invariably mounts guard at the feasts, to prevent disorders arising from such a concourse of people" (*Jewish War* II. 12. 1 [224]). It is reasonable to assume that the same was done in Jesus' time. As the throngs of pilgrims started to arrive well in advance of the festivals one can expect that the Romans mounted their troops on the roof at least days if not weeks before the actual festival arrived. Josephus mentions the formal assembling by the pilgrims "for the feast of unleavened bread, on the eight of the month Xanthicus [March-April]" (*Jewish War* VI. 5. 3 [290]).

6. Josephus remarks that "it is on these festive occasions that sedition is most apt to break out" (*Jewish War* I. 4. 3 [88]).

7. Concerning the right of the Jews to pass a sentence of death, the Jerusalem

Talmud states: "A *baraita* says, 'Forty years before the destruction of the Temple they took from Israel the right to inflict capital punishment'" (J.T. *Sanhedrin* 1:1, 7:2).

8 It was, however, employed by the Hasmonean king/high priest, Alexander Janneus (103-76 B.C.E.). He had eight hundred Pharisees crucified and ordered their wives and children to be slaughtered before them as they hung dying (*Jewish Antiquities* XIII. 14. 2 [380], *Jewish War* I. 4. 6 [97]).

9 Martin Hengel summarizes the horror associated with crucifixion:

> Crucifixion as a penalty was remarkably widespread in antiquity . . . . The chief reason for its use was its allegedly supreme efficacy as a deterrent; it was, of course, carried out publicly . . . . It was usually associated with other forms of torture, including at least flogging . . . . By the public display of a naked victim at a prominent place—at a crossroads, in the theatre, on high ground, at the place of his crime—crucifixion also represented his uttermost humiliation, which had a numinous dimension to it. With Deuteronomy 21:23 in the background, the Jew in particular was very aware of this . . . . Crucifixion was aggravated further by the fact that quite often its victims were never buried. It was a stereotyped picture that the crucified victim served as food for wild beasts and birds of prey. In this way, his humiliation was made complete. What it meant for a man in antiquity to be refused burial, and the dishonor which went with it, can hardly be appreciated by modern man. (Martin Hengel, *Crucifixion in the Ancient World and the Folly of the Message of the Cross*, Philadelphia: Fortress Press, 1977, pp. 86-88).

See also, Gerald G. O' Collins, "Crucifixion," *The Anchor Bible Dictionary*, ed. David Noel Freedman, New York: Doubleday, vol. 1, 1992, pp. 1207-1210.

10 This is not to say that the priesthood was devoid of all corruption or that there was no hostility toward those who took improper advantage of their privileged status. In the case of the Qumran community, opposition to the Temple ritual and to the priesthood was rooted in the view that the high

priest's office belonged to one particular branch of the descendants of Aaron. Therefore, adherents of the sect considered the claim of anyone else invalid. They were not against the Temple or its overall ritual, but against those usurpers who officiated in it and what they considered the latter's innovations. Thus, even when the Temple priesthood is denounced as corrupt the denunciation is in terms of what the Temple ought to have been.

[11] *Bereshit Rabba* 91:10.
[12] *Bereshit Rabba* 94:9.
[13] That is, if the size of the arresting party is not an exaggeration.
[14] *Jewish War* II. 14. 6 [293-295].
[15] *Jewish War* II. 14. 8 [301-303].
[16] *Jewish War* II. 14. 9 [305-306].
[17] *Jewish War* VI. 5. 3. [300-309].
[18] Valerius Gratus was prefect of Judea from 15-26 C.E. "Gratus deposed Ananus from his sacred office, and proclaimed Ishmael, the son of Phabi [15-16 C.E.], high priest. Not long afterwards he removed him also and appointed in his stead Eleazar, the son of the high priest Ananus [16-17 C.E.]. A year later he deposed him also and entrusted the office of high priest to Simon, the son of Camith [17-l8 C.E.]. The last mentioned held this position for not more than a year and was succeeded by Joseph, who was called Caiaphas [18-36 C.E.]. After these acts Gratus retired to Rome, having stayed eleven years in Judea. It was Pontius Pilate who came as his successor" (*Jewish Antiquities* XVIII. 2. 2 [34-35]).
[19] Both Caiaphas and Pilate were dismissed from office at approximately the same time. "[The Roman governor of Syria, Vitellius] ordered Pilate to return to Rome to give the emperor his account of the matters with which he was charged by the Samaritans. And so Pilate, after having spent ten years in Judea, hurried to Rome in obedience to the orders of Vitellius, since he could not refuse" (*Jewish Antiquities* XVIII. 4. 2 [89]). "[Vitellius also] removed from his sacred office the high priest Joseph surnamed Caiaphas, and appointed in his stead Jonathan, son of Ananus the high priest" (*Jewish Antiquities* XVIII. 4. 3 [95]).
[20] Jesus' name appears in identifying "a man named James, the brother of Jesus who was called the Christ" (*Jewish Antiquities* XX. 9. 1. [200]), in which case Josephus is focusing on James, not Jesus. Earlier, Josephus mentions Jesus in a statement that seemingly confirms his personal belief in Jesus as the

"Messiah": "About this time there lived Jesus, a wise man, if indeed one ought to call him a man. For he was one who wrought surprising feats and was a teacher of such people as accept the truth gladly. He won over many Jews and many of the Greeks. He was the Messiah. When Pilate, upon hearing him accused by men of the highest standing among us, had condemned him to be crucified, those who had in the first place come to love him did not give up their affection for him. On the third day he appeared to them restored to life, for the prophets of God had prophesied these and countless other marvelous things about him. And the tribe of the Christians, so called after him, has still to this day not disappeared (*Jewish Antiquities* XVIII. 3. 3 [63-64]).

Josephus' alleged positive statement about Jesus is spurious. The attestation that Jesus was the Messiah, the suggestion that he was more than human, the acceptance of his resurrection and the affirmation that his activities were foretold by the Hebrew prophets—*is a third or fourth century forgery*. Origen (c. 280) explicitly states that Josephus did not believe Jesus was the Messiah (*Contra Celsum* 1. 47). Eusebius (c. 324), however, does know of this passage (*Ecclesiastical History* 1. 11). Moreover, Josephus considers the revolutionary zealots and apocalyptic messianists responsible for the Jews' revolt against Rome and the consequent destruction of Jewish sovereignty. His loyalty to Rome and his strong sense of self-preservation would make doubtful any suggestion that he would risk his safety by affirming as Messiah a person whose followers the Imperial government held in disfavor.

[21] Mishnah *Sanhedrin* 6:4.
[22] Despite the claims of some Christian commentators, the Johannine Gospel does not represent Pilate as ratifying a sentence for a Jewish religious offense, which had already been passed by the Sanhedrin.
[23] Sometimes the title appears in works of art as *INRI*, abbreviated from the supposed Latin, *Iesus Nazarenus Rex Iudaeorum*.

BIBLIOGRAPHY

The Apocrypha and Pseudepigraha of the Old Testament in English. Ed. R.H. Charles. Oxford: Clarendon Press. Vols. 1, 2, 1913.

Arndt, W.F. and Gingrich, F.W. *A Greek-English Lexicon of the New Testament and Other Early Christian Literature.* Chicago: University of Chicago Press, 1957.

Baron, Salo Wittmayer. *A Social and Religious History of the Jews.* New York: Columbia University Press. Vol. 1, 1952.

Baum, Gregory. *Is the New Testament Anti-Semitic?* New York: Paulist Press, 1965.

___. *A Theological Reading of Sociology.* New York: Paulist Press, 1975.

Bereshit Rabba. Editors J. Theodor and Ch. Albeck. 3 vols. Jerusalem: Wahrmann, 1965.

Bowman, John. "The Fourth Gospel and the Samaritans." *Bulletin of the John Rylands Library* 40 (1958): 298-308.

Brown, Raymond. *The Community of the Beloved Disciple.* New York: Paulist Press, 1979.

___. "The Gospel According to John (XIII-XXI): Introduction, Translation, and Notes." *The Anchor Bible* 29A. Garden City, N.Y.: Doubleday. Vol. 29, 1970: 787-804.

Bratcher, Robert J. "'The Jews' in the Gospel of John." *The Bible Translator* 26 (1975): 401-409.

Bruce, F.F. *Word Biblical Commentary: 1 and 2 Thessalonians.* Waco: Word Books, 1982.

Bultmann, Rudolf. *The Gospel of John.* Philadelphia: Westminster Press, 1971 (Eng. Trans.).

Buchanan, George W. "The Samaritan Origin of the Gospel of John." *Religions in Antiquity: Essays in Memory of E.R. Goodenough.* Ed. Jacob Neusner. Leiden: E.J. Brill, 1968: 149-175.

Davies, Alan. Ed. *Anti-Semitism and the Foundations of Christianity.* New York: Paulist Press, 1979.

___. "The Aryan Christ: A Motif in Christian Anti-Semitism." *Journal of Ecumenical Studies* 12 (Fall 1975): 569-579.

Eckardt, A. Roy. *Elder and Younger Brothers.* New York: Scribner's, 1967.

___. "The Nemesis of Christian Anti-Semitism." *Journal of Church and State* 13 (Spring 1971): 227-244.

___. "Theological Approaches to Anti-Semitism." *Jewish Social Studies* 33 (October 1971): 272-284.

Eliav, Binyamin. "Anti-Semitism." *Encyclopedia Judaica.* Jerusalem: Keter Publishing House. Vol. 3, 1971: cols. 87-160.

Epp, Eldon Jay. "Anti-Semitism and the Popularity of the Fourth Gospel in Christianity." *Central Conference of American Rabbis Journal* 22 (Fall 1975): 35-57.

Eusebius. *Ecclesiastical History.* Translated by C.F. Cruse. Grand Rapids: Baker Books, 1987.

Feldman, Louis. *Jew and Gentile in the Ancient World: Attitudes and Interactions from Alexander to Justinian.* Princeton: Princeton University Press, 1993.

Finkel, Asher. "Yavneh's Liturgy and Early Christianity." *Journal of Ecumenical Studies* 18 (1981): 231-250.

Fitzmeyer, Joseph A. "Anti-Semitism and the Cry of 'All the People (Mt 27:25).'" *Theological Studies* 26 (December 1965): 667-671.

Flannery, Austin. Gen. Ed. *Vatican Council II: The Concilar and Post Concilar Documents.* North Point, N.Y.: Costello Publishing Co., Rev. Ed. 1992.

Flannery, Edward H. "Anti-Judaism and Anti-Semitism: A Necessary Distinction." *Journal of Ecumenical Studies* 10 (Summer 1973): 581-588.

Freed, Edwin D. "Did John Write the Gospel of John Partly to Win Samaritan Converts?" *Novum Testamentum* 12 (1970): 241-256.

___. "Samaritan Influence in the Gospel of John." *Catholic Biblical Quarterly* 30 (1968): 580-597.

Fuller, Reginald. "The 'Jews' in the Fourth Gospel." *Dialog* 16 (Winter 1977): 31-37.

Funk and Wagnalls Standard College Dictionary. New York: Funk and Wagnalls, 1973.

Ginzburg, Louis. *The Legends of the Jews*. Philadelphia: The Jewish Publication Society of America. Vol. 6, 1968.

Hare, Douglas R.A. "The Relationship Between Jewish and Gentile Persecution of Christians." *Journal of Ecumenical Studies* (1967): 446-456.

Hayes, Stephen R. "Changing Paradigms: Reformist, Radical, and Rejectionist Approaches to the Relationship Between Christianity and Antisemitism." *Journal of Ecumenical Studies* 32 (Winter 1995): 63-88.

Heil, John Paul. *The Death and Resurrection of Jesus: A Narrative Critical Reading of Matthew 26-28*. Minneapolis: Fortress Press, 1991.

Hengel, Martin. *Crucifixion in the Ancient World and the Folly of the Message of the Cross*. Philadelphia: Fortress Press, 1977.

Hoehner, Harold W. *Chronological Aspects of the Life of Christ*. Grand Rapids: Zondervan Publishing House, 1977.

The Holy Scriptures According to the Masoretic Text. Philadelphia: Jewish Publication Society of America, 1955.

Howard, George. *The Gospel of Matthew According to a Primitive Hebrew Text*. Macon, Ga.: Mercer University Press, 1987.

Jerome. *Letters of Saint Jerome*. Edited by Quasten & Burqhardt. New York: Paulist Press, 1963.

Josephus. *Works*. Trans. H. St. J. Thackery, R. Marcus, A. Wikgren, and L.H. Feldman. Loeb Classical Library. 9 vols. Cambridge, Mass.: Harvard University Press, 1926-1965.

Juvenal. *Satires*. Translated by Jerome Mazzaro. Ann Harbor: University of Michigan Press, 1965

Kennedy, H.A.A. "The Epistle to the Philippians." *Expositor's Greek Testament*. Ed. W. Robertson Nicoll. New York: George H. Doran Co. Vol. 3, n.d.

The King James Version of the Bible. *New York: New York Bible Society,* n.d.

Lowe, Malcolm. "Real and Imagined Anti-Jewish Elements in the Synoptic Gospels and Acts." *Journal of Ecumenical Studies* 24 (Spring 1987): 267-284.

Maccoby, Hyam. *The Sacred Executioner: Human Sacrifice and the Legacy of Guilt.* London: Thames and Hudson, 1982.

___. "Theologian of the Holocaust." *Commentary* 74 (December 1982): 33-37.

___. *Judas Iscariot and the Myth of Jewish Evil.* New York: The Free Press, 1992.

Macdonald, John. *Theology of the Samaritans.* Philadelphia: The Westminster Press, 1964.

Meeks, Wayne E. "Galilee and Judea in the Fourth Gospel." *Journal of Biblical Literature* 85 (1966): 159-169.

___. "'Am I a Jew'?: Johannine Christianity and Judaism." *Christianity, Judaism and Other Greco-Roman Cults.* Ed. Jacob Neusner. Leiden: E.J. Brill. Vol. 1, 1975.

Mishnayoth. Translated by Philp Blackman. New York: The Judaica Press, 1965.

Montgomery, James Alan. *The Samaritans: The Earliest Jewish Sect.* Philadelphia: The John C. Winston Co., 1907.

The New American Standard Bible. Carol Stream, Ill.: Creation House, 1971.

The New English Bible Version. Oxford University Press and Cambridge University Press, 1970.

The New York Times. "Pope Ties 'Unjust' Teachings to Anti-Semitism." November 1, 1997: A6.

O'Collins, Gerald G. "Anti-Semitism in the Gospels." *Theological Studies* 26 (December 1965): 663-666.

___. *Interpreting Jesus, Introducing Catholic Theology* 2. London: Geoffrey Chapman; Ramsey, N.J.: Paulist Press, 1983.

___. "Crucifixion." *The Anchor Bible Dictionary.* Ed. David Noel Freedman. New York: Doubleday. Vol. 1, 1992: 1207-1210.

Oesterreicher, John M. *Anatomy of Contempt.* South Orange, N.J.: Seton Hall University, n.d.

Origen. *Contra Celsum.* Translated by Henry Chadwick. Cambridge: Cambridge University Press, 1965.

Pannenberg, Wolfhart. *Jesus—God and Man.* Trans Lewis L. Wilkens and Duane A. Priebe. Philadelphia: Westminster Press, 1968.

Patai, Raphael. "Anti-Semitism." *The Encyclopedia Americana.* Danbury, Conn.: Grolier. Vol. 2, 1992: 74-75.

Philo. *The Works of Philo.* Translated by C.D. Yonge. Peabody, Mass.: Hendrickson Publishers, 2000.

Pines, Shlomo. *The Jewish Christians of the Early Centuries of Christianity According to a New Source.* Jerusalem: Central Press, 1966.

Przybylski, Benno. "The Setting of Matthean Anti-Judaism." *Anti-Judaism in Early Christianity.* Ed. Peter Richardson. Waterloo: Wilfred Laurier Press. Vol. 1, 1986: 181-200.

Purvis, James D. "The Fourth Gospel and the Samaritans." *Novum Testamentum* 17 (1975): 161-198.

___. *The Samaritan Pentateuch and the Origin of the Samaritan Sect.* Cambridge: Harvard University Press, 1968.

___. "The Samaritans." *The Cambridge History of Judaism.* Ed. W.D. Davies and Louis Finkelstein. Cambridge: Cambridge University Press. Vol. 2, 1989: 591-613.

Reuther, Rosemary R. "Theological Anti-Semitism in the New Testament." *The Christian Century* 85 (February 1968): 191-196.

___. *Faith and Fratricide.* New York: Seabury. 1974.

Richardson, Peter. *Anti-Judaism in Early Christianity.* Waterloo: Wilford Laurier Press. Vols. 1 and 2, 1986, 1987.

Saldarini, Anthony. *Matthew's Christian-Jewish Community.* Chicago: University of Chicago Press, 1994.

___. "Understanding Matthew's Vitriol." *Bible Review,* 13:2 (April 1997): 32-39, 44-45.

Sanders, E.P. *Paul and Palestinian Judaism.* Philadelphia: Fortress Press, 1977.

Sandmel, Samuel. *Anti-Semitism in the New Testament?* Philadelphia: Fortress Press, 1978.

Scobie, Charles H.H. "The Origins and Development of Samaritan

Christianity." *New Testament Studies* 19 (1972-1973): 390-414.

Scroggs, Robin. "The Earliest Hellenistic Christianity." *Religions in Antiquity: Essays in Memory of E.R. Goodenough*. Ed. Jacob Neusner. Leiden: E.J. Brill, 1968: 176-206.

The Septuagint Version: Greek and English. Translated by Lancelot C.L. Brenton. Grand Rapids, Mich.: Zondervan Publishing House, 1979.

Seutonius. *The Lives of the Caesars: Domitian*. Translated by J. Rolfe. Loeb Classical Library. Cambridge, Mass.: Harvard University Press, 1998.

Spiro, Abraham. "Stephen's Samaritan Background." Appendix V in *The Acts of the Apostles* by Johannes Munck. Rev. by W.F. Albright and C.S. Mann. *The Anchor Bible*. New York: Doubleday. Vol. 31, 1967: 285-300.

Schiffman, Lawrence H. *Who Was a Jew? Rabbinic and Halakhic Perspectives on the Jewish-Christian Schism*. Hoboken, NJ: Ktav Publishing House, 1985.

Stanley, Alexandra. "Pope Asks Forgiveness for Errors of the Church Over 2000 Years." *The New York Times*. March 13, 2000: A10.

Tacitus. *Histories*. Translated by John Jackson. Loeb Classical Library. Cambridge, Mass.: Harvard University Press, 9th edition, 1988.

Talmud, Babylonian. Edited by I. Epstein. London & New York: Soncino Press, 1935.

Talmud, Jerusalem. Zhitomer edition. Reprint. Jerusalem: Bene Ma'arav, 1979/80.

Thayer, Joseph Henry. *A Greek-English Lexicon of the New Testament*. Grand Rapids, Mich.: Zondervan, 1979.

A Theological Understanding of the Relationship Between Christians and Jews: A Paper Commended to the Church for Study and Reflection. New York: Office of the General Assembly of the Presbyterian Church (USA), 1987.

Tosephta. Translated by Jacob Neusner. Peabody, Mass.: Hendrickson, 2002.

Vermes, Geza. *The Religion of Jesus the Jew*. Minneapolis, Mn.: Fortress Press, 1993.

Weinfeld, Moshe. "The Charge of Hypocrisy in Matthew 23 and in Jewish Sources." *The New Testament and Christian-Jewish Dialogue: Studies in Honor of David Flusser*. Ed. M. Lowe. *Immanuel* 24/25 (1990): 52-58.

___. "The Jewish Roots of Matthew's Vitriol." *Bible Review*, 13:5 (October 1997): 31.

Westcott, B.F. and Hort, F.G.A. *Introduction to the New Testament in the Original Greek*, Peabody, Mass.: Hendrickson Publishers, 1988.

Whittaker, Molly. *Jews and Christians: Graeco-Roman Views*. Cambridge: Cambridge University Press. 1984.

SCRIPTURAL INDEX

THE HEBREW BIBLE

Genesis
Genesis 4:8—126
Genesis 11:26—239
Genesis 11:32—239
Genesis 11:32-12:1—239
Genesis 12:4—239
Genesis 12:6-7—242
Genesis 15:1-21—242
Genesis 16—63
Genesis 21—63
Genesis 21:9-21—63
Genesis 23:1-20—241
Genesis 23:16—241
Genesis 28:12—183
Genesis 33:19—241
Genesis 49:29-32—241
Genesis 49:29-33—241
Genesis 50:13—241

Exodus
Exodus 3:6—240
Exodus 3:12—242
Exodus 3:15—240
Exodus 12:4—137
Exodus 12:26-27—137
Exodus 19:5—78
Exodus 20:16—266
Exodus 20:17—240
Exodus (Septuagint) 20:18—265
Exodus (Septuagint) 20:19—265
Exodus 20:19—266
Exodus 26:35—74
Exodus 26:36—74
Exodus 30:1-10—74
Exodus 30:15-16—307

Leviticus
Leviticus 10:10—97
Leviticus 11:2-47—97
Leviticus 19:28—288
Leviticus 21:10—86
Leviticus 24:15-16—86, 287, 292
Leviticus 24:16—288
Leviticus 27:28—96

Numbers
Numbers 6:13-14—267
Numbers 30:15—71

Deuteronomy
Deuteronomy 2:5b—240, 241
Deuteronomy 2:5c—241
Deuteronomy 9:24—298
Deuteronomy 13:6—287
Deuteronomy 14:3-21—97
Deuteronomy 18:15—208, 210, 240, 246, 249
Deuteronomy 18:15-18—207
Deuteronomy 18:18—208, 210, 240, 246
Deuteronomy 18:20—287
Deuteronomy 19:15—191
Deuteronomy 21:6—131
Deuteronomy 21:22-23—287
Deuteronomy 21:23—308

Joshua
Joshua 24:32—241

Judges
Judges 3:16-22—272

2 Samuel
2 Samuel 1:16—135
2 Samuel 3:28-29—131
2 Samuel 20:1—279

1 Kings
1 Kings 8:43—244
1 Kings 19:10—67
1 Kings 19:18—60, 299
1 Kings 21:1-19—300

2 Kings
2 Kings 2:33—135

Isaiah
Isaiah 1:4—299
Isaiah 6:9-10—102, 103
Isaiah 6:9-13—104
Isaiah 6:11-12—102
Isaiah 6:13—105
Isaiah 7:14—286
Isaiah 9:6—286
Isaiah 10:22—59
Isaiah 26:13—201
Isaiah 40:8—143
Isaiah 42:2-3—145
Isaiah 53—168
Isaiah 53:9—271
Isaiah 66:1-2—244

Jeremiah
Jeremiah 7:18—243
Jeremiah 7:25-26—299
Jeremiah 18:1-6—140
Jeremiah 19:13—243
Jeremiah 26:15—135
Jeremiah 26:20-23—67
Jeremiah 29:7—24
Jeremiah 32:6-9—140

Ezekiel
Ezekiel 3:7—299

Hosea
Hosea 4:1-2—298
Hosea 13:1—60

Amos
Amos 5:25-27—243
Amos 5:27—243

Haggai
Haggai 2:7-8—78
Haggai 2:8—271

Zechariah
Zechariah 1:1—144
Zechariah 9:9—269, 305
Zechariah 11:12-13—140

Malachi
Malachi (Septuagint) 2:7—265

Psalms
Psalms 2:7—286
Psalm 22—168
Psalms 26:6—131
Psalms 69:26 (25)—147
Psalms 82:6—191
Psalms 110:1—286
Psalms 111:7-8—143
Psalms 132:5—243

Daniel
Daniel 7:13-14—286

2 Chronicles
2 Chronicles 24:20-21—144
2 Chronicles 24:20-22—67
2 Chronicles 36:14-16—67
2 Chronicles 36:16—102

THE NEW TESTAMENT

Matthew

Matthew 1:21—135
Matthew 1:22—115
Matthew 2:2—119
Matthew 2:6—135
Matthew 2:11—119
Matthew 2:16—119
Matthew 2:20—120
Matthew 4:16—135
Matthew 4:23—135
Matthew 5:12—145
Matthew 5:17—190
Matthew 5:17-19—120
Matthew 5:39—145, 164
Matthew 5:44—128, 145, 164
Matthew 6:1-18—123
Matthew 8:5-9—117
Matthew 8:10—117, 118
Matthew 8:11-12—117
Matthew 9:3—286
Matthew 9:11—79
Matthew 9:34—285
Matthew 10:2—81
Matthew 10:3—81
Matthew 10:4—80, 109
Matthew 10:5—209
Matthew 10:5-6—210, 266
Matthew 11:20-24—164, 165, 182
Matthew 12:1-2—122
Matthew 12:9-12—122
Matthew 12:14—122
Matthew 12:19-20—145
Matthew 12:24—285
Matthew 12:30—153
Matthew 13:3-9—103
Matthew 13:13—104
Matthew 13:15—135
Matthew 13:57—181
Matthew 14:10—123
Matthew 15:1-2—122
Matthew 15:1-20—97
Matthew 15:8—135
Matthew 15:12-14—98
Matthew 15:20—98
Matthew 15:21-28—118
Matthew 16:1—122
Matthew 16:4—144

Matthew 16:17—81
Matthew 16:21—297
Matthew 17:12-13—123
Matthew 17:17—144
Matthew 19:3—122
Matthew 20:18-19—297
Matthew 21:2—269
Matthew 21:2-7—305
Matthew 21:4-9—280
Matthew 21:4-11—35
Matthew 21:7-11—269
Matthew 21:9—183
Matthew 21:11—135
Matthew 21:12—35, 195, 270, 280
Matthew 21:12-13—270
Mathew 21:14-15—28
Matthew 21:33-43—117
Matthew 21:33-45—90
Matthew 21:39—110
Matthew 21:43—21, 91, 117, 200
Matthew 21:45—29, 90
Matthew 21:46—135, 277
Matthew 22:7—117
Matthew 22:15—154
Matthew 22:15-16—119, 122
Matthew 22:15-22—78
Matthew 22:21—35, 280
Matthew 22:34-36—122, 149
Matthew 23—9, 13, 123, 145, 164, 165
Matthew 23:1-33—123
Matthew 23:2-3—122, 126

Matthew 23:3-4—122
Matthew 23:4-7—126
Matthew 23:5-7—122
Matthew 23:15—121, 127
Matthew 23:23—122
Matthew 23:29—135, 136
Matthew 23:30—135
Matthew 23:31—124
Matthew 23:33—124
Matthew 23:34—135
Matthew 23:34-35—106, 124
Matthew 23:34-36—149
Matthew 23:35—67, 135, 296, 300, 304
Matthew 23:35-36—123
Matthew 23:36—124, 135, 144, 145
Matthew 23:37-38—125
Matthew 24:2—147
Matthew 26:3-4—9
Matthew 26:5—135
Matthew 26:24—145, 165
Matthew 26:37-38—145
Matthew 26:47—154, 271
Matthew 26:51—272
Matthew 26:52—272
Matthew 26:52-53—221
Matthew 26:56—219
Matthew 26:57—291
Matthew 26:57-65—290
Matthew 26:59-61—260
Matthew 26:61—83, 84, 260
Matthew 26:62—291
Matthew 26:63—84, 285, 293

Matthew 26:63-65—285, 292
Matthew 26:64—285
Matthew 26:65-66—286
Matthew 26:68—287
Matthew 26:69-74—221
Matthew 27:2—46
Matthew 27:3-5—139
Matthew 27:3-8—139
Matthew 27:4—135
Matthew 27:5—109
Matthew 27:9—129
Matthew 27:9-10—139
Matthew 27:11—35, 289
Matthew 27:15—109
Matthew 27:15-26—32
Matthew 27:16—130
Matthew 27:17—130, 157
Matthew 27:18—130, 197
Matthew 27:19—130, 135
Matthew 27:20—129, 130
Matthew 27:21—130, 157
Matthew 27:22—130, 133
Matthew 27:22-23—132
Matthew 27:22-24—29, 131
Matthew 27:23—34, 130
Matthew 27:24—30, 33, 130, 131, 133, 158
Matthew 27:25—9, 10, 30, 44, 67, 90, 106, 123, 124, 129, 133, 134, 135, 136, 145, 158, 171, 200, 276, 290, 296, 304
Matthew 27:26—157
Matthew 27:27-31—132
Matthew 27:37—200, 283, 294
Matthew 27:38—46
Matthew 27:39-40—260
Matthew 27:40—83
Matthew 27:54—118, 132, 146
Matthew 27:62-64—119
Matthew 28:10—217, 220
Matthew 28:11-15—220
Matthew 28:15—129
Matthew 28:16—217, 220
Matthew 28:18—136
Matthew 28:19—217, 220

Mark

Mark 2:1-3:6—93
Mark 2:7—93, 286
Mark 2:9-11—111
Mark 2:10—111
Mark 2:12a—111
Mark 2:16—78, 93
Mark 2:18—94
Mark 2:24—94
Mark 3:2—112
Mark 3:4—112
Mark 3:5—112
Mark 3:6—28, 89, 94, 112
Mark 3:17—81
Mark 3:18—80
Mark 3:20-21—77
Mark 3:22—285
Mark 3:31-35—77
Mark 4:1-9—103
Mark 4:11-12—103, 104

Mark 4:13—104
Mark 4:13-20—103
Mark 5:13—280
Mark 6:2-6—89
Mark 6:4—78, 181
Mark 7—97
Mark 7:1-23—95, 100, 294
Mark 7:2-4—95
Mark 7:9-13—95
Mark 7:11—81, 95
Mark 7:14-15—96, 120
Mark 7:18-19—96, 120
Mark 7:19b—98
Mark 7:20-23—97
Mark 7:24-30—118
Mark 7:25-30—98, 101
Mark 7:31-3—113
Mark 10:47—92
Mark 11:2—269
Mark 11:2-7—305
Mark 11:7-10—35, 280
Mark 11:7-11—269
Mark 11:9-10—183
Mark 11:10—92
Mark 11:11—86
Mark 11:13-14— 280
Mark 11:15-16—35, 86, 195, 270, 280
Mark 11:18—9, 28, 86, 87
Mark 11:27—119
Mark 12:1-12—90
Mark 12:8—110
Mark 12:12—29, 90, 277
Mark 12:13—119, 154
Mark 12:13-17—78

Mark 12:14-17—105
Mark 12:17—35, 280
Mark 12:35-37—92
Mark 12:35—92
Mark 12:37—92
Mark 13:2—147
Mark 13:32—262
Mark 14:1—28
Mark 14:10-11—139
Mark 14:13-14—269
Mark 14:16—269
Mark 14:43—83, 154
Mark 14:47—272
Mark 14:50—219
Mark 14:53—83
Mark 14:53-64—290
Mark 14:55—83, 84
Mark 14:56—28
Mark 14:57-58—260
Mark 14:58—83, 84, 147, 248. 260
Mark 14:59—83
Mark 14:60—291
Mark 14:61—84, 285, 293
Mark 14:61-64—285, 292
Mark 14:62—285
Mark 14:63—86
Mark 14:63-65—286
Mark 14:64—84, 287
Mark 14:65—287
Mark 14:66-71—221
Mark 15:1-14—77
Mark 15:1-15—34
Mark 15:—35, 88, 289
Mark 15:3—77

Mark 15:6-8—109
Mark 15:6-15—32, 290
Mark 15:7—79, 146, 275
Mark 15:9—34, 157
Mark 15:10—35, 77, 197
Mark 15:11—89, 129, 133, 146, 157
Mark 15:12—34
Mark 15:13—89, 133
Mark 15:14—33, 34
Mark 15:14-16—89
Mark 15:15—89, 91, 157, 158, 159
Mark 15:16-20—132, 160
Mark 15:16-20a—159
Mark 15:17-20—157
Mark 15:20—89
Mark 15:20b—159
Mark 15:24—89
Mark 15:26—76, 200, 283, 294
Mark 15:29—83, 147, 260
Mark 15:39—105, 146
Mark 16:7—217, 220
Mark 16:9-2—114
Mark 16:15—217
Mark 16:16—103, 104

Luke

Luke 1:3-4—159, 170
Luke 4:24—181
Luke 5:21—286
Luke 5:30—79
Luke 6:6-11—112
Luke 6:15—81
Luke 6:27—164
Luke 6:28—166
Luke 6:29—164
Luke 7:1-10—142
Luke 7:9—142
Luke 9:51—269
Luke 9:51-53—209
Luke 9:54-55—209
Luke 9:56—209
Luke 10:10-15—209
Luke 10:12—209
Luke 10:13-15—164, 165, 182
Luke 10:15—209
Luke 10:25-37—266
Luke 10:29-37—149
Luke 11:41—97
Luke 11:45—150
Luke 11:47-51—150
Luke 11:49—150
Luke 11:49-50— 106
Luke 11:49-51—124
Luke 11:50—67, 150
Luke 11:50-51—150, 296, 300
Luke 11:51—144
Luke 13:1—79
Luke 13:10-17—112
Luke 13:31—289
Luke 13:34-35—125
Luke 14:1-6—112
Luke 14:15-24—150
Luke 14:24—151
Luke 17:11-19—149, 266
Luke 18:32-33—161
Luke 18:33—160
Luke 19:1-11—153
Luke 19:11—152-153
Luke 19:11-27—151-152

Luke 19:12—152
Luke 19:13—152
Luke 19:14—152
Luke 19:15—152
Luke 19:15-26—152
Luke 19:26—153, 154
Luke 19:27—145, 152, 153, 154, 164, 296, 304
Luke 19:28—269
Luke 19:30—269
Luke 19:30-35—305
Luke 19:35-38—269, 280
Luke 19:35-39—35
Luke 19:37—218
Luke 19:38—211
Luke 19:39—28
Luke 19:45—35, 195, 280
Luke 19:45-46—270
Luke 20:9-16—90
Luke 20:15—110
Luke 20:16—69
Luke 20:19—29, 90, 119, 277
Luke 20:20—9, 46, 119, 154
Luke 20:20-26—78
Luke 20:25—35, 271, 280
Luke 21:6—147
Luke 22:10-11—269
Luke 22:13—269
Luke 22:36—271, 272
Luke 22:37—271
Luke 22:38—271, 272
Luke 22:42—262
Luke 22:49—219
Luke 22:52—155
Luke 22:57-60—221
Luke 22:63-65—160, 287

Luke 22:66—290, 291
Luke 22:66-71—290
Luke 22:67—293
Luke 22:67-71—285, 292
Luke 22:67-23:2—286
Luke 22:69—285
Luke 22:70—285
Luke 23:1—290
Luke 23:2—273, 283, 291, 292
Luke 23:3—35, 36, 289, 293
Luke 23:4—36, 291
Luke 23:5—36, 273, 291
Luke 23:6-12—171
Luke 23:7-12—167
Luke 23:11—157, 160
Luke 23:13—28, 133, 156, 158, 161, 171, 203
Luke 23:13-16—34
Luke 23:13-21—156
Luke 23:14—158
Luke 23:15—157
Luke 23:16—157
Luke 23:16-25—32
Luke 23:17—109
Luke 23:18—28
Luke 23:19—275
Luke 23:20—157
Luke 23:22—157
Luke 23:23—158
Luke 23:23-26—158
Luke 23:24—157, 158
Luke 23:24-25—157, 159
Luke 23:25—33, 157, 158, 203
Luke 23:26—159, 160, 161

Luke 23:30-31—159
Luke 23:33—162
Luke 23:34—161
Luke 23:34a—161, 162, 163, 164, 171
Luke 23:34b—161, 162
Luke 23:36—160, 161, 162
Luke 23:38—200, 283, 294
Luke 23:47—146, 162, 164
Luke 23:48—171
Luke 24:20—155, 159
Luke 24:21—229, 278
Luke 24:47-53—217, 220

John

John 1:11—188, 201
John 1:11-12—181
John 1:21a—143
John 1:42—81
John 1:43-48—210
John 1:44—263
John 1:45—181, 210
John 1:47—182
John 1:49—182
John 1:50—183
John 1:51—183
John 2:6—188
John 2:13—174, 188
John 2:13-16—270
John 2:14-15—195
John 2:14-16—35, 270, 280
John 2:18-21—173
John 2:19—83, 84, 147, 248, 260
John 2:21—83, 260
John 3:13—206
John 3:22—174
John 3:23—210
John 3:31—206
John 4—185, 206, 245
John 4:1-42—266
John 4:3—181
John 4:4—181
John 4:5-42—207
John 4:9—174, 188
John 4:19—208
John 4:21—208, 245
John 4:22—180, 188, 191, 304
John 4:23—180
John 4:25—207
John 4:26—208
John 4:39-40—181
John 4:39-42—179, 180
John 4:41-42—209
John 4:44—181
John 4:44-45—181
John 4:45—181
John 5:1—188
John 5:10-18—173
John 5:15-18—194
John 5:16—173
John 5:18—173
John 5:20—206
John 5:23—175
John 5:38-47—175
John 6:4—188
John 6:5-7—210
John 6:14—208
John 6:24—193
John 6:30—193
John 6:32-35—206

John 6:41—173, 193, 194
John 6:41-52—173
John 6:46—206
John 6:52—173, 193
John 6:70—175
John 7:1—173
John 7:2—174, 188
John 7:10-13—194
John 7:11-13—176
John 7:13—173, 205
John 7:16—206
John 7:19—205
John 7:20—184
John 7:28—175
John 7:32—191
John 7:35—173
John 7:40-41—208
John 7:41-42—178, 184
John 7:47-48—191
John 7:52—178, 181
John 8—9, 188
John 8:13—193
John 8:17—190, 205, 300
John 8:19—175
John 8:22—173
John 8:22 ff.—193
John 8:25—173
John 8:30—188
John 8:30-32—188, 189
John 8:31-32—188
John 8:32—189
John 8:32-35—206
John 8:33—189
John 8:37—173, 189
John 8:39—184, 189
John 8:39b—191
John 8:40—189
John 8:41—189
John 8:42—189
John 8:43—189
John 8:44—10, 17, 21, 44, 67, 106, 175, 190, 214, 296, 304
John 8:44a—191
John 8:44-47—189-190
John 8:45—188
John 8:47—175, 184, 201
John 8:48-49—184
John 8:48-57—173
John 8:52—184
John 8:58—190
John 9:13—191, 193
John 9:15—191
John 9:15-17—192
John 9:17—208
John 9:18—192
John 9:18 ff.—193
John 9:18-23—173
John 9:22—186, 187, 192, 205
John 9:40—191
John 10:19-21—173
John 10:20—184
John 10:30-33—286
John 10:31—173, 194
John 10:34—190, 206, 300
John 10:36—286
John 11:19—12
John 11:43-53—196
John 11:46—191
John 11:47—278
John 11:47-50—198

John 11:47-53—29
John 11:48—27, 248, 278
John 11:48-53—9
John 11:50—88, 278
John 11:51-52—196
John 11:53—197
John 11:53-54—179, 194
John 11:55—188
John 12:12-15—35, 280
John 12:13—183
John 12:14-15—269, 305
John 12:15—269
John 12:19—28, 191
John 12:21-22—210
John 12:37—173
John 12:42—187
John 13:27—175
John 14:8-9—210
John 15:18-25—175
John 16:1-3—175
John 16:2—187
John 18:3—29, 83, 155, 198, 199, 280
John 18:7-8—217
John 18:8—219
John 18:10—218
John 18:12—155, 197, 198, 199, 280
John 18:13—291
John 18:14—196
John 18:15-17—221
John 18:19—283, 291
John 18:19-28—291
John 18:20—104
John 18:22-23—145, 165

John 18:24—291
John 18:28-29—291
John 18:29—199, 212
John 18:30—199
John 18:30-31—204
John 18:31—191, 199, 204, 212, 275
John 18:33—174, 183, 289, 293-294
John 18:33-37—200, 208
John 18:33-38—292
John 18:35—188, 192, 204, 297
John 18:36—183, 192, 221, 228, 229, 294
John 18:37—35
John 18:38—33-34, 200
John 18:38b—297
John 18:39-40—32
John 18:39a—109
John 18:40—46
John 19:1—200
John 19:1-16—203
John 19:3—174
John 19:4—200
John 19:6—14, 200, 279
John 19:7—191, 200, 292
John 19:11—204
John 19:11-15—204
John 19:12—28, 32, 47 195, 200, 204
John 19:12-16—34
John 19:13—142
John 19:15—202
John 19:15b—200, 201

John 19:16—198, 202
John 19:17—110
John 19:19—183, 198, 200, 283, 294
John 19:20-22—183
John 19:23—198, 202
John 19:23-25—161, 162
John 19:31-34—203
John 19:36-37—203
John 19:38—198, 205
John 19:40—188
John 19:42—174, 188
John 20:19—195, 205 220
John 21:1—217, 220
John 21:15—81
John 21:16—81
John 21:17—81

Acts

Acts 1:3—81, 100
Acts 1:4—217, 220
Acts 1:6—229, 230, 278
Acts 1:7—230
Acts 1:7-11—229
Acts 1:13—81, 221
Acts 1:18—109
Acts 1:18-19—139
Acts 1:20—147
Acts 2:1 ff.—222
Acts 2:22-23—166
Acts 2:23—159, 161, 297
Acts 2:36—159, 166, 276, 297, 304
Acts 2:41—218, 222
Acts 2:46-47—222
Acts 2:47—222, 226
Acts 3:12-15—159
Acts 3:13—297
Acts 3:13-15—167
Acts 3:17—163
Acts 3:19—167
Acts 3:19-20—164
Acts 4:1-21—253
Acts 4:1-2—223, 226
Acts 4:1-3—87
Acts 4:4—222, 226
Acts 4:10—167, 223
Acts 4:17-18 —225, 226
Acts 4:25—92
Acts 4:25-27—161
Acts 4:27-28—167
Acts 4:33—223, 225
Acts 5:12-42—222
Acts 5:13—226
Acts 5:14—222, 226
Acts 5:28—223
Acts 5:30—167, 223
Acts 5:30-31—225
Acts 5:33—227
Acts 5:33-40—227
Acts 5:34—227
Acts 5:36-37—261
Acts 5:38a—234
Acts 5:38-39—234
Acts 5:40—225
Acts 6:1—236, 237, 238
Acts 6:1-5—235, 237
Acts 6:7—223
Acts 6:8-15—254
Acts 6:11—246, 247

Acts 6:13—83, 246, 247, 248, 251
Acts 6:13-14—260
Acts 6:14—83, 238, 245, 246, 248, 251
Acts 7—208, 209, 239, 242, 245, 266
Acts 7-8—210
Acts 7:2-51—238
Acts 7:2-53—248, 254
Acts 7:4—239
Acts 7:5—240
Acts 7:7—242
Acts 7:9-18—242
Acts 7:15-16—241
Acts 7:25—246
Acts 7:32—240
Acts 7:34—246
Acts 7:35—246
Acts 7:37—240, 246
Acts 7:38—246, 247
Acts 7:39—246
Acts 7:41-42—243
Acts 7:42—243
Acts 7:42-43—243
Acts 7:43—243, 246
Acts 7:44-45—244, 246
Acts 7:46—243
Acts 7:46-47—247
Acts 7:47-48—251
Acts 7:47-50—244
Acts 7:48—244, 247
Acts 7:49-50—244
Acts 7:51—245
Acts 7:51-53—169
Acts 7:53—246-247
Acts 7:54-60—254
Acts 7:55—238
Acts 7:56-59—250
Acts 7:60—171
Acts 8:1—226, 227, 250, 251, 253
Acts 8:1-4—252
Acts 8:4—251, 253
Acts 8:5-6—252
Acts 8:5-25—208
Acts 8:12—252
Acts 8:14-15—252
Acts 9:2—256
Acts 9:23-25—168, 233
Acts 9:26-30—168, 233
Acts 9:30—172
Acts 10:9-16—100
Acts 10:15—97, 99
Acts 10:28—101
Acts 10:34—101
Acts 10:39—159, 167
Acts 11:2-10—100
Acts 11:3—101
Acts 11:9—97
Acts 11:17—101
Acts 11:18—101
Acts 11:19—227
Acts 12:1-3—231
Acts 12:11—231
Acts 12:17—221
Acts 13:15—51
Acts 13:27-28—65, 66, 138, 167
Acts 13:46—69, 170

Acts 13:50—166, 233
Acts 14:2—166
Acts 14:11-12—212
Acts 14:19—166
Acts 15:5—99, 113, 225
Acts 15:7-29—100
Acts 15:19—99
Acts 15:29—99
Acts 16:1—53
Acts 16:3—53
Acts 16:19-24—233
Acts 17:4—169
Acts 17:5—166, 169, 233
Acts 17:5-6—169, 233
Acts 17:5-7—233
Acts 17:6 f.—233
Acts 17:13—166
Acts 18:6—170
Acts 18:12 ff.—166
Acts 18:13—233
Acts 18:15—212
Acts 19:23-41—233
Acts 21—267
Acts 21:20—52, 109
Acts 21:21—52, 53
Acts 21:23-24—52
Acts 21:23-26—253
Acts 21:24—52
Acts 21:26—51
Acts 21:27-28—52
Acts 21:28—52, 247
Acts 21:31-39—87
Acts 22:3—57, 109
Acts 23:2-3—165-166
Acts 23:6—57
Acts 23:6-10—224
Acts 23:7—58
Acts 24:1 ff.—166
Acts 24:5-6—232, 257
Acts 25:8—51, 247
Acts 26:5—51
Acts 28:17—51
Acts 28:28—170, 176

Romans
Romans 1:3—184
Romans 1:7—59
Romans 2:25-29—59
Romans 2:28-29—213
Romans 2:29—59
Romans 3:20—62
Romans 4:16—59
Romans 8:17—59
Romans 8:34—293
Romans 9-11—60
Romans 9—63
Romans 9:1—49
Romans 9:6—64
Romans 9:6-7—21
Romans 9:6-8—57, 191
Romans 9:8—59
Romans 9:24—57
Romans 9:27—59
Romans 9:31-32—62
Romans 10:4—120
Romans 10:13—293
Romans 11:1—60
Romans 11:4-5—60
Romans 11:5—57, 60
Romans 11:7—60, 61, 102

Romans 11:10—60
Romans 11:11-25—118
Romans 11:11-32—59
Romans 11:16-25—61
Romans 11:17—56, 62
Romans 11:23—70
Romans 11:25—61
Romans 11:25-26—62
Romans 11:25-32—62
Romans 11:26—60, 61
Romans 11:28-29—62
Romans 12:14—166
Romans 13:1-2—47
Roman 13:1-7—107
Romans 14:5-6—52
Romans 14:14—97, 98, 113
Romans 14:14-15—53, 99

1 Corinthians
1 Corinthians 1:23—220
1 Corinthians 1:31—293
1 Corinthians 2:16—293
1 Corinthians 7:18-19—54
1 Corinthians 9:19-23—51
1 Corinthians 9:20—53, 54
1 Corinthians 9:20-23—54
1 Corinthians 9:22—248
1 Corinthians 10:4—293
1 Corinthians 10:32-33—52, 54
1 Corinthians 15:47—293

2 Corinthians
2 Corinthians 3:4-6—58
2 Corinthians 3:14-15—62
2 Corinthians 4:4—293
2 Corinthians 11:22—237
2 Corinthians 11:22-23— 255
2 Corinthians 11:24—256
2 Corinthians 11:32-33— 168, 233

Galatians
Galatians 1:14—109
Galatians 1:18-24—168, 233
Galatians 1:20—50
Galatians 1:21—172
Galatians 2:7-9—211
Galatians 2:11-12—53, 99, 113
Galatians 2:11-14—248
Galatians 2:11-17—98
Galatians 2:12—225
Galatians 3-4—63
Galatians 3:5-14—58
Galatians 3:6-9—191
Galatians 3:7—20, 64
Galatians 3:10—62
Galatians 3:11—62
Galatians 3:13—288, 289
Galatians 3:16-18—265
Galatians 3:19—265
Galatians 3:24-26—57
Galatians 3:29—64, 69
Galatians 4:21-31—61, 63, 191
Galatians 4:24—63
Galatians 4:25—63
Galatians 4:26—63
Galatians 4:28—63

Galatians 4:30—63
Galatians 5:3—54
Galatians 5:4—54
Galatians 6:15—62
Galatians 6:16—21, 59, 61

Philippians
Philippians 1:15—50
Philippians 1:15-18—49
Philippians 1:16—55
Philippians 1:17—49, 50, 54, 55
Philippians 1:18—49, 50, 54
Philippians 2:6—293
Philippians 2:9-10—293
Philippians 3:2—57
Philippians 3:3—59, 64
Philippians 3:4-8—51
Philippians 3:5—57, 237, 256
Philippians 3:8—57

Colossians
Colossians 2:16—53, 97, 99
Colossians 2:20-22—53, 98, 99

1 Thessalonians
1 Thessalonians 2:13—65
1 Thessalonians 2:14—66
1 Thessalonians 2:14-15—10, 65, 66, 70, 178, 207
1 Thessalonians 2:14-16—13, 31, 64, 65, 68, 138, 169, 233
1 Thessalonians 2:15—58, 66, 68, 69
1 Thessalonians 2:15-16—66, 302
1 Thessalonians 2:16—66, 67, 69
1 Thessalonians 2:17—65

Titus
Titus 1:10—12

Hebrews
Hebrews 6:20—72
Hebrews 7:14—73
Hebrews 7:16—72
Hebrews 8:7—72
Hebrews 8:13—72, 120, 304
Hebrews 9:3-4—74
Hebrews 10:1—72
Hebrews 12:22—75
Hebrews 13:12 f.—110

1 Peter
1 Peter 2:9-10—91
1 Peter 2:13-14—47

Revelation
Revelation 2:1-3:22—213
Revelation 2:8-11—213
Revelations 2:9—184, 213, 296
Revelations 3:7-13—213
Revelation 3:9—213, 214, 296

SUBJECT INDEX

Abel, 124, 125, 126, 135, 150, 300
Abraham, 21, 57, 58, 59, 60, 63, 64, 69-70, 117, 121, 125, 126, 150, 184-185, 189-190, 239, 240, 241, 242, 243, 255, 264, 265, 267, 300, 304
Alexandria, 25, 42, 275
Ananus, 232-233, 309
Antonia fortress, 87, 270, 279, 307
Albinus, 281-282
Ananias, 165-166
Annas, 291
Anti-Jewish, *passim*
anti-Judaism, *passim*
anti-Judaic, *passim*
anti-Semitism, 14, 15-16, 43-45, *passim*

Baum, Gregory, 13-14
Barabbas, 31-34, 46, 79, 81, 89, 110, 129-131, 146, 156
birkat-ha-minim, 187, 211
Biryonim, 82

Blasphemy, 84-86, 111, 213, 246, 285-292
bloody commission, 154, 296
Brown, Raymond, 17, 206
Bultmann, Rudolf, 205

Caesar, 32, 33, 35, 36, 47, 78, 80, 119, 195, 200, 201, 202, 218, 262, 271, 273, 279, 280, 283, 286, 290
Caiaphas, 29, 34, 108, 196, 278, 279, 282, 291-292, 309
Cain, 126
Catholic Church, 12
Christendom, 11, 26, 204, 262
Circumcision, 12, 24, 41, 53-54, 57, 59, 64, 113, 116, 213, 259
Crucifixion, 18, 21, 27, 28, 29, 30, 33, 37, 43, 46, 57, 76, 79, 88, 112, 118, 129, 132, 134, 137, 138, 146, 147, 149, 156, 157, 158, 159, 160, 161, 162, 163, 164, 167, 171, 172, 200, 202, 203, 204, 215,

216, 217, 218, 220, 221, 222, 223, 226, 234, 274, 275, 276, 288-289, 291, 308

Damascus, 42, 168, 243, 255, 256
David, Davidic 28, 73, 74, 77, 92-93, 110, 131, 178, 183-184, 206, 207, 208, 210, 230, 243-244, 246, 250, 294
Davies, Alan, 14, 263
Diaspora, 28, 51-52, 115, 138, 187, 232, 233, 236, 238, 276
dietary laws, 24, 52, 97-101
Domitian, 23, 40

Eckardt, A. Roy, 45, 70, 205
Epp, Eldon Jay, 45, 204, 205
Eusebius, 116, 140, 141, 142, 310
expediency principle, 54

Feldman, Louis H., 41
Fiscus Iudaicus, 22, 23, 40
Flaccus, 25, 42
Flannery, Edward, 44-45
Florus, 281
Fuller, Reginald, 205, 206, 207

Gamaliel, 57, 227, 234, 261-262
Gamaliel II, 211

Gentile(s), *passim*
Godfearers, 56
Gospels, *passim*

Hadrian, 23
Hagar, 63
Haynes, Stephen R., 46
Hebrews, 57, 73, 210, 236-238, 254-257, 261, 263
Heil, John Paul, 134, 147
Hellenistic, 23, 24, 56, 75, 112, 168, 212, 234, 235-236, 239, 248, 251, 254-258, 260, 261
Hengel, Martin, 308
Herodians, 78, 89, 94, 109, 112, 119, 154
Herod, the Great, 36, 107-108, 109, 119, 231
Herod Antipas, 107-108, 122-123, 156, 157, 160, 167, 171, 172, 289
Herod Agrippa I, 42, 79, 107-108, 231-232, 235
Hoehner, Harold, 46-47
hoi Ioudaioi, 174, 177-178, 193, 205
Holocaust, 15, 16, 43, 44, 211
Howard, George, 142

Ishmael, 63
Israel, *passim*

James, 52, 53, 99, 113, 168, 221, 232, 309

Subject Index

Jesus, son of Ananias, 281-282
Jews, *passim*
John Paul II, 15-16
Josephus, 22, 31, 36, 40, 41, 42, 43, 46, 71, 82, 109, 209, 212, 231, 232, 233, 237, 241, 258, 261-262, 265, 280, 281, 284, 307, 309-310
Judas, 81, 82, 109, 138-139, 147, 155, 165, 175, 198, 204
Judaizers, 100, 217
Julian, 40, 147
Judaic, 11
Juvenal, 41

Lowe, Malcolm, 143

Maccoby, Haim, 43, 109
Macdonald, John, 73, 208, 209, 210, 264, 265
Messiah, 8, 33, 38, 40, 56, 57, 58, 59, 62, 63, 69, 70, 84-85, 92, 103, 116-117, 154, 187, 189, 201, 207-208, 210, 216, 218, 220, 225, 230, 246, 250, 253, 254, 256, 260, 269, 273, 278, 286, 290, 292, 293, 310

Nazarite vows, 52
Nostra aetate, 14

Oesterreicher, John M., 14

Oral Law, 93-94, 95, 98, 100, 112, 191, 288, 294
Origen, 116, 141, 146, 264, 310

pagan(s), 15, 16, 21, 24-26, 40, 41, 43, 56, 69, 70, 87, 113, 146, 159, 171, 186, 284, 297, 303
Pannenberg, Wolfhart, 146-148
Parkes, James, 45
Passover, 36, 109-110, 188, 215, 218, 219, 231, 261, 268-270, 274, 277-278, 283-284, 289
Paul, *passim*
Peter, *passim*
Pharisee(s), *passim*
Philo, 25, 31, 33, 34, 42, 46, 47, 75, 107, 239, 258-259, 264, 265, 367
Pontius Pilate, *passim*
Poppea, 42
Purvis, James D., 207, 263, 264-265, 266

Quintilius Varus, 36,
Qumran community, 121, 266, 295, 296, 308

Rabbis, 27, 68, 86, 94-95, 111, 112, 115, 120, 121-122, 127, 146, 211
Resurrection, 39, 69, 83, 136, 147, 148, 152, 218, 223-

224, 225, 226-227, 232, 259, 310
Reuther, Rosemary, 14, 40, 48
Roman(s), *passim*
Roman-Jewish War, 21, 25, 31, 42, 76, 80, 92, 133, 216

Sadducees, Sadducean 35, 58, 95, 110, 223-224, 226, 227, 258, 292, 293, 304
Samaritan(s), *passim*
Sanders, E.P., 13, 70
Sanhedrin (Council), 29, 57-58, 71, 83-84, 160, 181, 196, 215, 224, 225, 227, 232, 234, 246, 261, 265, 275, 276, 278, 285-286, 290, 291, 293, 310
Sarah, 63, 71
Satan, 7, 124, 175, 199, 211, 213, 214, 296
Schiffman, Lawrence H., 262
Scobie, Charles, H.H., 73, 74, 75, 207
second coming, 152, 153-154, 228, 230
seder, 137, 293
Sejanus, 46-47
Sicarii, 82
Stephen, 40, 73, 74, 75, 83, 156, 169, 171, 208, 210, 227, 237-255, 257, 264, 265, 266
supersession, 20, 40, 43, 58, 170, 143, 175, 191, 201

Tacitus, 31, 46, 69, 71, 108
Taheb, 179, 208-209, 246, 265
Timothy, 53
Titus, 12, 23, 36, 43

Vatican Council II, 15, 48
Valerius Gratus, 282, 309
Vespasian, 23
Vitellius, 309

Zealots, 46, 80, 81, 82